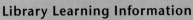

baby & toddler
healthy eating planner

mitchell beazley

amanda grant

baby & toddler
healthy eating planner

the new way to feed your child a balanced diet every day, featuring
over 350 recipes, meal planners, charts and nutrition guides

Baby & Toddler Healthy Eating Planner
by Amanda Grant

First published in Great Britain in 2008 by Mitchell Beazley,
an imprint of Octopus Publishing Group Limited,
2–4 Heron Quays, London E14 4JP
An Hachette Livre Company
www.octopusbooks.co.uk

The publishers will be grateful for any information that will assist them in keeping future
editions up to date. Although all reasonable care has been taken in the preparation of this
book, neither the publishers nor the author can accept any liability for any consequence
arising from the use thereof, or the information contained therein.

The *Baby & Toddler Healthy Eating Planner* is meant to be used as a general reference
guide and recipe book. While the author believes the information and recipes it contains
are beneficial to health, the book is in no way intended to replace medical advice, which
you should obtain from a state-registered dietician, paediatrician or health visitor. You are
therefore urged to consult your health-care professional about specific medical complaints.

ISBN 978 1 84533 439 0

A CIP record for this book is available from the British Library

Set in Praxis
Printed and bound in China by Toppan Printing Company Limited

Commissioning Editor: Rebecca Spry
Senior Editor: Leanne Bryan
Proofreaders: Abi Waters, Jo Murray
Indexer: Diana Lecore
Executive Art Editor: Yasia Williams
Designer: Lizzie Ballantyne
Special Photography: William Reavell, Francesca Yorke
Consultant Nutritionists: Tanya Carr, Fiona Hunter
Stylist: Juliet Harvey
Home Economy Assistant: Sibilla Whitehead
Senior Production Controller: Lucy Carter

To Toby and Henry – keep eating boys! –
and to Joseph, the gorgeous boy next door

information about this book

recipe symbols:

● The symbols used for each nutrient are for visual
identification only; they do not imply that your baby can
eat the food shown in that symbol.

● The 'rich in' symbol (*see* page 10) indicates that a
portion of a dish contains more than 25 per cent of your
baby's daily requirement of the listed nutrients.

recipes:

● All baby portion sizes are approximate, based on the
age group of the chapter, and the points listed are based
on the stated portion size. However, all babies' appetites
are different.

● Wash all fruit and vegetables that have not been peeled.

points system:

● The points system is only intended to be a guide.

● If you are successfully breastfeeding, assume as a guide
that your baby is consuming the same number of points of
each nutrient as is provided by the recommended amount
of formula milk.

nutrition:

● The 'most recently published recommended nutrient
intakes' refer to the UK Government's Recommended
Nutrient Intakes (RNIs).

**Note: The fresh recipes in this book are
mostly suitable for the whole family.
The frozen recipes are often not suitable
for adults, but you can make big batches
of them for freezing.**

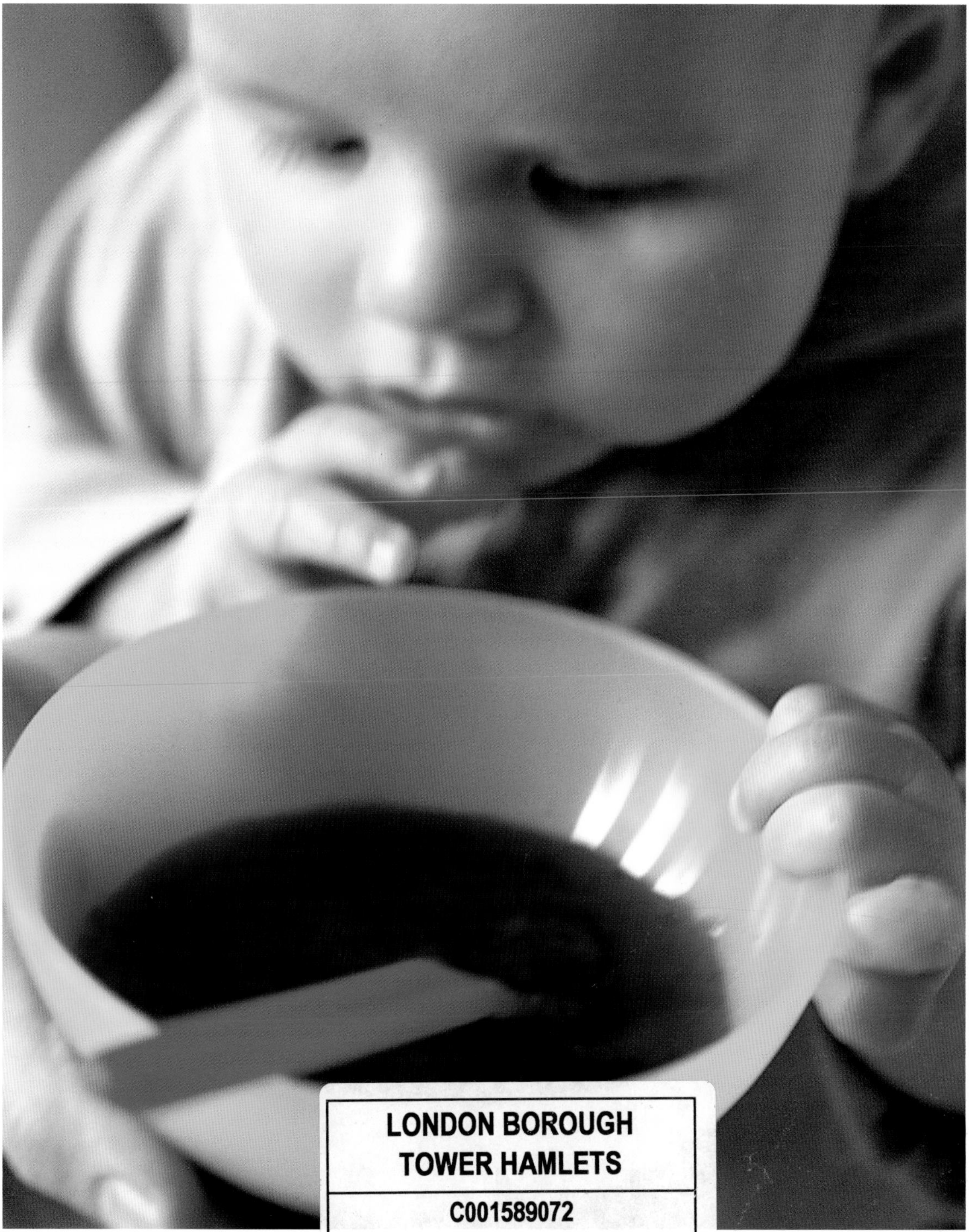

contents

It really does matter what children eat, so it is vitally important that you give your child a good diet if you want her to have the best start in life. This is achievable, even if you are a busy parent with a hectic schedule.

The food that your child eats in her formative years will set her up for the rest of her life: if she enjoys food and receives a varied and well-balanced diet she is more likely to develop and grow at a normal rate, be more alert, full of energy and suffer from fewer illnesses. There is a big difference between a child who is simply fed food each day and one that is optimally nourished.

It is a parent's responsibility to know and understand what it is that a child needs for her most favourable growth and function. Breast milk is by far the best first food and then when this no longer provides your child with all the nutrients she requires at around 6 months, other 'non-milk' or 'solid' foods are called for. This is the time to start giving your child fresh, unprocessed food in the form of purées or finger foods that contain a variety of nutrients. Keep life simple and follow recipes in this book that can be made at the same time as making food for you and the rest of the family. This will help with the transition period from baby to toddler when your child needs to move from simple first foods to sharing the same meals as all the family, at the same times. Making mealtimes fun and relaxed should ensure that your child looks forward to them.

The meal planners in this book are particularly useful if you need some weekly inspiration – we all know how difficult it can be to have to think of different meals for every day of the week. All the recipes are also easy and quick to make using readily available ingredients.

Good nutrition is about not only a well-balanced diet, but also your whole approach to food and eating. If your family embraces the idea that food is something to be enjoyed and shared, your child is likely to have this attitude too.

introduction

how to
use this book

how to use the charts and symbols

During the first year of your baby's life, five nutrients are particularly important: protein, iron, zinc, calcium and vitamin C. For toddlers of 1, 2 and 3 years, over 30 nutrients that are essential to health must be obtained from food and drink. However, in this age group the same five nutrients – protein, iron, zinc, calcium and vitamin C – are still particularly important. The 'nutrients required per day' chart on page 11 illustrates how I have converted the most recently published recommended nutrient intakes (see 'nutrition' on page 4), which are usually measured in grams (g), milligrams (mg) or micrograms (mcg), into points for each of these nutrients. Where the recommended daily nutrient intake does not convert exactly to points, I have rounded it up to the nearest quarter or half point. All my recipes have symbols illustrating how many points of each of these nutrients a single portion of the dish contains. So, using the 'nutrients required per day' charts as easy reference, you can count up the points for each nutrient that you've fed your baby or toddler in a day to check that he is getting the required amount. To help you further, points are calculated for four stages: 6 months, 7–9 months, 10–12 months and 1–3 years.

Of course, you must also ensure that your baby or toddler has a sufficient intake of the other important nutrients, in particular saturated and unsaturated fats, carbohydrates (starch and sugar), vitamins A, D, E and B group, and the mineral phosphorus. However, as long as he's enjoying a varied diet, he's likely to be getting enough of all of these nutrients. On pages 22–27 you'll find a guide to how much of each of these nutrients your baby or toddler needs and lists of which foods contain them. Recipes that are rich in one or more of these nutrients (apart from fats and carbohydrate) feature a symbol (see below and 'recipe symbols' on page 4).

The most important thing to remember is that this points system is designed to be used as a guide. Do bear in mind, however, that many babies and toddlers will need less than the recommended nutrient intake that the 'nutrients required per day' charts refer to, but a small minority will need slightly more – if in doubt, ask your health visitor. Some days your child will exceed the recommended nutrient intake for a particular nutrient and other days he'll fall short, but it's his average intake over weeks and months that's important. This unique points system will give you a good guide, but if you are ever in doubt about your baby or toddler's nutritional intake, always ask your family doctor or state-registered dietician for advice.

symbols

Each recipe in this book features a selection of these nutrient symbols. Each represents a nutrient and is accompanied by a number to show how many points of that nutrient a portion of the dish contains. The tick symbol shows that a portion of the dish gives more than 25 per cent of the recommended daily requirement of the nutrient listed alongside it.

protein

iron

zinc

calcium

vitamin C

rich in listed nutrient(s)

1+ suitable for babies over 1 year old

nutrients required per day

This chart shows how many points of each key nutrient your baby or toddler needs per day at each age (*see* pages 57, 69, 97, 141, 197, 243, and 289). While most professionals assess babies in terms of weight and age, I have used age only in order to simplify matters. Of course, babies' weights will vary, but on the whole this only affects how much they eat rather than the food types that are acceptable for their digestive and immune systems. Weight may, however, have an impact on nutritional requirements; if you have a heavy baby, follow the points system as a guide but slightly increase the amount of food given – this should compensate for any extra nutrients required.

Although the nutritional requirements of babies increases regularly throughout the first year because of the rapid development of their organs and brain, the guideline remains static for toddlers aged 1 to 3 (inclusive). I have based the figures for 1–3 years on age rather than weight, but weight may have an impact on nutritional requirements; if you are concerned, speak to your family doctor or state-registered dietician.

age	protein 1 point = 1.5g	iron 1 point = 1.5mg	zinc 1 point = 1mg	calcium 1 point = 105mg	vitamin C 1 point = 5mg
6 months	8½	3	4	5	5
7–9 months	9	5	5	5	5
10–12 months	10	5	5	5	5
1–3 years inclusive)	10	5	5	3½	6

how to build a daily meal plan for your child, based on a 7–9-month-old baby

This shows how to ensure that your baby or toddler gets enough nutrients by adding up the points in his daily food. It doesn't matter if the points requirement is exceeded, although you should not excessively exceed the intake.

time	food and milk	protein	iron	zinc	calcium	vitamin C
breakfast	Breast milk/200ml formula	2	1	1	½	2/4
	1 portion vanilla porridge	3	½	1	½	0
mid-am	Breast milk/200ml formula	2	1	1	½	2/4
lunch	1 portion quick pizza	3½	½	½	1	0
	1 portion pear and almond yogurt	3	0	½	1	¼
	water	0	0	0	0	0
mid-pm	Breast milk/200ml formula	2	1	1	½	2/4
supper	1 portion sweet potato and coconut curry	1½	½	0	½	2½
	1 portion rice cakes with mango purée	½	0	1	0	3
	water	0	0	0	0	0
bedtime	Breast milk/200ml formula	2	1	1	½	2/4
	total points	19½	5½	7	5	14/22

Good nutrition is vital to help your child's body to function, grow efficiently and repair itself – and to promote good health throughout life. All foods provide a mixture of nutrients, but no single food, apart from breast milk or formula milk during the first six months, provides them all. Introducing your child to a broad range of fresh, unrefined foods will help to ensure that, by the age of 12 months, she will be eating a varied diet.

As babies and toddlers have small appetites, they need small, frequent meals made up of nutrient-dense foods. A good variety of foods will keep your toddler interested at mealtimes, and your goal from 1–3 years should be to feed her the same foods as the rest of the family. Healthy snacks between meals are crucial to help maintain toddler energy levels.

baby and toddler nutrition

why nutrition
matters

'**Nutrition in the early years of life is a major determinant of growth and development and it also influences adult health**'
The Committee on Medical Aspects of Food Policy 'COMA' Report.

By far the best food for your baby in the first few months is breast milk. Ideally, you should try to breastfeed for at least the first six months (*see* pages 28–31). Once your baby reaches the age of 6 months you can start to wean her onto 'solid' foods – that is, foods and liquids other than milk (although the foods babies eat at this stage can hardly be described as 'solid'). The foods you choose to feed her should be the best foods for her development and growth (*see* pages 54–56).

your baby's immune system
Your baby's immune system is very immature at birth and it needs to develop to become healthy and strong. The strength of your baby's immune system is dependent on an optimal, balanced intake of nutrients. From birth, the first food to assist in building a strong immune system is colostrum, the liquid that comes from the breast before the milk comes in (*see* page 28). Colostrum contains many antibodies to combat bacteria and viruses, and so support your baby's immune system. Colostrum also contains a high concentration of zinc, which is essential for a child's growth and development. Formula milks are fortified with zinc.

your baby's digestive system
Your baby's digestive system is far from being fully developed in her first few weeks of life, which is why breast milk is the perfect food. It can take at least four months for your baby's intestines to develop and to produce the right enzymes for digesting foods. Similarly, her kidneys will not be able to cope with eliminating waste products from solid food. It makes sense that if solid foods are introduced too early, your baby's digestive system may become damaged. This is one of the reasons why it is advised to wean babies at 6 months old and not earlier.

essential nutrients
The reason for making sure that your baby's diet gradually becomes more varied and balanced is because she needs all of the essential nutrients to grow and develop, and to develop strong and healthy immune and digestive systems. Her diet needs to be varied, because no one nutrient works in isolation and a severe deficiency of one vitamin or mineral can adversely affect her development.

energy

Energy-dense foods are important for the first year, as your baby's demands for energy are high due to her rapid growth and development while her stomach capacity is small. Standard adult healthy eating advice (low-fat, high-fibre diets) should not be given to babies or children under 2 years.

fresh fruit and vegetables

Non-citrus fruit and vegetables make great first foods as they are unlikely to cause allergies in babies. They also contain a concentrated supply of vitamins, minerals, trace elements and beneficial enzymes, which can be quickly absorbed into your baby's system and bloodstream. Enzymes are important for your baby's health as they are essential to every stage of metabolism. They can be destroyed during cooking. At first, breast milk will provide all the essential enzymes your baby needs. After 9–10 months, to supplement your baby's enzyme intake, increase the amount of steamed fruit and vegetables you give so long as your baby is confident with chewing.

the importance of vitamins

I often mention antioxidant vitamins (such as vitamins A, C and E) in this book and, although we associate these with the prevention of cancer, heart disease and problems later in life, they also play a significant role in assisting the immune system and enabling the body to maintain good health.

toddler nutrition

There is an abundance of information on healthy eating and nutrition, and most parents have a fair idea of what constitutes a healthy diet. Nevertheless, the newspapers regularly carry stories about diet-related disorders among toddlers and food-related health problems among people of all ages. We are just beginning to see more clearly how a diet that is heavily dependent on processed foods and high in sugar, fat and salt is affecting the next generation.

Good nutrition benefits your toddler's behaviour and emotional well-being as well as her health. What your toddler eats during her formative years will have a significant impact on future health, and good eating habits formed now are likely to last a lifetime. As much as possible your toddler should be eating the same foods as the rest of the family and at the same times. This is assuming that the family as a whole is eating a well-balanced and varied diet. If not, having a toddler around is a great opportunity to pay more attention to what the whole family eats. Remember, however, that healthy eating guidelines intended for adults do not fully apply to pre-school children (age 1 to 5 years). Diets that are high in fibre or low in fat are not suitable for toddlers.

Your toddler will develop and grow at an amazing rate. Her new-found independence will spur her on to explore and test her world. All this increased activity and inquisitiveness requires fuel. Regular meals are particularly important for toddlers. They should have three meals a day, with two small, healthy snacks in between. This ensures that they get enough calories, but also enables you to give a wide range of foods in the space of a day.

Breakfast is the most important meal for toddlers because they have gone through the night without eating. A good breakfast, including carbohydrate (eg porridge) with some protein (eg milk), will set them up for the day. Lunch should include some protein (eg egg, chicken, pulses);

the fat can give an energy boost for afternoon activities and the protein can help with growth, development and repair. Carbohydrate foods such as pasta or rice are important at suppertime as they will help make your toddler feel full throughout the night, helping her to sleep more soundly.

Snacks should be as nutritious as possible, ideally fruit, vegetables or other healthy nibbles – sometimes, if your child had a late breakfast or lunch, just a drink of diluted fruit juice will be enough. Sugary snacks should only be given occasionally, preferably relatively soon after a meal to help prevent a blood sugar rush. Encourage your toddler to drink lots during the day – particularly water, with some milk (preferably organic) or very dilute fruit juice.

Good nutrition is not just about a well-balanced diet, it is also about your whole approach to food and eating. If your family embraces the idea that food is something to be enjoyed and shared, your toddler is likely to have this attitude too. While healthy eating should be your goal, try not to place too much emphasis on so-called 'good' or 'bad' foods. Inevitably toddlers are drawn towards processed foods, particularly because of their packaging. It is unrealistic to try to exclude them, and you may run the risk of exaggerating their desirability. It is far better to have the attitude that there are no 'good' or 'bad' foods, just that everything can be eaten in moderation.

food allergies and intolerances

Until recently special diets for children were relatively unusual, but research has indicated that many disorders, such as asthma, may be treated by restricting certain foods. Similarly, some disorders are linked to certain foods – for instance, some E-numbers in processed foods have been connected to hyperactivity. These kinds of allergies and intolerances are being reported with greater frequency.

When foods that are normally harmless (eg cow's milk, nuts or wheat) are perceived as foreign by the immune system, an allergic reaction can occur. Some reactions cause mild discomfort (eg a rash), whereas others can be life-threatening (eg anaphylactic shock). A serious allergy will become apparent minutes after your toddler has eaten a particular food. If you suspect an allergic reaction, speak to your family doctor immediately. If there is any family history of food allergies, avoid giving nuts or nut products before 3 years. Foods that have caused an allergic reaction in the family may need to be avoided: your doctor or dietician can advise about this. Food intolerances are less serious and may not be immediately apparent. They are indicated by milder symptoms, such as tummy ache, diarrhoea, asthma, eczema or poor growth. Allergies and intolerances can be treated by changing the diet, but always seek the advice of your family doctor or state-registered dietician before excluding any food to ensure that your child continues to get all the nutrients she needs.

the points system

To help make your life easier, I have chosen five of the key nutrients your baby or toddler needs (*see* page 10) and designed a points system around them. This is intended to help you easily get used to feeding your child a balanced diet. At the same time, it will reassure you that she is eating the recommended amount of each of these nutrients on a daily basis. There are, however, other nutrients that are also very important during the first four years of your child's life. (To find out how to ensure a healthy intake of all the key nutrients, *see* pages 17–27.)

nutrition for
babies and toddlers

key protein foods

These foods may not all be suitable for babies and toddlers in all age groups. *See* the relevant chapters for specific advice.

Protein foods providing all the essential amino acids include:
- Meat, such as chicken and lamb
- Fish, such as salmon and tuna
- Dairy products, particularly milk, cheese, eggs and yogurt
- Soya beans and soya products, such as tofu, soya cheese and soya milk.

Good vegetarian protein sources – other than the soya products mentioned above – include:
(These do not contain all the essential amino acids. However, in combination they can, for instance, vegetable burgers served with rice.)
- Beans and pulses, such as chickpeas, beans, lentils and butter beans
- Cereals and grain foods, such as rice, pasta, oats and muesli (with finely chopped nuts – do not give nuts or seeds to babies or toddlers under the age of 3 if there is a family history of food allergies)
- Ground nuts, such as hazelnuts and almonds, and smooth nut butters (*see* warning above)
- Ground seeds, such as sunflower seeds and sesame seeds (*see* warning above).

protein

Protein consists of building blocks called amino acids. There are two types of amino acids: essential and non-essential. Essential amino acids must be obtained directly from food, while the body can produce non-essential amino acids. Therefore you need to make sure that your baby or toddler's diet contains enough essential amino acids (*see* 'key protein foods', left).

why your child needs it

Protein is one of the most important nutrients for helping the body to build and repair muscles, tissues, hair and organs, and also maintain an effective immune and hormonal system. Considering how fast babies grow during their first year, this is definitely one of their key nutrients.

how to make sure your child gets it

An adequate intake of protein in particular should be ensured during weaning. This will be easy to achieve if you aim to feed your baby a diverse diet by the time she is 9 months old. 'Infants in the UK, whose diets rapidly diversify and who by the age of nine months are regularly consuming meat, fish, eggs or reasonable quantities of milk are unlikely to be protein deficient,' according to the UK Department of Health.

However, if you are feeding your baby or toddler a vegetarian or vegan diet you must make sure that she gets a good combination of protein-rich foods. Most plant foods are low in protein compared with foods of animal origin (with the exception of soya products such as tofu and soya milk), and the proteins from any single plant, unlike animal protein, do not contain all the essential amino acids. This is why it is important to feed your baby or toddler a mixture of plant foods to help make sure that the complete range of essential amino acids is provided (*see* vegetarian and special diets, pages 40–41). Mothers wishing to offer their child a vegan diet should seek specialist advice from a registered dietician.

Whole nuts are not recommended for children under 5.

iron

There are two main types of iron in food – haem iron from lean red meat and non-haem iron from plant sources, such as vegetables, dried fruits and finely chopped or ground nuts. (Do not give nuts to toddlers under the age of 3 if there is a family history of food allergies.)

why your child needs it

Iron is needed for healthy blood and muscles. A lack of iron can lead to a common form of anaemia. A significant number of babies under 12 months do not achieve good iron intake. It is very rare for babies to get too much of this mineral because they are physically unable to eat large quantities of it. Toddlers who are poor eaters, or on restricted diets, are also at risk. Normally toddlers who are affected by anaemia can seem listless and lethargic and have a general lack of appetite or interest in their food. However, the symptoms are not always so obvious. It is important to prevent iron-deficiency anaemia because it has been linked to poorer health, slower development and to specifically poor mental development. Studies into iron deficiency and anaemia in toddlers show that they are common among 2-year-olds in the UK, but become less common the older the child gets. If you have any concerns about your toddler's iron intake, speak to your family doctor or a registered dietician. Iron-deficiency anaemia is relatively easy to treat by changes to diet and with iron supplements.

how to make sure your child gets it

At birth, babies born at term (as close to 40 weeks as possible) need only a small amount of iron because they have laid down stores that will last them for six months.

The level of iron in breast milk is low, but since about 50 per cent or more of it is absorbed – which is a high rate of absorption for iron – this makes an important contribution for your breastfed baby during early weaning. Many formula milk powders are fortified with iron. The amount of iron contributed from breast and formula milk by the time the baby is 6 months old is insufficient to meet her increasing needs.

One of the main functions of weaning is to increase your baby's intake of iron. A large number of babies under the age of 12 months do not achieve the recommended level due to late weaning and inappropriate foods.

Babies, like adults, find it easier to absorb haem iron. They are capable of absorbing 20 to 40 per cent of the iron from meat and only 5 to 20 per cent of the iron available from vegetable sources. Consequently, you will need to feed your baby a good variety and quantity of vegetables to provide her with a good supply of iron. The absorption of iron is enhanced by the presence of adequate vitamin C in the diet.

You can help to increase iron absorption by giving your toddler certain combinations of foods at the same meal. Foods rich in vitamin C, particularly citrus fruits and some green vegetables, significantly help the absorption of iron. For example, serve red meat with green vegetables or fresh fruit juice with breakfast cereals. Similarly, meat and fish help to increase iron absorption from non-animal foods, such as pulses and vegetables. Fortified foods can also help to increase iron intake from the diet. Some foods, particularly those containing tannin or caffeine, such as tea or chocolate, or foods high in fibre, such as bran, can hinder iron absorption. You should only give these foods to your toddler in moderation. These points are particularly relevant if you are feeding your toddler a vegetarian or vegan diet (*see* page 40).

calcium

Calcium is a mineral needed for strong, healthy bones and teeth.

why your child needs it

Ninety-nine per cent of the body's calcium content is found in bones and teeth, with one per cent in blood plasma and soft tissues. During her formative years your baby or toddler needs calcium to help with the normal function of all cells as well as for bone and teeth development. Lack of calcium has been linked to the development of osteoporosis. Although this is rare in children, a diet that meets calcium requirements in childhood will help ensure healthy bones in adulthood.

how to make sure your child gets it

Your child can easily get sufficient calcium if she eats a good range of dairy produce and other calcium-rich foods. Products made from fortified white flour provide useful sources of calcium for toddlers. Ensuring vegan toddlers, or those on restricted diets, have enough calcium is more challenging (*see* pages 40–41).

zinc

The mineral zinc has many functions in your child's body. These include maintaining healthy blood function and an efficient immune system, helping wounds to heal and assisting in growth.

why your child needs it

Zinc deficiency can limit your child's growth. The most recent information from the British Food Standards Agency shows that around 14 per cent of children under 4 years have average intakes of zinc below recommended levels. In extreme cases the symptoms of zinc deficiency can include a lack of appetite, skin problems and poor healing of wounds.

how to make sure your child gets it

A significant number of babies under the age of 12 months do not achieve the recommended daily level of this nutrient from their diet. Meat and meat products are the richest sources of zinc, but these foods contribute only 10 per cent of the dietary zinc intake, so make sure your child's diet includes other good sources. A toddler given a diet that includes plenty of meat, fish and dairy products, is unlikely to be zinc deficient. Vegetables and other plant foods, such as pulses, are not such good sources of zinc, so you need to give your vegetarian or vegan toddler a wide variety of these foods (*see* page 40).

vitamin C

Vital for growth and healthy gums, teeth, bones and skin, vitamin C is particularly important for the healing of wounds. It is also needed to aid the absorption of iron. Vitamin C is one of the best-known antioxidant vitamins, which are well known for preventing life-threatening diseases, such as cancer. It also helps to boost the immune system and in particular helps to prevent common colds.

why your child needs it

It is important to give your child foods that contain vitamin C every day. Vitamin C is a water-soluble vitamin and the body cannot store excess amounts, it just uses what it needs. Severe vitamin C deficiency is characterized by several symptoms, including poor wound healing and swollen or inflamed gums. Breast and formula milks are normally good sources of this vitamin. However, if you are giving your toddler a wide range of fruits and vegetables, it is very unlikely that she will become vitamin C deficient.

how to make sure your child gets it

It is important that your child's diet provides a good combination of both raw and cooked fruits and vegetables. Vitamin C is very easily destroyed by heat and light, so include raw or very lightly cooked foods, such as steamed vegetables, in your baby or toddler's diet as much as possible. But remember, babies cannot cope with citrus fruits until they are 6 months old. Chunks of raw, soft fruits and vegetables make great snacks, but until she is confident with chewing and eating crunchier foods always stay with her while she is eating them.

key vitamin C foods

These foods may not all be suitable for babies and toddlers in all age groups. See the relevant chapters for specific advice.

- Kiwi fruit
- Strawberries
- Raspberries
- Oranges and other citrus fruits
- Mango and melon
- Papaya
- Nectarines
- Peaches
- Blackcurrants
- Red, green, orange and yellow peppers
- Broccoli
- Cabbage
- Mangetout and peas
- Grapefruit
- Cauliflower
- Spinach
- Potatoes and sweet potatoes
- Swede.

fats

Fats and oils are made up of molecules of three types of fatty acids, and glycerol. A fat is said to be saturated, mono-unsaturated or polyunsaturated, depending on which type of fatty acid is present in the largest proportion. Saturated fats, such as butter, are solid at room temperature and are sometimes referred to as 'bad' fats. Mono-unsaturated fats, such as olive oil, and polyunsaturated fats, such as sunflower oil, are liquid at room temperature.

why your child needs them

Fats are energy-dense foods and are essential to meet a baby's demands for her rapid growth and development. They also allow toddlers to obtain their energy requirements from a manageable amount of food. This is particularly helpful because toddlers have such small stomach capacities. Foods that contain fats provide not only a concentrated source of energy but also the fat-soluble vitamins A, D, E and K, all of which are vital for the healthy development of your child. Many parents are concerned about the amount of fat in their toddler's diet, but it is essential to include some fatty acids in the diet, both saturated and unsaturated, as they are essential to health. It is the 'quality' of fat that is more important than worrying about quantity for babies – let your baby's appetite guide you. Low-fat products and low-fat diets are not suitable for babies or toddlers, although semi-skimmed milk can be given to toddlers from 2 years as long as they are following a healthy balanced diet.

how to make sure your child gets them

Give your child a healthy, balanced diet, which includes both saturated and unsaturated fats. Essential fatty acids are found in plant and fish oils. They cannot be made in the body and so, like vitamins and minerals, they need to be present in your baby or toddler's diet. Fat is the greatest provider of energy to babies in the first months of life. More than 50 per cent of the energy from breast milk comes from fat. Infant formula milks and follow-on formula milks provide 30 to 56.6 per cent of their energy from fat.

carbohydrates

There are two types of carbohydrates: simple (sugars) and complex (starches and fibre). Both can be found in a natural form or they can be refined. Carbohydrates are the body's primary source of energy.

why your child needs them

Your baby or toddler needs a good source of carbohydrates to provide her with energy to get through each day but also to fuel her growth and development. It is very important that she gets the right balance of carbohydrates. Too much refined carbohydrate, such as sugar and honey, including cakes and biscuits that contain them, can lead to dental or weight problems. Similarly, too much fibre in unrefined carbohydrates, such as brown rice or wholewheat pasta, can inhibit the absorption of other nutrients and the release of energy.

starches and fibre

Starches and fibre can be refined or natural.

how to make sure your child gets starch and fibre

'Provided energy intake is adequate, the proportion of energy supplied as starch in the weaning diet should increase as the proportion derived from fat decreases' (COMA).

Starch is well tolerated and easily absorbed by babies, so even though it can be bulky, it is relatively easy to ensure that your baby will consume the right quantity. Foods such as cereals, vegetables and in particular rice starch, are perfect weaning foods for your baby. High-fibre diets are not suitable for children under 1 year old.

You should aim to give your toddler a variety of complex carbohydrates, such as cereals, vegetables, pasta and pulses every day.

sugars

Sugars can either be refined or found in a more natural form.

how to make sure your child gets sugar

Sugars provide energy but have little nutritive value. Your baby or toddler should find fruit and milk-based products sweet enough without you needing to add any extra sugar, because they contain natural sugars. Introducing your child to too many sweet foods, such as cakes and biscuits, early on can encourage her to develop a sweet tooth later in life, so they should only be given in moderation. A little sugar added to the occasional dessert will not hurt, but it really should only be occasional.

key starch foods

These foods may not all be suitable for babies and toddlers in all age groups. *See* the relevant chapters for specific advice.

Refined starch foods:
- Processed breakfast cereals, such as Weetabix and porridge
- White flour and white bread
- Biscuits and cakes
- Baby rice.

Natural starch foods:
- Potatoes and bread
- Breakfast cereals, such as nut-free muesli
- Sweetcorn
- Root vegetables, such as parsnips
- Nuts – finely chopped or ground (do not give nuts or seeds to babies or toddlers under the age of 3 if there is a family history of food allergies)
- Chickpeas
- Bananas.

key sugar foods

These foods may not all be suitable for babies and toddlers in all age groups. *See* the relevant chapters for specific advice.

Natural sugar foods:
- Fruit and vegetables
- Breast milk and full-fat milk.

Refined sugar foods:
- White- and brown-coloured sugar
- Biscuits, cakes and jellies.

These foods may not all be suitable for babies and toddlers in all age groups. *See* the relevant chapters for specific advice.

- Breast milk, infant formula milk or full-fat cow's milk
- Liver and liver products
- Oily fish, such as herring, mackerel
- Full-fat cheese and unsalted butter
- Fortified margarine
- Egg yolks.

Good beta-carotene sources include:

- Sweet potatoes
- Mangoes
- Papayas
- Old (rather than baby) carrots
- Pumpkins
- Puréed or finely chopped dried unsulphured apricots
- Yellow-fleshed melons, such as cantaloupe
- Tomatoes
- Leeks
- Courgettes
- Red, yellow and orange peppers
- Green beans
- Broccoli
- Spinach
- Dark green cabbage.

vitamin A

Vitamin A is found in animal products. Beta-carotene is a substance found in plant foods and converted by the body into vitamin A.

why your child needs it

Vitamin A is needed for growth, development, healthy skin and hair, and good colour and night vision. It also helps the development of healthy teeth.

how to make sure your child gets it

Only a limited number of foods contain vitamin A other than breast milk, infant formula milk or full-fat milk. For this reason, the UK Department of Health still recommends vitamin drops for babies, to ensure that they have an adequate intake, especially those who are still being breastfed after 6 months or taking less than 500ml formula milk a day. Ask your family doctor or health visitor or paediatric doctor for more information.

If your toddler is being given a healthy well-balanced diet she should get all the vitamin A or beta-carotene she needs. Speak to your family doctor or state-registered dietician before giving a vitamin A supplement, as too much vitamin A can be detrimental to your toddler's health.

vitamin B group

The vitamin B complex comprises vitamin B_1 (thiamine), B_2 (riboflavin), B_3 (niacin), folic acid, B_5 (pantothenic acid), B_6 (pyridoxine) and B_{12} (cyanocobalamin).

why your child needs them

The B vitamins play many roles: they are essential for your baby or toddler's metabolism and for helping with the conversion of carbohydrate into energy. They are also vital for the maintenance of healthy nervous and immune systems, mucous membranes and a healthy brain. They assist in the production of red blood cells, skin and hair.

how to make sure your child gets them

Some foods, such as red meat, contain all the B vitamins. If your child is being fed a well-balanced diet she should get all the B vitamins she needs. However, if she is being fed a restricted diet, she may need supplements (*see* pages 40–41); babies breastfed by vegan mothers may receive low levels of vitamin B_{12} from the breast milk; similarly, babies weaned onto vegan diets and toddlers following vegan diets may need supplements, as they are at risk of becoming deficient in vitamin B_{12}. All the B vitamins are water-soluble, so where you can, give your child raw or uncooked fruit and vegetables, bread and cheese to maximize her B vitamin intake. Chunks of raw, soft fruits and vegetables make great snacks, but until she is confident with chewing and eating crunchier foods always stay with her while she is eating them.

key vitamin B foods

These foods may not all be suitable for babies and toddlers in all age groups. *See* the relevant chapters for specific advice.

B_1:
- Brazil nuts and peanuts – finely chopped or ground (don't give nuts to babies or toddlers under the age of 3 if there is a family history of food allergies)
- Potatoes
- Bacon and red meat
- Bread and cereal products
- Full-fat milk.

B_2:
- Liver and red meat
- Full-fat milk and cheese
- Fortified cereals and eggs.

B_3:
- Meat
- Potatoes, bread and cereal products
- Dried fruit
- Nuts – finely chopped or ground (*see* warning above).

Folic acid:
- Green leafy vegetables, such as spinach, broccoli and Brussels sprouts
- Oranges
- Yeast extract
- Cereal products and bread fortified with folic acid
- Nuts – finely chopped or ground (*see* warning above).

B_6:
- Red meat and liver
- Fish and eggs
- Bananas and avocados
- Cereal products.

B_{12}:
- Meat
- Full-fat milk products.

key vitamin D foods

These foods may not all be suitable for babies and toddlers in all age groups. *See* the relevant chapters for specific advice.
- Oily fish, such as sardines
- Eggs and unsalted butter
- Fortified margarine
- Full-fat milk, yogurt and cheese
- Fortified cereals.

vitamin D

Vitamin D is mainly made by the skin in the presence of sunlight, hence its nickname the 'sunshine vitamin'.

why your child needs it

Vitamin D is essential for the absorption of calcium and the normal growth and healthy development of strong bones and teeth. It also plays a role in maintaining a healthy immune system.

how to make sure your child gets it

Vitamin D is naturally present in only a few foods, and these are all of animal origin. Breast milk contains little vitamin D and breastfed babies rely on their stores at birth and exposure to sunlight to maintain satisfactory levels. Infant formula milks are fortified with vitamin D. Some other products, such as breakfast cereals and margarine, are also fortified and should be included in your child's diet. For this reason all babies and toddlers should spend at least 30 minutes outdoors each day – if this is not possible your child may need a supplement: speak to your family doctor or state-registered dietician (*see* 'supplements', opposite).

key vitamin E foods

These foods may not all be suitable for babies and toddlers in all age groups. *See* the relevant chapters for specific advice.
- Unsalted butter
- Meat
- Vegetable oils
- Wheatgerm and wholegrain cereal
- Nuts and seeds – finely chopped or ground (don't give nuts or seeds to babies or toddlers under the age of 3 if there is a family history of food allergies)
- Tomatoes and avocados
- Sweet potatoes
- Spinach and watercress
- Mangoes
- Egg yolks
- Oily fish, such as sardines and salmon
- Blackberries.

vitamin E

Vitamin E is an antioxidant that is thought to play an important role in reducing the risk of diseases such as cancer and heart disease.

why your child needs it

Vitamin E is needed to help develop and maintain strong healthy cells, especially in the blood and nervous system.

how to make sure your child gets it

Vitamin E is pretty widely available from the diet, including, for babies, breast milk and infant formula milk. If your child is being given a balanced diet she should get all the vitamin E she needs.

phosphorus

Phosphorus is a mineral that works in a way similar to calcium.

why your child needs it
Phosphorus is vital for energy production. It helps to build and maintain healthy bones and teeth. It also aids the absorption and transport of many other nutrients.

how to make sure your child gets it
About half your child's phosphorus will come from milk. Phosphorus is present in nearly all foods.

key phosphorus foods
These foods may not all be suitable for babies and toddlers in all age groups. *See* the relevant chapters for specific advice.
- Breast milk or full-fat dairy products
- Bread and cereal products
- Red meat and poultry
- Fish
- Eggs
- Pulses, such as chickpeas
- Potatoes
- Yeast extract
- Pumpkin seeds (do not give nuts or seeds to toddlers under the age of 3 if there is a family history of food allergies)
- Fruit and vegetables
- Nuts – finely chopped or ground (*see* warning above).

supplements
Current UK Government guidelines recommend that all children between 6 months and 5 years should be considered for receiving vitamin A, C and D drops. If your child is a good eater and being given a healthy, well-balanced diet, including a wide range of foods, she will probably not need any drops. However, problem eaters, those who were born prematurely, those on restricted diets such as vegans (*see* page 40) or children with little chance of being outside in the sunlight, may need them. Always speak to your family doctor or registered dietician before giving any supplements to your child. Vitamin drops may be available free of charge to certain families, but this does vary from area to area.

milk for babies and toddlers

breast is best

Breast milk provides all the essential nutrients your baby needs for development during her first six months. From then on, she requires a combination of milk and solids.

Breast milk is the only food naturally designed for your baby, and research studies have suggested that the health benefits of breast milk can be significant and lifelong. My advice would be to at least start by breastfeeding, as some breastfeeding is better than none. Even premature babies who are given breast milk often do better than those given formula milk.

Breastfed babies can be easier to wean because they have had traces of your diet in their breast milk. Breastfeeding has many advantages for you, too – it helps you to get your shape back and it encourages your womb to contract more quickly. Best of all, breastfeeding is practical; it takes little time to do and the milk is always at the right temperature.

Breastfeeding is natural, but it does not come naturally to every mum. Don't be afraid to ask for help if you are finding it hard. There are books on breastfeeding, as well as organizations that provide information on solely on that subject and counsellors trained to help mothers with difficulties. Breastfeeding is encouraged and supported by most baby experts and health professionals, so persevere. I had a difficult time with my firstborn in the first three months and used to dread the next feed, but I sought help with remarkable results.

colostrum

The first liquid your breasts produce is colostrum. This is the perfect nutrition for your baby during her first few days. Colostrum has more protein and vitamins and less carbohydrate and fat than the mature milk that arrives between days 3 and 5. It also provides antibodies that protect your baby's health while she is building up her immune system and developing long-term resistance to infections. There is no artificial equivalent of colostrum, so the first few days at the breast gives your baby a head start.

breast milk

Breast milk is different in appearance, texture and nutritional composition to colostrum. Breast milk provides the balance and concentration of nutrients in a digestible form and it contains enzymes that aid the digestive process. The make-up of milk varies during your baby's feed: 'fore' milk is produced at the beginning of the feed, and is high in volume and low in fat; as your baby progresses she will reach the 'hind' milk that will help her go for longer between feeds. This is why your baby should drink for a certain amount of time from one breast before being transferred to the next. As a guide, once your baby is a week old, she should be spending 25–30 minutes on the first breast

key nutrients in milk

	breast milk (100ml)	formula milk (100ml)
energy:		
kilojoule (kJ)	293kj	280–310kj
kilocalorie (kcal)	70kcal	67–74kcal
protein	1.3g	1.4–1.8g
carbohydrate	7g	7.2–9.3g
fat	4.2g	3.3–3.6g
vitamins:		
A	60µg	64–78µg
D	0.01µg	0.9–1.4µg
E	0.35mg	0.4–1.3mg
C	3.8mg	8.2–9mg
K	0.21µg	0–6.7µg
B vitamins:		
B_1 (thiamine)	16µg	40–100µg
B_2 (riboflavin)	30µg	73–150µg
B_3 (niacin)	620µg	760–960µg
B_5 (pantothenic acid)	260µg	270–450µg
B_6 (pyridoxine)	6µg	40–60µg
B_{12} (cyanocobalamin)	0.01µg	0.14–0.2µg
Folic acid	5.0µg	4.9–13µg
minerals:		
calcium	35mg	46–81mg
phosphorus	15mg	26–48mg
zinc	295µg	500–920µg
iron	76µg	650–1300µg
potassium	60mg	64–85mg
sodium	15mg	16–22mg
chloride	43mg	41–43mg
magnesium	3mg	5–7mg
copper	39µg	17–50µg
iodine	7µg	8.1–12µg

Important note: The rate of absorption of nutrients from breast milk is significantly higher than it is from formula milk. This is particularly relevant in relation to micronutrients such as minerals. That means although most infant formula milks contain higher levels of certain nutrients than human milk, your baby will more easily absorb the nutrients in the latter.

g = gram
mg = milligram
(one-thousandth of a gram)
µg = microgram
(one-millionth of a gram)

Breast-milk data from COMA report, 'Weaning and the Weaning Diet' (1995). Formula milk range taken from the first milks from the following brands: SMA Gold, Hipp Organic, Cow & Gate Premium and Aptamil.

before being transferred. Recent studies have found that breastfeeding can optimize brain development and minimize the chances of neurological problems. There is also evidence to suggest that breastfed babies can have higher IQs than bottle-fed babies because of the essential fatty acids and other key nutrients in breast milk.

Breastfeeding also helps prevent your baby suffering from minor infections, supporting her underdeveloped immune system for as long as it is offered.

allergies

Breast milk is less likely to cause allergies in your baby than formula milks, most of which are based on cow's milk protein. This is particularly true in families with a strong history of food allergies, eczema or asthma. If, however, during breastfeeding, you notice any symptoms such as diarrhoea, vomiting or rashes, or if you have a family history of allergies to food, speak to your family doctor.

your diet when breastfeeding

Your diet affects both the flavour and nutritional composition of your milk. It is important to eat a balanced, varied diet when breastfeeding. You need to eat foods from all the main food groups, providing all the essential nutrients. Eat small, frequent meals and drink at least 2 litres of water a day. Try to get plenty of rest (easier said than done), especially if this is not your first baby. You may wish to increase the intake of certain vitamins and minerals while breastfeeding. Vitamin D supplementation of 10µg per day is often recommended. For more information, ask your family doctor or state-registered dietician.

why organic

In recent years many people have become concerned about levels of pesticide residues and other by-products of intensive farming, such as antibiotics, that are found in non-organic food. Although these are permitted levels, deemed safe by the UK Government, there has been an increase in the production and consumption of organic food, in which the levels are much lower. So if you choose more organic foods you will certainly consume fewer pesticides. Going organic is a personal choice, and many parents find it too expensive.

advantages of breastfeeding for mum

Your uterus will return to its pre-pregnancy state much faster if you breastfeed than if not. Hormones are released during feeding which help you relax. Also, you may find it easier to get your shape back because the extra fat your body lays down in preparation for lactation is used to feed your baby. Some mums believe that breastfeeding relieves long-term pre-menstrual tension.

disadvantages of breastfeeding for mum

I found the one disadvantage of breastfeeding occurred when it was time to return to work and I had to express more milk. There are many ways to cope with this, and the National Childbirth Trust or La Leche League provide excellent information.

bottle-feeding

Some mothers have to give up breastfeeding or find that it does not suit them and choose to stop. If you find breastfeeding too difficult, you should not be pressured to continue.

It is more important to ensure you and your baby are happy. There is a school of thought that your baby may suffer emotionally if you stop breastfeeding. My mother breastfed me only for the first few days of my life and no one could have had a stronger bond than she and I had.

If you have decided to bottle-feed your baby from day one, your hospital should provide you with ready-made formula milk. When you leave hospital, I would recommend choosing an organic brand of formula milk to ensure it contains no artificial additives, chemical pesticides or GM ingredients.

toddlers and milk

Milk, whether breast, formula or cow's, makes a vital contribution to your toddler's nutrition. Breast milk is a naturally nutrient-rich food that is easily digested by your toddler, and if you wish you can continue to breast-feed a toddler up to 2 years. La Leche League, a voluntary organization that promotes breastfeeding, believes that antibody production in breast milk increases after one year of breastfeeding, which helps boost your child's immune system. Breast milk is also free!

milk substitutes

Breast, formula and follow-on milks (offered later on) should be the main drinks in the first year. Cooled, boiled tap water may be given in between feeds (cooled, boiled bottled water is safe unless labelled 'natural mineral water', in which case it can contain higher concentrations of solutes such as sodium and fluoride). Other drinks, such as diluted fruit juice, should be given only at meal times once you are weaning, in a feeding cup. It is wise to consult your doctor, midwife, health visitor, nurse, state-registered dietician or pharmacist for more information on breast-milk alternatives before choosing.

infant formula milks

These provide a sole source of nourishment for babies for the first four to six months. Infant formula milk is more likely to trigger an allergic reaction than human milk because it is based on cow's milk protein. If you have a family history of allergies, seek advice before you start formula-milk feeding.

organic infant formula milks

Made with organic ingredients and guaranteed to be GM free.

soya infant formula milks

There are concerns about the long-term health effects of soya-based infant formula, particularly that babies with a risk of allergies may also become sensitive to soya protein. There has only been one study examining long-term implications and, although it did not find any adverse effects, it is recommended (by the British Nutrition Foundation) that soya-based formulas should only be fed to infants on the advice of a doctor or state-registered dietitian.

follow-on milk

Unlike infant formula milks, these are not intended to be a sole source of nutrition but part of a mixed diet. The levels of some nutrients in follow-on milk are higher than in human or cow's milk, with a minimum level of iron twice that specified for infant formula milk.

Fresh cow's, goat's or sheep's milk should not be given as a drink to babies under the age of 1. Similarly, soya drinks, other than soya infant formula milk, should not be given during weaning.

From the age of 1 it is possible to make the transition from breast or formula milk to pasteurized full-fat cow's milk. Infant formula is normally based on cow's milk and is the main alternative to breast milk in the first six months. After 6 months you can introduce 'follow-on' milks – these are similar to formula, but with different nutritional qualities (however, if your baby is getting a broad range of foods as she is being weaned, ordinary formula will be just as good). After 1 year there is no reason to continue giving formula or follow-on milk, as cow's milk can now be given as a drink.

cow's milk

From the age of 6 months, cow's milk can be used in cooking, but it should not be given as a drink until your baby is at least 1 year old.

Toddlers over 1 year need a minimum of approximately 350ml full-fat milk a day, inclusive of milk used in food. Most toddlers need up to 565ml full-fat milk per day, with approximately 350ml of that being given as a drink. Milk makes an important contribution to a toddler's diet, providing a substantial proportion of their daily intake of protein, fat, zinc, calcium and B vitamins, particularly riboflavin. Often, at this stage, growth may slow down and your toddler's appetite may slacken off. Giving milk will help to ensure that your child is receiving many essential nutrients in one hit.

When giving cow's milk as a drink to toddlers under the age of 2, always make sure it is full fat. The fat content of milk is an important source of energy for 1- to 2-year-olds. Also, the vitamins A, D and E are found mainly in the milk's cream. Toddlers aged 2 to 4 are generally eating a wider range of foods, so they do not need to rely on cow's milk so much. At this stage, as long as your toddler is a good eater, with a varied diet that provides sufficient good fats, semi-skimmed milk can be introduced. Skimmed milk should not be given to children under the age of 5.

Cow's milk contains all essential nutrients. However, the concentrations of some of these are different in cow's milk to in breast milk and formula. For example, full-fat cow's milk contains less iron and vitamin D compared to breast milk. Most toddlers will be consuming sufficient amounts of these nutrients from other foods and, in the case of vitamin D, through the action of sunlight on the skin, so there is no cause for concern. In a few cases where your toddler's diet is restricted or she cannot make enough vitamin D because she is not getting enough exposure to sunlight, your family doctor may recommend continuing formula feeding and giving vitamin supplements.

milk intolerance

A small number of young children may not be able to tolerate cow's milk. This may be for one of two reasons. Cow's milk contains the milk sugar lactose, and some people may be intolerant to this as they may lack or have an insufficient amount of the enzyme lactase in the gut to help digest this sugar. Symptoms include digestive problems such as stomach pain and diarrhoea. Cow's milk also contains cow's milk protein, which a small percentage of young children may be allergic to. This means their immune system views this protein as something foreign and reacts against it, resulting in various symptoms such as asthma and eczema. Most children grow out of both of these intolerances. In both cases, a dairy-free diet may be recommended by the doctor or dietician. Some toddlers who are lactose-intolerant may be able to tolerate a small amount of dairy foods, whereas with cow's milk protein allergy, a dairy-free diet will certainly be recommended until the child grows out of it.

milk alternatives

When cow's milk is not an option, breast milk should ideally be promoted, depending on the age of the child. If that is not possible, soya products enriched with calcium are suggested as the next option. This is because they have a high-quality protein equivalent to cow's milk and because the calcium is as equally well absorbed as that from dairy. If a child cannot tolerate soya, some other alternatives such as pasteurized goat's and sheep's milk may be suggested. However, both of these are low in iron and vitamin D. Goat's milk is also deficient in folic acid. When these are recommended by health professionals, vitamin drops are also suggested.

organic

Milk is one of the biggest organic sellers in supermarkets. Organic milk is different from ordinary milk because the cows feed on organic pastures, hay and silage. The other feeds they are given are vegetable based and so will not contain animal by-products, such as fishmeal. This is one of the main reasons why organic milk has, in my opinion, a noticeably better flavour than non-organic milk. Organic milk is guaranteed to be free from antibiotics, as the routine use of antibiotics is prohibited in organic farming. Organic goat's and sheep's milk are also becoming more widely available.

soya drink

Regular calcium-enriched soya drinks and yogurt alternatives can be given to young children as part of a healthy balanced diet, but not as the main source of milk under 2 years of age. If your toddler has an intolerance to cow's milk, or you have chosen to give her a vegan diet, you will need an alternative milk source. The UK Government recommends breast milk as the best main drink for your toddler so, if you can, continue to breastfeed. It is important, where there is an allergy or intolerance, or if you choose a cow's, breast or formula milk alternative, to seek advice from your family doctor or registered dietician, who may recommend a hydrolyzed cow's milk formula or soya infant formula.

bottle, breast or beaker

By 9 months, bottle-fed babies should be drinking all of their water, diluted juice and most of their milk feeds from a beaker. By the age of 1, all drinks, with the exception of breast milk (unless you are expressing), should now be given in a beaker or cup.

Having reached this stage, the transition from formula milk to cow's milk will be only a matter of taste. I feel that because formula is based on cow's milk, which you will have been using in cooking, the change is relatively easy. If you are switching from beaker-fed breast milk, you may need to make the change more gradually.

However, if you have managed to breastfeed into your toddler's first year, you may want to wean her from the breast during her second year. This will require more careful planning, because it is a far more emotional transition. For each breastfeed that you are giving your baby, you need to allow five to seven days to drop it. In my experience the night-time feed is the most difficult to drop, so leave that one until last. Start by reducing each feed by around five minutes, topping up with cow's milk given in a beaker. This will also help your body to adjust to the change, preventing blocked milk ducts, which can lead to sore and painful breasts.

food
purity

organic food

Babies and toddlers have unique and delicate physiologies; their digestive systems are far more efficient at absorbing food than those of adults. This enables nutrients to be used quickly, but also makes babies and toddlers vulnerable to toxins, especially from additives, pesticides and other chemical residues often found in non-organic food. Research has found that babies and toddlers are more exposed to these substances than adults because, weight for weight, they eat larger quantities of a small range of foods than adults, which are often the ones most contaminated with residues, such as bananas and cow's milk. In addition, a baby's immature kidneys cannot excrete harmful substances efficiently so they circulate around the body for longer.

The Soil Association, a UK-based organic certifying body, describes organic farming as a 'safe, sustainable farming system, producing healthy crops and livestock without damage to the environment'. Organic food is produced without the use of synthetic pesticides, fungicides, fertilizers and growth hormones. The residues of these chemicals in non-organic foods cause concern. They have been used in food production for years but we still don't know the health impacts of long-term exposure to them.

Buying certified organic produce guarantees that food has been grown and processed according to strict standards, set out in law to prohibit the use of certain chemicals and retain the 'integrity' of the food. These stringent regulations must be followed, not only by food producers and growers, but also by food manufacturers, processors, packers and importers. There are even stricter regulations for baby foods. I'd advise you to list the five foods you most often give to your baby or toddler and resolve to buy organic, even if it is just basics such as milk, bread, apples and potatoes. Staple foods, such as baby rice, wheat products, fruit and vegetables, are often the worst offenders when non-organic.

Many parents argue that organic food is too expensive. As organic farming is more labour intensive than conventional farming, organic food costs more to produce and can be more expensive to buy than non-organic. But as its production is becoming more widespread, prices are falling. There are ways to buy cheaply without compromising on quality: buy unprocessed organic foods such as fruit, vegetables and meat seasonally from markets, farm shops or local producers and cook with them at home rather than buying expensively packaged organic processed supermarket food.

genetically modified foods

Throughout history different crops and animals have been bred specifically to produce certain desirable qualities. Genetic modification (GM) permits scientists to move DNA from one plant or animal species to another. This means that a vegetable may contain a small part of an animal gene, which has the effect of making it resistant to a certain herbicide or antibiotic.

As it develops, GM technology seems to provide solutions to many problems in world agriculture and food production. However, in recent years a vociferous anti-GM movement has emerged. There has been little research into the long-term effects of such foods on the environment and on human health. All foods containing GM products are now required by British law to be clearly labelled, making it easy for you to decide whether to buy them or not. All organic food is certified non-GM.

additives and preservatives

There are thousands of food additives in the form of preservatives, antioxidants, artificial colourings and flavourings, flavour enhancers, artificial sweeteners, stabilizers and thickeners. Their main purpose is to give processed food a longer shelf-life and to make it more palatable. Although some additives help to make food safe to eat, most have no health benefits or nutritional value. Few additives are known to be completely safe, and the quantity of additives children consume can be large. (According to the Food Commission, by the time children have reached the age of 17 they have typically consumed their own weight in food additives.) Research is still being carried out into their long-term effects on human health. An official study into the link between food colouring and children's tantrums found that colourings induce hyperactive behaviour in 25 per cent of children. Other studies have shown a link between food additives and conditions such as asthma, eczema, allergies and behavioural problems.

Some additives are permitted in certain foods, usually because they have a specific role, such as stopping a product going rancid. Additives approved for use in the European Union (EU) have an 'E-number' allocated to them. Read labels carefully. All food labels in the UK must list all E-numbers or the actual name of the additives contained in the product in the ingredients list.

There are more than 900 approved E-numbers. E-numbers have been banned from use in baby food in the EU, but when your child is weaned and begins to eat what the rest of the family eats, she may be exposed to them. Some foods are not regarded by manufacturers as 'children's foods' and so contain high quantities of additives and salt. Try to cut out foods that are high in additives for all the family, and eat home-cooked food as much as possible.

the importance of freshness

There are many reasons why fresh, home-cooked food is the best choice for your baby or toddler. Most importantly, freshly prepared food will maximize your child's intake of essential nutrients, especially if it is served raw when appropriate, or cooked for the shortest time possible. Fresh foods will often look, smell and taste better than processed foods. Giving them to your baby or toddler, especially when you eat them yourself, will help her to develop an appreciation for freshly prepared, unprocessed foods, which will hopefully last a lifetime. Always remember that even organic ready-made food will always be inferior to fresh, home-made versions. Even the best baby foods have been processed, cooked and packaged and will inevitably have lost some of their nutritional value. If you are feeding your family home-made food, you can easily adapt the meal for your baby or toddler.

Sometimes it is just not possible to juggle work and family life and still have time to make fresh meals every day. There is a vast range of convenience foods out there and they are not all bad. By choosing carefully and reading labels, you can buy certain things that will save you lots of time and, if you add some fresh ingredients to them, they can make up a useful part of your child's diet. For example, if you are buying baby food in jars, add a little mashed banana or avocado to up the nutrient content. Adding some chopped fresh ripe tomatoes to beans on toast is also a good idea.

labels

Most pre-packaged food for babies and toddlers is strictly regulated, but get into the habit of reading labels – this is the best way to prevent your child from eating large quantities of additives. Look out for and avoid, if possible, the following: salt (often listed as sodium); sugars – sucrose, dextrose, glucose, fructose, lactose, maltose, honey, invert sugar syrups and fruit syrups; meat or vegetable extracts, hydrolyzed vegetable protein or yeast in savoury foods, which often indicate over-processing; processed starches, because they are often used to counteract the overuse of water – they are low-nutrient fillers, such as modified cornflour, maltodextrin, rice starch and wheat starch, and they dull the flavour of the food. Their presence often means the food will need flavouring or added sugar or salt to make it taste better; flavourings – these are unnecessary for babies and toddlers and only introduce your child to artificial tastes.

'children's foods'

Many parents assume that their children need to be cooked for separately, rather than eating what the adults eat. They also find themselves under pressure from their child who, influenced by her peers, wants foods that are not always good for her. Many parents rely on pre-packaged foods – marketed as 'children's foods' or 'convenience' foods – and it can be a hard habit to get out of. A cartoon-covered pot of brightly coloured yogurt is irresistible to most toddlers, and there is a huge range of these foods available. If the whole family has a healthy diet, you can feed your toddler what the rest of the family eats – just simplify it or chop it up as appropriate. The recipes in this book are designed for the whole family. Inevitably, it will be almost impossible to avoid junk food altogether, and being too prohibitive will only make the issue more contentious, just keep it to a minimum (*see* page 30).

first
cooking

Preparing food at home gives you control over what goes into the dish and it is usually cheaper than buying ready-made food. Yet the main advantage is nutritional. How you cook the food will affect its nutrient content. One of the best ways to prepare vegetables for your baby is to steam them. When she is confident with chewing, give her chunks of steamed vegetables, such as carrots, to get her used to the texture and taste.

steaming and boiling
When you do cook, especially fruit and vegetables, do it for the shortest time needed. If you boil food, only add just enough water to cover, and if a purée needs thinning, use some of the cooking water.

microwaving
Some scientists are concerned about the effect of microwave radiation on food, particularly on its ability to deplete breast milk's disease-fighting capabilities. I have concerns about the health implications of giving babies microwaved food. I do not use a microwave when I cook for my children; I find steaming, baking and boiling are all preferable alternatives.

freezing
It is a good idea to make more home-cooked food than you need and freeze the excess, especially when you are weaning. Most purées freeze brilliantly; exceptions include those made with banana or avocado. For fruit and vegetable purées, you just need some sterilized, rubber ice-cube trays and new freezer bags. As your baby gets older, small ramekins are great for freezing baby-sized meals that need to be reheated. But don't freeze a huge amount of purée because your baby will never get through it! All the recipes in the freezer sections of this book have instructions on when to freeze and how to reheat, but there are a few general rules:
- Cool food quickly that is to be frozen.
- Always label and date the food; after a long time its taste and texture will deteriorate.
- Ideally, defrost food in the refrigerator overnight, although for small cubes of purée this is not necessary – just reheat them in a bowl over a pan of boiling water.
- Make sure that food is thoroughly reheated and never refreeze.
- Freeze breast milk for up to a month.
- Freeze food containing dairy produce for up to six weeks.
- Freeze food made only from fruit or vegetables for up to eight weeks.
- Freeze food containing meat and fish for up to three months.

first
kitchen

equipment

If you are breastfeeding, you won't need any kitchen equipment, but as you start to wean your baby from breast to bottle, whether you are using breast milk or formula milk, there are a few basics you will need: bottles, teats and sterilizing equipment (*see* below). A bottle insulator is useful for transporting milk when you and your baby are out and about, and is also good for night feeds. An expressor is invaluable when you are breastfeeding, as it will enable you to prepare feeds in advance, giving you some independence from your baby. Both manual and electric ones are available. It's worth asking your hospital if they lend out electric ones.

As your baby starts to eat solid food, you will need an unbreakable bowl, spoons without hard edges and a large supply of bibs. A stainless-steel saucepan is best because non-stick ones are coated in plastic, which can contaminate food. A steamer is also useful, although a metal colander or sieve on top of a wide saucepan, covered with a lid, makes a good alternative. For making purées, a hand-held blender with a detachable blade is quick and easy to clean, and it can travel with you. A mouli or ricer, or even a nylon sieve, will do the job, but it takes longer. Rubber ice-cube trays are the best for freezing small quantities of baby food, and you'll also need airtight containers and ziplock bags for freezing.

hygiene

Most kitchen hygiene is common sense, but with a baby you will need to take extra care.
- Always wash your hands before preparing feeds and, as your baby becomes old enough to hold food or feed herself, wash her hands before and after meals.
- Make sure all your equipment is clean and sterilized correctly (*see* below).
- Put raw meat and fish at the bottom of the refrigerator, ensuring it cannot drip onto fresh food, and use different chopping boards for raw and cooked food.
- Cook food thoroughly and don't use food past its sell-by date.
- Keep pets out of the kitchen.
- Keep food covered.
- Never save uneaten food from the feeding bowl or undrunk milk from the bottle.
- Sterile bottles of breast milk or formula milk can be kept chilled in the refrigerator for up to 24 hours – after that they must be thrown away.

sterilizing

Whether feeding breast milk or formula milk, it is essential that all the equipment you use is thoroughly sterilized. Warm milk is the perfect feeding ground for bacteria. If teats and bottles are not washed thoroughly, your baby could become very ill. Most tummy upsets in babies are caused by poor hygiene when feeding.

There are three main methods of sterilizing: boil all the equipment for at least ten minutes in a large pan; soak the equipment in sterilizing solution for two hours and then rinse with boiling water; use an electric steam sterilizer. I found the steam sterilizer to be the easiest and most convenient method; just follow the instructions carefully.

As your baby is weaned onto solid food, it is best to sterilize her bowl and feeding spoons. However, as soon as she can crawl and put everything in reach into her mouth there is no need to continue sterilizing these items. Nevertheless, you should continue to sterilize any bottles you use for milk feeds up to the age of 1. With equipment that it is impractical to sterilize, such as saucepans and sieves, make sure you wash these items thoroughly in hot water and detergent, and rinse them well to remove any residues. There are two key things to remember:

● Sterile bottles of breast milk or formula milk can be kept chilled in the refrigerator for up to 24 hours. Follow manufacturer's guidelines for bottle insulators.

● Once your baby has finished feeding, get into the habit of rinsing and washing bottles ready for sterilizing. Always throw away any milk left over from a feed.

washing and drying equipment

Use an organic detergent, if possible, because they are much milder and far less likely to irritate if they come into contact with your baby's skin. If you have a dishwasher, make use of it, because the water goes to a high temperature and the crockery will be air dried. Let equipment air dry as much as possible and avoid drying with a tea-towel that may harbour germs, use kitchen paper instead.

essential equipment

- Bottles
- Teats
- Bottle cleaner
- Sterilizing equipment
- Expressor
- Bottle insulator
- Rubber ice-cube trays
- Ziplock freezer bags
- Airtight containers

- Steamer
- Nylon sieve
- Hand-held blender or electric food processor or blender
- Stainless-steel saucepan
- Plastic feeding bowl
- Shallow baby spoons
- Bibs

vegetarian
toddlers

Vegetarians do not eat meat or fish, but they do eat dairy produce, eggs and honey. A varied, balanced vegetarian diet provides all the nutrients for healthy growth and development, but a diet that keeps an adult vegetarian in good health is not necessarily appropriate for a toddler. A toddler's rapid growth and development means that she needs energy- and nutrient-dense foods daily, such as milk, cheese, pulses and nut butters. A vegan diet excludes all animal-derived produce, including honey. Talk to your family doctor, health visitor or registered dietician before you begin feeding your toddler such a diet.

For vegetarian and vegan diets you need to pay particular attention to the following nutrients (*see* pages 17–27 for more information):

protein – milk and milk products are rich in protein, as are pulses, soya products, nuts, nut butters and seeds (do not feed seeds or nuts or their products to toddlers under the age of 3 if there is any family history of food allergies). Bread and cereal-based products (eg pasta, noodles, rice) and potatoes are useful sources. As plant sources of protein (except for soya) do not contain all the essential amino acids, it is important to feed your toddler a variety of plant foods.

iron – good sources include eggs, green vegetables, dried fruit, beans and tofu. Foods containing vitamin C (eg citrus fruits) will aid iron absorption. Avoid high-fibre foods (eg bran) or any containing tannin or caffeine (ie tea and coffee), as they inhibit iron absorption.

calcium – milk and milk products are the best sources for vegetarians. Other sources include leafy green vegetables, fortified white bread and breakfast cereals, dried fruit (eg apricots), nuts and tahini (*see* warning above), calcium-fortified soya drink, tofu and miso.

zinc – good sources include oats, wholemeal bread, nuts (*see* warning above), rice, pulses, soya products including tofu and miso, parsley and bean sprouts. Be careful not to feed your baby too many wholemeal foods as they can adversely affect the absorption of zinc. Try to feed her low-fibre foods instead.

vitamin D – milk is the best source for vegetarians. Other sources include fortified breakfast cereals and margarine. However, vitamin D is mainly made by the skin in sunlight. It is important for your toddler to be outside for at least 30 minutes daily between the months of March and October in the Northern Hemisphere or she may need a supplement (*see* page 27).

vitamin B$_{12}$ – milk and milk products are good sources for vegetarians. Also fortified breakfast cereals and yeast extract. Vegans are likely to need a supplement (*see* page 25).

riboflavin (vitamin B$_2$) – milk, fortified breakfast cereals, eggs and some fortified soya drinks provide vitamin B$_2$. Vegans are likely to need a supplement (*see* page 25).

fibre – with a wide variety of foods, your vegetarian or vegan toddler's fibre intake will be adequate. Avoid bran, which can impair the absorption of minerals, particularly calcium and zinc.

special toddler
diets

diabetes

Type one diabetes is a condition where the body does not produce enough insulin, which is needed to process glucose into energy. A toddler suffering from diabetes often experiences drastic swings in energy levels as her blood sugar fluctuates. Untreated diabetes can be fatal. About one in 500 children have this kind of diabetes. It can develop suddenly, with the child often feeling unwell for a couple of weeks, feeling thirsty and going to the toilet frequently. If you notice these sorts of symptoms speak to your family doctor – a simple urine test can provide a quick diagnosis. This type of diabetes can be managed through a combination of monitoring blood sugar levels, insulin injections and a well-balanced diet. Type two diabetes usually develops later in life – its onset has been linked to excess weight and obesity, where eating a high-fat and high-sugar diet has contributed to this.

obesity

An obese toddler weighs 20 per cent or more above her ideal weight. While your child's weight and shape is partially predetermined by genetics, her diet and lifestyle plays an important role, and it is this that you can control. The fat and sugar content of toddlers' diets has increased significantly recently, particularly in 'children's' foods. Today's toddlers are also less active than they were a generation ago. Obesity at a young age can be detrimental to your child's health as an obese child is predisposed to obesity later in life. If you are concerned, take her to see your health visitor or family doctor to check her growth. However, many toddlers may look plump, or just be larger than average. If your child is over-weight or obese, the first approach in young children is to maintain weight so that as they grow their weight levels itself out with the child's increased height. The best course is to give your toddler a healthy, well-balanced diet with regular mealtimes. Take time to read labels if you are buying processed foods and find out what your child is eating if and when she is out of your care. Don't offer food as comfort. And encourage her to enjoy active play and to walk as much as possible. After the age of 4, an obese child is likely to remain fat, so it is important to address the causes of obesity during this stage of toddlerhood.

coeliac disease

This is a condition in which the lining of the gut is damaged by gluten, a protein found in wheat and rye. Coeliacs are also affected by similar proteins present in barley and possibly oats. The damage that occurs significantly reduces the absorption of nutrients from the gut, causing weight loss, diarrhoea and poor growth if not treated. It is easily treated by excluding gluten from the child's diet. Advice should be given by your doctor and state-registered dietician.

Aim to breastfeed for at least the first six months of your baby's life, as breast milk is the perfect food for a baby. It's much easier to breastfeed if you establish a routine early on. Conversations with midwives, state-registered paediatric dieticians and breastfeeding counsellors, as well as my own experience and that of close friends, have convinced me that it is possible and beneficial to start getting into a routine that suits you and your baby while your baby is still young. Achieving this may not be plain sailing, but the hard work will pay off when you find you can enjoy some quality time without having a screaming baby to cope with.

0–5 months

what's happening to
your baby

Your baby may be able to hold something at 3 months, but then again he may not be able to do so until he's 4 months old. Both are quite normal and every child is different. These sections on your baby's development are meant as a guide; if you are concerned about any aspect of your baby's development, never be afraid to talk to your health visitor or family doctor.

your baby's weight and height

Your baby will undergo considerable change during these early months. One of the first things that you are likely to notice is his weight. It's normal for your baby to lose weight after birth before he regains it. This is especially common among breastfed babies. Formula-fed babies may not lose weight, or may lose only a little and quickly put it back on.

Once your baby has regained his birth weight, he will probably gain about 25g a day. To help you relax about his growth, your health visitor, midwife or doctor should give you a book containing growth charts, or something similar, which will enable you to plot your baby's weight and height over time. Whatever your baby's length at birth, he will gain about 2cm every month. But there will always be variations, such as twins, triplets and premature babies, as well as the child's position in the family (first child, second child, etc).

your baby's responses to the world

You will begin to notice how your baby responds to the outside world. Almost from the time he is born he will be startled by sudden, loud noises. In the first few weeks he will gradually start to focus on your face when it is close to him. By 2 weeks he will recognize both your face and voice.
At around 1 month he may be able to lift his head briefly while lying on his stomach. An exciting milestone is when he smiles back at you, which can happen from around 6 weeks. At this stage, his eyes may be able to follow brightly coloured toys, and by the second month he may begin to make cooing noises and grasp an object if put in his hand.

By 4 months, your baby is likely to be more settled and to have a routine. You will be able to tell whether he is happy or not and he will often indicate this by smiling and laughing out loud. He can recognize your smell and voice and increasingly will be able to focus on objects close to him, in particular, your face. When you put him on the floor, he may be able to roll over in one direction. At this stage he will also be staying awake for longer during the day and will be more alert. This is a great time to start playing simple games and having conversations. He is very likely to be amused by seeing his reflection in a mirror; try putting him in front of one and watch him chat away.

your
routine

The traditional belief is that babies should be fed on demand. However, juggling family and work can leave you feeling exhausted and inadequate. For me, establishing a routine seemed a logical solution. I spoke to many midwives and health professionals and read extensively on the subject before creating a routine that made my life easier and, in turn, helped my children feel happy and secure. It was not always easy, but it was worth the effort, especially when, by 4 months, both my girls were sleeping through the night. The books that I found most useful included *Birth to Five* by the NHS and *The Contented Little Baby Book* by Gina Ford (Vermilion).

The routines I devised are relaxed and, in my experience, easily achievable by a busy modern mum. One of the main advantages of establishing a good routine is that you can quite quickly begin to understand your baby's needs. I was confident that if my girls had slept well and eaten well but were still crying, there was a reason for their stress or discomfort, which was often just that they needed to be held or changed. This knowledge helped me to feel more in control and calm, which in turn helped to make Ella, Jasmin and Finley relaxed babies.

And remember that it is crucial that you do not forget to think about yourself. Sleep whenever you can during the day, eat healthy snacks in between meals and drink lots of water.

weeks 1 and 2

your baby's first feeds

The first feed is very important and should be offered within the first hour of life outside the womb. This is when your baby is most alert and the instinct to suck is strong, and so is the ideal opportunity to commence breastfeeding. For the first few days your breasts produce a liquid called colostrum (*see* page 28). Feeding should be on demand for a normal weight, healthy-term baby. Hopefully, this will be little and often. However, many babies, naturally shocked by their birth, spend the first few days sleeping more than they will later on in order to recover. If your baby tends not to wake for feeds in the first few days, offer the breast every three or four hours to prevent long gaps. Waking him may seem a little unfair, but it will help to ensure an adequate milk supply on day three or four, help you to establish a routine and prevent your baby cramming lots of feeds into a short space of time. The length of feeds is individual and, as long as it is not painful to you, your baby should be left to suck. The feeding time can shorten when the milk comes in because greater volume is achieved with less effort; after time, it will gradually increase again.

your baby's feeds from 4 days old

After about four days your body stops producing colostrum and produces milk instead. By now your baby should be sucking on one breast for 15 to 20 minutes for each feed. It is important to remember which breast he drank from last so you can offer the other at the next feed. Each breast produces 'fore' and 'hind' milk. The fore milk is thirst-quenching and low in calories, but the hind milk is richer and more concentrated. By making sure each breast is emptied you will ensure he has drunk both types of milk. If your baby only drinks the fore milk he may be constantly hungry. As his appetite increases you will need to start offering him the second breast at each feed; if he's not lasting three hours between feeds he is probably ready for more milk.
During the day, aim to feed approximately every three hours.

expressing milk

Even if you get into the habit of feeding your baby frequently this is rarely enough to ensure you make sufficient milk to meet his demands during growth spurts. So if at all possible try to establish an expressing routine in the second or third week of feeding, once your milk has come in. This encourages your body to make more milk than your baby may need, but you will be producing enough milk for those times when his demand increases, preventing the need to feed more frequently, especially during the night. I know mums who have had to feed every two hours at night to help stimulate more milk during their baby's growth spurts. This is often when tiredness pushes mums to the limit and they either give up the routine or stop breastfeeding completely.

I found the best times of day for expressing were first thing in the morning, when sitting in bed, and at bedtime. An electric pump makes this easier. I then froze the milk for future use. If a breast is not empty after you have finished expressing, start the next feed on that breast. Express before or after his first and last feeds – approximately 50 to 75ml each time. During growth spurts, stop expressing and offer your baby the breast for longer.

your baby's sleeps

Aim to have a regular getting-up time and bedtime for your baby, which will hopefully fit in with your daily routine. Most families start their day about 7am. Try to get him used to being settled at night by 11-ish. Let him have about four hours', continuous sleep at a time during the night, as he needs frequent feeds to keep his energy levels up. For more advice speak to your registered paediatrician. During the first two weeks try to aim for the following:

- After breakfast: approximately 1½ hours.
- After lunch: 2–2½ hours, ideally between midday and 2–2.30pm.
- Mid-afternoon: one hour at around 3.30pm.
- Bedtime: around 7pm, but wake him up at 10-ish for a feed and then roughly every four hours.

weeks 3 and 4

quantity of milk

The amount you should aim to feed your baby largely depends on his weight. Health authorities advise that a baby under 4 months of age will need to eat 150ml per kilogram of his body weight per day (eg a 3.5kg baby will need 525ml of milk a day). This is only a guide; hungrier babies may need an extra 25ml at some feeds. Larger feeds are best given early in the day or late at night. Avoid big feeds in the middle of the night so that your baby associates daytime with feeding and night-time with sleeping. This routine applies for breastfed and bottle-fed babies.

your baby's feeds

During the day, aim to feed every three hours. You may notice by this stage that your baby needs to drink for 25 to 30 minutes on the first breast to empty it, and he may need more from the second as his appetite increases. Begin the next feed with the second breast so he always gets all the hind milk.

expressing milk

In order to compensate for the extra demand for food during this growth spurt, you will need to reduce the amount you express at the expressing times (before or after your first and last feeds).

your baby's sleeps

- After breakfast: approximately 1½-hours.
- After lunch: 2–2½ hours, ideally between midday and 2–2.30pm.
- Mid-afternoon: one hour at around 3.30pm.
- Bedtime: around 7pm, but wake him up at 10-ish for a feed and then every four hours.

weeks 5 to 8

your baby's weight gain

If your baby gains weight at a steady 150–200g a week, he can move on to the next routine. If his weight gain is low, you may need to keep him on the same routine as weeks 3 and 4 until it improves. Speak to your health visitor, family doctor or registered paediatrician about any weight-gain concerns.

your baby's feeds

Start to leave slightly more time between the first three feeds of the day – up to 3½ hours, but keep the 7pm and 10pm feeds as before. If your baby is not as interested in his breakfast feed as he used to be, he may still be full from his night-time feed, in which case you could start to reduce the amount of milk he drinks during the night. You can encourage him to accept this by offering cooled, boiled water before the breast at night feeds – he won't like it to begin with, but it does work as he will soon drink more at other times to compensate and will stop waking in the night when he realizes that all he is going to get is water! Take this at your own pace.

expressing milk

Before or after your first and last feeds – approximately 50 to 75ml each time – but it is a good idea to reduce the amount you express at 7am or stop expressing milk at this time completely.

your baby's sleeps

As your baby gains weight and is taking most of his food during the day, he should be able to sleep for longer during the night.

- After breakfast: up to one hour.
- After lunch: 2–2½ hours, ideally between midday and 2–2.30pm.
- Mid-afternoon: 45 minutes at around 3.30pm, if required.
- Bedtime: around 7pm, but wake him up at 10-ish for a feed.

week 9 to 4 months

Things are getting simpler by the day; all your effort in the first weeks is really starting to pay off!

your baby's feeds

At around 9 weeks babies often go through a growth spurt. Increase the feed for breastfed and bottle-fed babies at their early morning, mid-morning and suppertime feeds. Keep the first three feeds up to about 3½ hours apart, but keep the 7pm and 10pm feeds as before.

expressing milk

Only express at the last feed.

your baby's sleeps

With a routine, Ella and Jasmin started sleeping through the night at around 4 months. But they woke up, hungry, earlier than usual, so I gave them a small amount and finished off the feed at 7am. Before long they could last until breakfast again. As a guide, if your baby weighs about 5.5kg and is taking all of his daytime feeds, you can assume he's ready to sleep through the night. As a result, he'll need less sleep in the day (about three-and-a-half hours in total).

- After breakfast: about 45 minutes.
- After lunch: 2 hours (2¼ hours maximum), ideally between midday and 2pm.
- Mid-afternoon: 30 minutes at about 3.30pm if required (by 4 months he will probably not need it anymore).
- Bedtime: around 7pm, but wake him up at 10-ish for a feed.

teething and sitting up

There is no fixed time for teething, but on average your baby's first teeth could appear at around 5 months. He may start to chew his hand or suck his thumb and even put his feet in his mouth – babies often chew and suck everything in sight! This can alleviate the pain of teething. He will begin to learn to sit and hold his head unsupported, and he will reach for things to hold and chew – these are good indications that he will soon be approaching the time when he can be weaned because he will have the co-ordination to pick up and move the spoon from bowl to mouth, although you will need to feed his at this stage. It is often during feeding when you discover that, as well as being able to coo with pleasure, your baby can squeal and scream with annoyance. *See* the next chapter for advice about weaning.

weaning
before the sixth month

In 2003 the UK Government changed its advice to be in line with the World Health Organization about the recommended age for babies to start solids.

It is strongly recommended that mothers breastfeed for at least the first six months, preferably a year and introduce 'solid foods' (non-milk foods) at around 6 months.

All babies are different. Some parents may feel that their babies need to be weaned slightly earlier than 6 months. If you do decide to do this, please discuss it with your health visitor first. The Department of Health states that solid food should not be introduced before the end of your baby's fourth month (20 weeks).

Rushing weaning can be more damaging for your baby's health than continuing breast milk or formula milk feeds, because a baby's immature digestive system cannot cope with solid foods. Solid food can hinder a baby's ability to absorb nutrients, particularly iron, from breast milk or formula milk. There is growing evidence that giving solids too early increases the likelihood of your baby developing serious food allergies and intolerances.

If you do decide to introduce your baby to solid food before 6 months, begin with the first weaning foods as recommended on page 56 and make sure that you avoid the foods listed below. You will also have to wait until around the sixth month before you can introduce finger foods.

foods to avoid before 6 months
Wheat, gluten, eggs, fish, shellfish, meat, liver, citrus fruits and soft and unpasteurized cheeses.

Similarly it is best that weaning is not delayed for too long after the sixth month as your baby needs more than just milk to help him to grow and develop.

Remember never to leave your baby alone while eating, instead talk to your baby quietly and offer him words of encouragement.

Always speak to your health visitor or family doctor before you begin weaning, especially if your baby was premature.

During your baby's first six months her birth weight is likely to double. To sustain this growth she will eventually need more than just breast milk or formula milk. The Department of Health changed its weaning advice from 4 to 6 months in 2003 to come in line with with the World Health Organization.

Up until 6 months, breast milk (or infant formula milk) is still providing all the nutrients that your baby needs. At 6 months most babies have strong necks and can sit up if they are supported. Their hand–eye co-ordination is also likely to have developed to the extent that they can reach out and start to grasp food and grip it in their palms.

6

months

the weaning **process**

The Department of Health advises that parents should begin the weaning process with puréed or mashed foods. But it also recommends including finger foods in your baby's diet as soon as you feel your baby is ready to do so. Some parents feel that their babies are ready almost straight away.

You may have heard of Baby-led Weaning (often abbreviated to BLW). This means forgetting baby purées and weaning spoons and simply letting your baby feed herself. Many parents do this without even realizing it, especially with second or subsequent children. Babies do love to copy and if they have older siblings they may try to copy them or grab food from their plates, and they may feel happier being able to do the same as their siblings.

Some experts believe that babies who are allowed to feed themselves by being offered a selection of nutritious finger foods can easily join with family meals from the start and are less likely to refuse foods or become fussy eaters as they grow older.

However, not all babies like to feed themselves and there are only a limited number of foods that you can make into suitable shapes for your baby to hold during this initial weaning stage. So it is advisable to offer mashed and puréed foods too. This way you will be able to make sure that your baby is having a varied diet.

There is also some concern that if babies are only fed purées for the first few months they are not encouraged to learn how to chew food. Hence it is also a good idea gradually, after the first few weeks, to make purées with texture by mashing the foods rather than puréeing them.

Weaning is a natural process in which you introduce your baby to 'solid' or 'non-milk' foods gradually until your baby is eating the same foods as the rest of your family. There are two main reasons for weaning; one is nutritional and the other is social.

Breast milk, or formula milk, is a complete food. It provides all the nutrients, energy and liquid that your baby needs during her first six months. However, it is quite a dilute food, containing a high percentage of water. As your baby grows, breast milk alone will not satisfy her. From 6 months your baby has developed so that she is able to eat solid foods. Your baby now needs to learn how to eat other foods as she will need more nutrition than milk alone can provide.

The very early stages of weaning are more about social change than nutrition. Breast or formula milk is still the main food. At this stage, babies are most receptive to new tastes. Babies given a large variety of non-allergy forming foods tend to accept a wider range of foods at 1 year than those weaned on a restricted diet. Children given lots of sweet things often prefer sweet foods through to at least the age of 2.

Solid foods are far more concentrated in terms of nutrients than breast milk, so tiny amounts will help to satisfy your baby. While a single solid food, such as puréed carrot, may be high in certain nutrients, it may be low in others, so it is important that your baby has a varied and balanced diet of solid foods to ensure healthy development.

when to wean

Begin to wean as she is beginning her sixth month, by which time she should be able to sit up with support and her neck should be strong. The most obvious sign that your baby is ready for weaning is that she appears to still be hungry even though you have tried increasing milk feeds for a few days. She may be irritable and start to chew her hand or toys before the next feed is due, or she may begin to wake earlier than usual, especially at night.

Another good way to judge whether a baby is ready to be weaned is by testing her tongue-thrust reflex. If you put a tiny amount of bland purée onto the end of your finger and gently put it onto the tip of your baby's tongue she will poke both the food and her tongue out almost immediately. This reflex clears any foreign bodies, including food, out of her mouth and so protects her from choking. This reflex disappears just before the sixth month. Experiment with your baby and see how she reacts. If she sucks your finger instead of spitting out the food, she is ready to try a little solid food.

Other, less obvious, indications are:
● She may show an interest in the food you are eating, particularly by drooling – don't be tempted to give her your food.
● She wants to chew and her first teeth may be developing.
● Her weight may level off.
● She may be able to hold objects and put them to her mouth.
Don't ignore these signs and leave weaning too late, as babies can be less receptive and less willing to try different flavours of food after 8 months or so.

how to wean

Weaning requires patience and will entail a lot of mess, especially if your baby is keen to feed herself too! But it's a rewarding and essential experience because your baby learns to eat with the family.

A plastic sheet or newspaper under the chair and a bib that catches food may prove to be useful. Try to feed your baby some solid food at family mealtimes. Even if you are by yourself, try to eat something at the same time – babies learn through example.

Make sure that your baby is sitting up straight and is facing forward. A highchair is best as this way your baby is able to explore foods better and will be less likely to choke.

Start by offering a small amount of baby rice mixed with breast or formula milk or mashed vegetable or fruit (*see* first food, page 56) after a milk feed or in the middle of one. Lunchtime is the best time of day to try this, as babies are generally alert and satisfied from their breakfast milk.

If the food is hot, make sure that you stir it and test it before giving it to your baby.

Offer small tastes on the end of a plastic, shallow weaning spoon. (Never use a metal spoon – they can be sharp or too hot.) She may spit it out, but persevere.

All that is needed is a small bowlful to start – she may only want a few teaspoons of food at first, she may want more. Your baby will be learning about new tastes and textures and that food does not always come in a continuous flow. Try to wait for your baby to open her mouth when you offer her food. Don't force your baby to eat, if she is not interested in the food, leave it and then try again later. Let your baby touch the food in the dish or on the spoon and let her feed herself as soon as she shows an interest (*see* finger foods, page 56).

As your baby becomes used to the new texture, you can begin to offer different fruits or vegetables every couple of days or so, after her milk feed. Let your baby set the pace. Your aim is to gradually introduce a range of foods and textures to taste. How much food your baby eats is less important than getting used to the idea of food rather than milk.

You can begin to introduce the second feed after her milk at suppertime, before bed. This will help to keep her satisfied until morning.

If any purée seems to be too thick, dilute it with breast milk or formula milk.

Take weaning reasonably slowly – it's better for both of you. Don't make any sudden changes.

first **food**

In the very early days of weaning the introduction of 'solid' foods is primarily to help your child become used to eating solids, and to learn how to suck food off a spoon, pass food from hand to mouth and to chew (very often with gums!) and swallow solid food. It then gradually becomes important from a nutritional point of view.

It is recommended to offer soft, bland food when you first start weaning as this will help with the transition from milk to food. First foods the world over are soft and bland – usually mushy blends of staple foods that are easily digested, such as rice, non-citrus fruit or vegetables. It is also a good idea to cook any fruits or vegetables to begin with as this makes the food easier to eat and digest. Mashed cooked vegetables like carrots, parsnip, potato, rice or yam are all great first foods. Mashed banana, avocado, cooked apple or pear can also be quite quickly introduced.

Try as much as possible to cook your own food or use mashed up family food when you can, this way you will know the ingredients of the food and you will be getting your baby used to what you eat. Don't add salt or sugar to food for your baby.

Stick to single-ingredient purées for the first couple of weeks in order to identify any food to which your baby may have an adverse reaction. Your baby will be able to move on from this first-food stage quite quickly. A more varied range of purées and soft finger foods can then quite quickly be given to encourage your baby to chew and swallow and to broaden her appetite.

Always wash fruits and vegetables before you cook them. Never leave a baby alone while feeding.

nutrition
for **immunity**

It is a good idea to give your baby foods that will help boost her immature immune system. This will aid her body's natural defence system, which fights off infections and diseases. The most important nutrients are:

Vitamin C – a powerful, immune-boosting vitamin that is great for helping to fight colds. It is also essential for assisting iron absorption. Carrots, mangoes and broccoli are all good early weaning foods and great sources of vitamin C.

Vitamin E – an antioxidant vitamin vital for helping protect the body from diseases that occur later in life. Sweet potatoes and avocados are good sources and great early weaning foods.

Betacarotene – the body converts beta-carotene into vitamin A, which is a good antioxidant. Good weaning foods high in this nutrient include carrots and sweet potatoes.

Zinc – essential for a healthy immune system. Good sources for babies of this age include rice and green vegetables, such as peas and spinach.

which nutrients **are key**

nutrients required per day

Milk provides a baby with all the nutrients she needs until she is 6 months old. I've assumed, per 100ml of milk, the lowest level of nutrients provided by the common brands on which the milk chart on page 29 is based. The quantity of milk (1000ml) and nutrients required (based on the Recommended Nutrient Intake) are based on a larger than average baby. If you're breastfeeding, your baby should get all nutrients she needs from you. *Although it seems babies need extra calcium from solids, because babies absorb nutrients more easily than adults this is not needed.

	protein 1 point = 1.5g	iron 1 point = 1.5mg	zinc 1 point = 1mg	calcium 1 point = 105mg	vitamin C 1 point = 5mg
total points recommended	8½ (12.7g)	3 (4.3mg)	4 (4mg)	5 (525mg)	5 (25mg)
milk (1000ml of formula) provides	9½ (14g)	3½ (5mg)	5 (5mg)	4½ (460mg)	16½ (82mg)
points required from food	0	0	0	½*	0

finger **food**

This is the time that your baby will be learning how to take food from a spoon. But some babies may also like or even prefer to feed themselves with soft finger foods.

You should only start to offer your baby finger foods when she is over 6 months old and when you are really confident that your baby can sit upright, hold her neck well and can hold food and move it from her hand to her mouth. This all indicates that the risk of choking will be minimal.

Choking – babies can still choke so you will need to be especially careful with hard foods like apple pieces or small, round foods like grapes. Cook vegetables like carrots first as raw vegetables are too hard. When you begin to introduce fish and meat (*see* page 100), remove all skin and bones and be careful with food with skins eg sausages.

If your baby has special needs and has impaired chewing skills or fine motor skills she may not be able to feed herself successfully and so finger foods at this stage would not be suitable.

When you first offer your baby finger foods it is a good idea to do this at a family mealtime. This way she is more likely to copy everyone else at the table. Finger foods encourage babies to feed themselves and to practise chewing.

When you first introduce finger foods it is also a good idea to offer foods that are easy to hold. The best foods are those that are shaped like a big chip, or alternatively foods that have a natural 'handle' for the baby to hold eg a cooked broccoli spear. Small babies cannot always hold small things as they have not yet developed their pincer grip. Only offer finger foods that are suitable for your baby's age and stay with her while she is eating at all times. Pieces of banana, cooked carrot, cooked broccoli or avocado are all fine. When you make the purées cook extra fruits and vegetables that she can hold as finger foods (*see* sample meal planner, pages 64–65).

At first she may just play with the food or she might grab pieces of food with her fist and start to suck on them. Keep offering her some puréed food alongside the finger foods, so that she becomes used to eating from a spoon as well as feeding herself. You will be able to work out how to do this between you. Some babies will be happy with a rest from feeding themselves, while others may want you to feed them some purée once they have finished their finger food. Let your baby help you to decide what is best for her.

If you have any family history of food allergies, digestive problems or food intolerances or if your baby was born prematurely do talk to your health visitor or family doctor before you start weaning and especially before you offer finger foods.

foods to eat and
foods to avoid

It is important to wean your baby on as wide a range of foods as possible because she will learn to enjoy and appreciate food. However, you should introduce new foods gradually. Some foods are not suitable at this stage, usually either because of the danger of food allergies or choking, and so these foods are not introduced until your baby is older. If there is any family history of allergies, you should always seek advice from your doctor or state-registered dietitian.

new foods to eat at 6 months

Give your baby a wide selection of non-citrus fruits and vegetables with her milk feeds. The best first fruits and vegetables are detailed in the vegetable and fruit purée recipes in this chapter (*see* pages 66–92). All fruits and vegetables should be washed and carefully peeled before being prepared. Always remove the core, pips and any discoloured areas. Most should be cooked at this stage; bananas, avocados and cucumbers are the exception. Make sure vegetables and fruits are ripe or they might be indigestible and need extra cooking, which will diminish their nutritional content. If any of your purées are too runny or too thick, add baby rice or breast milk or formula milk as appropriate to achieve a consistency that's easy for your baby to suck off the spoon. Similarly, you can use these ingredients to soften flavours that are too strong for your baby at this stage.

foods to avoid at 6 months

● Foods containing gluten, such as wheat cereals and wheat flour, including bread and breakfast cereals, rye, barley and oats.
● Eggs – the yolk and white are high in protein, which babies find hard to digest. They may also contain salmonella bacteria, which cause food poisoning.
● Citrus fruits, including juice, are too acidic. Their high sugar and fruit-acid content can contribute to tooth decay and may trigger an allergic reaction.
● Nuts and peanut butter can trigger a fatal nut allergy.
● Sugar is unnecessary; mix tart non-citrus fruit with sweeter non-citrus fruit to sweeten it.
● Honey can contain botulism spores that cause food poisoning.
● Salt can stress immature kidneys and cause dehydration.
● Dairy products can trigger allergic reactions. Soft cheeses may contain the food-poisoning bacteria listeria, which some babies are sensitive to.
● Fish and shellfish.
● Excessively hot or spicy foods that can burn or inflame a baby's stomach.
● Tea and coffee contain tannins, which inhibit iron absorption, and caffeine. Caffeine is a stimulant that babies cannot tolerate.

drinks

At 6 months, milk is still the most important source of nutrition – your baby should be getting all the nutrients she needs from her milk feeds. When you start to introduce solid foods, you need to continue to give your baby most of her milk feed first, then a little solid food, and then the remaining milk. This way you can ensure that your baby will drink as much milk as she needs and just have a taste of the solid foods.

As your baby gradually takes more solid food she will start to take less milk. However, milk is still a very important part of her diet and she will continue to need 800–1000ml a day.

The 'recommended daily volume of foods' chart on page 61 is intended to be a guide. Obviously all babies have different needs, depending on many factors, including weight.

You will have to follow your baby's direction and use your initiative when deciding how much to feed her each day. For example, if, after a week of weaning, you introduce a suppertime solid feed to your baby's routine only to find that she is too tired to eat it, you may need to start that feed a little bit earlier in the day.

You will need to keep breastfeeding or feeding formula milk in between the solid feeds up until she is 1 year. Cow's milk is not suitable as a drink until your baby is 12 months old. However, it can be used in cooking (see page 32).

The only other drink your baby will need is water. Boil tap water and then leave it to cool. This is especially important for babies who are being formula fed, whereas breast milk is a drink as well as a food.

If you choose to give fresh fruit juice to your baby, which is not something that they need, please dilute it one part juice to ten parts water.

If you are breastfeeding and you wean your baby too quickly, your breasts will become extremely sore; they may get engorged and blocked and you could get mastitis.

Never add any food to your baby's bottle of milk, this is dangerous.

If you are bottle feeding it can be a comfort to a baby to suck on a bottle, which can become a habit that is hard to break. Try to introduce a cup at 6 months and aim to have your baby off the bottle by her first birthday. Using a cup is better for your baby's teeth.

Soya-based infant formulas should only be used on the advice of your health visitor or family doctor. Some babies who are allergic to cow's milk may also be allergic to soya. Infant formulas based on goat's milk protein have not been approved for use in Europe.

recommended
daily intake

The chart below is intended as a guide. Babies have different needs, depending on many factors, including weight. Follow your baby's direction and use your initiative when deciding how much to feed her. For example, if towards the end of week 1 of weaning you introduce a suppertime solid feed to your baby's routine only to find that she is too tired to eat it, try starting that feed earlier in the day.

recommended daily volume of foods

	6 months old, week 1	6 months old, weeks 2–3	6 months old, week 4
Note	You may choose to gradually introduce finger foods too, but do this at a pace that suits both you and your baby	You may find it easier to feed the second solid food at lunchtime instead of breakfast; be guided by your baby and do what suits you both best	
Breakfast, 7–8am	milk	milk; at a pace that suits you and your baby you can begin to gradually introduce solid food at this time too – cereal and/or fruit purée (mash)	milk, cereal and/or fruit purée (mash), finger foods* (see note, page 64)
Lunch, 11.45am-ish	milk, puréed baby rice and/or vegetable purée	milk	milk, vegetable purée/mash, finger foods* (see note, page 64)
Mid-pm, 3pm	milk, cooled, boiled water	milk, cooled, boiled water	milk, cooled, boiled water
Supper, 6.30pm-ish	milk; towards the end of the first week you and your baby may want to introduce some vegetable and/or fruit purée at this time too	vegetable purée/mash and/or finger foods* (see note, page 64)	vegetable purée/mash and/or finger foods* (see note, page 64)
Night-time, 10pm	milk	gradually stop this milk feed as soon as your baby is ready: this will depend on how much solid food she is eating	gradually stop this milk feed as soon as your baby is ready: this will depend on how much solid food she is eating
TOTAL MILK	Breast milk or about 800–1000ml formula, depending on the size of the baby	breast milk or about 800ml formula, depending on the size of the baby, inclusive of milk used in sauces and cereals	breast milk or about 800 ml formula, depending on the size of the baby

your
routine

your baby's feeds

In the early days of weaning, continue to offer a small amount of milk before the solid food, finishing with more milk. It is a good idea at the very beginning of weaning to only introduce a new savoury or fruit or vegetable purée every two to three days to help prevent any problems with your baby's digestion – worth bearing in mind when you plan her menu (*see* pages 64–65 for meal planners).

Ideally, at between 5 and 6 months old your baby will not need any milk after 7pm. To help achieve this, gradually reduce the amount of milk that you give her at 10pm and offer cooled, boiled water instead of milk. Babies soon realize that there is little point in waking up for water.

By the end of the sixth month ideally she will be enjoying two to three small solid food meals a day. Offer more vegetables so that she becomes used to the taste of savoury foods not just sweet. Try and focus on the lunchtime feed as the most important, and during this feed, try to alternate between milk and solids. Towards the end of the sixth month, gradually start to separate the solid feed from the milk feed at suppertime. Give her the solid feed at around 5pm with a drink of water and then the milk feed at bedtime.

your baby's sleeps

In an ideal world, your baby needs to sleep for approximately 45 minutes after breakfast and for two to two-and-a-quarter hours after lunch. I have suggested that you put your baby to sleep for a quick nap in the morning and then a longer sleep after lunch because this is what really worked for my girls and many of my friends' babies. But if it is impossible to fit this into your schedule, then change the routine to suit you. Do make sure, though, that your baby is awake by 3pm because this helps to ensure that she will be tired again by bedtime, at 7pm-ish.

frustration when eating

Some babies cry between spoonfuls of solid food, usually because they are frustrated. It may take them a little while to get used to the fact that solid-food feeding isn't continuous but interrupted, and that solids will satisfy their hunger. If you feel they are ready for finger foods (*see* page 58) this may help to relieve some of the frustration in between the puréed food.

messy eating

Don't worry if there is more purée over your kitchen than inside your baby. The weaning process in the early stages is more about getting her used to the food's taste and texture and the spoon than providing her with food. Milk will still satisfy all her nutritional needs. Her lack of enthusiasm may be because she is not hungry; towards the end of the sixth months try reducing the amount of milk feed you give before the solid food.

reluctance to eat

Never force your baby to eat solid food; it's unpleasant for her and she may choke. Eating is quite a difficult process for your baby to get the hang of because she is used to sucking. When you start feeding, use a flat spoon and let her suck the food off the end. Gradually she will learn to take the food and swallow without relying on the sucking reflex. Never try to force-feed by mixing solid food with milk in a bottle; this takes away her right to 'say' no to solid food and to take weaning at her own pace. It can also make her choke.

a baby with a sweet tooth

Do not always give sweet food after savoury – it helps prevent your baby from believing that green vegetables are unpleasant and sweet foods a treat.

a stressed baby who won't eat

Sit her on your lap to reduce any stress she may feel.

breast to bottle-feeding

Don't switch from breast to bottle-feeding at the same time as weaning. Two major changes can be too much and make the baby confused, stressed and less likely to adapt well during the transition stage.

trouble shooting

sample meal planners

Always use the meal planner key (page 104)

6 months old, week 1

	breakfast	lunch	mid-afternoon	supper	10pm
days 1–3	milk	milk, alternated with a few tsp baby rice	milk, possibly cooled, boiled water	milk	milk
days 4–7	milk	Milk alternated with a few tbsp purée e.g. carrot purée	milk, possibly cooled, boiled water	milk, possibly pear or apple purée*	milk

* you and your baby need to decide if she is ready for solid foods at suppertime.

6 months old, weeks 2–3

	breakfast	lunch	mid-afternoon	supper	10pm
day 1	milk	milk, alternated with a few tsp courgette purée	milk, possibly cooled, boiled water	milk, sweet potato and carrot purée	small milk
day 2	milk	milk, alternated with a few tsp courgette purée	milk, possibly cooled, boiled water	milk, vegetable purée/mash, steamed broccoli finger foods	small milk
day 3	milk	milk, alternated with a few tsp courgette purée	milk, possibly cooled, boiled water	milk, vegetable purée/mash, steamed broccoli finger foods	small milk
day 4	milk	milk, alternated with a few tsp courgette purée	milk, possibly cooled, boiled water	milk, vegetable purée/mash, steamed broccoli finger foods	small milk
day 5	milk	milk, alternated with a few tsp courgette purée	milk, possibly cooled, boiled water	milk, vegetable purée/mash, steamed broccoli finger foods	small milk
day 6	milk; at a pace that suits you and your baby gradually introduce cereal mixed with papaya or mango purée. You may also like to try mango pieces as a finger food	milk, alternated with a few tsp courgette purée	milk, possibly cooled, boiled water	milk, root vegetable medley, steamed parsnip 'chips'*	small milk
day 7	milk, cereal and/or fruit purée plus finger foods*	milk, vegetable mash or purée plus finger foods*	milk, root vegetable medley, steamed parsnip 'chips'*	milk, root vegetable medley, steamed parsnip 'chips'*	small milk
Total milk	Breast milk or about 800ml formula, depending on the size of the baby, this will depend on how much solid food she is eating				

*see advice on finger foods on page 58. Make sure that your baby is really ready before you introduce finger foods.
It is a good idea to have a combination of purée or mashed food with some finger foods.

6 months old, week 4

If you and your baby want to include finger foods at this stage too, steam a little extra fruit and vegetables at the same time as you make the purées and then give a few pieces to your baby to hold while you feed her the purée.

NB remember, too, to cook enough of the fruits and vegetables for the whole family, not just enough for the purée; this will help cut down on your cooking time.

	breakfast	lunch	mid-afternoon	supper	10pm
day 1	milk, apple and cinnamon purée	milk, pumpkin and leek purée, chip-size pieces of pumpkin, water	milk, water	courgette purée, steamed courgette 'chips', melon purée, melon 'chips', water, milk	small milk (possibly no milk)
day 2	milk, then apple and cinnamon purée	milk, pumpkin and leek purée, chip-size pieces of pumpkin, water	milk, water	courgette purée, steamed courgette 'chips', melon purée, melon 'chips', water, milk	small milk (possibly no milk)
day 3	milk, papaya and raspberry purée, chip-size pieces of papaya	milk, pumpkin and leek purée, chip-size pieces of pumpkin, water	milk, water	broccoli purée, apricot purée, florets of steamed broccoli, chip-size pieces of melon, water, milk	small milk (possibly no milk)
day 4	milk, papaya and raspberry purée , chip-size pieces of papaya	milk, carrot purée, chip-size pieces carrot, water	milk, water	courgette purée, steamed courgette 'chips', apple purée, water, milk	small milk (possibly no milk)
day 5	milk, mango and peach purée, chip-size pieces of mango and/or peach	milk, parsnip and potato purée, water	milk, water	swede and carrot purée, apple purée, water, milk	small milk (possibly no milk)
day 6	milk, mango and peach purée, chip-size pieces of mango and/or peach	milk, parsnip and potato purée, water	milk, water	beetroot and carrot purée, steamed carrot 'chips', water, milk	small milk (possibly no milk)
day 7	milk, then apple and cinnamon purée	milk, pumpkin and leek purée, chip-size pieces of pumpkin, water	milk, water	root vegetable medley, steamed parsnip/carrot/potato 'chips', water, milk, pear and blackberry purée, chip-size pieces of ripe pear (start with them peeled)	small milk (possibly no milk)

fresh breakfasts

blueberry and pear purée

makes: 3 baby portions or 1 baby portion and 1 adult portion as a smoothie base

storage: up to 24 hours in the refrigerator

1 ripe pear, eg Williams
4–5 tbsp water
large handful of fresh blueberries

Keep an eye out for the wild version of blueberries, known as bilberries. They are available in late summer and are very distinctive because they have a really bright blue juice. For a smoothie, add apple juice to taste.

1 Peel and core the pear and cut into bite-size chunks.
2 Put into a saucepan with the water and the blueberries.
3 Simmer for a few minutes until the pear is tender and the blueberries just burst.
4 Whiz with a hand-held blender (or in a food processor or blender) until smooth. Leave to cool before serving.
5 For just-weaned babies, pass the purée through a nylon sieve.

papaya and raspberry purée

makes: 3 baby portions or 1 baby portion and 1 adult portion as a smoothie base

storage: up to 24 hours in the refrigerator

1 ripe papaya
handful of fresh raspberries

Most fruits for babies at this age need to be cooked. A really ripe papaya should have a wonderful scent of the fruit and should just give when gently squeezed. For a smoothie, add orange juice to taste.

1 Cut the papaya in half and scoop out the seeds. Peel each half and cut the flesh into cubes.
2 Put the papaya and raspberries in a pan with 2 tbsp water and simmer for a few minutes, or until the raspberries have burst.
3 Whiz the papaya with the raspberries using a hand-held blender (or in a food processor or blender) until smooth.
4 For just-weaned babies, pass the purée through a nylon sieve.

Before feeding your baby any of these purées, please read the section on weaning (pages 54–56) and the 6 month sample meal planners (pages 64–65).

melon mania purée

½

½

1

4 **C**

makes: 4 baby portions or 1 baby portion and 2 adult portions as a smoothie base

storage: up to 24 hours in the refrigerator

200g piece of cantaloupe melon

200g piece of galia melon

baby rice or mashed ripe banana, to thicken

Melons have a high water content, so they don't need cooking and are easily digested. This is a particularly lovely purée to serve on a hot day because it is naturally cooling. If the purée is a little too thin, add some mashed banana or baby rice, which will also help offset the melon's sweetness. For a smoothie, add a little lime juice. Alternatively, just make half the recipe, which is sufficient for two baby portions. Note that melon is mildly laxative.

1 Scoop out the seeds from each piece of melon and then spoon out the flesh of the fruit – use only the flesh that can easily be scooped out. If you find you have to scrape hard to get the flesh away from the edges, it will not be ripe enough for your baby to eat.

2 Steam or simmer the melon with 2 tbsp water for a few minutes, until soft.

3 Whiz the melon with a hand-held blender (or in a food processor or blender) until smooth. Add enough baby rice or mashed banana to thicken to a purée consistency before serving.

mango and peach purée

½

½

5 **C**

makes: 3 baby portions or 1 baby portion and 1 adult portion as a smoothie base

storage: up to 24 hours in the refrigerator

1 ripe small mango

1 ripe small peach

Mango is one of many tropical fruits that are naturally sweet and don't need cooking. However, it can also be quite intensely flavoured, so at first you may wish to dilute it with a little baby rice. Some mangoes can be a bit fibrous, so it is best to pass a purée of a particularly stringy mango through a nylon sieve.

1 Slice through the mango on either side of the stone. Peel, then cut the flesh into cubes.

2 Put the peach in a bowl and pour over boiling water. Leave for 2 minutes. Drain and rinse with cold water. Peel the skin off the peach, remove the stone and cut the flesh into chunks.

3 Steam or simmer the peach and mango with 3 tbsp water for a few minutes, until soft.

4 Whiz the mango and peach with a hand-held blender (or in a food processor or blender) until smooth.

apricot and banana purée

½

1 C

makes: 3 baby portions or 1 baby portion and 1 adult portion as a smoothie base

storage: up to 24 hours in the refrigerator

3 ripe fresh apricots
1 ripe small banana

Choose bananas that are fully ripe – that means ones with small black spots. Just make sure they are not split or bruised. Bananas often have high levels of pesticide residues, so if you can buy organic bananas this is advisable. They are now widely available, and many supermarkets also sell the smaller varieties, which means less waste! Apricots have an intense fresh taste that babies love – choose fruits that feel heavy for their size and have a strong apricot scent.

1 Remove the stones from the apricots. Peel them and cut the flesh into small pieces. Put into a saucepan with 4 tbsp water.
2 Heat gently for about 4–5 minutes, until the apricots are soft and pulpy. Cool the fruit.
3 Peel the banana. Whiz the apricots and banana together with a hand-held blender (or in a food processor or blender) until smooth.
4 For just-weaned babies, pass the purée through a nylon sieve.

peach and raspberry purée

½

8 C

makes: 2 baby portions or 1 baby portion plus 1 small adult portion as a smoothie base

storage: up to 24 hours in the refrigerator

1 ripe small peach
handful of fresh raspberries

Just like adults, babies appreciate food that is interesting to look at as well as tasting good. This purée is a fabulous vibrant pink – great for encouraging a less-than-keen baby to try some solid food!

1 Put the peach in a bowl and pour over boiling water. Leave for 2 minutes. Drain and rinse with cold water. Peel the skin off the peach, remove the stone and cut the flesh into chunks.
2 Put the raspberries and peach into a pan with 2–3 tbsp water and heat gently for a few minutes, until soft. Cool.
3 Whiz together the raspberries and peach with a hand-held blender (or in a food processor or blender) until smooth.
4 For just-weaned babies, pass the purée through a nylon sieve.

quick bites **breakfasts**

At first, weaning is not about giving your baby nutrients through solid foods, but rather it is about introducing new textures and tastes and encouraging your baby to have an interest in food. All these quick ideas use ingredients that take very little time to prepare or cook.

things to purée with banana

Take ½ ripe banana (look for little brown spots on the banana's skin to make sure it is really ripe), peel and cut the flesh into small pieces.

2 **C** ½ 🥚

blueberries

handful of ripe blueberries
½ ripe banana, cut into small pieces

Put the blueberries in a saucepan with 1 tbsp water and cook for 2–3 minutes, until the fruit just starts to burst open. Transfer to a bowl, add the chopped banana and whiz with a hand-held blender (or in a food processor or blender) until smooth. For just-weaned babies, pass the purée through a nylon sieve.

2 **C** ½ 🥚

peach

½ ripe peach
½ ripe banana, cut into small pieces

Peel and chop the peach and put it into a small pan. Add 2 tbsp water and cook for 5 minutes, until the flesh is just soft. Add the chopped banana and whiz together with a hand-held blender (or in a food processor or blender) until smooth.

3 **C**

papaya

½ ripe papaya
½ ripe banana, cut into small pieces

Peel and chop the flesh of the papaya and put it into a small pan. Add 2 tbsp water and cook for 3–4 minutes. Add the chopped banana and whiz with a hand-held blender (or in a food processor or blender) until smooth or mash.

1 **C**

pear

1 ripe pear
½ ripe banana, cut into small pieces

Peel and core the pear and cut the flesh into pieces. Put the pieces into a small pan. Add 2 tbsp water and cook for 5 minutes. Add the chopped banana and whiz together with a hand-held blender (or in a food processor or blender) until smooth.

things to purée with baby rice

Make up 2 tbsp baby rice following the instructions on the packet, using breast or formula milk or cooled, boiled water.

mango

½ ripe mango
2 tbsp baby rice made as above

Peel the mango and cut the flesh into small pieces. Put into a pan with 2 tbsp water and cook for a few minutes, until just soft. Add the baby rice and whiz with a hand-held blender (or in a food processor or blender) until smooth.

pear

1 ripe pear
2 tbsp baby rice made as above

Peel and core half a pear. Cut the flesh into small pieces. Put into a pan with 2 tbsp water and simmer gently for 5 minutes, or until soft. Add the baby rice and whiz with a hand-held blender (or in a food processor or blender) until smooth.

banana

½ ripe banana
2 tbsp baby rice made as above

Peel the banana and chop the flesh into small pieces. Add the baby rice and whiz with a hand-held blender (or in a food processor or blender) until smooth.

apple

1 eating apple
2 tbsp baby rice made as above

Peel and core the apple, then cut into small pieces and put into saucepan with 2 tbsp water. Simmer gently for 5 minutes, or until soft. Add the baby rice and whiz with a hand-held blender (or in a food processor or blender) until smooth.

quick things to cook with apple purée

Take 1 eating apple, eg Cox's orange pippin. Peel, core and cut into small pieces.

carrot

1 small carrot
1 eating apple, chopped as above

Peel the carrot, then cut it into small pieces. Put it into a saucepan with the apple pieces and a little water and cook until just tender – approximately 3–5 minutes. Drain off a little water and then whiz with a hand-held blender (or in a food processor or blender) until smooth.

parsnip

1 small parsnip
1 eating apple, chopped as above

All quick bites make 1 portion unless otherwise stated.

Peel the parsnip, then cut it into 1.5cm pieces. Put into a saucepan with a little water and cook for 5–10 minutes. Add the apple pieces and continue to cook for a few minutes until the apple is just tender. Drain off a little water and whiz with a hand-held blender (or food processor or blender) until smooth. For just-weaned babies, pass the purée through a nylon sieve.

breakfasts to freeze

cherry and apple purée

makes: 3 baby portions

storage: up to 2 months in the freezer

**handful of fresh cherries
3 eating apples, eg Cox's
orange pippin**

Make this purée in early summer, when there is a glut of cherries and they are not too expensive. The larger, darker cherries tend to be sweeter. If you have the time or are doing this in bulk, it may be easier to stone the cherries before you cook them – do this over a clean bowl so that you can catch all the juice. Cherry stoners are available in most kitchen shops.

1   Remove any stalks or leaves from the cherries.
2   Peel and core the apples and cut into chunks. Put into a pan with 4 tbsp water. Add the cherries and heat gently until the apples are soft and pulpy and the cherries are releasing their juice. Allow to cool.
3   Pass the fruit through a nylon sieve, or purée using a mouli.
4   Spoon the purée into ice-cube trays. Cover with foil or put into a freezer bag and seal. Freeze.
5   To serve, thaw thoroughly.

plum and pear purée

makes: 3 baby portions

storage: up to 2 months in the freezer

**3 ripe plums, eg Victoria
plums or greengages
2 ripe pears, eg Williams**

Before feeding your baby any of these purées, please read the section on weaning (pages 54–56) and the 6 month sample meal planners (pages 64–65).

This is a great autumnal purée. Try different varieties of plums to see which your baby likes. Victoria plums have a mild flavour; greengages can be sharper if they are not fully ripe, so make sure you choose sweet-smelling and slightly soft fruits. Swirl a little through some yogurt for a quick breakfast for yourself.

1   Remove the stalks from the plums. Halve the fruit, remove the stones. Peel, and cut the flesh into chunks.
2   Peel and core the pears and cut into chunks.
3   Put both the fruits into a pan with 3 tbsp water and heat gently until the fruit is soft and pulpy. Whiz with a hand-held blender (or in a food processor or blender) until smooth. For just-weaned babies, pass through a nylon sieve.
4   Spoon the purée into ice-cube trays. Cover with foil or put into a freezer bag and seal. Freeze.
5   To serve, thaw thoroughly.

raspberry and pear purée

 makes: 2 baby portions or 1 baby portion and 1 small adult portion as a smoothie base

storage: up to 2 months in the freezer

1 ripe pear, eg Williams
50g or large handful of fresh raspberries
4–5 tbsp water

The colour of this purée is particularly appealing. To make a smoothie, just add apple juice to taste.

1 Peel and core the pear and cut it into bite-sized chunks.
2 Put the pear into a saucepan with the raspberries and water. Simmer for a few minutes until the pear is tender and the raspberries have just burst open – it won't take long.
3 Whiz with a hand-held blender (or in a food processor or blender) until smooth, then leave to cool before serving.
4 For just-weaned babies, pass the purée through a nylon sieve.
5 Spoon the purée into ice-cube trays. Cover with foil or put into a freezer bag and seal. Freeze.
6 To serve, thaw thoroughly.

apple and cinnamon purée

½ **makes:** 2 baby portions

½ **storage:** up to 2 months in the freezer

4 eating apples, eg Cox's orange pippin
10 tbsp water
¼ tsp ground cinnamon

This is a great purée to make in the autumn, when there is a glut of apples. Look for locally grown apples and do a bit of experimenting with different varieties – many British eating apples cook just as well as cookers and have a much fruitier taste. As with all weaning foods, resist the temptation to sweeten the purée with sugar if you feel it is a little tart. Try feeding first; if it's not successful, sweeten with another fruit such as bananas. A little spice, such as cinnamon, can be introduced once your baby has been taking solids for at least a month.

1 Peel and core the apples. Slice.
2 Put the apples into a saucepan with the water and cinnamon.
3 Heat gently for 15–20 minutes, until the apples are soft and pulpy, mashing occasionally with a wooden spoon. Cool.
4 Whiz with a hand-held blender (or in a food processor or blender) until smooth.
5 Spoon the purée into ice-cube trays. Cover with foil or put into a freezer bag and seal. Freeze.
6 To serve, thaw thoroughly.

apple and pear purée

½
2

makes: 2 baby portions

storage: up to 2 months in the freezer

2 eating apples,
  eg Cox's orange pippin
2 pears
½ tsp cinnamon

This is a great purée to make in the autumn, when there are lots of apples and pears. You could always make a larger quantity and add a good dollop to your breakfast cereal or yogurt. A little spice, such as cinnamon, can be introduced once your baby has been taking solids for at least a month.

1   Peel and core the apples and pears and slice.
2   Put into a saucepan with 10 tbsp water and the cinnamon.
3   Heat gently until the fruit is soft and pulpy, mashing occasionally with a wooden spoon; this will take about 15–20 minutes. Allow to cool.
4   Whiz with a hand-held blender (or in a food-processor or blender) until smooth. Spoon the purée into ice-cube trays. Cover with foil or put into a freezer bag and seal. Freeze.
5   To serve, thaw thoroughly.

apricot and mango purée

1

makes: 3 baby portions

storage: up to 2 months in the freezer

4 dried apricots
1 small ripe mango

Most dried apricots are treated with sulphur dioxide, a preservative that can cause an allergic reaction. Organic apricots are untreated and tend to be harder and darker in colour but, if anything, have a more intense and apricot-y flavour. This is another beautifully coloured purée – and the little frozen cubes make great summer treats for toddlers.

1   Put the apricots in a small bowl and pour over 4 tbsp boiling water. Leave to soak until they are soft and plump (about half an hour).
2   Slice through the mango either side of the stone. Peel, then cut the flesh into cubes.
3   Drain the apricots, reserving the soaking liquid, and finely chop them.
4   Put the mango, chopped apricots and apricot-soaking liquid into a pan. Cook gently until the mango has broken down and the apricot pieces are soft (about 5–10 minutes). You may need to add 2–3 tbsp water if the fruit becomes too dry. Cool.
5   Whiz the fruits together with a hand-held blender (or in a food processor or blender) until smooth.
6   For a just-weaned baby, pass the purée through a nylon sieve.
7   Spoon the purée into ice-cube trays. Cover with foil or put into a freezer bag and seal. Freeze.
8   To serve. thaw thoroughly.

fresh savouries

avocado and cucumber purée

makes: 2 baby portions

storage: eat immediately

¼ small cucumber

½ ripe avocado

This is a simple, no-cook purée with a texture that most babies love. To make the most of the avocado, slice the remaining half and add it to a salad or sandwich for your lunch. Avocados contain healthy unsaturated fats that are essential to help keep your energy levels up when you are breastfeeding. They are also good for your skin.

1 Peel the cucumber and slice in half lengthways. Scrape out the seeds with a teaspoon. Chop into small chunks.
2 Peel, stone and chop the avocado.
3 Whiz the cucumber and avocado with a hand-held blender (or in a food processor) until smooth. For just-weaned babies, pass the purée through a nylon sieve.

pea, mint and potato purée

makes: 3 baby portions

storage: up to 24 hours in the refrigerator

1 small floury potato,
  eg King Edward

100g peas, fresh or frozen

1 fresh mint leaf

Vitamin B₁

Adding a small amount of fresh herbs or seasonings is a great way to stimulate your baby's appetite and to broaden her palate. Mint and peas have a natural affinity with each other, and using potatoes as the base is a good way to introduce new vegetables gradually into your baby's diet.

1 Peel the potato and cut into small dice. Bring a small pan of water to the boil, add the potatoes and cook until tender (approximately 10–12 minutes).
2 A couple of minutes before they are cooked, add the peas. Continue to simmer until just tender.
3 Drain, add the mint and allow to cool slightly before whizzing with a hand-held blender (or in a food processor or blender) until smooth.
4 For just-weaned babies, pass the purée through a nylon sieve.

Before feeding your baby any of these purées, please read the section on weaning (pages 54–56) and the 6 month sample meal planners (pages 64–65).

sweet potato and onion purée

makes: 5 baby portions or 1 baby portion and 2 adult portions as the base for a soup

storage: up to 24 hours in the refrigerator

Vitamin A

1 small mild onion, finely chopped

1 medium sweet potato, peeled and finely chopped

Look for white sweet potatoes, which actually have deep yellow flesh, rather than the big red sweet potatoes (also known as yams). The white ones are less rich and have a fluffier texture when cooked, which babies seem to love. You can substitute them for ordinary potatoes in almost any recipe. A little pinch of ginger will accentuate their flavour and make the purée more interesting for your baby.

1 Put the onion and potato in a saucepan and just cover the vegetables with water.

2 Bring to the boil and simmer gently until the potato is soft (approximately 15 minutes). Drain and cool.

3 Whiz with a hand-held blender (or in a food processor or blender) until the purée is smooth.

4 For just-weaned babies, pass the purée through a nylon sieve.

potato and sweetcorn purée

makes: 2 baby portions

storage: best eaten immediately or stored for up to 24 hours in the refrigerator

1 medium floury potato, eg King Edward

1 cob fresh sweetcorn or 85g frozen sweetcorn

This is another great combination – potato is the most fantastic base for almost any vegetable purée, and it's particularly good for just-weaned babies. Look for organic sweetcorn, which is now available frozen. Non-organic sweetcorn is one of the most commonly genetically modified foods and is often specifically modified to make it sweeter, which means it loses its delicious nuttiness. A little chopped parsley or chives would be a great addition to this purée.

1 Peel the potato and cut into small chunks.

2 Remove the outer leaves of the sweetcorn and any stringy bits clinging to the cob. Using a sharp knife, cut the kernels away from the cob, turning it around as you go.

3 Bring a pan of water to the boil and add the potato and corn. Bring to the boil and simmer for about 6 minutes, or until the vegetables are tender. Drain and cool.

4 Whiz with a hand-held blender (or in a food processor or blender) until smooth. Add breast or formula milk to achieve the desired consistency.

5 For just-weaned babies, pass the purée through a nylon sieve.

avocado and pea purée

makes: 2 baby portions

storage: best eaten immediately or within 2 hours

60g peas, fresh or frozen
1 ripe medium avocado

Vitamin B₁

Another beautifully coloured purée, provided you don't leave it hanging around too long because avocado does have a tendency to discolour. Ripe avocado has a lovely rich and creamy texture, which babies love. For babies used to herbs, add a couple of fresh coriander leaves to the purée to give it a little zing. If there is any of this purée left over, spread it on toast and top with Parma ham for a quick snack for you.

1 Bring a pan of water to the boil, add the peas and then bring back to the boil and cook until just tender (approximately 3–4 minutes). Drain and leave to cool.
2 Peel, stone and chop the avocado.
3 Whiz the peas and avocado together with a hand-held blender (or in a food processor or blender) until smooth.
4 For just-weaned babies, pass the purée through a nylon sieve.

pumpkin and leek purée

makes: 3 baby portions

storage: up to 24 hours in the refrigerator

200g pumpkin flesh
1 medium leek

Vitamin A

Pumpkin and squash tend to be rather neglected as a baby food, but their creamy texture and sweet nuttiness are always popular with babies. When I lived in South America for a couple of years during my childhood, my mother frequently cooked pumpkin and squash in many inspirational ways. This purée is best given once the baby has eaten a few other purées and is used to different flavours, because the leek can be quite strong. You may prefer to use slightly less leek.

1 Scrape away the seeds and stringy flesh from the pumpkin and peel off the skin. Chop into small chunks.
2 Remove any tough outer leaves from the leek and trim the ends of the vegetable. Slice lengthways and clean under running water to remove any grit. Cut into 1.5cm chunks.
3 Put the vegetables into a steamer or colander over a pan of boiling water.
4 Cover with a lid and steam for 8 minutes, until they are tender.
5 Allow to cool slightly before whizzing with a hand-held blender (or in a food processor or blender) until smooth. For just-weaned babies, pass the purée through a nylon sieve. Leave to cool a little more before serving.

quick bites veggie purées

Some parents like to start their baby off on single-food purées. This is a great way to introduce your baby to a variety of tastes. You may need to add breast milk or formula milk or a baby rice to these purées to make the desired consistency.

asparagus

makes 2 portions
4 fresh asparagus stalks

Asparagus is great for the immune system and is a good source of beta-carotene, essential for healthy skin and lungs. It also contains vitamin C, potassium, folic acid and riboflavin. Use fresh asparagus (look for stalks with clean, pale-green ends) and choose medium-size stalks. Asparagus is best eaten on the day it is bought. Snap off the tough ends of the stalks. Cut each stalk into 4 pieces and steam for 5–10 minutes, then whiz with a hand-held blender (or in a food processor or blender) until smooth, with no stringy bits.

beetroot

1 raw, firm medium beetroot

Beetroot is a good source of vitamins and minerals, especially vitamins B_6 and C, beta-carotene, potassium, calcium, iron and folic acid. It is a great immune-boosting food. Cut off the stalk ends of the beetroot. Boil for 25–30 minutes, until tender. Drain and leave to cool, then peel. Whiz the flesh with a hand-held blender (or in a food processor or blender) until smooth.

avocado

1 ripe avocado

Avocados are rich in monounsaturated fats, which promote healthy skin. They are also easily digested, making them great for babies. Avocados can be served raw; pick a ripe one that gives slightly when pressed around the neck. Cut the avocado in half, twist to separate. Scrape the flesh from one half into a bowl. Mash with a fork or a blender to make a purée. Make this just before serving.

peas

handful of frozen peas

Peas are rich in vitamin C, the B vitamins and iron. Put the peas in a pan of boiling water, bring back to the boil and cook for 1 minute. Whiz with a hand-held blender until smooth or, for just-weaned babies, pass through a sieve. Fresh peas should be cooked for longer, puréed and sieved for babies up to 6 months.

3 C 1 🍷 broccoli

makes 2 portions
1 medium broccoli head

Broccoli is an excellent source of iron, particularly because it is a good source of vitamin C, essential in aiding the absorption of iron. It is also an immune-boosting food. Cut off the hard stalk from the broccoli head. Remove a quarter of the florets and steam them for 5–10 minutes until tender. Whiz with a hand-held blender (or in a food processor or blender) until smooth.

½ 🍷 cauliflower

florets and tender leaves
of ¼ small cauliflower

Cauliflower has high levels of vitamin C and folic acid. Try adding some tender green inner leaves to the purée, as this will increase its vitamin C content. Put the cauliflower florets and tender leaves into a steamer and steam for 10 minutes, or boil for 8 minutes, until tender. Whiz with a hand-held blender (or in a food processor or blender) until smooth.

✓ ½ C 1 📹 ½ 🍷 carrot

Vitamin A

1 medium carrot

Carrots are an excellent first food for babies because they rarely trigger an allergic reaction. Smaller carrots may be sweeter, but older, darker carrots have a higher nutrient content. Carrots are also a good treatment for diarrhoea. If you buy organic carrots there is no need to peel them; just scrub them well. Non-organic carrots will need to be peeled. Chop the carrot into small pieces and boil or steam until tender (approximately 5 minutes). Whiz with a hand-held blender (or in a food processor or blender) until smooth.

½ C 1 📹 ½ 🍷 parsnip

1 medium parsnip

Parsnips are a good source of minerals and vitamins. They also help to relieve constipation. Top and tail the parsnip and peel and cut it into small pieces, then steam over boiling water for 6–8 minutes, until tender. Whiz with a hand-held blender (or in a food processor or blender) until smooth.

✓ 3½ C ½ 📹 ½ 🍷 courgette

Vitamin A, B₁

2 small courgettes

Courgettes are rich in vitamin C, folic acid and potassium. Choose small, young courgettes, which will not need to be peeled, as they have tender, soft skins. It is better to choose organic, as any pesticide residues would be found in the skin. Remove the ends from the courgettes and slice into small rounds. Steam or boil until tender (10–15 minutes). Whiz with a hand-held blender (or in a food processor or blender) until smooth, with no stringy bits.

All quick bites make 1 portion,
unless otherwise stated.

savouries to freeze

sweetcorn and squash purée

½

makes: 5 baby portions

storage: up to 2 months in the freezer

½ small butternut squash
1 cob fresh sweetcorn

Try to choose organic fresh sweetcorn to make sure that it has not been genetically modified. If you cannot find fresh corn on the cob, use frozen sweetcorn because this is normally picked and frozen while still very fresh.

1 Cut the squash in half, scoop out the seeds and remove the peel. Cut the flesh into small chunks.
2 Remove the leaves from the sweetcorn and any stringy bits clinging to it. Using a sharp knife, cut the kernels away from the cob, turning it around as you go.
3 Bring a pan of water to the boil and add the squash and corn (if using frozen corn, add later). Return to the boil, then simmer until the vegetables are tender. Drain and cool.
4 Whiz with a hand-held blender (or in a food processor or blender) until smooth.
5 For just-weaned babies, pass the purée through a nylon sieve. Spoon the purée into ice-cube trays. Cover with foil or put into a freezer bag and seal. Freeze.
6 To serve, thaw thoroughly and then reheat.

beetroot and carrot purée

Vitamin A

makes: 3 baby portions

storage: up to 2 months in the freezer

1 fresh medium beetroot
2 small carrots

Before feeding your baby any of these purées, please read the section on weaning (pages 54–56) and the 6 month sample meal planners (pages 64–65).

If you cannot find whole, fresh beetroot, use cooked beetroot – but do make sure that it has not been pickled in vinegar. Beetroot does have quite an intense flavour, so you may like to mix this purée with a little baby rice when you first introduce it.

1 Cut the top off the beetroot's stem. Bring a pan of water to the boil and add the beetroot. Cook until tender (about 30 minutes). Drain and leave to cool. Slip the skin off (wearing clean rubber gloves) and cut the flesh into small dice.
2 Peel the carrot and cut into dice. Bring a pan of water to the boil, add the carrot and cook until tender (approximately 3–4 minutes).
3 Drain and add to the beetroot. Whiz with a hand-held blender (or in a food processor or blender) until smooth. For just-weaned babies, pass the purée through a nylon sieve. Spoon into ice-cube trays, cover with foil and seal. Freeze.
4 To serve, thaw thoroughly and then reheat.

sweet potato and carrot purée

½

½ **C**

✓
Vitamin A

makes: 5 baby portions

storage: up to 2 months in the freezer

2 medium carrots
1 small sweet potato

Adding a little chopped fresh coriander to this purée will give it a bit of zing, and the herb goes really well with the carrots. Both sweet potatoes and carrots are excellent sources of beta-carotene, an antioxidant that helps to fight disease.

1 Peel and chop the carrots. Peel the sweet potato and cut into small chunks.
2 Put the vegetables into a steamer or colander over a pan of boiling water.
3 Cover with a lid and steam for 8 minutes, until the vegetables are tender. Cool before whizzing with a hand-held blender (or in a food processor or blender) until smooth.
4 Spoon the purée into ice-cube trays. Cover with foil or put into a freezer bag and seal. Freeze.
5 To serve, thaw thoroughly and then reheat.

root vegetable medley

½ **C**

makes: 5 baby portions

storage: up to 2 months in the freezer

1 medium parsnip
2 medium carrots
1 small floury potato,
  eg King Edward

A great purée for the winter months. Try adding some chopped fresh herbs to make it more interesting for your baby. Parsnips can be quite sweet and have a lovely nutty flavour, making this purée especially popular. You may need to thin this purée down slightly with breast milk or formula milk or cooled, boiled water before serving.

1 Peel and chop all the vegetables into small dice.
2 Put them into a steamer or colander over a pan of boiling water.
3 Cover with a lid and steam for 10 minutes, until all the vegetables are tender.
4 Allow to cool slightly before whizzing with a hand-held blender (or in a food processor or blender) until smooth.
5 Leave to cool before freezing.
6 Spoon the purée into ice-cube trays. Cover with foil or put into a freezer bag and seal. Freeze.
7 To serve, thaw thoroughly and then reheat.

swede and carrot purée

makes: 3 baby portions

storage: up to 2 months in the freezer

Vitamin A

1 small or ½ large swede
2 medium carrots

Swede is an often forgotten vegetable, but it has a lovely mellow taste that is popular with babies. Steaming swede helps to preserve its flavour, which may be lost if the vegetable is boiled. Try adding a little pinch of ginger or cinnamon, which will enhance it further.

1 Peel the vegetables and cut into small chunks.
2 Put into a steamer or colander over a pan of boiling water.
3 Cover with a lid and steam for 10 minutes, until all the vegetables are tender.
4 Allow to cool slightly before whizzing with a hand-held blender (or in a food processor or blender) until smooth.
5 Spoon the purée into ice-cube trays. Cover with foil or put into a freezer bag and seal. Freeze.
6 To serve, thaw thoroughly and then reheat.

brussels sprout and pea purée

makes: 3 baby portions

storage: up to 2 months in the freezer

15 small Brussels sprouts
100g peas, fresh or frozen

Big, old sprouts can be quite bitter and unpleasant tasting, so choose the smaller ones. Steaming sprouts will also help prevent them getting too watery. The peas give a lovely sweetness to the purée. Try adding some chopped herbs to make it a little more interesting for your baby.

1 Remove the outer leaves from the sprouts and cut off the base. Bring a pan of water to the boil and steam the sprouts until just tender (about 7 minutes).
2 A couple of minutes before the sprouts are cooked, add the peas to the boiling water and cook until just tender.
3 Drain and whiz the vegetables with a hand-held blender (or in a food processor or blender) until smooth. You may need to add 2–3 tsp cooled, boiled water to help blend the vegetables.
4 For just-weaned babies, pass the purée through a nylon sieve.
5 Spoon the purée into ice-cube trays. Cover with foil or put into a freezer bag and seal. Freeze.
6 To serve, thaw thoroughly and then reheat.

fresh puddings

mango and fresh apricot purée

makes: 3 baby portions or 1 baby portion and 1 adult portion as a smoothie base

storage: up to 24 hours in the refrigerator

1 ripe mango
2 fresh apricots

This is a gorgeous purée, and it's definitely worth making extra so you can have a smoothie yourself. Just add some apple or orange juice or coconut milk and a squeeze of lime.

1 Slice through the mango on either side of the stone. Peel, then cut the flesh into cubes.
2 Stone and peel the apricots and cut the flesh into small pieces.
3 Put the mango and chopped apricots into a pan. Add 4 tbsp water and cook gently until the mango has broken down and the apricot pieces are soft (approximately 5–10 minutes). Cool.
4 Whiz the fruits together with a hand-held blender (or in a food processor or blender) until smooth.
5 For a just-weaned baby, pass the purée through a nylon sieve.

apple and plum purée

makes: 2 baby portions

storage: up to 24 hours in the refrigerator

1 eating apple, eg Cox's orange pippin
1 ripe plum
pinch of ground cinnamon

Apples and plums are in season at the same time, making them a good match. You could always add a little pinch of ginger to this purée instead of cinnamon if you want extra spice, but because this is hotter, ginger might be more suitable for older babies.

1 Peel, core and slice the apple. Peel and halve the plum, remove the stone and chop the flesh into small pieces.
2 Put the apple and plum into a saucepan with 2 tbsp water and the cinnamon. Heat gently until the apple is soft and pulpy (approximately 5 minutes) stirring occasionally. Cool.
3 Whiz with a hand-held blender (or in a food processor or blender) until smooth.
4 For just-weaned babies, pass the purée through a nylon sieve.

Before feeding your baby any of these purées, please read the section on weaning (pages 54–56) and the 6 month sample meal planners (pages 64–65).

pear and blackcurrant purée

makes: 1 baby portion

storage: up to 24 hours in the refrigerator

1 ripe pear
handful of fresh ripe blackcurrants

If you can't find fresh blackcurrants, use frozen. Pear and redcurrant is another delicious combination. If the blackcurrants are not quite ripe or are too sharp, add more pear. Blackcurrants are exceptionally rich in vitamin C, having four times as much as the equivalent weight of oranges.

1 Peel, core and slice the pear.
2 Put the pear and blackcurrants into a saucepan with 1 tbsp water.
3 Heat gently until the pear is soft and pulpy and the blackcurrants have burst open (about 4–5 minutes).
4 Whiz with a hand-held blender (or in a food processor or blender) until smooth.
5 Pass the purée through a nylon sieve before serving.

nectarine and peach purée

makes: 2 baby portions or 1 baby portion and 1 small adult portion

storage: up to 24 hours in the refrigerator

1 ripe peach
1 ripe nectarine

Make this in the summer, when these fruits are plentiful. It's really not worth it at other times of the year because the fruit will be imported, and consequently expensive and often of poor quality.

1 Halve the peach and nectarine, remove their stones and chop the flesh into small pieces.
2 Put the fruit into a small saucepan with 2 tbsp water and cook gently until it is soft and pulpy (approximately 5 minutes). Cool.
3 Whiz the fruits together with a hand-held blender (or in a food processor or blender) until smooth.
4 For a just-weaned baby, pass the purée through a nylon sieve.

mango and melon purée

makes: 3 baby portions or 1 baby portion and 1 adult portion as a smoothie base

storage: up to 24 hours in the refrigerator

1 ripe mango
½ ripe small melon, eg Galia

Mangoes are a great source of nutrients. When they are cheap, cook and then whiz up lots of the pulp and freeze in ice-cube trays, then add to purées, smoothies and breakfast cereals. All forms of melon are mildly laxative.

1 Slice through the mango on either side of the stone. Peel, then cut the flesh into cubes.
2 Cut the melon in half, scoop the seeds out and separate the skin from the flesh. Cut the flesh into small cubes.
3 Put the mango and melon in a pan with 2–3 tbsp water and cook for a few minutes, until soft.
4 Whiz the fruits using a hand-held blender (or in a food processor or blender) until smooth. For a just-weaned baby, pass the purée through a nylon sieve.

blueberry and banana purée

makes: 2 baby portions or 1 baby portion and 1 small adult portion as a smoothie base

storage: up to 24 hours in the refrigerator

150g blueberries
pinch of ground cinnamon
1 ripe small banana

The starch in bananas is not very easy for babies to digest, but when bananas are ripe most of the starch has turned to sugar. This is why it is so important to choose ripe bananas for all baby food – look for those with little brown specks all over the skin. A little spice, such as cinnamon, can be introduced once your baby has been taking solids for at least a month. So, either serve this purée with or without the cinnamon; you decide if your baby is ready for a new taste.

1 Put the blueberries and cinnamon into a small saucepan with 3 tbsp water. Heat gently until the berries are just beginning to burst. Cool.
2 Whiz the blueberries and banana together using a hand-held blender (or in a food processor or blender) until smooth.
3 For a just-weaned baby, pass the purée through a nylon sieve.

quick bites fruit purées

You may need to add breast milk or formula milk or a baby rice to these purées to make the desired consistency.

Vitamin A 3½ C ½ ½

makes 2 portions
1 ripe mango

mango

Mango is naturally sweet and easy to digest. Rich in vitamin C, minerals and antioxidants, it is great for the immune system and for convalescing babies. Choose ripe mangoes; unripe ones can cause stomach upsets. Peel the fruit, then wash the peeling knife before chopping. Slice the mango down each side of the stone. Scoop out the flesh using a spoon (if you can't do this the fruit is probably not ripe enough). Steam or simmer in 2–3 tbsp water for a few minutes, until soft. Whiz with a hand-held blender (or in a food processor or blender) until smooth. Mangoes can be stringy and need passing through a nylon sieve.

½

1 medium eating apple

apple

When cooked, apples' sweet, soft purée is always popular with babies. Apples are rich in antioxidants, so they are a good immune-boosting food. They are also good for diarrhoea and constipation. Buy organic, tree-ripened apples. Peel and core the apple. Cut it into small pieces and simmer in water or steam for 5 minutes, until soft. Whiz with a hand-held blender (or in a food processor or blender) until smooth. You can also bake apples. Cut the fruit in half and scoop out the core. Score a line around its middle and bake at 180°C/350°F/gas mark 4 for 25 minutes, until soft. Scoop the flesh from the skin and mash.

2 C

1 ripe medium banana

banana

Bananas are a great first food, but the purée can be a bit thick for a baby to swallow, so add a little boiled water or breast or formula milk. Buy really ripe fruit, as the starch will have turned to sugar, making it easier on a baby's delicate digestive system. Bananas are also good for diarrhoea and constipation. Peel the banana and mash or purée. Dilute it with water or breast or formula milk as necessary. Alternatively, bake a banana in its skin for 20 minutes at 180°C/350°F/gas mark 4. Cool and peel, then mash the flesh.

blueberry

handful of blueberries

Blueberries can be hard for babies to digest, so they are best puréed and sieved or put through a mouli until weaning has been underway for at least four months. Blueberries have natural antibacterial properties, which help to prevent mild colds and they are also excellent for treating diarrhoea. Put the blueberries in a saucepan with a little water and simmer gently until the fruit bursts open. Whiz with a hand-held blender (or in a food processor or blender) until smooth. For just-weaned babies, pass the purée through a nylon sieve.

cherry

handful of cherries

Cherries have good cleansing and antioxidant properties, which make them great for building up resistance. They are also good for constipation. They have high levels of vitamin C, potassium and magnesium. Stone the cherries, then cook them in a small pan with a little water. When they are soft, cool and then whiz with a hand-held blender (or in a food processor or blender) until smooth. For just-weaned babies, pass the purée through a nylon sieve.

apricot

1 apricot

Apricots are rich in beta-carotene, which the body converts into vitamin A. They are good for constipation – especially dried apricots, but these are best given to babies over 6 months. Apricots also have high levels of iron and potassium. First skin your fruit by putting it in boiling water. Leave for 1 minute, then slip the skin off using a sharp knife. Finely chop and cook with 1 tbsp water until soft. Whiz with a hand-held blender (or in a food processor or blender) until smooth.

melon

chunk of melon

Cantaloupe, galia and charentais are the sweetest varieties. Melons are good for digestion, but are also a mild laxative. Simmer the melon with a little water for a few minutes, until soft. When buying melon, choose ones that feel heavy for their size and have a sweet aroma. Peel the melon and remove the seeds. Whiz with a hand-held blender (or in a food processor or blender) until smooth.

pear

1 ripe pear

Pears are a great first food because they have a fairly neutral flavour. They relieve constipation and are good for convalescence. Peel and core the pear and cut into bite-size pieces. Cook gently in a small pan with a little water until soft. Whiz with a hand-held blender (or in a food processor or blender) until smooth.

All quick bites make 1 portion unless otherwise stated.

puddings to freeze

raspberry and apple purée

½**C**

makes: 3 baby portions

storage: up to 2 months in the freezer

3 eating apples, eg Cox's
  orange pippin
150g raspberries

Use fresh raspberries when they are in season; otherwise frozen ones are just as good, especially if you buy organic. This is also delicious stirred through some natural yogurt as a pudding or breakfast for mum. If your baby is used to spice, try adding a pinch of cinnamon, as it really brings out the flavour of both the apples and the raspberries.

1   Peel and core the apples, then cut into bite-sized pieces. Put them into a small pan with 6 tbsp water and cook gently until the apples are just beginning to soften (approximately 10–15 minutes).
2   Add the raspberries to the pan and cook for a further 3 minutes. Remove from the heat and cool.
3   Whiz the fruits using a hand-held blender (or in a food processor or blender) until smooth.
4   For a just-weaned baby, pass the purée through a nylon sieve.
5   Spoon the purée into ice-cube trays. Cover with foil or put into a freezer bag and seal. Freeze.
6   To serve, thaw thoroughly.

blueberry purée

½**C**

makes: 3 baby portions

storage: up to 24 hours in refrigerator

1 ripe pear, eg Williams
4–5 tbsp water
50g blueberries

Before feeding your baby any of these purées, please read the section on weaning (pages 54–56) and the 6 month sample meal planners (pages 64–65).

Just a hint of spice is a good thing occasionally to get your baby's palate used to different flavours.

1   Peel and core the pear and cut it into bite-sized chunks.
2   Put the pear into a saucepan with the water and blueberries.
3   Simmer for a few minutes, until the pear is tender and the blueberries have just burst open (it won't take long).
4   Whiz with a hand-held blender (or in a food processor or blender) until smooth. Leave to cool before serving. For just-weaned babies, pass the purée through a nylon sieve. Freeze.
5   To serve, thaw thoroughly.

At this stage in his life, your baby goes through a period of rapid growth and development. Milk will still provide most of the nutrients he needs, but solid food is becoming more important. As your baby becomes more used to solids, you can start to vary tastes and textures. You will also be able to increase the amount that he eats. Try to react to your baby's appetite, so if your baby is still hungry you can give a little more. Your baby is the best guide to how much solid food you need to give him.

This stage is still about encouraging your baby to enjoy food, which will help to form the basis of healthy eating habits that can last a lifetime.

7–9 months

what's happening to
your baby

Your baby will now be more alert, especially visually, and he will take far more notice of things around him. He will be begin to be selective about the people around him and may be wary of strangers. He will sleep less during the day and will gradually become more active. He will be more mobile and able to roll over onto his tummy, lift his head, sit unsupported and perhaps stand while being held or hold on to pieces of furniture. He will be able to wave hello and goodbye and may even be able to crawl. You will become increasingly aware of him babbling because he starts to make more recognizable sounds, such as ga-ga, ma-ma and da-da. Now is a good time to introduce a few simple games; for example, show him a picture of a cow, say 'moo', and watch his response.

eating and drinking

Your baby's physiological development will aid the weaning process – he will have better hand–eye co-ordination, so he is very likely to really enjoy steering hand-held foods towards his mouth while he sits unaided. He may start to teethe, which will help him to cope with lumpier food, and he will have learned how to swallow food rather than suck it from a spoon. His appetite will increase as he becomes more active, and he will see other people eating and drinking and want to imitate them. He is ready for new eating experiences. Try to feed him some meals at the same time as the rest of the family eats, so that he feels he belongs and can copy what other family members are doing.

Your baby will be receptive to a wide range of tastes and textures now; even mildly spiced food might be accepted, if only on the third try. His taste buds will really develop over a six- to eight-week period. It is important to give your baby lots of different foods at this stage, especially foods with stronger flavours – for example, vegetables such as carrots, broccoli, spinach, turnip and avocado, and white fish and lean meat. After this development period, especially as he becomes more aware, he will have acquired strong preferences for certain foods, and introducing new flavours will become more difficult – particularly if you have fed your baby only ready-prepared baby foods, which are often bland.

Different babies develop at different rates and only you will know at what point your baby is likely to be confident with chewing. At this stage of his development, your baby is likely to progress from puréed to mashed food and possibly to chunks of food, depending on his teeth and confidence with chewing. The most important thing is, never leave a baby alone while feeding.

Breast milk is still the primary source of nutrition for your baby, but the nutrients he gets from solids are becoming more important. Up to this point, you will have fed your baby only fruits, vegetables and baby rice. As he starts to stay awake for longer periods he will need more food. Give foods that are nutrient-dense and high in energy, such as finely ground nuts and seeds and oils (do not give nuts to babies if there is a family history of food allergies). Foods that are high in carbohydrates should also be added to his diet. A good source of protein will be needed. Iron is especially important at this stage, too, as babies are born with a natural store of this nutrient, which becomes depleted at around 6 months old.

vegetarian and vegan babies

Follow the same basic rules as any mum (*see* pages 17–27), paying particular attention to:

Protein – good sources include beans, cereals, pulses, finely ground nuts and seeds (do not feed nuts to babies if there is any family history of food allergies) and tofu.

Iron – good sources include bread, pulses, green vegetables and chopped dried fruit.

Calcium – dairy produce can be given in small quantities at this age. Good sources for a vegan diet are green vegetables, chopped dried fruits, ground nuts and fortified foods such as bread.

Iodine – good sources include grains and vegetables. You may also like to include an iodine supplement. Speak to your family doctor or state-registered dietician for more information.

Vitamin D – this is made in your baby's skin when he's exposed to sunlight, so make sure that your baby has at least half an hour outside every day. Vegetarian babies can have a little dairy produce, which will boost their vitamin D. Vegan babies should be given vegan margarine, which is fortified with vitamin D.

Vitamin B$_2$ – ground wholegrain cereals, leafy green vegetables and ground almonds.

Anyone considering providing their baby with a vegan diet should consult a state-registered dietician.

which nutrients
are key

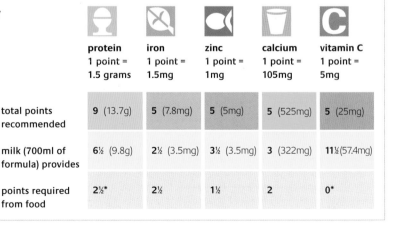

nutrients required per day

Milk provides your baby with much of his nutritional needs from 7 to 9 months – for this book I've assumed the lowest level provided by the common brands on which the milk chart on page 29 is based. If you're successfully breastfeeding, your baby should get at least these levels from your milk.

* If you feed your baby a healthy balanced diet of fresh food, you will almost certainly give him much more protein and vitamin C than he needs. Do not worry, as this will not damage his health at these levels.

	protein 1 point = 1.5 grams	iron 1 point = 1.5mg	zinc 1 point = 1mg	calcium 1 point = 105mg	vitamin C 1 point = 5mg
total points recommended	9 (13.7g)	5 (7.8mg)	5 (5mg)	5 (525mg)	5 (25mg)
milk (700ml of formula) provides	6½ (9.8g)	2½ (3.5mg)	3½ (3.5mg)	3 (322mg)	11½ (57.4mg)
points required from food	2½*	2½	1½	2	0*

second-stage
weaning

The purpose of this stage of weaning is to establish a regular eating pattern and to increase the range of nutritionally rich foods you give your baby, so that solids will become his main source of nutrients rather than breast milk. Once your baby is comfortable eating three meals a day, with finger foods and water in between, you can start to offer breast milk or formula milk as an after-solids drink only. This is best begun first thing in the morning, when your baby will be at his hungriest. Gradually, breakfast can become the largest meal of the day.

new foods

As your baby learns to swallow and chew and his teeth grow, you can gradually introduce new foods. Remember that babies develop at different paces, and that some babies will be comfortable with new foods earlier than others. Try foods that have a coarser texture; mince or mash purées rather than blending them. This is important to help encourage your baby to chew. Always wash and peel fruit and vegetables and remove pips. Never leave a baby alone with food at any time.

As your baby's digestive system matures and his appetite increases, add more foods to his diet. Fish, lean meat and poultry should be offered at least once a week to increase his protein and iron intake. (Check fish for bones, then grill or poach. Always mash the cooked food.) Babies find the flavour of protein strong when cooked on its own, so try mixing it with a blander food such as potato.

Iron is particularly important at this stage (*see* page 97). If your baby is being given a vegan diet and is relying on pulses such as beans and lentils for protein, he will need iron from other sources too, such as green vegetables, especially broccoli, spinach and watercress, and puréed, cooked dried fruit such as prunes and unsulphured apricots. Always make sure pulses are thoroughly cooked, because they are high in fibre and can be hard for babies to digest. Similarly, avoid giving babies high-fibre breakfast cereals at this stage because their digestive systems will not be able to cope.

Towards the end of this age group, if your baby is confident with chewing you can introduce wheat and wheat-based foods, such as pasta and cereals. These are great for encouraging babies to chew and use their jaw muscles. Bread, bread sticks and unsalted rice cakes can also be cut into finger-size pieces – but check their labels for salt and sugar content before you buy. At this stage babies often particularly love finger foods; try pieces of ripe, soft peeled fruit or cooked soft vegetables. Chop these foods large enough to hold and chew on, rather than bite-size to minimize the risk of choking – and always keep an eye on him (see finger food, page 58). Now that your baby is having finger foods always wash his hands before his meals.

Small amounts of full-fat cow's milk can be given if incorporated into a dish rather than as a drink. And it is important to give your baby cooled, boiled tap water between meals.

Begin to add different food and different tastes. Use lots of the foods you already cook for yourself. Just mash a small amount of cooked food without any added salt or sugar.

Don't rush the meals or force feed. Most babies know when they have had enough to eat. Go at your baby's pace. Try to be patient, I know it is not always easy. If your baby shakes his head, turns away or refuses to open his mouth take the food away from him and try again later.

allergic reactions

Occasionally, potentially harmless foods such as nuts or cow's milk can trigger an allergic reaction in babies. Some reactions cause mild discomfort, while others can be life-threatening. Allergies in children, particularly asthma and eczema, are on the increase.

Babies are more likely to develop allergies if there is a family history of eczema, asthma or hayfever. For these families, exclusive breastfeeding is recommended for the first six months. Seek advice from your health visitor, family doctor or a state-registered dietician or registered nutritionist.

common myths

myth: eating utensils must be sterilized
Up to the age of 7 months, sterilize all of your baby's eating utensils (see page 38–9). After 7 months, just wash and rinse them well and allow them to air-dry.

myth: low-fat diets are good
It is more important to make sure babies get a wide variety of foods and enough energy for their rapid development than to worry about their fat intake.

myth: high-fibre diets are good
A fibre-rich diet can be detrimental to your baby's health. His stomach capacity is too small for most high-fibre meals. Fibre can also hinder the absorption of nutrients.

myth: ready-made baby foods are better
While ready-prepared baby foods have their uses, there is no substitute for real food. Its nutrient content is far superior and, although home-made purées will have a coarser texture or less consistent flavour, this will help to instil in your baby an appreciation for fresh food with real flavours.

myth: allergies are common in babies
If you introduce foods at the correct stage, there is no reason why your baby should have an adverse reaction unless there is a history of allergy in your family. Do not restrict your baby's diet by cutting out food on the basis of unproven tests or without expert advice.

foods to eat and
foods to avoid

new foods to eat at 7–9 months

It's important to remember that babies develop at different paces, and will learn to chew at different rates, so only you will know. They should never be left alone with food at any time.

● Mashed lean meat, poultry and fish (except shellfish) at least once a week; this can increase gradually to once a day by the time he reaches 10 months. Avoid salty/smoked food.

● Pulses, such as lentils, chickpeas, haricot beans, flageolet beans and kidney beans.

● Later on, wheat or wheat-based foods, such as pasta and sugar-free unrefined cereals.

● Small amounts of full-fat dairy produce, such as natural yogurt, a little well-cooked egg, pasteurized cheese, or calcium-enriched soya dairy alternatives to milk, yogurt and desserts.

● Citrus fruits – but mix with other fruits to counteract their sugar and acid content.

● Introduce puréed dried fruits gradually. Mix with other fruits as they might cause an upset stomach.

● Water, boiled and cooled, as a drink between meals.

● Eggs are a quick, nutritious and cheap source of protein, but make sure that they are thoroughly cooked until both the white and yolk are solid.

● Finely ground nuts and smooth nut butters, assuming there is no family history of allergies.

foods to avoid at 7–9 months

● Cow's milk should not be given as a drink, although small amounts can be used in meals.

● Shellfish can trigger allergic reactions. Avoid until your child is at least 2 years old.

● Unpasteurized cheese may contain the bacteria listeria, which can cause food poisoning.

● Soft-boiled eggs and runny yolks may contain the food-poisoning bacteria salmonella, to which babies are far more sensitive than adults. Eggs should always be hard boiled.

● Salt cannot be processed by a baby's digestive system; it causes dehydration. A diet high in salt often leads to high blood pressure. Particular foods to avoid at this stage are yeast extracts such as Marmite or Vegemite and stock cubes. Most food labels refer to salt as sodium.

● Refined or unrefined sugar provides calories but few nutrients. It's a major cause of tooth decay and can lead to health problems such as obesity. It is not necessary to add sugar to your baby's food. Check labels because sugar may be present as sucrose, glucose, fructose, lactose, hydrolyzed starch, invert sugar and products such as treacle, honey and golden syrup.

● Never give your baby artificial sweeteners.

● Honey may contain botulism spores, which can cause food poisoning, and this is far more serious in babies than it is in adults.

● Avoid excessively hot or spicy foods, which can burn or inflame babies' stomachs.

● Tea and coffee contain tannins that inhibit iron absorption. Babies cannot tolerate caffeine.

Breast milk or formula milk continue to be the primary source of nutrition for your baby when he is 7–9 months old. However, the nutrients that are provided by solid food are becoming more and more important to him, and this is the time to establish a routine in which your baby eats three meals a day, with finger foods. Cooled, boiled tap water needs to be given in-between those meals.

recommended
daily intake

Until now, you have offered your baby breast milk or formula milk before giving him any solid food, in order to ensure that he drinks it all and gets the nutrients he needs. Now start to offer breast milk or formula milk as an after-solids drink. Begin this at breakfast time, when your baby will be at his hungriest and so will eat more solids. Eventually breakfast can become the largest meal of the day.

This is also the time for introducing new foods to your baby's diet. Until now, he has eaten mainly fruit, vegetables and baby rice. See page 100 for details of foods to introduce. Use the chart below as a guide to how much to feed your baby each day, remembering that all babies have different needs, depending on many factors, including weight. Follow your baby's direction and use your own initiative when deciding how much to feed him. Include finger foods at each of these meals as seems appropriate for your baby. Try to get into the habit of cooking extra fruits and vegetables and offer these to your baby in big chip-size pieces alongside the purées.

recommended daily volume of foods

milk = breastfeed or approx 200ml formula

	7 months old	8 months old	9 months old
Breakfast 7–8am	1 portion breakfast, milk	1 portion breakfast, milk	1–2 portions breakfast, milk
Lunch 11.45am-ish	1 portion lunch, alternating during feed with milk, gradually changing from milk to cooled, boiled water	1 portion lunch, cooled, boiled water	1 portion lunch plus occasionally 1 small portion fruit purée or healthy snack, cooled, boiled water
Mid-pm, 3pm	milk	milk	milk
Supper 6.30pm-ish	1 portion supper plus occasionally 1 portion pudding, cooled, boiled water, milk, in bed by 7pm-ish	1 portion supper plus occasionally 1 portion pudding, cooled, boiled water, milk, in bed by 7pm-ish	1 portion supper plus occasionally 1 portion pudding, cooled, boiled water, milk, in bed by 7pm-ish
Night-time 10pm	small milk feed if needed	small milk feed if needed	small milk feed if needed
TOTAL MILK	breast milk or 600–700ml formula, depending on baby size, inclusive of milk used in sauces, cereals	breast milk or 600–700ml formula, depending on baby size, inclusive of milk used in sauces, cereals	breast milk or 600–700ml formula, depending on baby size, inclusive of milk used in sauces, cereals

your
routine

your baby's feeds

Solids are becoming more important because milk cannot provide all the nutrients your baby now needs. To help him to eat the right amount of solids, you will need to reduce some of his milk feeds gradually. The best way to start is to reduce the amount of milk he drinks at lunch. Keep alternating food and milk during the lunchtime feed until you feel he is ready to have just solid foods with a drink of water. By 7 months, he should be eating supper with a drink of water and having his milk feed later, just before bed.

If you haven't already done so this is a great time to offer foods that your baby can hold and feed to himself. Finger foods help your baby feel a little more independent, and they can help to keep him interested in food: its shapes, colours and textures. By 9 months, it is also worth aiming to give your baby all of his drinks, other than milk, in a beaker. This will help when you come to stopping the bottle later on.

your baby's sleeps

Most babies at this age still need a quick nap after breakfast for up to 45 minutes. However, he may be ready to cut this sleep out. If you would like to encourage this, you may like to feed him lunch slightly earlier so that his after-lunch sleep is a little earlier; he'll still need at least a couple of hours at lunchtime. Then, when he is used to lasting the morning, you can gradually move lunchtime back again to a time that fits in with the rest of the family.

I remember feeling quite excited when Ella and Jasmin were only having one sleep during the day; it made life quite a lot easier if I wanted to go out and about. The important thing is to not make any changes that affect the night sleep. You need to try and keep him sleeping through, for your sake as much as his. If he does start to wake up during the night, you may want to offer water instead of milk to discourage it from becoming a habit. If he is eating well during the day, he should not need any more food at night-time.

when teething affects your baby's eating pattern

When teeth start to grow through your baby's gums, the pressure can cause some discomfort and may even affect his eating patterns. Most babies love to suck and chew things when teething so this is an ideal time to introduce finger foods.

involving your baby in feeding

Give your baby a piece of finger food or a spoon dipped in a purée to encourage independence and help him become more co-ordinated. Letting him chew and suck a spoon will also help him get used to the feel of it in his mouth.

no enjoyment of mealtimes

Most families talk at the table – it makes mealtimes far more enjoyable. Talking to your baby while you are feeding him encourages enthusiasm about mealtimes. Even saying things like 'yum yum' or congratulating him when he has managed to eat something will have positive effects.

no interest in food

Try to give your baby your undivided attention when you are feeding so he doesn't lose interest in the food.

if your baby dislikes a food

There will be some foods your baby does not like – every baby has different tastes. If a particular purée is not a hit, try it again a few days later. Some purées, especially vegetables such as beetroot or cauliflower, can have quite intense flavours, so try diluting them with baby rice, potato or breast milk or formula milk to make them more palatable.

avoiding dehydration

Always make sure your baby has plenty of water to drink. The fluid will prevent constipation, which can occur when solid foods are increased. Babies can now be encouraged to drink cooled, boiled water, given in a 'first cup'. The best way to do this is to offer it consistently at the same time each day, for example at lunch, and between every few mouthfuls of food. You may need to experiment with different types of cups to see which one your baby prefers.

a full baby

Your baby will close his mouth and turn his head away when he is full. Never try to force him to eat more than he wants. Respect his appetite.

trouble shooting

sample meal planners

key to meal planners

each milk feed:
Breastfeed or 200ml formula milk
portions:
After 6 months, all servings of food referred to in the meal planners are 1 portion
water:
Always give cooled, boiled water or very dilute fruit juice. After 9 months, all drinks should be served in a beaker.
mealtimes: These are intended as a guide
breakfast 7–8am
lunch 11.45-ish
mid-afternoon 3pm
supper 6.30pm-ish, for bed at 7pm-ish

At 7–9 months, solids start to become a more important source of nutrition. On page 97 you'll find a chart showing how much of each of the key nutrients your child generally needs to obtain from solid food. For some of these nutrients, in particular vitamin C and protein, you'll inevitably exceed these recommended intakes if you cook your baby fresh food; do not worry, as this will not harm your child. Equally, do not worry if your baby doesn't get enough points every single day, as all babies have cranky days. The important thing is to ensure that, on average, your baby is getting the recommended intake. If your baby is getting a good variety and mix of foods, all other essential nutrients that haven't been allocated points should be more than covered.

The key thing you need to achieve at mealtimes during these months is a regular eating pattern of three meals a day. Once your baby is comfortable with this, with snacks and water in between, you can offer milk after solids rather than before. Once your child starts to teethe and becomes more confident with chewing, you can begin to offer him coarser-textured foods. Your baby's digestive system will be more developed now, as well as his teeth, so you can introduce many new foods (see page 100).

7 months old, any week

	breakfast	lunch	mid-pm	supper	10pm
day 1	milk, then strawberry, apple and mint purée, water	guacamole, water	milk, water	creamy mushroom pasta sauce, water, milk	small milk if needed
day 2	milk, then strawberry, apple and mint purée, water	minestrone, water	milk, water	sweet potato and coconut curry, water, milk	small milk if needed
day 3	milk, then vanilla porridge, water	potato purée, sweetcorn and carrot, water	milk, water	creamy tomato soup, water, milk	small milk if needed
day 4	milk, then fruity muesli, water	ratatouille, water	milk, water	baked pot with 2 cheeses, dried fruit, water, milk	small milk if needed
day 5	milk, then plum yogurt with muesli, water	poached fish with spinach sauce, water	milk, water	tomato and mozzarella couscous, mango and banana fool, water, milk	small milk if needed
day 6	milk, then papaya and rice, water	courgette and mint purée, water	milk, water	salmon, broccoli and pasta, water, milk	small milk if needed
day 7	milk, then apple and banana purée, water	tomato and aubergine beef, water	milk, water	potato salad, water, milk	small milk if needed

8 months old, any week

	breakfast	lunch	mid-pm	supper	10pm
day 1	milk, banana and peach smoothie, toast, water	baked potato with 2 cheeses, water	milk, water	lamb with butternut squash, water, milk	small milk if needed
day 2	milk, then fruity muesli, water	chicken with sesame seeds, water	milk, water	bubble and squeak with cheese, water, milk	small milk if needed
day 3	milk, then mango lassi, water	creamy tomato soup, water	milk, water	salmon, broccoli and pasta, mango and banana fool, water, milk	small milk if needed
day 4	milk, then papaya and rice, water	fruity Moroccan chicken, peach yogurt, water	milk, water	sweet potato and coconut curry, water, milk	small milk if needed
day 5	fruity muesli, water, then milk	minestrone, water	milk, water	macaroni and cauliflower cheese, rice pudding with blueberries, water, milk	small milk if needed
day 6	peach and cinnamon purée, water, then milk	creamy mushroom pasta sauce, water	milk, water	butterbean and carrot pâté, choc b&b pud, water, milk	small milk if needed
day 7	apricot and vanilla purée, water, then milk	tomato and aubergine beef, water	milk, water	tomato and mozzarella couscous, water, milk	small milk if needed

9 months old, any week

	breakfast	lunch	mid-pm	supper	10pm
day 1	plum yogurt with muesli, water, then milk	fruity Moroccan chicken, water	milk, water	peanut butter soldiers; vegetable sticks, water	small milk if needed
day 2	mango, kiwi and banana purée, water, then milk	bubble and squeak with cheese, peach yogurt, water	milk, water	creamy tomato soup, water	small milk if needed
day 3	pear and apple muffins, water, then milk	potato salad, mango and peach purée, water	milk, water	chicken with sesame seeds, water	small milk if needed
day 4	raisin bread in milk with banana, water, then milk	mushrooms with tuna, water	milk, water	fish with spinach sauce, pear/almond yog, water	small milk if needed
day 5	papaya and rice, water, then milk	sweetcorn and potato soup, muesli bar, water	milk, water	salmon, broccoli and pasta, water	small milk if needed
day 6	prune and banana porridge, water, then milk	herby tomato pasta sauce, water	milk, water	fish fingers with carrot, banana teabread, water	small milk if needed
day 7	apricot couscous, water, then milk	quick pizza, pear and blackcurrant purée, water	milk, water	macaroni and cauliflower cheese, water	small milk if needed

fresh breakfasts

vanilla porridge

makes: 3 baby portions or 1 baby portion and 1 adult portion

storage: best eaten fresh or up to 24 hours in the refrigerator

½ vanilla pod
200ml breast milk or formula milk
125ml water
60g oats
1 tbsp finely chopped or puréed mango (optional)

Vanilla is another flavour that babies seem to love and it is a really easy way to make porridge a little more interesting. Ella, my eldest, who is 3, still loves eating sugar-free vanilla porridge.

1   Split the vanilla pod lengthways.
2   Put all the ingredients into a saucepan and heat gently for 5 minutes, stirring often, until the mixture has thickened. Remove the vanilla pod.
3   Purée with a hand-held blender (or in a food processor or blender), adding more milk or cooled, boiled water to create a runnier consistency if necessary.
4   If wished, serve with finely chopped or puréed mango, depending on your baby's confidence with chewing.

strawberry, apple and mint purée

makes: 3 baby portions or 1 baby portion and 1 adult portion as a smoothie base or cereal topping

storage: best eaten fresh

handful of strawberries
½ small eating apple, eg Cox's orange pippin
1 mint leaf

Mint goes really well with strawberries, but try adding it to other fruit purées, too, especially melon. This is a great purée to give a baby who may be constipated, because strawberries are rich in both soluble and insoluble fibre, which help to relieve the condition.

1   Hull the strawberries.
2   Peel and core the apple, then roughly chop. Put it into a small saucepan with 2 tbsp water and heat gently until the apple is soft and pulpy.
3   Cool, then add the strawberries and the mint. Whiz with a hand-held blender (or in a food processor or blender) until smooth, or mash.

Note: not all recipes in this section are suitable for all babies in the age group. Please read the introductions carefully before serving them.

plum yogurt with muesli

makes: 2 baby portions

storage: best eaten fresh or up to 24 hours in the refrigerator

1+

1 ripe plum, eg Victoria
  or greengage
a tiny pinch of ground ginger
2 tbsp natural full-fat yogurt
1 tbsp ground baby muesli
breast milk or formula milk,
  to serve

Small amounts of spices can be added to lots of different purées, not only to make them more interesting to your baby but also to educate his palate. It is at this early stage that a lifetime's eating habits can be influenced, so be bold! You could also include a little fresh grated ginger instead of ground ginger. Avoid muesli that contains nuts if there is any family history of allergies.

1 Remove the plum's stone and roughly chop.
2 Put the plum in a saucepan with the ginger and 2 tbsp water and heat gently until the plum is soft. Leave to cool.
3 Mash the plum into a purée, then add the yogurt, muesli and enough breast milk or formula milk to create the desired consistency. Mix together well.

prune and banana porridge

makes: 3 baby portions or 1 baby portion and 1 adult portion

storage: best eaten fresh or up to 24 hours in the refrigerator

Vitamin B$_{12}$

1+

125ml boiling water
2 prunes, stoned and finely
  chopped (only for babies
  of 9 months or older)
200ml breast milk or
  formula milk
60g oats
½ ripe medium banana,
  roughly chopped

A great purée for any older baby who is prone to constipation, because prunes are a natural laxative. But dried fruits can be difficult to digest, so I'd advise keeping this one for babies in their ninth month plus. As with all fruit for babies, make sure the bananas are ripe – they should have black spots. Unripe bananas can be indigestible for babies, as well as causing wind.

1 Pour the boiling water over the prunes and then leave them to soak for half an hour.
2 Put the soaked prunes in a pan with all the other ingredients except the banana, and then heat gently for 5 minutes, stirring often, until the mixture has thickened.
3 Add the banana and purée with a hand-held blender (or in a food processor or blender), adding a little more milk or cooled, boiled water, to thin, if necessary. Alternatively, mash.

mango, kiwi and banana purée

makes: 3 baby portions or
1 baby portion and 1 adult
portion as a smoothie base

storage: best eaten fresh

½ ripe mango
1 ripe kiwi fruit
1 ripe small banana
lime juice (optional)

This is a really zingy purée, but try adding a little bit of lime juice to help bring out the flavours of the fruit and give the purée an extra kick. Surprisingly, lots of older babies and toddlers really enjoy the sour taste of citrus fruits. My 3-year-old daughter, Ella, loves to suck on slices of lemon.

1 Remove the peel from the mango and then roughly chop the flesh into small pieces.
2 Peel and roughly chop the kiwi fruit and banana.
3 Put the fruit into a bowl and whiz with a hand-held blender (or in a food processor or blender) until smooth, or roughly mash.

apple and banana purée

makes: 2 baby portions

storage: best eaten fresh or
up to 24 hours in the
refrigerator

75ml boiling water
1 small eating apple,
  eg Cox's orange pippin
1 ripe small banana, roughly
  chopped

This simple purée is always a favourite with babies, who love the taste of banana and the sweetness of apple.

1 Peel and core the apple, then chop into small pieces. Put it in a pan with a little boiling water and simmer gently until the apple is soft and pulpy (approximately 5 minutes), adding a little more water if necessary. Cool.
2 Whiz the banana and apple mixture together using a hand-held blender (or in a food processor or blender) until smooth, or roughly mash.

quick bites **breakfasts**

6 **C** 1 🥚 ### melon and raspberry fruit salad

¼ ripe melon, eg Ogen
good handful of raspberries

Deseed, peel and finely chop the melon. Finely chop the raspberries. Mix the fruits together and mash with a fork or potato masher.

½ **C** ½ 🥚 ### apple yogurt

makes **2** portions
1 eating apple
2 tbsp natural full-fat yogurt

Peel, core and grate the apple. Put it into a saucepan with 1 tbsp water. Cook gently for 2–3 minutes. Leave to cool, then mix the apple into the yogurt and mash with a fork.

4 **C** ½ 🥛 ½ 🍶 1½ 🥚 ### banana and peach smoothie

makes **2** portions
¼ ripe small banana
1 small peach, stone removed
100ml breast milk or formula milk

Peel and chop the banana and peach. Mix with the breast milk or formula milk and whiz with a hand-held blender (or in a food processor or blender) until smooth.

4 **C** ½ 🥛 ½ 🍶 1½ 🥚 ### mango lassi

makes **2** portions
1 small mango
5 tbsp natural full-fat yogurt

Cut through the mango on either side of the fruit's stone. Peel off the skin and then cut the mango flesh into cubes. Put the mango into a bowl. Add the yogurt and whiz with a hand-held blender (or in a food processor or blender) until smooth.

½ 🥛 ½ 🍶 1½ 🥚 ### banana and fig yogurt

makes **2** portions
1 ripe small banana
1 fresh fig
3 tbsp natural full-fat yogurt

Peel and chop the banana, then put it in a bowl. Wash, stalk and finely chop the fig. Mash the banana, add the fig, mash again, then stir into the yogurt. This recipe is only suitable for babies who are confident with chewing.

2 **C** 1 🍶 1½ 🍶 4 🥚 ### fruity muesli

50g ground baby muesli
1 ripe apricot
50ml apple juice

Put the muesli into a bowl. Cut the apricot in half, remove the stone and chop the flesh. Put the fruit into a bowl and purée with a hand-held blender. Add to the ground muesli with the apple juice and mix together. Remember, do not serve muesli containing nuts if there is any family history of allergies.

1 C **½** 🥛 **½** 🍴 **3½** 🥚

raisin bread soaked in milk with banana

1 slice of raisin bread (only for babies of 9 months or older)
100ml breast milk or formula milk
1 ripe pear

Tear the raisin bread into small pieces and put it in a bowl. Pour over the breast milk or formula milk and leave to soak for 5–10 minutes. Peel and core the pear and finely chop the flesh. Stir through the softened bread. Mash with a fork.

Vitamin B₁

3 C **1** 🥛 **1** 🍴 **3½** 🥚

Weetabix with banana

1 Weetabix
100ml breast milk or formula milk
1 ripe small banana

Break the Weetabix into small pieces and put in a bowl. Add the breast milk or formula milk. Peel and mash the banana, then mix all the ingredients together and serve. This is only suitable for babies who are confident with chewing.

1½ C **1½** 🍴 **2** 🥚

apricot couscous

makes 2 portions
100g couscous
50ml apple juice
3 fresh apricots

Put the couscous in a bowl and pour over the apple juice and 50ml boiling water. Cover and leave for 10 minutes. Remove the stones from the apricots and peel (optional), then roughly mash. Fluff the couscous with a fork and mix with the mashed apricots. This is only suitable for babies who are confident with chewing.

3 C **½** 🥛 **½** 🥚

peach and cinnamon purée

1 ripe peach
pinch of ground cinnamon

Stone and peel the peach, then mash the flesh in a bowl until smooth. Add a pinch of ground cinnamon and mix well.

3 C **½** 🥚

soft bread

1 slice of white bread
2 tbsp natural full-fat yogurt
2 tbsp breast milk or formula milk

Tear the bread into small pieces and put it into a bowl. Add the yogurt and breast milk or formula milk and then leave for 5–10 minutes to soften. This recipe is only suitable for babies who are confident with chewing.

6 C **2** 🥛 **½** 🥛 **2½** 🍴 **1½** 🥚

papaya and rice

makes 2 portions
1 ripe medium papaya
3 tbsp baby rice
3 tbsp breast milk or formula milk

Cut the papaya in half, remove the seeds and then peel. Finely chop the flesh of the fruit and then put it into a bowl. Mix together the baby rice and breast milk or formula milk. Add to the papaya and whiz with a hand-held blender (or in a food processor or blender).

6 C **½** 🍴 **½** 🥚

melon and mashed blueberries

¼ ripe melon, eg Ogen
75g fresh blueberries

Peel the melon and finely chop it. Put the fresh blueberries into a bowl, mash roughly and mix with the melon.

All quick bites make 1 portion unless otherwise stated.

breakfasts to freeze

buttermilk and nut scones

2

½

1+

makes: 20 baby portions

storage: up to 2 months in the freezer

450g self-raising flour
pinch of ground cinnamon
60g unsalted butter
2 tbsp finely ground nuts
  (optional)
284ml buttermilk
6 tbsp breast milk or
  formula milk

These little scones are quick to make and freeze brilliantly. Serve them soaked in a little formula milk or soya drink to babies who are confident with chewing. For older babies they make great nibbles when teething. Remember, if there is any history of allergy, particularly nut allergy, it is best to leave the nuts out.

1 Preheat the oven to 180°C/350°F/gas mark 4. Sieve the flour and cinnamon into a large bowl. Rub in the butter, then stir in the nuts (if using) and buttermilk.
2 Add enough breast milk or formula milk to make a soft, sticky dough.
3 Drop teaspoonfuls of the mixture onto a buttered baking sheet. Bake for 12–14 minutes, until golden and cooked through.
4 Leave to cool on a wire rack, then freeze in freezer bags.
5 To serve, thaw thoroughly.

apricot and vanilla purée

½

2 C

makes: 4–5 baby portions

storage: up to 2 months in the freezer

8 ripe fresh apricots, stoned
4 tbsp water
4 tbsp fresh orange juice
1 vanilla pod

Note: not all recipes in this section are suitable for all babies in the age group. Please read the recipe introductions carefully before serving them to your baby.

Vanilla is a fantastic ingredient for babies and children. It gives dishes a lovely, natural, sweet flavour without the addition of sugar. It also helps bring out the flavour of many soft fruits, apricots and peaches in particular. Once you have used the vanilla pod, wash it and leave it to dry on kitchen paper. You can then reuse it, or put it into a jar of golden caster sugar to use for baking.

1 Chop the apricots into small pieces and put them into a small saucepan with the water and orange juice.
2 Split the vanilla pod lengthways and add to the pan. Heat gently until just simmering and cook until the apricots are soft (approximately 10 minutes).
3 Remove from the heat and cool. Remove the vanilla pod before whizzing the fruit with a hand-held blender (or in a food processor or blender) until roughly blended.
4 Spoon the purée into ice-cube trays. Cover with foil or put into a freezer bag and seal. Freeze.
5 To serve, thaw thoroughly.

oatcakes

makes: 10 baby portions

storage: up to 3 months in the freezer

125ml boiling water
1 tsp unsalted butter
150g fresh medium oatmeal

A great stand-by, these are quick to make and older babies who are confident with chewing love them. Your baby shouldn't have too much butter in his diet, and always make sure it is unsalted. In fact, it's a good opportunity to change to unsalted butter for all the family. Only serve these to babies who are confident with chewing.

1 Preheat the oven to 180°C/350°F/gas mark 4.
2 Put the boiling water into a bowl and stir in the butter until it has melted. Stir in the oatmeal and leave to stand for 5 minutes.
3 Turn the dough out onto a floured surface and roll out to 0.5cm thick. Using a sharp knife, cut into small 2.5cm squares.
4 Put the oatcakes onto a lightly greased baking sheet and then cook for 8–10 minutes, or until just turning brown. Cool and layer between greaseproof paper in a freezerproof container. Freeze.
5 To serve, thaw thoroughly.

raspberry and blueberry compote

makes: 3–4 baby portions

storage: up to 2 months in the freezer

200g raspberries, fresh or frozen
200g fresh blueberries
6 tbsp water

Always pick over soft fruit for leaves and bugs – the easiest way to do this is to lay them on something white, such as kitchen paper. In the autumn, look out for bilberries, a type of blueberry that has a distinctive bright-blue juice and a delicious flavour.

1 Put the raspberries and blueberries into a small saucepan with the water. Heat gently until just simmering and cook until all the fruit has burst and the raspberries are pulpy.
2 Remove from the heat and cool before whizzing with a hand-held blender (or in a food processor or blender).
3 Spoon the purée into ice-cube trays. Cover with foil or put into a freezer bag and seal. Freeze.
4 To serve, thaw thoroughly.

pear and apple muffins

½

Vitamin B₁₂

1⁺

makes: 16 baby portions

storage: for up to 2 months in the freezer

185g plain flour
1 tsp baking powder
1 tsp bicarbonate of soda
80g golden caster sugar
1 large free-range egg
125ml breast milk or
  formula milk
3 tbsp unsalted butter,
  melted
150g mixed pear and apple,
  peeled and finely chopped

Try making these in mini-muffin cases, which will help to keep the muffins fresher and more moist for longer. Muffins are always popular with babies, especially when they are beginning to teethe – but only serve them to babies who are confident with chewing. The fruits can be substituted with almost any other soft fruit.

1 Preheat the oven to 200°C/400°F/gas mark 6.
2 Butter the mini-muffin tins.
3 Sift the flour, baking powder and bicarbonate of soda into a bowl.
4 Make a well in the centre. Add the remaining ingredients, gently folding everything together to make a wet batter.
5 Spoon the batter into the buttered tins. Bake for about 12 minutes, or until the muffins are golden brown and firm to the touch.
6 Cool on a wire rack, then freeze in freezer bags.
7 To serve, thaw thoroughly.

apple and dried apricot purée

½

1**C**

makes: 3 baby portions

storage: for up to 2 months in the freezer

6 dried apricots (only for
  babies of 9 months or
  older)
100ml boiling water
4 eating apples, eg Cox's
  orange pippin

Dried fruits can be difficult to digest, so I'd advise keeping this one for babies of 9 months or older. Make this purée in the autumn, when apples are plentiful and cheap; look out for different varieties.

1 Roughly chop the apricots and then put them into a bowl. Pour over the boiling water. Leave to soak for at least an hour, but preferably overnight. (The longer you soak the apricots, the more water they will absorb.)
2 Peel and core the apples, then cut into small chunks. Put into a small saucepan with the soaked apricots and, if the fruit looks dry, a little extra water. Bring to simmering point and cook gently until the apples are soft and pulpy.
3 Remove from the heat and cool before whizzing with a hand-held blender (or in a food processor or blender).
4 Spoon the purée into ice-cube trays. Cover with foil or put into a freezer bag and seal. Freeze.
5 To serve, thaw thoroughly.

fresh savouries

fruity Moroccan chicken

14

1½

1

½

2 **C**

Vitamin B₁, A

1+

makes: 4 baby portions or 2 baby portions and 1 adult portion

storage: up to 24 hours in the refrigerator

1 tbsp olive oil
1 large onion, chopped
1 clove garlic, finely
  chopped
450g raw chicken, finely
  chopped
100g dried apricots, finely
  chopped and 75g sultanas
  (only for babies of
  9 months or older)
pinch of ground cinnamon
400ml tomato passata
200ml water
couscous, to serve

The classic Moroccan combination of fruit, meat and mild spices is always popular with babies. You could make this with lamb or beef mince instead of chicken – just change the cooking time accordingly. Serve with couscous. Non-organic dried fruits are treated with the preservative sulphur dioxide, which may provoke allergic reactions, so buy organic when possible. This is only suitable for babies of 9 months or older, who are confident with chewing.

1 Heat the oil in a small frying pan and fry the onion and garlic until soft and pale golden.
2 Add the chicken and fry, stirring often, until browned.
3 Add the apricots, sultanas, cinnamon, tomato passata and water.
4 Bring the mixture to the boil, then reduce the heat and simmer gently for 20 minutes.
5 Meanwhile, cook the couscous following the packet's instructions.
6 Serve the chicken mixture (mashed if necessary) with couscous.

baked potato with two cheeses

10½

½

1½

2

1 **C**

1+

makes: 1 baby portion
storage: best eaten fresh

1 medium potato
3 tbsp cottage cheese
25g Cheddar cheese, grated

Note: not all recipes in this section are suitable for all babies in the age group. Please read the introductions carefully before serving.

Don't waste time and energy by cooking just one baked potato – cook a few. Have one for lunch and use the flesh from the others to make a purée or mash that can be frozen and reheated. You could use a sweet potato for this recipe instead.

1 Preheat the oven to 180°C/350°F/gas mark 4. Wash the potato and stick it on a metal skewer or cut a cross in the top.
2 Cook for 1 hour, or until the potato is cooked through. Meanwhile, strain the cottage cheese. Allow the potato to cool slightly, and then cut in half and scoop out the flesh. Mash the potato with the cheeses and purée if necessary.

chicken with sesame seeds

makes: 2 baby portions or 1 baby portion and 1 small adult portion

storage: best eaten fresh

1 raw chicken breast
1 small broccoli head, cut into small florets
1 tbsp olive oil
2 tsp sesame seeds, ground

14

2

2

1

4

1+

If you have the time, toast the sesame seeds to give them a more pronounced nutty flavour. You could also add a dash of sesame oil to the olive oil. This recipe makes enough for lunch for an adult as well; if you don't fancy eating it, just quarter the recipe. Do not feed seeds to babies if there is any family history of allergies.

1 Cut the chicken into thin strips.
2 Bring a pan of water to the boil and cook the broccoli until just soft (approximately 3–4 minutes).
3 Heat the oil in a pan and fry the chicken until golden. Add the cooked broccoli and sesame seeds and cook for 5 more minutes, until the chicken is cooked through.
4 Chop the chicken and broccoli into small pieces and mash, or serve in big chip-size pieces.

tomato and aubergine beef

makes: 8 baby portions or 2 baby portions and 3 adult portions

storage: up to 3 days in the refrigerator

10

1

3

1

Vitamin B_{12}

1+

2 tbsp olive oil
500g beef mince
1 onion, finely chopped
1 clove garlic, finely chopped
1 small aubergine, chopped into small dice
400g fresh vine tomatoes or 400g tin chopped tomatoes
200ml no-salt vegetable stock (page 332)
1 tbsp tomato purée
1 tbsp chopped fresh mixed herbs or just parsley (or pinch of dried herbs)
tiny pasta shapes, or rice, to serve

I am not a fan of baby books that encourage you to make mince dishes with just 100g of meat. If you are going to cook mince, you may as well make it worth your while and do enough to feed the whole family. Adding aubergine to the mince is not only a great way of making it go further – it also gives it a lovely rich flavour.

1 Heat a frying pan until really hot. Add 1 tbsp of the olive oil and fry the beef until it is really brown all over (approximately 5–10 minutes). Transfer the meat to a plate.
2 Heat the remaining oil in the pan and fry the onion, garlic and aubergine until they are soft and golden, stirring often.
3 Return the beef to the pan and add the tomatoes, vegetable stock, tomato purée and dried herbs (if using), then cover and simmer for 25 minutes.
4 Meanwhile, bring a large pan of water to the boil and cook the pasta or rice following the packet's instructions.
5 Add the fresh herbs to the sauce, cook for a further 1–2 minutes, then mash. Spoon the sauce over the pasta or rice and serve as is, or purée a small amount of each together in a small bowl, then serve.

butterbean and carrot pâté

makes: 3 baby portions or 1 baby and 1 adult portion

storage: up to 24 hours in the refrigerator

200g carrots, peeled
and chopped
2 tbsp olive oil
200g tin butterbeans
pinch of paprika
1 tsp chopped fresh
coriander (optional)
toast, to serve (optional)

Vitamin A

As your baby gets older and increasingly used to solids, you can start to introduce more fibrous foods – as long as they are well cooked and puréed. Beans and pulses are an excellent source of many nutrients, but especially protein, and so are ideal for vegetarian babies. Canned beans are fine, although some can have high levels of salt, so check the labels and make sure you rinse them well before use.

1   Put a pan of water on to boil and cook the carrots in a steamer over the pan, until they are soft (about 4 minutes).
2   Put the carrots and all the other ingredients into a blender (or food processor) and whiz until smooth.
3   If your baby is confident with chewing, spread the pâté onto toast and cut it into fingers.

minestrone

makes: 3 baby portions or 1 baby portion and 1 adult portion

storage: up to 3 days in the refrigerator

1 tbsp olive oil
2 spring onions, finely
chopped
1 small carrot, peeled
and diced
½ leek, washed and finely
chopped
200g tin chopped tomatoes
300ml no-salt vegetable
stock (page 332)
100g tiny pasta shapes
1 tbsp freshly grated cheese,
eg Parmesan

Vitamin B₁, A

When using vegetable stock, make sure it is a no-salt brand because too much salt can be dangerous for small babies. If you can't find a brand without salt, just use water. Many varieties of tinned tomatoes often have added sugar and salt, so you should always check the labels and look for ones without these unnecessary ingredients.

1   Heat the olive oil in a large pan. Add the spring onions, carrot and leek, and cook until the vegetables are soft and the spring onions are just golden.
2   Add the tomatoes and vegetable stock and bring to the boil. Simmer for 15–20 minutes, until the vegetables are tender.
3   Add the pasta and cook following the packet's instructions, stirring often.
4   Stir in the grated cheese and serve as is, or purée then serve.

quick bites savouries

tomato and mozzarella couscous

50g couscous
1 ripe tomato
2 slices of mozzarella cheese
(approximately 40g)

Put the couscous into a bowl and add 50ml boiling water. Cover and leave for at least 10 minutes. Fluff the couscous with a fork. Finely chop the tomato and mozzarella cheese, then add to the couscous. Mix all of the ingredients together and then mash them slightly with either a fork or a potato masher.

potato salad

2 new potatoes
2 fresh mint leaves
2 tbsp natural full-fat yogurt
1 tsp lemon juice

Peel the potatoes and put them into a saucepan with a little water. Bring to the boil and simmer until just tender (approximately 7–10 minutes), then drain. Chop the potatoes into small pieces and finely chop the mint leaves. Mix together the yogurt, lemon juice and mint in a bowl. Add the potatoes and toss all the ingredients together. Mash the mixture with either a fork or a potato masher.

Vitamin B₁

guacamole

1 avocado (of which you
will use ½)
2 fresh coriander leaves
1 ripe small tomato (optional)
a little baby rice, to serve

Peel and halve the avocado, leaving the stone in the half you are not using in order to delay browning. Finely chop the coriander and tomato. Mash the flesh of the avocado half with the coriander. Add the tomato if your baby is confident with chewing. Serve with a little baby rice mixed with breast or formula milk.

avocado and cheese tortillas

1 avocado (of which you will use ½)
1 flour tortilla
25g mild or medium Cheddar cheese

Peel and halve the avocado, leaving the stone in the half you are not using in order to delay browning. Mash the avocado, then spread it onto a flour tortilla. Grate the cheese and sprinkle it over the avocado. Roll up the tortilla and cut into small circles. This is only suitable for babies who are confident with chewing.

Vitamin B₁

courgette and mint purée

1 small courgette
5 green beans
handful of fresh or frozen peas
2 fresh mint leaves

Finely chop the courgette and put into a steamer or saucepan with the green beans, peas and mint leaves. Cook for 5 minutes, or until just tender. Drain and whiz with a hand-held blender (or in a food processor or blender). Serve with little fingers of soft bread or roll if your baby is confident with chewing.

Vitamin B₁, A   ½ ½ ½ 6

fish fingers with puréed carrot

2 fish fingers
2 small carrots

Grill the fish fingers following the pack's instructions, then cut them into small pieces. Peel and chop the carrots, then put them into a pan with a little water and bring to the boil. Simmer until tender (approximately 4–5 minutes). Drain and purée with a hand-held blender or potato masher. Serve the fish fingers with the carrot purée. This is only suitable for babies who are confident with chewing.

2 C 1 1 ½ 3½

hummus and tomato with pitta

1 ripe small tomato
3 tbsp hummus
2 tbsp full-fat or natural yogurt
pitta fingers, to serve

Finely chop the tomato. Put the hummus (which can be bought or home-made) into a bowl, and add the yogurt and tomato. Mix together well. Serve with little pitta fingers. This is only suitable for babies who are confident with chewing.

Vitamin B₁, A   4 C 1 ½ 3½

potato purée with sweetcorn and carrot

1 medium potato
1 small carrot
handful of fresh or frozen sweetcorn

Peel and roughly chop the potato and carrot. Put the potato into a saucepan with a little water, bring to the boil and simmer for 5 minutes. Add the carrot and sweetcorn. Continue to cook for another 5 minutes, until all the vegetables are just tender. Drain and purée with a hand-held blender or potato masher.

Vitamin B₁₂   2 C ½ ½ 8

mushrooms with tuna

2 chestnut mushrooms, cleaned
knob of butter
50g tinned tuna
1 ripe small tomato
piece of fresh bread (optional)

Finely chop the mushrooms. Heat the butter in small frying pan and sauté the mushrooms until they are really soft. Add the tinned tuna. Finely chop the tomato and mix into the other ingredients. Lightly mash with a fork. Serve on its own or, if your baby is confident with chewing, with pieces of fresh bread.

Vitamin B₁₂   ½ 3 ½ 9½

lamb with mint and yogurt

2 slices of cooked lamb
2 tbsp full-fat natural yogurt
2 fresh mint leaves
1 pitta bread (optional)

Finely chop the cooked lamb and mix with the yogurt. Finely chop the mint and mix into the dish. Lightly mash with a potato masher or fork. Serve with a portion of sweet potato and onion purée (*see* page 78).

Vitamin B₁   ½ C 1½ ½ 12½

avocado with chopped cooked chicken

1 avocado (of which you will use ½)
½ small cooked chicken breast
2 fingers of fresh bread

Peel and halve the avocado, leaving the stone in the half you are not using in order to delay browning. Mash the avocado and finely chop the cooked chicken breast, then mix the two together. Serve with a couple of fingers of fresh bread. This recipe is only suitable for babies who are confident with chewing.

All quick bites make 1 portion unless otherwise stated.

savouries to freeze

salmon, broccoli and pasta

makes: 6 baby portions

storage: up to 2 months in the freezer

10
½
1
2
3
in B₁, B₁₂, A
1+

100g tiny pasta shapes
200g broccoli, cut into small
   florets
200ml formula milk or
   calcium-enriched soya drink
20g plain flour
20g unsalted butter
freshly ground black pepper
100g Cheddar cheese, grated
200g cooked salmon, cut
   into small chunks

This is the sort of food I grew up on. Cool the sauce before adding the other ingredients and then freeze, so that the cooked fish is only reheated once.

1 Bring a pan of water to the boil and cook the pasta following the packet's instructions. Cook the broccoli over the boiling pasta water in a steamer, until just tender (approximately 5 minutes). Drain and reserve.

2 Preheat the oven to 180°C/350°F/gas mark 4.

3 Mix together the milk, flour and butter in a saucepan. Heat gently, stirring constantly with a whisk, until you have a smooth sauce.

4 Season with pepper, add half the cheese and stir until melted, then stir in the cooked pasta. Stir in the salmon and broccoli and pour into an ovenproof dish. Sprinkle with remaining cheese. Bake for 25 minutes, until golden. Cool and freeze.

5 To serve, thaw thoroughly and bake at 180°C/350°F/gas mark 4 for 15–20 minutes, or until hot through, then serve as is or chopped into tiny pieces.

macaroni and cauliflower cheese

makes: 4–6 baby portions

storage: up to 2 months in the freezer

4
½
1
½
6
amin B₁, B₁₂
1+

100g macaroni
400g cauliflower florets
200ml formula milk
20g plain flour
20g unsalted butter
freshly ground black pepper
2 tbsp finely chopped parsley
100g Cheddar cheese, grated

Keep some of the tiny tender cauliflower leaves to steam with the florets and add to the dish for extra vitamins if your baby is confident with chewing.

1 Bring a pan of water to the boil and cook the macaroni following the packet's instructions. Cook the cauliflower over the boiling water in a steamer, until just tender (approximately 5 minutes). Drain and reserve.

2 Preheat the oven to 180°C/350°F/gas mark 4.

3 Mix together the milk, flour and butter in a pan. Heat gently, stirring with a whisk, until you have a smooth sauce. Season with pepper, then add the herbs and half the cheese. Stir until the cheese has melted, then stir in the macaroni.

4 Arrange the cauliflower in an ovenproof dish. Pour over the macaroni cheese and sprinkle over the remaining cheese. Bake for 15 minutes until golden brown.

5 Leave to cool completely, wrap in foil and freeze.

6 To serve, thaw thoroughly and bake at 180°C/350°F/gas mark 4 for 15–20 minutes, or until hot through, then serve as is, chop into tiny pieces or mash.

Note: not all recipes in this section are suitable for all babies in the age group. Please read the introductions carefully before serving.

sweet potato and coconut curry

1½

½

½

2½ **C**

Vitamin A

makes: 10 baby portions

storage: up to 2 months in the freezer

25g unsalted butter
1 tbsp olive oil
1 onion, chopped
1 garlic clove, crushed
1–2 tsp mild curry powder
1cm fresh root ginger,
  peeled and finely chopped
1 small butternut squash,
  peeled and finely diced
1 small sweet potato, peeled
  and cut into small dice
1 carrot, cut into small dice
200g tin chopped tomatoes
400ml coconut milk
300ml no-salt vegetable stock
  (page 332)

Older babies and children enjoy a creamy, coconut curry – in fact, having Thai curry is a great treat for Ella, my eldest. Try adding a little lime juice to give it a bit of a kick. This recipe is designed to feed the whole family, but if you only want enough for a few meals for the baby just halve the recipe. Do not feed coconut to babies if there is any family history of allergies.

1 Heat the butter and oil in a large pan, add the onion and garlic and cook until soft (approximately 5 minutes).
2 Add 1 tsp curry powder and ginger and cook for 1 more minute, stirring the mixture often. Add the butternut squash, sweet potato and carrot and then cook for 2 minutes, stirring.
3 Add the tomatoes, coconut milk and stock and bring to the boil. Simmer for 15–20 minutes, until the vegetables are just tender.
4 Leave to cool completely, then spoon into a freezerproof container. Freeze.
5 To serve, thaw thoroughly. Put into a saucepan and heat through for 10–15 minutes, or until hot through. Lightly mash or, for a smoother purée, whiz with a hand-held blender (or in a food processor or blender).

creamy tomato soup

½

½

1

1 **C**

Vitamin A

makes: 10 baby portions

storage: up to 2 months in the freezer

10g unsalted butter
1 small red onion, finely
  chopped
1 small garlic clove, crushed
1 small carrot, peeled and
  finely chopped
1 small potato, peeled
  and diced
500g ripe tomatoes, chopped
1 tbsp tomato purée
600ml no-salt vegetable stock
a few torn basil leaves
50g full-fat cream cheese or
  50ml formula milk

This soup is absolutely delicious and freezes brilliantly. The quantities are easily doubled if you are feeding a family.

1 Heat the butter in a large saucepan. Add the onion, garlic and carrot and cook until soft and golden (about 5 minutes). Add the potato and cook for another 5 minutes.
2 Add the tomatoes, tomato purée, stock and basil. Stir and bring to the boil, then simmer for 8–10 minutes, until the potatoes are soft.
3 Whiz with a hand-held blender (or in a food processor or blender) until smooth, then pass through a nylon sieve.
4 Leave to cool, then pour into a freezerproof container. Freeze.
5 To serve, thaw thoroughly. Stir in the cream cheese or milk and reheat gently.

sweetcorn and potato soup

2

½

½ C

makes: 10 baby portions

storage: up to 2 months in the freezer

1 tbsp olive oil
2 unsmoked streaky bacon
rashers, finely chopped
10g unsalted butter
1 small onion, finely chopped
1 small garlic clove, crushed
1 medium potato, peeled
and cut into small dice
250g tin sweetcorn, drained
1 tbsp parsley, finely chopped
175ml no-salt vegetable
stock (page 332)
125ml formula milk or
calcium-enriched soya drink

If you make this soup in the summer, use a couple of new potatoes instead of a single large potato and just scrub them well instead of peeling. This will increase the fibre content of this dish, which is fine for babies that are used to solids. Also, because most of the nutrients in potatoes are stored just under the skin, they will be retained.

1 Heat the oil in a large pan and fry the bacon until crisp and golden. Reserve on a plate.
2 Add the butter to the pan and use it to fry the onion and garlic until soft and pale golden (approximately 5 minutes). Add the potato and cook for a further 5 minutes, stirring often. Add the sweetcorn, cooked bacon and fresh parsley and stir well.
3 Pour in the stock, bring to the boil, then simmer gently for 15 minutes.
4 Whiz with a hand-held blender (or in a food processor or blender) until smooth, then pass through a nylon sieve.
5 Leave to cool, then pour into a freezerproof container. Freeze.
6 To serve, thaw thoroughly. Add the milk and reheat gently before serving.

creamy mushroom pasta sauce

½

½

makes: 6 baby portions

storage: up to 2 months in the freezer

1 tbsp olive oil
3 spring onions, finely
chopped
300g mushrooms, sliced
1 tbsp fresh parsley, finely
chopped
freshly ground black pepper
100ml no-salt vegetable
stock (page 332)
50g full-fat cream cheese
baby pasta or rice, cooked

Mushrooms are perennially popular with babies and young children. They shouldn't be washed because they soak up water easily – it's best to gently wipe them well with some damp kitchen paper. Try using brown cap mushrooms because they have more flavour than ordinary button mushrooms.

1 Heat the oil in a large frying pan, add the spring onions and cook until soft and translucent (approximately 5 minutes).
2 Add the mushrooms and fry until they are golden and just beginning to lose their liquid. Add the parsley and black pepper and stir well. Pour in the stock and cook over a gentle heat until the mushrooms are soft (about 4 minutes).
3 Stir in the cream cheese, then spoon into a freezerproof container. Freeze.
4 To serve, thaw thoroughly. Whiz with a hand-held blender (or in a food processor or blender) until smooth, then pour over cooked baby pasta or rice.

quick bites finger foods

By this stage it is very likely that your baby will be able to move food from hand to mouth quite easily, enabling you to offer him more 'finger foods'. He will also be able to cope with foods that have more of a texture, rather than just purées, so start experimenting with a few new shapes and sizes.

home-made bread sticks

1½

makes 2 portions
2 thick slices of bread
olive oil

Cut each slice of bread into strips. Put them onto a baking sheet and drizzle with the olive oil. Bake at 180°C/350°F/gas mark 4 for 10–15 minutes, until golden, then turn them over and bake for another 10 minutes. Leave to cool, then store in an airtight container.

rice cakes

2 unsalted rice cakes

There are many types and brands of rice cakes. The most important thing is to go for a variety that has no added salt, and I'd recommend choosing an organic brand to ensure there are no GM ingredients. They are a great snack for vegetarian babies and for babies on a gluten-free diet. They are delicious spread with cream cheese.

rice cakes with mango purée

Vitamin A   3 C   1   ½

½ ripe mango
2 unsalted rice cakes

Remove the stone from the mango and peel. Cut the flesh into small pieces, put them into a bowl and mash with a fork. Spread the mango purée on the rice cakes.

tomato bread

2 C   ½   ½   ½   2½

1 ciabatta loaf (of which you will use ⅛)
1 ripe medium tomato
1 fresh basil leaf
1 tbsp olive oil

Cut the ciabatta into four pieces. Slice one of the quarters in half horizontally, repeat with the other pieces and place on a baking sheet. Mash the tomato in a small bowl and spread on the bread, removing the skin as you push (it should come off easily). Finely chop the basil leaf. Drizzle with the olive oil and scatter over the basil. Put under a hot grill for 2–3 minutes, then leave to cool slightly.

Vitamin B₁

peanut butter soldiers

1 slice of brown bread
1 tbsp smooth peanut butter

Lightly toast the bread and spread with the peanut butter. Cut the toast into fingers. Do not serve nut products to babies if there's a family history of allergies.

toast with boiled egg

tamin B₁₂

1 free-range egg
1 slice of bread, toasted

Put the egg into a pan of water, bring to the boil and simmer for 5 minutes; ensure the egg yolk is firm, with no runny bits. Peel away the shell and cut the egg into small pieces. Serve with the toast cut into soldiers.

fruit bun and apple

...uit bun (only for babies of 9 months or older)
½ eating apple
1 slice of bread

Cut the fruit bun half into fingers. Peel and core the apple, then simmer in 2 tbsp water until soft. Serve the bun and the apple purée together.

tortilla with cream cheese and banana

makes 2 portions
1 ripe small banana
1 soft flour tortilla
1 tbsp full-fat cream cheese

Peel and mash the banana. Spread the flour tortilla with the cream cheese and the mashed banana. Roll the tortilla into a long sausage and then chop into small circles, approximately 2cm in diameter.

easy cheese straws

makes 8 portions
375g puff pastry
6 tbsp grated Cheddar cheese

Cut the sheet of puff pastry lengthways into eight equal strips. Sprinkle over the Cheddar cheese and press onto the pastry slightly. Carefully twist each strip to make a long, thin, twisted straw. Place the strips on a baking sheet and bake for 8–10 minutes at 180°C/350°F/gas mark 4. Leave to cool and store in an airtight container.

eggy bread fingers

Vitamin B₁₂

1 free-range egg
1 tbsp full-fat milk
tiny drop of vanilla extract (optional)
a little butter
2 slices of bread

Lightly beat the egg and place in a bowl. Add the milk and vanilla extract and mix together. Rub a little butter over the base of a frying pan and heat the pan. Dip the slices of bread into the egg mixture, making sure the bread is completely covered with egg, then put them straight into the pan. Fry gently for a couple of minutes on each side until golden. Cut into fingers and leave to cool slightly.

All of these quick bites are only suitable for babies who are confident with chewing.

All quick bites make 1 portion unless otherwise stated.

fresh puddings

mango and banana fool

makes: 4 baby portions or 2 baby portions and 1 adult portion

storage: best eaten fresh or up to 24 hours in the refrigerator

Vitamin B₁₂, A

200ml formula milk or calcium-enriched soya drink
1 vanilla pod, split lengthways
3 free-range egg yolks
1 tsp golden caster sugar
1 tbsp cornflour
1 ripe mango
1 ripe small banana, peeled and cut into chunks
100g natural full-fat yogurt

Calcium-enriched soya drink can be used in place of formula milk. Freeze the left-over egg whites or use them to make meringues for the rest of the family.

1 To make the custard, heat the milk with the vanilla pod in a saucepan until just below boiling point.
2 In a bowl, mix the egg yolks, caster sugar and cornflour together, then pour the hot milk into this mixture, stirring constantly. Return the custard to the saucepan and heat it gently, stirring constantly, until the mixture thickens (approximately 10 minutes). Do not allow to boil, because it will curdle.
3 Once the custard has thickened, leave it to cool.
4 Meanwhile, cut the mango flesh on either side of the stone, then peel the fruit and cut it into chunks.
5 Put the mango into a bowl with the banana chunks and whiz together with a hand-held blender (or in a food processor or blender) until you have a smooth purée.
6 Gently fold together the cooled custard and the yogurt. Swirl through the fruit purée to make a rippled fool.

pear and almond yogurt

makes: 2 baby portions

storage: 24 hours in the refrigerator

150g natural Greek yogurt
1 tbsp ground almonds
1 ripe pear

Note: not all recipes in this section are suitable for all babies in the age group. Please read the introductions carefully before serving.

This is a delicious combination, which goes well with muesli for breakfast. Pears are one of few fruits that ripen naturally after they have been picked, so it's best to buy ones that are firm (not quite ripe) if you are not going to use them straight away. Do not feed nuts to babies if there is any family history of allergies.

1 Put the yogurt into a large bowl, add the almonds and mix together well.
2 Cut the pear into quarters, then peel and core them.
3 Grate each quarter directly into the bowl of yogurt so you catch the juice and mix again.
4 Mash lightly. Alternatively, serve large pieces of peeled and quartered pear with the yogurt.

rice pudding with blueberries

2½

½

½

1 C

Vitamin B₁₂

1+

makes: 8 baby portions or
2 baby portions and 3 adult
portions

storage: best eaten fresh or
24 hours in the refrigerator
(but must not be reheated)

**150g short-grain
pudding rice**

**500ml formula milk or
calcium-enriched soya drink**

100ml water

2–3 drops of vanilla extract

**small knob of unsalted
butter**

200g blueberries

Vanilla gives many desserts a natural sweetness, so you really don't need to add sugar. It's best to let your baby get used to the sweet taste of fruits in desserts without extra sugar, so that he doesn't develop a sweet tooth.

1 Put the first four ingredients into a saucepan and stir.
2 Bring to the boil, then reduce the heat and simmer the rice for 15–20 minutes, stirring often to prevent the mixture from sticking on the bottom. If necessary, add a few more tablespoons of water.
3 Add the butter; mix well and cook for another minute.
4 Put the fruit into a small saucepan with 1–2 tbsp water and heat gently until the berries are just at bursting point. Mash slightly or whiz with a hand-held blender (or in a food processor or blender) until smooth.
5 Swirl the blueberries through the rice pudding before serving.

apple and raspberry custard

2½

½

1

½

1 C

Vitamin B₁₂

1+

makes: 4 baby portions

storage: 24 hours in the
refrigerator

**200ml formula milk or
calcium-enriched soya drink**

1 vanilla pod, split lengthways

**3 medium free-range egg
yolks**

1½ tsp golden caster sugar

1 tbsp cornflour

**1 eating apple, eg Cox's
orange pippin**

**large handful of fresh
raspberries**

2 tbsp water

Home-made custard is a million miles away from the stuff made from instant custard powder. This has a subtle, delicate vanilla flavour that babies love. Don't worry about the possibility of it curdling – just don't rush!

1 To make the custard, gently heat the milk with the vanilla pod in a saucepan until just below boiling point.
2 In a bowl, mix the egg yolks, 1 tsp of the sugar and cornflour together, then pour the hot milk over this mixture, stirring constantly. Return the custard to the saucepan and heat gently, stirring constantly, until the mixture thickens (approximately 10 minutes). Do not allow it to boil, because it will curdle.
3 Once the custard has thickened, remove the vanilla pod and leave to cool.
4 Peel and core the apple, chop into small pieces and put into a saucepan with the raspberries. Add the water and the remaining sugar. Heat gently until the apple is soft and pulpy (approximately 5 minutes).
5 Mash the fruit purée or whiz with a hand-held blender (or in a food processor or blender) until smooth.
6 Serve the custard with a swirl of apple and raspberry purée.

baked apples stuffed with fruits

makes: 3 baby portions

storage: up to 24 hours in the refrigerator

4 small cooking apples,
   eg Bramley
100g dried fruit, eg prunes,
   apricots, mango, raisins
   (only for babies of 9
   months or older)
2 tbsp porridge oats
small knob of unsalted
   butter

As with potatoes, don't waste time just baking one apple – bake lots and scrape the flesh out to purée and freeze. If the apples are very tart, add a little golden caster sugar to taste; the dried fruits should add enough natural sweetness to make this quantity of sugar ample.

1 Preheat the oven to 180°C/350°F/gas mark 4.
2 Core the apples and score the skin around the middle of each apple. This will stop them from bursting in the oven. Finely chop the dried fruits and put into a bowl.
3 Add the oats and butter and mix together well.
4 Fill the cavity of each apple with the stuffing.
5 Put the apples into a lightly greased, ovenproof dish and bake for 45 minutes until the apples are tender. Scoop out the flesh and dried fruits. Serve as is, or finely chop and serve.

summer pudding

makes: 4 baby portions or 2 baby portions and 2 adult portions

storage: up to 24 hours in the refrigerator

500g mixed berries,
   eg strawberries,
   raspberries, blackberries,
   blueberries, fresh or frozen
1 tbsp golden caster sugar
6 tbsp water
6 slices of day-old white
   bread, crusts removed

This is easy-peasy and makes a delicious pudding for all the family. You could just as easily use a bag of frozen summer or forest fruits. This recipe is only suitable for babies who are confident with chewing.

1 Put the berries into a saucepan with the sugar and water. Bring to the boil and then simmer for 5–6 minutes, until the fruits are bursting.
2 Cut the bread in quarters into triangles. Arrange half of the triangles in the bottom of a shallow dish. Using a slotted spoon, spoon over three-quarters of the warm fruit.
3 Arrange the remaining bread triangles over the fruit and pour over the juice and remaining fruit. Press down lightly to ensure all the bread is covered with fruit juice. Leave to stand for at least an hour in a cool place before serving.
4 Serve as is, or mash or finely chop and serve.

quick bites puddings

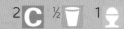

blueberry and pear yogurt

1 ripe small pear
small handful of blueberries
2 tbsp natural full-fat yogurt

Cut the pear into small pieces and cook in 1 tbsp water until pulpy. Put the pieces into a bowl and mash with a small handful of blueberries, then mix with the yogurt. Pears are great to give to your baby if he is constipated.

fruity yogurt

2 large strawberries
2 tbsp natural full-fat yogurt

Hull and crush the strawberries until they are puréed, then mix them with the yogurt and serve.

apple and carrot

2 tbsp grated eating apple
2 tbsp grated carrot

Mix together the grated apple and carrot and cook in 1 tbsp water until pulpy (approximately 4–5 minutes). Lightly mash with a hand-held blender until smooth.

fruit porridge

2 dried apricots or figs and 1 tbsp raisins
(only for babies of 9 months or older)
3 tbsp cooked porridge (page 106)

Make porridge more interesting by adding puréed dried fruit. Cook the dried fruits in 3 tbsp boiling water until soft and then purée. Mix them with the porridge and serve.

cheese and grapes

4 seedless red grapes
1 tbsp full-fat cream cheese
1 oatcake (page 114)

Children love grapes. Finely chop the grapes, mix into the cream cheese and spread onto an oatcake. This is only suitable for babies who are confident with chewing.

baked apples

1 eating apple
a tiny pinch of cinnamon
25g raspberries

Baking apples is an easy way to get a soft apple purée. Core your apple and score around its middle with a sharp knife. Put into a greased ovenproof dish and sprinkle with a tiny pinch of cinnamon. Bake for 20–25 minutes. Leave to cool and scoop out the flesh. Mash the raspberries and mix into the apple. (To save time bake a few apples at once and freeze the purée.)

prune custard

1 tbsp prunes (only for babies of 9 months or older)
4 tbsp custard (page 128)

Cook the prunes in a saucepan with 1 tbsp boiling water and then mash. Mix them with the warm custard.

peach yogurt

6 C ½ 1 3½

Vitamin B₁

1 ripe peach
2 tbsp natural full-fat yogurt

Peel the peach by plunging it into some boiling water for a couple of minutes and then draining it and peeling away the skin. Remove the stone and then mash the flesh well before stirring it into the natural full-fat yogurt. Alternatively, serve unmashed peach pieces alongside the yogurt.

iced pineapple

½ C

makes 2 portions
50g fresh pineapple

Cut the pineapple into large chunks. Freeze it for about 2–3 hours. Serve when it is semi-frozen to babies who are confident with chewing.

mango and banana smoothie

4½ C 1

makes 2 portions
1 ripe mango
1 ripe medium banana, peeled
150ml coconut milk

Cut a mango either side of the stone and peel the flesh. Slice the banana. Put both fruits into a bowl. Add the coconut milk and whiz with a hand-held blender until smooth. Do not serve coconut if there is any family history of allergies.

strawberry lassi

6 C ½ 2

Vitamin B₁₂

makes 2 portions
1 ripe medium banana, peeled
100g strawberries
100ml natural full-fat yogurt

Slice the banana and hull and slice the strawberries. Mix the yogurt, banana, and strawberries together in a bowl. Whiz with a hand-held blender (or in a food processor or blender) until smooth.

baked banana

½ C ½

1 date (only for babies of 9 months
or older)
1 ripe medium banana

Finely chop the date. Leaving the skin on the banana, cut a slit into it lengthways. Stuff the banana with the date. Wrap the whole thing in kitchen foil. Bake in an oven at 190°C/375°F/gas mark 5 for 20 minutes. Leave to cool and then lightly mash. This recipe is only suitable for babies who are confident with chewing.

baked plums

½ C ½ ½ 3½

4 plums
1 tsp soft brown sugar
2 tbsp full-fat cottage cheese

Halve the plums, remove the stones and put the fruit on a greased baking tray. Sprinkle with the sugar and roast for 20 minutes in an oven at 180°C/350°F/gas mark 4. Cool, then cut two halves into small pieces and mash with the cottage cheese. Keep the rest covered in the refrigerator for up to 48 hours.

All quick bites make 1 portion
unless otherwise stated.

puddings to freeze

blackberry and apple crumble

makes: 6 baby portions

storage: up to 3 months in the freezer

3 medium cooking apples, eg Bramley

200g blackberries

3–4 tsp golden caster sugar (or more if the fruit is tart)

4 tbsp water

for the crumble:

100g plain flour

50g unsalted butter

50g porridge oats

2 tsp golden caster sugar

pinch of ground cinnamon

A great time-saver is to make a big batch of crumble topping and then freeze it in bags ready to throw on fruits. Cooking fruit that is in season is cheap and easy. This recipe is not suitable for babies who are not confident with chewing.

1 Peel and core the apples, then cut into bite-size pieces. Put them into a pan with the blackberries, sugar and water. Heat gently until the berries are just starting to give up their juice.

2 For the crumble, put the flour into a bowl and rub in the butter until the mixture resembles breadcrumbs. Stir in the oats, sugar and cinnamon.

3 Put the fruit in a shallow ovenproof dish or into 5 or 6 small ramekins and leave to cool, then cover and freeze. Put the crumble mix in a freezer bag and freeze.

4 To serve, thaw the fruit and crumble mixture thoroughly. You will need 4–5 tbsp crumble mix for each small ramekin. Preheat the oven to 180°C/350°F/gas mark 4. Sprinkle the crumble over the fruit and bake in the oven for 25 minutes, until the crumble is crisp and golden on top. Serve as is, or lightly mash.

banana fruit ice

makes: 10 baby portions

storage: up to 2 months in the freezer

3 ripe medium bananas

1 tsp golden caster sugar

50ml formula milk

100g natural Greek yogurt

pinch of ground cinnamon

Note: not all recipes in this section are suitable for all babies in the age group. Please read the introductions carefully before serving.

The easiest pudding ever! Your baby may find this mixture too cold, so just leave to soften before serving.

1 Put all the ingredients into a bowl and whiz with a hand-held blender (or whiz in a food processor or blender) until smooth.

2 Pour into a plastic tub, cover and freeze for 2 hours.

3 Remove from the freezer and whiz the mixture again until really smooth to remove any ice crystals that may have formed.

4 Return to the freezer for at least 2 hours, until firm. Alternatively, spoon into ice-cube trays, cover with foil or put into a freezer bag, seal and freeze.

5 Serve immediately, or leave to soften for 5–10 minutes before serving.

drop scones

makes: 20 baby portions

storage: up to 2 months in the freezer

225g self-raising flour
1 large free-range egg
300ml formula milk or
    calcium-enriched soya drink
15g unsalted butter, melted

To make these scones more exciting, try adding a pinch of ground cinnamon and a few tablespoons of blueberries or finely chopped banana. These are just as good for breakfast as they are for a pudding. Once you have defrosted the drop scones, they are best warmed briefly in an oven at 150°C/300°F/gas mark 2 before serving. This is only suitable for babies who are confident with chewing.

1 Sift the flour into a bowl. Whisk together the egg and half the milk. Make a well in the centre of the flour and pour in the egg mixture. Using a whisk, gradually beat the mixture until all the flour is incorporated and you have a thick batter. Gradually beat in the remaining milk.

2 Lightly brush a heavy-based frying pan with melted butter and heat. Drop small teaspoons of the mixture into the pan. Cook over a medium heat until the top of each scone bubbles (approximately 2–3 minutes), then flip it over using a palette knife. Cook for a further 2 minutes.

3 Repeat until all the mixture is used up. Eat immediately or freeze, putting greaseproof paper between the layers of scones.

4 To serve, thaw thoroughly.

apricot and hazelnut muesli bars

makes: 12 baby portions

storage: for up to 2 months in the freezer

Vitamin A

150g unsalted butter
50g golden caster sugar
125g golden syrup
250g porridge oats
25g hazelnuts
50g dried apricots
    (only for babies of
    9 months or older)

These are definitely for older babies, especially those who are teething – they will love the chewy nuttiness of these bars. Because they are quite sweet, just give small pieces, ideally with a little fresh fruit on the plate, too. Remember, do not feed nuts to babies if there is a family history of allergies. This recipe is only suitable for babies who are confident with chewing.

1 Preheat the oven to 180°C/350°F/gas mark 4.

2 Put the butter, sugar and syrup in a pan and heat until the butter has melted.

3 Put the oats, hazelnuts and apricots into a food processor and whiz until ground.

4 Pour the oat mixture into the saucepan with the melted butter and mix well.

5 Tip into a greased baking tin (approx 35cm x 25cm), smooth the top and bake until golden (approximately 10–15 minutes). Mark into squares with a knife and cool in the tin. Tip out of the tin, cut and freeze, or store in an airtight container for up to a week.

6 To serve, thaw thoroughly.

choc bread and butter pudding

makes: 5–6 baby portions

storage: up to 2 months in the freezer

300g fruit bread, eg raisin bread, sliced and crusts removed (only for babies of 9 months or older)

25g unsalted butter

3 tsp cocoa

25g golden caster sugar

1 tbsp boiling water

2 large free-range eggs

568ml formula milk or calcium-enriched soya drink

6½

1

1

1½

½ **C**

✓ vitamin B₁₂, A

1+

This is a new version of a classic nursery pudding that children of all ages love. Remember, the chocolatey-ness of the finished dish will depend on the quality of cocoa you use; some cocoas are much stronger than others, so vary the amount accordingly.

1 Spread the fruit bread with the butter and cut into quarters in small triangles.

2 Lay half the triangles on the base of a buttered ovenproof dish.

3 In a mixing bowl, mix together the cocoa, sugar and boiling water. Beat the eggs and milk together and add them to the cocoa mixture, mixing them together thoroughly.

4 Pour half of the milk mixture over the bread in the ovenproof dish. Arrange the remaining triangles over the top and pour the remaining liquid over them.

5 Leave to stand for 30 minutes to allow the bread to absorb the liquid. Wrap in foil and freeze.

6 To serve, thaw thoroughly. Preheat the oven to 170°C/325°F/gas mark 3. Bake in the oven for 35–40 minutes, until the top is crisp and golden. Serve as is, or mash roughly and serve.

banana and cinnamon teabread

2½

½

½

✓ Vitamin B₁₂, A

1+

makes: 8–10 baby portions

storage: up to 2 months in the freezer

150g unsalted butter

100g golden caster sugar

2 medium free-range eggs

2 ripe small bananas, mashed

2 tbsp formula milk or calcium-enriched soya drink

4 tbsp natural Greek yogurt

pinch of ground cinnamon

150g self-raising flour

½ tsp baking powder

This is a great bread because it's not too sweet – the bananas are a natural sweetener. Try to use really ripe, black-spotted fruits because they will give the best flavour. My children love a slice of this spread with a mashed banana and cut into fingers. This is only suitable for babies who are confident with chewing.

1 Preheat the oven to 180°C/350°F/gas mark 4.

2 Cream the butter and sugar together until pale and fluffy. Beat in the eggs. Add the mashed bananas, milk, yogurt and cinnamon and mix well.

3 Sift the flour and baking powder over the mixture and fold in.

4 Pour the mixture into a lightly greased 500g loaf tin and bake for 55–65 minutes, until a skewer inserted in the centre comes out clean. Slice and freeze with greaseproof paper between the slices. Alternatively, store in an airtight container for a few days.

5 To serve, thaw thoroughly and cut into fingers.

As your baby approaches toddlerhood, mealtimes will become more exciting and involving for her. She should have an established routine, with healthy snacks and finger foods in between meals to maintain the energy levels needed for this period of rapid growth and development. As her co-ordination increases, she will continue to enjoy feeding herself – albeit messily – that will enable her to participate more fully in family meals. This will give her a sense of her place in the world, a feeling of security and confidence in her abilities.

10–12 months

what's happening
to your baby

This is the stage at which your baby really begins to appreciate the routine of mealtimes, making her feel more secure and like part of the family – especially if you eat as many meals together as possible. Her coordination and appreciation of colour and texture will also be developing. She will be able to point at objects, pick things up with her finger and thumb, and maybe even put things into and out of her bowl.

At mealtimes your baby will enjoy using a spoon to feed herself, and will particularly enjoy feeding herself finger foods. She will be able to hold a feeder cup to drink from. She will also learn to let go of things deliberately. Things may start to get messy, but this is when your baby really begins to learn about, and appreciate, good food. Get into the habit of feeding her foods that you enjoy – my daughter Jasmin's love of spicy food began at about 10 months, when I gave her a little of my favourite Thai green curry.

Your child will now have a sense of humour; even saying 'boo' will make her laugh. She will enjoy playing, especially at bathtime, and hearing you sing nursery rhymes will be a great source of entertainment to her. She may be able to say 'mama' and 'dada', and can indicate what she wants by gesturing instead of crying, both of which will make play more exciting.

Your baby is likely to begin to explore the world on foot by around 11 months, and it is important not to rush this. Often she will move by holding on to pieces of furniture and negotiating small distances between them with a little help from you. She may even be able to stand alone for a few seconds and will gradually learn to walk unaided.

However, it is also at this stage that babies begin to assert their independence by saying 'no'! Your baby will also begin to understand the word 'no' when you say it, but won't necessarily obey it. Try not to get too frustrated. At mealtimes, having smaller amounts of food on the plate often helps; otherwise, just take the food away and don't be tempted to offer sweet alternatives. Try creating interest at mealtimes by involving your baby in the preparation – even if it is only watching you chop carrots. For snacks, give food that can easily be held by small fingers – steamed carrot sticks are great.

At this stage it is important to encourage your baby to eat new things to ensure she is getting a wide range of nutrients. Adequate energy will be crucial for her as she starts to crawl and move about. Fat will be an essential energy-dense nutrient in the diet. Remember, it's the quality of the fat that matters – try using more unsaturated fats.

As your baby is crawling, she'll need more energy-rich food, particularly at the start of the day. Foods such as cereals and fresh fruits that are rich in slow-releasing carbohydrates are best for breakfast because they give your baby a steady flow of energy until her next feed. Many mums see all types of sugar as an easy way to give their baby energy; sugar is a carbohydrate, but it gives only short bursts of energy and has little nutritional value, so ideally it should be avoided. Sugar is also a major cause of tooth decay, to which first teeth are susceptible. Too much sugar can lead to health problems such as obesity later in life. It is not necessary to add sugar to your baby's food, even when foods are tart; just use other ripe fruits or apple juice to sweeten them.

Protein is essential for the healthy growth of every single one of the body's cells, and it is constantly being used and replaced. Because your baby is growing so rapidly, she will need more protein in relation to her weight than an adult. Good sources of protein for babies at this stage include meat, poultry, fish, full-fat dairy products, eggs, beans, pulses, soya products such as tofu, and calcium-enriched soya drinks and yogurt alternatives. Protein from animal sources is generally a complete protein; vegetarian and vegan babies need a combination of cereals, pulses and vegetables to get complete protein, as no non-animal source but tofu is a complete protein.

To help keep your baby's bowel movements regular, begin to introduce a little fibre in her diet. Her digestive system is still immature and she will not be able to cope with the bulky fibre found in brown rice, wholewheat and bran. Instead, include foods such as peas, fruits and vegetable juices, which are easier for her system to tolerate. Also ensure she drinks enough liquid, as too little fluid is one of the main causes of constipation in babies.

which nutrients are key

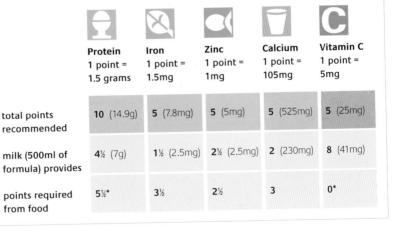

nutrients required per day

At this stage, different formula milks provide different proportions of each nutrient required. For this book, we've assumed the lowest level provided by the common brands on which the milk chart on page 21 is based. The quantity of formula given is based on the recommended quantity (page 139). Assume breastfed babies receive the equivalent nutrient intake from milk. Solids play a greater role in the provision of nutrients now.
* If your baby enjoys a healthy balanced diet, she'll probably get more protein and vitamin C than she needs. Do not worry.

	Protein 1 point = 1.5 grams	Iron 1 point = 1.5mg	Zinc 1 point = 1mg	Calcium 1 point = 105mg	Vitamin C 1 point = 5mg
total points recommended	10 (14.9g)	5 (7.8mg)	5 (5mg)	5 (525mg)	5 (25mg)
milk (500ml of formula) provides	4½ (7g)	1½ (2.5mg)	2½ (2.5mg)	2 (230mg)	8 (41mg)
points required from food	5½*	3½	2½	3	0*

third-stage
weaning

Your baby should still be having 500–600ml of breast milk or formula milk a day, but her solid food will be just as important as a source of nutrition. Breakfast should be her biggest meal, giving her lots of energy. This should be an easy habit to get into because she will be at her hungriest after a good night's sleep. Make use of baby-friendly, sugar-free cereals and whiz them in a food processor to make their texture easier for your baby to cope with. Finely ground nuts (as long as there is no history of allergy in your family), are a valuable source of protein, especially for vegetarians.

Between meals, your baby should be given cooled, boiled water to drink from a cup and healthy snacks to maintain her energy levels. Finger foods have a harder texture now, especially as your baby begins to teethe. Give bread and even toast or home-made rusks once your baby is confident with chewing. Steamed vegetable sticks – and even raw sticks of softer vegetables such as cucumber – can be given, but always stay nearby in case your baby chokes. At this stage your baby will be able to cope with dried fruit, although it can cause upset stomachs so I still wouldn't get too carried away. If you want to reduce the amount of artifical preservatives in your baby's diet, try and buy organic dried fruit or, at the very least, fruit that has not been treated with preservatives. Sulphur dioxide, the most commonly used preservative, has been shown to contribute to the causes of asthma in young children.

It is important to reduce your baby's milk intake to allow more room in her small tummy for solid food. Often parents are tempted to give milk when a baby of this age cries; try to give her solid foods instead – they will keep her satisfied for longer. One of the best ways to reduce milk intake is to dilute the mid-morning feed with cooled, boiled water; do this gradually as you reduce her overall milk consumption. Giving milk and other drinks in cups rather than bottles will help, and is recommended for the development of a baby's healthy teeth.

As your baby's appreciation of colour and texture develops, give her foods that will stimulate her senses and not just her appetite. Brightly coloured finger foods, such as steamed carrot sticks, were always a hit with my children. Try adding peas or little pieces of carrot to mash, or serving chopped fruit with a different coloured fruit purée. But remember, babies develop at different paces, and some can chew earlier than others, so use your own judgement and never leave your baby alone with food at any time.

Food can now be minced or finely chopped. You can give your baby almost all the foods you eat yourself; just remember not to season them with salt during cooking and either finely chop them or give her big pieces that she can hold. It is a good idea to introduce new foods in small quantities and with something familiar so that your baby does not feel overwhelmed. The main aim of this stage of weaning is to be able to include your baby at all the family meals and not have to cook separate meals for her, although obviously you will have to chop or mash as necessary. Many of the recipes in this book are suitable for the whole family.

Most importantly, you can begin to introduce foods that have more intense flavours. Herbs, such as parsley, oregano, basil and coriander, give standard dishes a much more interesting flavour. Onions and garlic can be used, as well as mild spices such as cinnamon and ginger, and the ever-popular vanilla pod. These natural ingredients will encourage your child to enjoy a variety of tastes and show her that delicious flavours can be natural rather than artificial.

Bottles for drinks other than milk should be phased out at this stage, primarily to ensure healthy teeth. Drinks from cups will be drunk quicker than those from a bottle, minimizing the time they are in contact with a baby's vulnerable first teeth. This is especially important if you are giving diluted fruit juices, which should never be given in a bottle. It is also good to begin to teach your baby how to hold a cup and drink with other children and adults; it will make her feel part of the family. Always make sure you wash the spout of a drinking cup regularly (*see* pages 38–39).

common myths

myth: snacks are bad
Babies and children have small stomachs and expend a lot of energy. Snacking is an easy way for them to top up their energy levels without spoiling their appetite for bigger meals. Many of the huge range of snacks available for babies and children are sugary and highly processed with additives to make them palatable. This is the perfect time, while your baby is not influenced by peer pressure, to encourage her to nibble on healthy snacks, such as steamed or lightly cooked vegetable sticks, fingers of bread and fresh fruits.

myth: fat is bad
Babies need fat. They need the calories that it provides for energy, and also to absorb fat-soluble vitamins. Make sure that you feed your baby full-fat dairy products, such as yogurt, fromage frais and cheese. Unsaturated fats are also very good at this stage.

myth: it's healthy to give fresh fruit juice between meals
Freshly squeezed fruit juices contain more nutrients than fruit-flavoured squashes or fizzy drinks, but first teeth are particularly susceptible to damage from the sugar all these drinks contain. A small amount of freshly squeezed juice, preferably non-citrus, is fine, but always dilute it and give it at mealtimes in a cup rather than a bottle to minimize the time the drink is in contact with teeth. Cooled, boiled water is best for quenching thirst.

foods to eat and
foods to avoid

new foods to eat at 10–12 months

It's important to remember that babies develop at different paces, and they should never be left alone with food at any time.

- As the amount of solid food in your baby's diet increases, she will need some fibre to help keep her bowel movements regular. Soluble fibre, found in foods such as peas, fruit and vegetable juices, is sufficient because her immature digestive system will not be able to cope with the bulky fibre found in brown rice and whole wheat.
- At least one baby portion of animal protein or its vegetable equivalent should be given each day. A wider range of fish can be introduced, especially oily fish such as mackerel and tuna (but not in brine).
- Whole well-cooked eggs.
- Small amounts of full-fat cow's milk, but only as part of a larger dish, such as custard.

foods to avoid at 10–12 months

- Cow's milk or soya milk as a drink.
- If there is any history of allergy in your family, avoid nuts, nut products or foods containing nuts until your child is at least 3 years old and seek professional advice from your doctor or state-registered dietitian. Whole peanuts should never be given to children under the age of 5 as there is a risk of choking.
- Shellfish can trigger allergic reactions in young babies, especially if there's a history of it in their family.
- Unpasteurized cheese may contain the bacteria listeria that can cause food poisoning. Babies are more sensitive to this bacteria.
- Too much salt can't be processed by a baby's immature digestive system; it causes dehydration. A diet high in salt often leads to high blood pressure later. Particular foods to avoid at this stage are yeast extracts, such as Marmite or Vegemite, stock cubes and smoked fish.
- Refined or unrefined sugar provides calories but has little nutritional value. Always give sweet things, such as fruit, at mealtimes so the acid that damages teeth is diluted; cheese is particularly good at doing this. Check food labels carefully since sugar may be present as sucrose, glucose, fructose, lactose, hydrolyzed starch, invert sugar, and products such as treacle, honey and syrup.
- Never use artificial sweeteners.
- Avoid honey until your baby is 1; it may contain botulism spores that can cause food poisoning.
- Excessively hot or spicy foods can burn or inflame babies' stomachs.
- Tea and coffee contain tannins that inhibit iron absorption. Caffeine is a stimulant, which babies cannot tolerate. Most fizzy drinks also contain caffeine.

A 10-month-old baby will begin to appreciate the routine of mealtimes, making her feel more secure and part of the family – especially if you eat as many meals together as possible.

Three key changes to a baby's diet take place at 10 months. The first is her milk intake; it is important to reduce this in order to allow more room in her small tummy for solid food. Often parents are tempted to give milk when a baby of this age cries; try to give solids instead – they will keep her satisfied for longer as she becomes more active. But be sure to give your baby plenty of liquids aside from milk, such as water and well-diluted juice, to avoid constipation.

The second key change is the balance of nutrition. Immune-boosting foods continue to be important, but the real focus is on strength. Your baby needs more starch, protein, sugar and fats to enable her to build up the strength to crawl and walk.

The third key change is volume. Your baby is likely to start really enjoying food now. Her coordination and appreciation of colour and texture will be developing, so try to encourage her to eat well by giving her lots of variety. However, it is also at this stage that babies begin to assert their independence by saying 'no'. Try not to get too frustrated over this; having smaller amounts of food on the plate often helps prevent it; otherwise, just take the food away and don't be tempted to offer your baby sweet alternatives.

recommended
daily intake

recommended daily volume of foods

milk = breastfeed or 150ml formula

	10 months old	11 months old	12 months old
breakfast	breastfeed or milk from a cup, alternating during feed with 1 portion breakfast and 1 portion fruit, water	breastfeed or milk from a cup, alternating during feed with 1–2 portions breakfast	breastfeed or milk from a cup, alternating during feed with 1–2 portions breakfast
lunch	1 portion lunch, also sometimes 1 portion pudding or snack, water or well-diluted fruit juice from a cup	1 portion lunch, also sometimes 1 portion pudding or snack, water or well-diluted fruit juice from a cup	1 portion lunch, also sometimes 1 portion pudding or snack, water or well-diluted fruit juice from a cup
mid-pm	milk or drink, alternating during feed with 1 portion snack or finger food	milk or drink, 1 portion snack or finger food	milk or drink, 1 portion snack or finger food
supper	1 portion supper, also sometimes 1 portion pudding, drink, milk	1 portion supper, also sometimes 1 portion pudding, drink, milk	1 portion supper, 1 portion pudding, drink
10pm	small milk feed if needed	small milk feed if needed	small milk feed if needed
TOTAL MILK	breast milk or 500–600ml formula each day, inclusive of milk used in sauces, cereals, etc	breast milk or 500–600ml formula each day, inclusive of milk used in sauces, cereals, etc	breast milk or 400–500ml formula each day, inclusive of milk used in sauces, cereals, etc

your
routine

your baby's feeds

Solid food is becoming nutritionally more important each day, week and month of your baby's life. By 10 months, your baby should be quite comfortable with eating a wide range of solid foods, and she should be enjoying three meals and two healthy snacks, such as fruit, in-between meals. Ideally she should be eating with the rest of the family, by the time she is 1 year old.

You may begin to notice that your baby does not want to drink all of her bedtime milk feed. If this does start to happen, you will need to stop the mid-afternoon milk feed if you have not already done so. If she is already having water in the afternoon, then make sure that she is not eating too many solid foods or snacks at this time instead. This is important because she still needs to be drinking her evening milk feed to make sure that she sleeps through the night.

your baby's sleeps

If your baby is still having a quick nap (anything up to 45 minutes) in the morning after breakfast, you may start to notice that she is waking up earlier after her lunchtime sleep. Rather than having two short naps, try to stop the early morning sleep and keep to one long sleep, approximately 1½–2¼ hours, after lunch. Ideally, try to make sure she is up and awake from 2.30pm to be confident that she will go to sleep successfully from bedtime at around 7pm. Aim to get her into a routine of just one sleep by the time she is 1 year old.

coping with fussy eaters

As your baby learns to assert her independence she may begin to say 'no' to certain foods, often pushing them away. While this will be frustrating for you, try not to show disappointment. Try again briefly and, if her mouth remains closed, just remove the food and don't offer an alternative, especially not anything sweet, because this will only create problems.

throwing food on the floor

As your baby becomes more coordinated she may be able to feed herself with a spoon. She may throw food onto the floor, which is often a sign that she has had enough or is bored with the food. Try adding interest by introducing new textures and flavours. If throwing persists, just take the food away and never offer alternatives – children eat sweet foods even if they are full.

spills from self-feeding

As your baby learns to feed herself, there may be a lot of spills. Try giving her a spoon to hold with a little food on it, or a stick of finger food, while you feed her with a separate spoon – she will get enough to eat but feel she has some control over proceedings. The more you let her try to feed herself, the quicker she will become more coordinated.

worries about food at the childminders

If you are sending your baby to a childminder or nursery and you are concerned about the food that she is being fed, just send your baby with food for the day. Every childminder and nursery is different and each will feed babies and toddlers what they feel is the right sort of food. However, nearly all of them will be more than willing to feed your baby with food you have provided, should you wish to do so. This way you can be certain that she will be getting exactly the right sort of diet and one that you can keep an eye on.

refusal to eat at mealtimes

If your baby is not willing to eat at mealtimes or messes with her food and does not concentrate on eating, there may be a simple answer. Some babies just prefer to have company when eating and enjoy watching and mimicking others. Even if it is the wrong time of day for you to eat a meal, it may be worth eating a little so that she does not feel she is eating alone.

trouble shooting

sample meal planners

key to meal planners

each milk feed:
Breastfeed or 200ml formula

portions:
After 5 months, all servings of food referred to in the meal planners is 1 portion

water:
Always give cooled, boiled water or very diluted fruit juice. After 9 months, all drinks should be served in a beaker.

mealtimes

breakfast 7–8am

lunch 11.45am-ish

mid-afternoon 3pm

supper 6.30pm-ish, for bed at 7pm-ish

At 10–12 months, solids are as important a source of nutrition as milk. On page 141 you'll find a chart showing how much of each of the key nutrients your child generally needs to obtain from solid food. For some of these nutrients, in particular protein, you'll inevitably significantly exceed these recommended intakes if you cook your baby fresh food – do not worry, as this will not harm your child. Equally, do not worry if your baby doesn't get enough points every single day, as all babies have cranky days. The important thing is to ensure that, on average your baby is getting the recommended intake. If your baby is getting a good variety and mix of foods, all other essential nutrients which we haven't allocated points to should be more than covered.

The key things you need to achieve during these months are feeding your baby three meals a day with healthy snacks between meals – you'll find lots of quick ideas on pages 180–183. And, of course, you still need to provide plenty of cooled, boiled water between meals. You can now aim to include your baby in all the family mealtimes, as she can enjoy most of the foods that the whole family eats – just remember to remove her portion before adding salt. You should also be encouraging finger foods at this stage to help teach your baby to chew.

10 months old, any week

	breakfast	lunch	mid-afternoon	supper	10pm
day 1	plum and ginger yogurt, water, then milk	cheese and ham on toast, water	milk, alternated with cucumber sticks, water	lamb chops with pea mash, water, milk	small milk if needed
day 2	really quick muesli, water, then milk	stuffed baked potatoes, water	milk, alternated with apricots and cream cheese, water	fish baked in orange juice, water, milk	small milk if needed
day 3	French toast with cinnamon, water, then milk	leek and ham mash, water	milk, alternated with apple and raisin toast, water	leek/chive macaroni, nutty yogurt, water, milk	small milk if needed
day 4	fresh and dried fruit compote, water, then milk	peanut noodles, rice pud with dried fruits, water	milk, alternated with dried fruit/vanilla yogurt, water	sweet potato gratin, mango/ raspberry soup, water, milk	small milk if needed
day 5	fruity couscous, water, then milk	tuna and tomato mash, water	milk, alternated with steamed veg sticks, water	chicken goujons, berry sponge, water, milk	small milk if needed
day 6	tropical yogurt, water, then milk	broccoli, chicken, rice, muesli bar yogurt, water	milk, alternated with rice cakes, water	tortelloni, strawberries and passionfruit, water, milk	small milk if needed
day 7	chunky spiced apple sauce, water, then milk	lamb burgers, water	milk, alternated with pieces of banana, water	Moroccan beef, water, milk	small milk if needed

11 months old, any week

	breakfast	lunch	mid-afternoon	supper	10pm
day 1	blueberry and cinnamon porridge, water, then milk	chickpea and bacon stew, water	milk, alternated with apple flapjack, water	sardines on toast, baked almond peach, water, milk	small milk if needed
day 2	fig and honey yogurt, toast, water, then milk	curried parsnip soup, muesli bar with yogurt, water	milk, alternated with pieces of apple, water	ham and pea pasta, apple flapjack, water, milk	small milk if needed
day 3	scrambled eggs, toasted bun, water, then milk	pesto and pea mash, water	milk, alternated steamed veg/cottage cheese, water	beans, tuna and cheese, muesli bar, water, milk	small milk if needed
day 4	papaya and coconut lassi, easy muesli, water, milk	Spanish tortilla, fruit smush, water	milk, alternated with pitta bread fingers, water	cottage pie, water, milk	small milk if needed
day 5	chunky plum yogurt, toast, water, then milk	tuna pasta, water	milk, alternated with malt loaf with mashed bananas, water	savoury crumble, vanilla pears, water, milk	small milk if needed
day 6	toast with bacon and tomatoes, water, then milk	beetroot and spinach with rice, apple flapjack, water	milk alternated with popcorn, water	baked bean gratin, fruit with cream cheese, water, milk	small milk if needed
day 7	banana porridge, water, then milk	pasta with cheese and bacon, water	milk, alternated with pieces of pear, water	home-made fish fingers, rice pudding, water, milk	small milk if needed

12 months old, any week

	breakfast	lunch	mid-afternoon	supper	10pm
day 1	carrot/pineapple smoothie, vanilla porridge, water, milk	fish and courgette gratin, nutty yogurt, water	milk, alternated with raisins	eastern rice with veg, baked bananas, water, milk	small milk if needed
day 2	fruit muffin, water, then milk	sweetcorn/ham mash. rice pud with dried fruits, water	milk, alternated with popcorn	pasta, spinach/cheese, apple/ Cheddar crackers, water, milk	small milk if needed
day 3	coconut muesli with banana, water, then milk	pasta with pesto and peas, water	milk, alternated with raw vegetable sticks	baked beans with sausage, water, milk	small milk if needed
day 4	potato scramble, water, then milk	tomato risotto, water	milk, alternated with dried apricots	green bean with tuna gratin, tropical fruits with raspberry sauce, water, milk	small milk if needed
day 5	creamy banana toast, water, then milk	bacon and mushrooms in cheese, water	milk, alternated with cherry tomato pieces	chicken/sesame balls, banana/ apple crumble, water, milk	small milk if needed
day 6	nut bread, water, then milk	chickpeas and bacon stew, water	milk, alternated with cream cheese soldiers	lamb chops with pea mash, fruit trifle, water, milk	small milk if needed
day 7	scrambled eggs with bacon, water, then milk	cheese and corn muffins, water	milk, alternated with satsuma segments	sausage, apple, parsnip pie, autumn rice pud, water, milk	small milk if needed

fresh breakfasts

coconut muesli with banana

makes: 20 baby portions or a mixture of baby and adult portions

storage: keep in an airtight container for up to 4 weeks

75g hazelnuts or almonds
50g sunflower seeds
50g desiccated coconut
4 tbsp wheatgerm
300g rolled or porridge oats
pinch of ground cinnamon
100g dried fruit, eg dried
   cranberries, raisins or
   apricots, finely chopped
breast milk, formula milk or
   full-fat cow's milk, to serve
½ medium banana or mango,
   finely chopped or mashed,
   to serve (optional)

Vitamin B₁

As your baby grows, she will start to enjoy slightly more challenging textures. Muesli is a great way to incorporate a wide variety of nuts, seeds and oats into her diet: all fantastic sources of protein and energy-providers. Make a large batch of this muesli and keep it in an airtight tin; just make sure you buy the ingredients from a shop with a good turnover so they are as fresh as possible. Do not give nuts or seeds to babies if there is any family history of allergies.

1   Dry-fry the nuts and seeds in a frying pan, stirring constantly until golden brown (approximately 5 minutes). Leave to cool.
2   Transfer to a food processor or blender, add the coconut and wheatgerm, and whiz to a powder. Tip into a bowl, add the oats and cinnamon and mix everything together.
3   Finely chop the dried fruit, then put a pan on the hob with 4–5 tbsp water and cook for approximately 5 minutes. Beat the fruit to a purée.
4   Spoon 5–6 tbsp of the muesli into a bowl, pour over some milk and top with the dried fruit purée and mashed banana, if using.
5   Leave to sit for 5 minutes to soften slightly before serving.

plum and ginger yogurt

makes: 3 baby portions or 1 baby portion and 1 adult portion

storage: up to 48 hours in the refrigerator

1cm fresh root ginger
5 ripe red plums, stoned
2 tbsp natural full-fat yogurt

Vitamin B₁

Note: do not feed chopped food to your baby until she is confident with chewing.

Fresh ginger has a hot flavour and is known for its stimulating and warming properties. It is particularly helpful for fighting off colds and chills. If you can't find any, just use a little pinch of dried ginger instead.

1   Peel the ginger, then put into a saucepan with the plums and 2–3 tbsp water. Cook gently for 5–10 minutes, or until the plums are soft.
2   Remove the ginger. Leave the plums to cool then serve, or mash if necessary. Mix 2 tbsp with the same amount of yogurt.

toast with bacon and tomatoes

6

1

1½

2 C

Vitamin B₁

1⁺

makes: 1 baby portion

storage: best eaten fresh

1 rasher unsmoked back
   bacon, preferably organic,
   rind removed
1 ripe tomato, halved
1 slice of brown bread

When you are cooking for babies, it is important to use good-quality meat. They eat such small amounts that it is especially worthwhile. Good bacon should cook without a white scum forming on the surface – this scum is made up of added salt, water and preservatives.

1 Preheat the grill on high.
2 Grill the bacon and tomato until the bacon is cooked through but not too crispy, and the tomato is soft.
3 Toast the bread. Place the tomato halves cut-side down on the toast, peel away their skin, and mash the flesh onto the toast. Cut the toast into soldiers.
4 Cut the bacon into small pieces and scatter over the top.

really quick muesli

5

1

1½

2

Vitamin B₁

1⁺

makes: 15 baby portions or a mixture of baby and adult portions

storage: keep in an airtight container for up to 4 weeks

2 tbsp sesame seeds, ground
2 tbsp poppy seeds, ground
50g ground almonds
200g rolled or porridge oats
pinch of ground nutmeg
100g dried fruits, eg mango
   or pear, finely chopped
natural full-fat yogurt, to
   serve (optional)

This is so easy – and a delicious alternative to all those high-in-sugar, packaged cereals for all the family. Home-made muesli can be stored for up to four weeks in a jar or airtight tin. Remember, do not give nuts or seeds to babies if there is any family history of allergies.

1 Dry-fry the ground sesame seeds, poppy seeds and almonds for a couple of minutes. Transfer to a bowl and leave to cool.
2 Add the oats and nutmeg.
3 Cook the dried fruits in 5 tbsp water for approximately 5 minutes, then purée.
4 Sprinkle 4–5 tbsp muesli over 4 tbsp yogurt, top with the purée, and serve.

french toast with cinnamon

makes: 2 baby portions or 1 baby portion and 1 small adult portion

storage: best eaten fresh

1 large free-range egg, lightly beaten

1 tbsp full-fat milk

drop of vanilla extract

knob of unsalted butter, for greasing

3–4 slices fruit bread

pinch of ground cinnamon

Vitamin B₁₂

You can make this as a savoury breakfast instead of a sweet one simply by omitting the cinnamon and vanilla and using ordinary bread – or a loaf with herbs, onion or cheese.

1 Put the egg, milk and vanilla in a bowl and whisk together.

2 Heat a frying pan over a medium heat and then grease it with a little unsalted butter.

3 Dip 2 slices of bread into the egg mixture and put into the hot frying pan. Cook the bread for 2 minutes on each side, until golden. Repeat with the remaining bread.

4 Cut into fingers and sprinkle with cinnamon.

scrambled egg with a toasted bun

makes: 1 baby portion

storage: best eaten fresh

small knob of unsalted butter

2 large free-range eggs

2–3 tbsp full-fat milk or calcium-enriched soya drink

freshly ground black pepper (optional)

1 tbsp fresh herbs (optional), chopped

1 fresh wholemeal bun

unsalted butter, for spreading

Vitamin B₁₂, A

Scrambled eggs are one of the quickest and most versatile meals for all the family – this could just as easily be served for lunch or supper. For breakfast, keeping it simple is often best, but you can add lots of things to scrambled eggs: peas, chopped herbs (especially chives), mushrooms – the list is endless.

1 Melt the butter in a non-stick pan. Whisk the eggs and milk together and season with a little black pepper and fresh herbs, if using.

2 Pour the eggs into the pan and cook over a gentle heat, stirring constantly until they are scrambled and well cooked, with no runny bits.

3 Slice the bun in half and toast until just pale golden. Spread with a little butter.

4 Cut one half of the bun into fingers. Top with half the scrambled egg. Serve the remaining bun and scrambled egg on a plate for you.

quick bites **breakfasts**

tropical yogurt

½ small mango, peeled and roughly chopped
70g natural full-fat yogurt
1 tbsp unsweetened shredded coconut

Mash the mango with a fork and mix into the yogurt with the coconut. For older children, split open a fresh coconut and just peel and grate the flesh. Do not serve coconut to babies if there is any family history of allergies.

fig yogurt

1 fresh fig
50g natural full-fat yogurt

Cut the fig in half and scrape out the flesh, then mash with the yogurt. This is also good spread on toast.

chunky plum yogurt

1 slice of raisin bread
70ml natural full-fat yogurt
1 plum, stoned and finely chopped

Lightly toast the bread and cut it into small pieces. Stir it into the yogurt with the chopped plum. If the mixture is a little thick, thin it with some breast milk, formula milk or full-fat milk. Leave to soak for at least 10 minutes. (The longer you leave this, the softer the toast will become.)

hazelnut milk and banana smoothie

50g skinned hazelnuts
250ml cold water
½ ripe banana, peeled and chopped

Whiz the nuts and water with a hand-held blender for 2–3 minutes, until you get a thick milk. Add the fruit and whiz again. For smaller babies, pass through a nylon sieve. Do not serve nuts to babies if there is any family history of allergies.

creamy banana toast

50g full-fat cream cheese
½ banana
1 piece of wholemeal toast

Mash the cream cheese with the banana and spread on the toast. Try cream cheese and peanut butter, too, so long as there is no family history of allergies.

Weetabix with strawberries and yogurt

1 Weetabix
70–90ml full-fat milk
1 tbsp natural Greek yogurt
50g strawberries, mashed

Weetabix are great because they go mushy naturally in milk. Adding fresh fruit will considerably increase the vitamin content of your baby's breakfast. Crumble the Weetabix into a bowl. Add the milk, yogurt and strawberries and mix everything together.

blueberry and cinnamon porridge

2 C ½ ½ ½ 2

1 portion prepared porridge (page 204)
30g blueberries, mashed
pinch of ground cinnamon

When you are making porridge for the rest of the family, just weigh out some for your baby. Mix it with the blueberries and cinnamon.

banana porridge

1 C ½ ½ 2

1 portion prepared porridge (page 204)
½ ripe medium banana, finely chopped, or roughly mashed

Porridge is really versatile – you can add almost any fruit to it. Sometimes adding banana can make it quite thick, so you may need to thin it with a little full-fat milk.

fruity couscous

1 C ½ 1

100ml fresh orange juice
30g couscous
50g raspberries, mashed

Heat the orange juice in a pan to just below boiling point and then pour it over the couscous. Leave to soak for 5 minutes, fluff with a fork then add the mashed raspberries.

papaya and coconut milk lassi

✓ 2½ C 1 ½ 2

Vitamin B$_{12}$

½ ripe papaya, peeled and chopped
50ml coconut milk
50ml natural full-fat yogurt
50ml full-fat milk

Put all the ingredients together in a bowl and whiz with a hand-held blender (or in a food processor or blender) until smooth. Lassis are great because they are less acidic than smoothies. You can use pretty much any soft fruit to make this drink. Do not serve coconut to babies if there is any family history of allergies.

carrot and pineapple smoothie

✓ 2½ C 1½ ½

Vitamin A

100g fresh pineapple, peeled
100ml carrot juice, fresh if possible
½ banana, chopped
1 tsp fresh ginger, peeled and grated

Cut the pineapple into chunks. Put all the ingredients into a bowl and whiz with a hand-held blender (or in a food processor or blender) until smooth. Add the fresh ginger for a zingy smoothie that will help to keep colds at bay.

potato scramble

1½ C ½ 2 1 6

75g potato, peeled, boiled
tiny knob of unsalted butter
1 large free-range egg, beaten
chopped fresh parsley (optional)

Chop the potatoes into small pieces. Melt the butter in a heavy-based frying pan and fry the potato until it is just golden. Add the egg and cook, stirring often with a wooden spoon until the egg is well cooked, with no runny bits. Add a little chopped fresh parsley if you have some to hand.

scrambled eggs with bacon

✓ 1 1½ 6½

Vitamin B$_1$, B$_{12}$, A

1 rasher unsmoked back bacon, grilled
3–4 tbsp scrambled egg, made with a little full-fat milk and unsalted butter (page 153)

Cut any rind off the bacon, then finely chop it and stir into the scrambled eggs. You could also add chopped herbs, cooked mushrooms, grated cheese or grilled tomato. Ensure the eggs are well cooked, with no runny bits. Serve with fingers of toast.

All quick bites make 1 portion unless otherwise stated.

breakfasts to freeze

bacon and apple bread

makes: 10 baby portions (1kg loaf)

storage: up to 3 months in the freezer

Vitamin B₁₂

2 rashers unsmoked back bacon, rind removed
200g self-raising flour
½ tsp baking powder
1 eating apple, peeled and grated
2 tbsp fresh parsley, chopped
4 tbsp olive oil
1 medium free-range egg
85ml full-fat milk
50g medium Cheddar cheese, grated

This is a lovely, moist scone bread that freezes fantastically. It is great on its own or spread with cream cheese or mashed banana. Choose unsmoked bacon, which will have a less overpowering flavour – I have added only a small amount of bacon because it is quite high in salt.

1 Preheat the oven to 180°C/350°F/gas mark 4. Grease and lightly flour a 1kg loaf tin.
2 Grill the bacon until crisp, then cut into very small pieces.
3 Sieve the flour and baking powder into a bowl. Stir in the apple, parsley and bacon, then make a well in the middle.
4 Mix together the oil, egg, milk and cheese and pour into the well. Mix everything together but do not beat.
5 Spoon the mixture into the prepared tin and bake for 25 minutes until risen and golden.
6 Cool slightly and serve – or cool, slice, wrap each slice individually in foil and freeze. To serve, thaw thoroughly.

banana scones

makes: 20 baby portions

storage: up to 3 months in the freezer

450g self-raising flour
pinch of ground cinnamon
60g unsalted butter
1 very ripe medium banana, roughly mashed
284ml buttermilk
4–6 tbsp full-fat milk

Note: babies develop at different rates; do not feed chopped food to your baby until she is confident with chewing.

Once you have made a batch of these, they are a great stand-by for mornings when time is really short. Scones are particularly good for teething babies – and a healthier alternative to shop-bought rusks. Try serving them with some chunks of banana or spread with a little mashed banana.

1 Preheat the oven to 180°C/350°F/gas mark 4.
2 Sieve the flour and cinnamon into a large bowl, then rub in the butter until the mixture resembles breadcrumbs. Stir in the banana and buttermilk.
3 Add enough milk to make a soft sticky dough. Drop little spoonfuls onto a greased baking sheet. Bake for 14–16 minutes, until golden and cooked.
4 Leave to cool on a wire rack.
5 Freeze in a freezerproof container. To serve, thaw thoroughly.

chunky spiced apple sauce

½

½ C

1+

makes: 4–5 baby portions

storage: up to 2 months in
the freezer

4 eating apples, eg Cox's
   orange pippin
pinch of allspice
4 dried apricots, finely
   chopped
12 tbsp water

This is a brilliant stand-by and is great served with yogurt, muesli or baby rice. Only add sugar if the apples are tart. Remember your baby will have less of a sweet tooth than you.

1 Peel and core the apples and put into a saucepan with the allspice, apricots and water. Cook over a gentle heat until the apples are soft and pulpy (approximately 15–20 minutes). Stir often to prevent them sticking.

2 Cool and freeze in freezer bags or in a freezerproof container. Thaw thoroughly before using.

fruit muffins

1

½

½ C

1+

makes: 15 baby portions

storage: up to 3 months in
the freezer

150g plain flour
½ tsp baking powder
pinch of ground cinnamon
1 large free-range egg
125ml full-fat milk
50g unsalted butter, melted
75g golden caster sugar
125g fresh blueberries

You can make these with any soft fruit – blueberries, raspberries, apples or bananas – and in any combination. Use what is plentiful and cheap! They are a brilliant breakfast stand-by for all the family, and are especially good for packed lunches or picnics.

1 Preheat the oven to 200°C/400°F/gas mark 6. Grease a muffin tin or line with paper cases.

2 Sift the flour, baking powder and cinnamon into a large bowl. In another large bowl, mix together the egg, milk, melted butter, sugar and blueberries.

3 Pour the flour mixture over the wet ingredients and quickly fold in – don't over-mix. The mixture should look lumpy and uneven.

4 Spoon the mixture into the prepared tin and bake for 15 minutes until risen and golden. Serve or cool on a wire rack and freeze.

5 To serve, heat through from frozen in a pre-heated oven at 180°C/350°F/gas mark 4 for 5–6 minutes and cut into small pieces.

nut bread

makes 10 baby portions

storage: up to 3 months in the freezer

400g plain white flour
400g wholemeal flour
50g hazelnuts, ground
25g sesame seeds, ground
25g sunflower seeds or
 flaked almonds, ground
approx 360ml warm water
1 tsp golden caster sugar
6g (2 level tsp) dried yeast

6½

2

1½

1

Vitamin B₁

1+

This is a really easy bread to make, and it has a lovely nutty flavour. Once you get into the habit of breadmaking, it needn't take up much time and the results are so much nicer than shop-bought loaves. The quantities are easily doubled. Do not serve nuts or seeds to babies if there is any family history of allergies.

1 Grease a 1kg loaf tin.
2 Put the flour into a large bowl and mix in the nuts and seeds.
3 Put 100ml warm water into a measuring jug, stir in the sugar, then the yeast and leave somewhere warm for 10–15 minutes until a froth has formed on the top.
4 Make a well in the centre of the flour and pour in the yeast. Stir with a wooden spoon, gradually adding the rest of the warm water. Use your hands to form a smooth dough that comes away from the edges of the bowl, adding a little more water if necessary.
5 Knead the dough briefly for approximately 5 minutes on a floured surface and then shape into an oblong and drop into the prepared tin.
6 Sprinkle the loaf with flour, cover with a warm damp cloth and leave to rise in a warm place for 30–40 minutes.
7 Preheat the oven to 200°C/400°F/gas mark 6 then bake the bread for 40 minutes. Remove from the tin and bake upside down on a baking tray for 10–15 minutes to crisp up the sides and the bottom. When the loaf is cooked, it will sound hollow on the bottom when tapped.
8 Cool completely on a wire rack. Wrap in foil and freeze or slice and wrap each slice in foil and freeze. To serve, thaw thoroughly.

fresh and dried fruit compote

makes: 5–6 baby portions

storage: up to 2 months in the freezer

3 dried apricots, finely
 chopped
50g dried apple, finely
 chopped
3 ready-to-eat prunes,
 finely chopped
100ml apple juice
50ml water
3–4 fresh pears, peeled,
 cored and finely chopped

½

1C

1+

This is great served with a little natural full-fat yogurt, apple purée or muesli. In the winter you can serve it warm, and it's also great served with porridge.

1 Put the dried fruits, apple juice and water into a saucepan.
2 Bring to the boil and simmer gently for 5 minutes.
3 Transfer to a bowl and add the fresh pears. Leave for at least 20 minutes.
4 Once cool, spoon into a freezerproof container or freezer bags and freeze. To serve, thaw thoroughly.

fresh lunches

tomato risotto

makes: 6 baby portions or 2 baby portions and 2 adult portions

storage: rice should not be reheated, but can be served cold up to 24 hours after cooking

25g unsalted butter
3 shallots, chopped finely
175g arborio rice
300ml of tomato passata or tinned chopped tomatoes
475ml light no-salt vegetable stock (page 332)
2 tbsp fresh basil, torn
50g Parmesan, grated

Make this at the weekend when everyone is at home, because it makes enough to feed a family of four. Alternatively, halve the quantities. This risotto is particularly easy because constant stirring isn't required – you just bung it in the oven.

1 Preheat the oven to 180°C/350°F/gas mark 4.
2 Melt the butter in a heavy-based pan and fry the shallots slowly, without colouring, until softened (approximately 5–10 minutes). Turn the heat up slightly and add the rice to the pan and stir, thoroughly coating it with the buttery shallots.
3 Stir for 1–2 minutes, until you hear the rice make a hissing sound, which means it's time to add the liquid. Add the tomato passata and stir well. Let it bubble and then add the stock and 1 tbsp basil. Bring up to simmering point, stir once and transfer to a warm ovenproof dish, without covering. Put the dish in the middle of the oven. After 20 minutes, remove from the oven and stir once.
4 Return to the oven for 15 minutes. When the rice is cooked but has a little bite, stir in the Parmesan and remaining basil. Leave for 2 minutes, cool then serve.

cheese and ham on toast

makes: 1 baby portion

storage: best eaten fresh

little knob of unsalted butter
2 slices of white bread
2 slices of cooked ham
50g medium Cheddar cheese, grated

Vitamin B₁, A

When you make this, toast only one side of the bread; this keeps the toast slightly softer than normal to compensate for the lack of teeth! Use a cheese with a decent flavour that also melts well, eg Cheddar, Cheshire or Lancashire.

1 Lightly butter the bread.
2 Chop the ham finely and scatter over the slices of bread.
3 Sprinkle the cheese on top and then grill until the bread is golden around the edges and the cheese has melted.
4 Cut into fingers.

Note: babies develop at different rates; do not feed chopped food to your baby until she is confident with chewing.

spanish tortilla

6½
1
1
½
1½ C

Vitamin B₁, B₁₂, A

1+

makes: 4 baby portions or 2 baby portions and 1 adult portion

storage: best eaten fresh or up to 24 hours in the refrigerator

450g floury potatoes, peeled and halved

2 tbsp olive oil

1 onion, thinly sliced

4 large free-range eggs, beaten

This delicious potato omelette is wonderful with a sprinkling of finely chopped cooked ham or crumbled cooked bacon, or some quickly sautéed mushrooms to help to make it a little more substantial.

1 Bring a pan of water to the boil.

2 Cook the potatoes in the pan of boiling water until they are soft on the outside but still firm in the middle (approximately 5–7 minutes). Drain and cut into thin slices.

3 Heat the olive oil in a frying pan and add the sliced onion. Cook slowly for 10 minutes until the onion is soft. Add the sliced potatoes and cook for a further 5 minutes.

4 Preheat the grill to high.

5 Pour the beaten eggs over the potato and onion mixture and cook over a medium heat until it has set on the bottom. Put the pan under the grill to finish cooking the top.

6 Cut a quarter of the omelette into slices small enough for your baby to hold.

sweet potato hummus

4½
1½
1
1
2 C

Vitamin B₁, A

1+

makes: 3 baby portions

storage: up to 48 hours in the refrigerator

2 medium sweet potatoes, well scrubbed

400g tin chickpeas, drained and rinsed

1 tbsp tahini

1 garlic clove, chopped

juice of ½ lemon

1 tbsp olive oil

to serve:

a few fingers of pitta bread (optional)

selection of soft vegetables for dipping, eg peeled cucumber or cooked beetroot, cut into sticks

This is fantastic for mums and dads as well as babies. Chickpeas are one of the most nutritionally valuable pulses, and a great source of protein for vegetarians, so tinned chickpeas are a useful store-cupboard ingredient. Do not serve tahini to babies if there is any family history of allergies.

1 Preheat the oven to 190°C/375°F/gas mark 5.

2 Score a cross in each sweet potato and bake until they are soft and tender (approximately 40 minutes).

3 Scoop the potato flesh into a food processor, discarding the skins. Add the chickpeas, tahini and garlic and whiz together. Add the lemon juice and enough oil to make the desired consistency.

4 Serve with toasted fingers of pitta bread, if using, and vegetable sticks.

bacon and mushrooms in cheese

This dish is easy to make and tastes delicious. This would also make a good supper dish for an adult, especially if served with a baked potato.

3

½

½

1 **C**

Vitamin B₁, A

1⁺

makes: 4 baby portions or 2 baby portions and 1–2 adult portions

storage: up to 24 hours in the refrigerator

4 Portobello mushrooms
2 rashers unsmoked back bacon, rind removed
1 tbsp olive oil
3 plum tomatoes
4 tbsp full-fat cream cheese
2 tbsp finely chopped flat-leaf parsley (or other herbs of your choice),
freshly ground black pepper
2 tbsp breadcrumbs
2 tbsp unsalted butter, melted

1 Preheat the oven to 180°C/350°F/gas mark 4.
2 Remove the stalks from the mushrooms and finely chop them. Fry the bacon in a little oil in a frying pan until crisp, golden and cooked through. Cut it into very small pieces and put into a bowl.
3 Add a little more oil to the pan and, when hot, add the mushroom stalks. Cook for a few minutes.
4 Chop the tomatoes, add to the bacon with the cooked mushroom stalks, cream cheese, herbs, and freshly ground black pepper.
5 Place the mushroom caps on a baking sheet. Spread the cream cheese mixture onto the mushrooms, then sprinkle over the breadcrumbs. Drizzle with the melted butter and cook in the preheated oven for 10–15 minutes.

leek and ham mash

A friend of mine, Lou, swears that she can get her children to eat any vegetables by mixing them with mashed potato. It's a good trick but hopefully your children will have got into the veg habit early on – especially if you are careful not to give them the idea that sweet things are nicer than vegetables.

4

1

1

½

2 **C**

Vitamin B₁

1⁺

makes: 3 baby portions or 1 baby portion and 1 adult portion

storage: best eaten fresh

10g unsalted butter
2 small leeks, washed and finely chopped
2 medium potatoes, peeled and cut into 4
6 tbsp full-fat milk or calcium-enriched soya drink
2 slices of cooked ham, finely diced

1 Heat the butter in a heavy-based frying pan and fry the leeks until soft and pale golden (approximately 3–5 minutes).
2 Bring a pan of water to the boil and cook the potatoes until tender (approximately 10–12 minutes). Drain.
3 Add the milk to the potatoes and mash, then add the leeks and ham and mash again briefly.

quick bites **lunches**

things with pasta or noodles

Bring a large pan of water to the boil. Add 75g noodles or small pasta shapes and cook following the packet's instructions until just tender. Drain.

½ 2½ 1½ 18

Vitamin B₁

2 tbsp smooth peanut butter
½ cooked chicken breast, finely chopped
75g cooked noodles

peanut noodles

Add the peanut butter and chicken to the noodles, then toss. Serve as is or finely chop. Do not feed nut products to babies if there is a family history of allergies.

½ 1 1 6½

Vitamin B₁, A

2 chestnut mushrooms
knob of unsalted butter
2 tbsp full-fat cream cheese
75g cooked pasta

cheese and mushroom pasta

Finely chop the chestnut mushrooms and fry them in the butter until soft. Add the cream cheese and the cooked pasta, then mix all the ingredients together. Serve as is or finely chop.

4 3½ 1 21

Vitamin B₁, B₁₂, A

50g Cheddar cheese
2 rashers unsmoked back bacon, rind removed
75g cooked pasta

cheese and bacon pasta

Grate the Cheddar cheese and grill the bacon rashers until they are cooked and slightly crisp. Finely chop the bacon and stir into the pasta with the cheese. Serve as is or finely chop.

4 2½ 1½ 23

50g Cheddar cheese
50g tinned tuna in oil, drained
75g cooked pasta

tuna pasta

Grate the Cheddar cheese. Add the tuna and grated cheese to the pasta, then toss everything together and serve as is or mash slightly.

4 C 1 1 7

Vitamin B₁

a handful of cooked peas
2 tsp pesto
75g cooked noodles

pesto and peas

Simply mix together the cooked peas and pesto and then stir the mixture into the cooked noodles. Serve as is or finely chop.

things with mashed potato

Bring a large pan of water to the boil. Peel and chop 1 medium potato or 1 sweet potato and cook until just tender (approximately 10–12 minutes). Drain, then mash with approximately 2 tbsp breast milk, formula milk or full-fat cow's milk.

sweetcorn and ham

✓ Vitamin B₁

2 [C] 1½ 🥫 ½ 🗙 6 🥚

a handful of cooked sweetcorn
1 slice of cooked ham, finely chopped
1 portion of mash (recipe above)

Mix the cooked sweetcorn and finely chopped ham into the mash and heat through gently for 2 minutes.

pesto and pea mash

✓ Vitamin B₁

2½ [C] 1 🥫 1 🗙 4 🥚

2 tsp pesto
a handful of cooked peas
1 portion of mash (recipe at top of page)

Mix the pesto and the cooked peas into the mashed potatoes and lightly mash again.

cheese and onion mash

2 [C] 2 🥛 1½ 🥫 ½ 🗙 8 🥚

1 tsp olive oil or unsalted butter
½ medium onion, finely chopped
2 tsp Cheddar cheese, grated
1 portion of mash (recipe at top of page)

Heat the olive oil or unsalted butter in a frying pan and sauté the onion until it is really soft (approximately 5 minutes). Add the onion to the mash with the grated Cheddar cheese and mix together.

tuna and tomato mash

min B₁, B₁₂, A

3 [C] 1 🥫 1 🗙 12 🥚

50g tuna tinned in oil, drained
1 ripe tomato, finely chopped
1 portion of mash (recipe at top of page)

Mix the tuna and finely chopped tomato into the mash, then lightly mash the mixture again.

things with rice

Mix 50g baby rice with breast milk or formula milk or full-fat cow's milk to achieve the desired consistency. Alternatively, mash 50g boiled basmati rice.

beetroot and spring onion

1 [C] ½ 🥛 ½ 🥫 ½ 🗙 2 🥚

1 tsp olive oil or unsalted butter
1 spring onion, finely sliced
1 small cooked beetroot, finely chopped
1 portion of rice (recipe above)

Heat the olive oil or unsalted butter. Add the spring onion and sauté until really soft (3–4 minutes). Add the beetroot and mix with the rice, then lightly mash with a fork or potato masher.

broccoli and chicken

3 [C] ½ 🥛 1½ 🥫 ½ 🗙 12 🥚

1 broccoli floret
1 portion of rice (recipe above)
¼ cooked chicken breast, finely chopped

Bring a small pan of water to the boil. Add 1 broccoli floret and cook until just tender (about 3 minutes). Finely chop the broccoli and add to the rice with the chopped cooked chicken breast, then lightly mash. Alternatively, serve the broccoli and chicken in pieces large enough for your baby to hold.

All quick bites make 1 portion
unless otherwise stated.

lunches to freeze

chickpea and bacon stew

makes: 7–8 baby portions

storage: up to 2 months in the freezer

4

1

1

½

1½ **C**

Vitamin B₁, A

1+

1 tbsp olive oil
130g pancetta or unsmoked
   back bacon, in small pieces
1 red onion, chopped
1 leek, washed and chopped
1 carrot, peeled and chopped
2 garlic cloves, chopped
2 ripe tomatoes, chopped
400g tin tomatoes
400g tin chickpeas, drained
   and rinsed
450ml no-salt vegetable stock
   (page 332)
1 tbsp fresh parsley, chopped
sprig of fresh rosemary

Introduce pulses gradually, or else they can be a little overwhelming for a baby's immature digestive system. Pulses are notorious for their 'windiness', but as long as they are well-cooked, you should have no problems. Interestingly, parsley can help to counteract this side-effect, which is why I have added a little to this recipe.

1 Heat the oil in a heavy-based saucepan. Fry the pancetta or bacon until crisp, golden and cooked through. Using a slotted spoon, transfer the meat to a plate.

2 In the same pan, sauté the onion, leek, carrot and garlic until they are soft (approximately 5–6 minutes).

3 Add the tomatoes and chickpeas and simmer for 5 minutes.

4 Add the stock, rosemary, parsley and pancetta or bacon, then simmer for another 30 minutes.

5 Leave to cool, then spoon into a freezerproof container or small freezer bags and freeze.

6 To serve, thaw thoroughly. Remove the rosemary, heat through and serve as is or roughly purée.

cheese and corn muffins

makes: 15 baby portions

storage: up to 3 months in the freezer

2

½

1+

100g tinned sweetcorn
150g plain flour
½ tsp baking powder
1 large free-range egg
125ml full-fat milk
50g unsalted butter, melted
50g Cheddar cheese, grated
pinch of mild chilli powder
1 tbsp fresh parsley, chopped

These muffins are popular with children of all ages. Serve them with cheese and chopped tomato and avocado. They are also good served with soup.

1 Preheat the oven to 200°C/400°F/gas mark 6. Grease a mini-muffin tin or line with paper cases. Drain and mash the sweetcorn.

2 Sift the flour and baking powder into a large bowl. In another large bowl, mix together the egg, milk, melted butter, cheese, sweetcorn, chilli and parsley.

3 Pour the flour mixture over the wet ingredients and quickly fold in. Don't overmix, as it should look lumpy. Spoon into the tin and bake for 15 minutes until risen and golden. Cool on a wire rack and freeze in a freezerproof container.

4 To serve, heat through from frozen in a preheated oven at 180°C/350°F/gas mark 4 for 5–6 minutes.

mild curried parsnip and pear soup

2

½

1

1+

makes: 10 baby portions

storage: up to 3 months in the freezer

1 tbsp olive oil
25g unsalted butter
1 small onion, chopped
1 garlic clove, chopped
1 medium potato, peeled and chopped
600g parsnips, peeled and chopped
1 tsp mild curry powder
1 litre water
1 ripe pear, peeled, cored and chopped
300ml full-fat milk, to serve

My whole family loves this soup – the pears work really well and the curry powder brings out the parsnip flavour. Try serving it with some warm, Indian-style bread, such as naan, which is soft and easy for babies to chew. This is quite a thick soup, which should make it slightly easier for your baby to eat without making too much of a mess.

1 Heat the oil and butter in a heavy-based saucepan.

2 Fry the onion and garlic until soft, then add the potato, parsnips and curry powder and cook for a further 1–2 minutes. Stir the mixture to prevent it sticking to the pan.

3 Add the water and pear and bring up to the boil. Simmer gently for 20 minutes, until the parsnips are soft.

4 Blend with a hand-held blender (or in a food processor or blender) until really smooth.

5 Freeze in a freezerproof container or freezer bags.

6 To serve, thaw thoroughly, add the milk and reheat gently in a saucepan without boiling.

fruity Moroccan lamb burgers

3

1

Vitamin B$_{12}$

1+

makes: 20 baby portions

storage: up to 2 months in the freezer

1 tbsp olive oil
3 spring onions, finely chopped
pinch of ground coriander
500g lean minced lamb
50g dried dates, finely chopped
1 tsp fresh coriander, chopped (optional)

These burgers can be fried, grilled or cooked in the oven. If you are grilling them, be careful not to let the edges burn. Giving babies any food that has very dark or crispy edges, such as chargrilled or barbecued food, should be avoided. Only use fresh (not previously frozen) minced lamb for this recipe.

1 Heat the oil in a heavy-based frying pan and fry the onions until just soft (approximately 5 minutes). Add the ground coriander and cook for a further 2 minutes, stirring often.

2 Transfer the onions to a bowl, then add the lamb, dates and coriander and mix together well with your hands.

3 Mould the mixture into about 20 little burgers. Wrap in clingfilm or foil and freeze.

4 To serve, thaw thoroughly. If oven cooking, preheat the oven to 200°C/400°F/gas mark 6. Cook the burgers for 15 minutes, or until cooked through. If grilling, preheat the grill to high. Grill the burgers for 5 minutes on each side until cooked through. Test if the burgers are cooked by inserting a skewer into the middle of the burger – the juices should run absolutely clear.

fish and courgette gratin

White fish is a brilliant food for babies – it's a great source of protein, but is relatively easy for them to digest. This is a delicious cheesy gratin that is suitable for all the family. All you need to serve with it is some green vegetables, such as spinach or broccoli.

17½

½

1½

3

1 C

amin B₁,B₁₂, A

1+

makes: 4 baby portions

storage: up to 2 months in the freezer

25g unsalted butter
25g plain flour
600ml full-fat milk
pinch of freshly grated nutmeg
freshly ground black pepper
100g pasta shells or twists
2 medium courgettes, thinly sliced
450g white fish, skinned, boned and cut into small jpieces
150g Cheddar cheese, grated

1 Preheat the oven to 180°C/350°F/gas mark 4. Make an all-in-one sauce by putting the butter, flour and milk into a saucepan. Heat gently, stirring constantly until the sauce thickens. You may like to use a whisk to prevent any lumps from forming. Add the nutmeg and a little freshly ground back pepper.

2 Bring a large pan of water to the boil and cook the pasta following the packet's instructions. Put the courgettes into a steamer and cook over the pasta for a few minutes until just tender.

3 Put the fish and courgettes into a gratin dish. Add the pasta and mix everything together. Cover with the sauce, then scatter over the cheese. Bake at 180°C/350°F/gas mark 4 for 20–25 minutes. Leave to cool, wrap up in clingfilm or foil and freeze.

4 Thaw thoroughly. Preheat the oven to 180°C/350°F/gas mark 4. Cook for 15–20 minutes, until thoroughly heated through and golden on the top. Lightly mash.

stuffed baked potatoes

These are really quick and easy. Make and freeze a big batch of them for maximum convenience. There are lots of ingredients you can add to the fillings: sautéed mushrooms and parsley, spinach and cheese, ham and tomato or baked beans and cheese.

10

½

1

2

1 C

Vitamin B₁,B₁₂, A

1+

makes: 2 baby portions

storage: up to 2 months in the freezer

1 medium potato
10g unsalted butter
50g tinned tuna in oil, drained and flaked
50g Cheddar cheese, grated
1 tsp fresh parsley, chopped
freshly ground black pepper

1 Preheat the oven to 180°C/350°F/gas mark 4. Bake the potato for 1 hour, until soft.

2 Remove from the oven, carefully cut the potato in half, and scoop out the flesh. Mash the flesh in a bowl with the butter, tuna, half the cheese and the parsley. Season with black pepper.

3 Refill the potato skin and sprinkle with the remaining cheese. Freeze.

4 Thaw thoroughly. Bake on a baking sheet in a preheated oven at 180°C/350°F/gas mark 4 until the filling is hot and the cheese is golden brown and bubbling (approximately 15 minutes). Leave to cool slightly before serving and, if necessary, chop into very small pieces.

fresh suppers

chicken goujons

makes: 6 baby portions or 2 baby portions and 2 adult portions

storage: best eaten fresh

200ml natural full-fat yogurt
2 tbsp fresh herbs,
   eg parsley, basil, sage,
   finely chopped
2 raw chicken breasts, cut
   into thin strips 1.5cm thick
freshly ground black pepper
75g fine fresh breadcrumbs
large pinch of paprika
olive oil, to drizzle

Sadly, chicken nuggets, one of the most popular foods among kids, are often packed with some of the worst ingredients for small children (or adults for that matter). They can be notoriously high in additives and made from poor quality meat. It may take a little more effort to make your own, but it will be worth it in the long run. Only serve this to babies who are very confident with chewing.

1 Preheat the oven to 180°C/350°F/gas mark 4.
2 Mix the yogurt and herbs together and divide in two.
3 Stir the chicken into half the yogurt, making sure the meat is all coated. Leave to marinade for at least an hour, or overnight in the refrigerator if possible.
4 Season the remaining half of the yogurt mixture with black pepper, then cover and keep as a dip for the goujons.
5 Grease a baking sheet. Mix the breadcrumbs with the paprika and black pepper. Dip each goujon into the breadcrumb mixture and lay on the baking sheet.
6 Drizzle with olive oil and cook for 20–25 minutes, until the goujons are golden and cooked through.

baked bean gratin

makes: 2 baby portions

storage: best eaten fresh

1 large potato, peeled
   and halved
2 good-quality low-salt pork
   sausages, cooked
420g tin baked beans,
   preferably sugar-free
50g Cheddar cheese, grated

Vitamin B₁, B₁₂

Note: babies develop at different rates; do not feed chopped food to your baby until she is confident with chewing.

There are lots of convenience foods that make life with children much easier. However, it's best not to rely on them and, if you do use them, make sure you cook or serve them with fresh vegetables or fruits as appropriate.

1 Bring a pan of water to the boil and cook the potato until tender (approximately 10 minutes). Drain. Preheat the oven to 180°C/350°F/gas mark 4.
2 Cut the cooked sausages into very small bite-size pieces – if they are too big there is a danger of choking.
3 Pour the baked beans into a gratin dish. Sprinkle over the sausage pieces.
4 Slice the potato halves and lay over the sausage and beans. Sprinkle with the cheese and bake in the oven for 20 minutes, until the top is golden and bubbling and it is hot all the way through. Serve as is or lightly mash before serving.

chicken and potato cakes

makes: 10 baby portions

storage: keep covered in the refrigerator for up to 48 hours

Vitamin B₁₂

2 large free-range eggs, beaten

200ml full-fat milk

125g plain flour

450g potatoes or sweet potatoes, peeled and coarsely grated

1 large onion, thinly sliced

2 cooked chicken breasts, finely chopped

200g tinned sweetcorn, drained

freshly ground black pepper

1 tbsp fresh coriander, chopped

This variation on fish cakes is really popular in my household. If you fancy eating some of these yourself, you may like to dip them into a little soy and/or sweet chilli sauce.

1 Whisk the eggs and milk together, then beat in the flour thoroughly to make a smooth batter.

2 Bring a small pan of water to the boil. Add the potatoes and onion and blanch for 2–3 minutes, then drain well, pressing out as much liquid as possible.

3 Stir the chicken into the batter with the sweetcorn, potato and onion, black pepper and coriander.

4 Rub a heavy-based frying pan with an oiled kitchen towel and heat. Drop rounded teaspoons of batter into the pan (or dessertspoons, if you want larger cakes), flatten a little with a spatula and cook for 2 minutes on each side until golden if they are small, and 3–4 minutes each side if larger.

5 Keep warm, uncovered, in an oven at 150°C/300°F/gas mark 3. Repeat until the mixture is used up. Serve warm.

eastern rice with baby veg

makes: 4 baby portions or 2 baby portions and 2 adult portions

storage: rice should not be reheated, but can be served cold up to 24 hours after cooking

3 mange-tout

3 baby carrots

3 baby corn

200g basmati rice

400ml water

10g creamed coconut, crumbled

4 cardamom pods

1 cinnamon stick

squeeze of lime juice

handful of chopped fresh coriander, (optional)

You and your partner might enjoy this dish served with grilled chicken or steamed fish. Do not serve coconut to babies if there is any family history of allergies.

1 Thinly slice the mange-tout, baby carrots and baby corn into even-size pieces to make sure that they cook evenly.

2 Put the rice, water, creamed coconut, cardamom pods and cinnamon stick into a saucepan, stir well, then cover and bring up to simmering point. Simmer for 11 minutes without removing the lid.

3 Remove the pan from the heat. Throw the sliced vegetables on top of the rice and quickly replace the lid, then cook for another 14 minutes.

4 Remove the cardamom pods and cinnamon stick. Add the lime juice, toss everything together well and scatter in a little fresh coriander, if using. Mash if necessary.

lamb chops with pea mash

makes: 5 baby portions or 1 baby portion and 2 adult portions

storage: best eaten fresh

450g potatoes, peeled and roughly chopped
150g frozen peas or petits pois
15g knob of unsalted butter
100ml full-fat milk
5 lamb chops
mint sauce, to serve (optional)

vitamin B₁, B₁₂

1+

Flavoured mash is really popular with my children, especially this pea one, because it is lovely and sweet. If you like, add a little chopped fresh mint, or a tiny bit of mint sauce to the mash. Cook as many lamb chops as you need. I have suggested five, as you can cook one for the baby and two each for you and your partner.

1 Bring a large pan of water to the boil. Add the potatoes and cook until just tender (approximately 10 minutes). Just before they are cooked, add the peas and bring back to the boil. Drain. Add the butter and milk and, using a potato masher, mash together.

2 Cook the lamb chops under a hot grill for 4–5 minutes on each side.

3 Chop one lamb chop into small pieces. Alternatively, chop the lamb chop into pieces large enough for your baby to hold. Serve with some mash and a little mint sauce, if using.

savoury crumble

makes: 5 baby portions or 1 baby portion and 2 adult portions

storage: up to 24 hours in the refrigerator

25g unsalted butter
25g plain flour
300ml full-fat milk
freshly grated nutmeg
freshly ground black pepper
75g broccoli or cauliflower
75g carrots, peeled
150g cooked chicken
75g frozen peas
1 tbsp finely chopped fresh parsley

for the crumble:
50g strong Cheddar cheese, grated
2 tbsp fresh herbs, chopped
40g fresh breadcrumbs
40g nuts, ground

vitamin B₁₂, A

1+

You could just as easily use tinned tuna instead of the chicken or, for a vegetarian meal, just add cooked quorn or tofu instead. If you have any cold leftover vegetables use those, too. As with sweet crumble, it's great to have a bag of this topping made up and kept in the freezer. Remember, only serve nuts to babies if there is no family history of allergies.

1 Preheat the oven to 180°C/350°F/gas mark 4.

2 Make an all-in-one sauce by putting the butter, flour and milk into a saucepan. Heat gently, stirring constantly, until the sauce thickens. You may like to use a whisk to prevent lumps from forming. Add the nutmeg and a little black pepper.

3 Cut the broccoli or cauliflower and carrots into small pieces. Also cut the chicken into bite-sized chunks.

4 Bring a large pan of water to the boil. Cook the broccoli or cauliflower and carrots until they are just tender, then drain.

5 Gently stir the cooked vegetables, peas, chicken and parsley into the sauce and pour into a gratin dish.

6 To make the crumble, mix together all the ingredients. Scatter over the chicken and vegetables.

7 Bake in the preheated oven for 30 minutes until cooked through and golden on the top. Finely chop or mash before serving.

quick bites **suppers**

Vitamin A ✓ 1**C** 🥛 ½ 🧈 1 🥚

carrot and courgette pasta

1 small carrot, peeled and grated
½ medium courgette, grated
small knob of unsalted butter
2 tbsp full-fat cream cheese
75g pasta, freshly cooked

Fry the carrot and courgettes in the butter until tender. Stir in the cream cheese and heat gently until it has melted. Pour over the pasta and finely chop or lightly mash before serving.

1**C** 2🥛 1🧈 1✉ 8🥚

sweetcorn and cheese pasta

small knob of unsalted butter
75g tinned sweetcorn
30g Cheddar cheese, grated
1 tsp fresh parsley, finely chopped
75g pasta, freshly cooked

Heat the butter in a pan and add the sweetcorn. Heat through, then add the rest of the ingredients and mix together well. Finely chop or lightly mash before serving.

2**C** ½🥛 ½🧈 ½✉ 7🥚

ham and pea pasta

75g frozen peas
75g pasta, freshly cooked
1 tsp finely chopped fresh parsley
½ slice of cooked ham, finely chopped

Mix the peas, pasta and parsley together in a saucepan and heat gently. When heated through. If you wish, add a little full-fat cream cheese or tomato passata to make more of a sauce. Remove from the heat and stir in the finely chopped cooked ham. Finely chop or lightly mash before serving.

2**C**1½🥛 1🧈 1✉ 3🥚

creamy spinach pasta sauce

75g green pasta, freshly cooked
75g fresh spinach, chopped and cooked
2 tbsp full-fat cream cheese
pinch of grated nutmeg
freshly ground black pepper

Mix the pasta, spinach and cream cheese together in a pan and heat gently until heated through. Add the nutmeg and a pinch of finely ground black pepper. Finely chop or lightly mash before serving.

½🥛 ½🧈 ½✉ 3🥚

tortelloni with buttered breadcrumbs

75g tortelloni
small knob of unsalted butter
30g fresh breadcrumbs
1 tsp finely chopped fresh parsley
freshly ground black pepper

Cook the pasta following the packet's instructions. Drain. Meanwhile, melt the butter in a pan and fry the breadcrumbs until golden. Add the cooked pasta and parsley. Stir gently and season with black pepper. Serve as is or finely chop or lightly mash before serving.

tomato baked beans on toast

75g baked beans
1 tomato, finely chopped
1 slice of wholemeal bread

Heat the beans in a pan with the tomato until hot. Toast the bread and serve cut into fingers with the beans.

baked beans with sausage

Vitamin B₁₂

1 good-quality low-salt
pork sausage
75g baked beans

Cook the sausage under a grill so that the fat drains away. Meanwhile, heat the beans until warmed right through. When the sausage is cooked through, chop it finely and stir it into the beans. If you can, buy sausages made with herbs or leeks to make this more tasty. If necessary, lightly mash before serving.

baked beans with tuna and cheese

Vitamin B₁₂

75g baked beans
30g tinned tuna in oil, drained and flaked
15g Cheddar cheese, grated

Heat the beans with the tuna in a small pan. When they are just simmering, stir in the cheese. If necessary, lightly mash before serving.

spaghetti with mushrooms

50g mushrooms, finely chopped
dash of olive oil
75g tinned spaghetti in tomato sauce

Fry the mushrooms in the olive oil. When they are golden, add the spaghetti and cook until heated through. If necessary, lightly mash before serving.

spaghetti with sweetcorn

75g tinned spaghetti in tomato sauce
50g tinned sweetcorn

Heat the spaghetti and stir in the sweetcorn, then cook until heated through. Lightly mash before serving if necessary.

fish baked in orange juice

Vitamin B₁₂

5g piece raw white fish, skinned and boned
4 tbsp fresh orange juice
bread and butter or mashed potato, to serve

Put the fish into a baking dish with the orange juice. Cover with foil and bake in a preheated oven at 180°C/350°F/gas mark 4 until cooked through (approximately 5–10 minutes). Finely chop or lightly mash before serving with a piece of bread and unsalted butter or mashed potato.

mexican couscous

Vitamin B₁

50g couscous, cooked
50g cold cooked chicken, finely chopped
¼ ripe avocado, peeled and finely chopped
lemon juice (optional)
fresh coriander, finely chopped (optional)

Mix together the cooked couscous, cooked chicken and avocado, adding a little lemon juice and coriander if you have them to hand. If necessary, lightly mash before serving.

All quick bites make 1 portion
unless otherwise stated.

suppers to freeze

sausage, apple and parsnip pie

8½

1½

1½

2

3 **C**

Vitamin B₁, B₁₂

1+

makes: 4 baby portions

storage: up to 2 months in the freezer

4 good-quality low-salt pork sausages

2 medium potatoes, peeled and halved

1 tbsp olive oil

1 small onion, finely chopped

1 garlic clove, crushed

1 leek, cleaned and sliced

2 parsnips, peeled and diced

2 eating apples, peeled, cored and sliced

1 tbsp parsley, finely chopped

150ml no-salt veg stock

50ml apple juice

50g Cheddar cheese, grated

Choose sausages with a high meat content – at least 80 per cent meat. This dish makes a great family supper and freezes well.

1 Preheat the oven to 200°C/400°F/gas mark 6. Put the sausages on a baking tray and cook for 20 minutes, turning occasionally, until cooked through and golden all over. Cook the potatoes in boiling water until just tender (approximately 10–15 minutes). Drain and slice thinly.

2 Meanwhile, heat the oil in a heavy-based frying pan and fry the onion and garlic until soft. Add the leek, parsnips and apples and cook for a further 15 minutes, stirring often. Add the parsley, stock and apple juice and 100ml boiling water and bring to the boil.

3 Slice the sausages and scatter over the bottom of an ovenproof dish. Pour over the vegetable mixture and top with the potato slices. Leave to cool.

4 Wrap in foil and freeze. To serve, thaw thoroughly. Cover with foil and bake for 35 minutes at 200°C/400°F/gas mark 6. Remove the foil, sprinkle with cheese and bake for a further 20 minutes. If necessary, finely chop or mash before serving.

sweet potato and coconut gratin

1

1 **C**

Vitamin A

1+

makes: 15 baby portions

storage: up to 3 months in the freezer

600g potatoes, peeled

250g sweet potatoes, peeled and very thinly sliced

3 spring onions, finely sliced

2 tsp mild curry powder

400ml coconut milk

2 tbsp coriander, finely chopped

Note: do not feed chopped food to your baby until she is confident with chewing.

This is a delicious dish, but do not serve coconut to babies if there is any family history of allergies.

1 Preheat the oven to 180°C/350°F/gas mark 4. Bring a pan of water to the boil, add the ordinary potatoes and parboil for 5 minutes. Drain and slice thinly.

2 Layer some of both types of potato into the bottom of a buttered ovenproof dish. Scatter some of the spring onions over the top and sprinkle with a little of the curry powder. Repeat until all of the potatoes have been used up.

3 Mix the coconut milk and 150–200ml water together, then pour onto the potatoes. Bake for 40–50 minutes, until the potatoes are tender. Scatter over the coriander and finely chop or mash before serving. Alternatively, leave to cool, wrap in foil and freeze. Thaw thoroughly, then reheat for 20–30 minutes at 180°C/350°F/gas mark 4 until hot right through, then finely chop or mash.

home-made fish fingers

makes: 3 baby portions

storage: up to 2 months in the freezer

300g fresh cod fillet, skin and bones removed and cooked

approx 3 tbsp plain flour, for dusting

pinch of freshly ground black pepper

pinch of paprika

1 large free-range egg, beaten

75g breadcrumbs

vegetable oil, for frying

Vitamin B₁₂

My girls love these more than the shop-bought variety and they take very little time or effort to make. Serve with a few peas or baked beans and a little mashed potato for a healthy and tasty supper.

1 Cut the cod into 2cm-wide strips and, if they are too long, cut these strips in half. Season the flour with a little black pepper and paprika. Dip the fish into the flour and shake off any excess.

2 Dip the seasoned fish into the beaten egg, then roll it in the breadcrumbs until it is evenly coated.

3 Layer with sheets of greaseproof paper in a freezerproof container and freeze.

4 To serve, thaw thoroughly, resting on kitchen paper, then heat enough oil to cover the base of a large non-stick frying pan. Arrange the defrosted fish fingers in the pan (you may have to cook them in batches), and fry them over a medium heat for 3–4 minutes on each side until crisp and golden. Drain on kitchen paper and serve as finger foods. (If necessary, finely chop or mash before serving.)

mini quiches

makes: 6 baby portions

storage: up to 2 months in the freezer

for the pastry:
175g plain flour, sieved

90g unsalted butter, cut into small pieces and kept in the refrigerator

1 egg yolk plus 1 tbsp cold water, or just 2–4 tbsp cold water

Vitamin B₁ B₁₂, A

for the fillings:
15g unsalted butter
1 small onion, finely chopped
125g courgettes, thinly sliced
125g broccoli, in small pieces
50g Gruyère cheese, grated
2 large free-range eggs plus 1 extra egg yolk
270ml full-fat milk

These can be made with lots of different fillings – use whatever you have to hand. Mini versions of things seems to go down really well with children.

1 Put the flour into a food processor or blender and whiz for a minute to aerate. Add the butter and whiz until the mixture resembles fine breadcrumbs.

2 Add the egg yolk (if using) and cold water, and whiz until the pastry draws together. Turn onto a floured surface and knead to form a flat round.

3 Use the pastry to line six chilled 10cm quiche tins, trim the edges and chill for 1 hour. Preheat the oven to 190°C/375°F/gas mark 5. Cover the pastry cases with greaseproof paper and baking beans and bake blind for 5 minutes. Remove the paper and beans and cook until just lightly golden (about 5 minutes). Remove from the oven and reduce the heat.

4 For the filling, heat the butter in a frying pan and soften the onion for 5 minutes. Add the courgettes and brown a little, turning frequently. Spoon into the pastry cases with the broccoli and top with the grated cheese.

5 Beat the eggs and yolk, then whisk in the milk. Pour over the filling, place the quiches on a baking tray, and bake until the centres are set and the fillings are golden and puffy (20–25 minutes). Cool slightly, then serve. Alternatively, leave to cool, wrap in foil and freeze. Thaw thoroughly, then bake at 180°C/350°F/gas mark 4 for 5 minutes. Serve. (If necessary, finely chop or mash before serving.)

chicken and mushroom broth

makes: 4 baby portions

storage: up to 3 months in the freezer

Vitamin B₁, A

1 tbsp olive oil

200g raw chicken, breast or thigh, cut into chunks

1 large onion, chopped

2 medium carrots, peeled and chopped

150g chestnut mushrooms, sliced

1 tbsp fresh herbs, eg rosemary, tarragon, parsley, finely chopped

1 tbsp tomato purée

500ml no-salt light veg stock

125g noodles, chopped

Many of the recipes in this book use herbs. If you have bought fresh herbs for a recipe and find that you do not need them all, finely chop any leftover herbs and put into ice-cube trays with a little water, then freeze. That way you won't waste them and you have handy herb cubes to add to other dishes.

1 Heat the oil in a casserole. Fry the chicken until just golden, remove with a slotted spoon and reserve. Fry the onion and carrots until soft and translucent (approximately 5 minutes). Add the mushrooms and cook over a high heat stirring often until they begin to lose their juice.

2 Add the herbs, tomato purée and vegetable stock, then return the chicken to the pan and bring to the boil. Simmer for 10 minutes, until the chicken is cooked.

3 Leave to cool. Freeze in a freezerproof container or in freezer bags.

4 To serve, thaw thoroughly and then reheat in a saucepan by simmering for at least 10 minutes, until piping hot. Add the noodles and cook for another 5 minutes. Serve, or if necessary, finely chop or mash before serving.

veggie burgers

makes: 8 baby portions

storage: up to 2 months in the freezer

Vitamin B₁, B₁₂, A

450g potatoes, peeled and cut into chunks

30g unsalted butter

200g cooked vegetables, eg carrots, courgettes, peas, leeks – all well drained

50g tinned butterbeans, rinsed, drained and mashed

2 tbsp fresh herbs, eg parsley, thyme, finely chopped

50g Cheddar cheese, grated

freshly ground black pepper

1 large free-range egg, beaten

90g dried breadcrumbs

vegetable oil, for frying

Shop-bought veggie burgers are often one of the most disappointing convenience foods. These are easy to make and freeze really well, so it's worth making a double batch.

1 Cook the potatoes in boiling water until tender (approximately 10 minutes). Drain and mash with the butter.

2 Stir in the cooked vegetables, mashed butterbeans, herbs, cheese, and pepper.

3 Using your hands (wet hands are probably easiest), form the mixture into approximately 16 balls and then flatten into patties.

4 Dip each patty in beaten egg and then into breadcrumbs, making sure each side is well-covered, then lay on a plate. Layer with greaseproof paper in a freezerproof container. Freeze.

5 To serve, thaw thoroughly on kitchen paper. Pour enough oil into a frying pan just to cover the bottom. Fry the patties over a medium heat until golden on both sides (approximately 6–8 minutes). Blot on kitchen paper and serve immediately. Serve, or if necessary, finely chop or mash before serving.

quick bites finger foods

apple and raisin toast

1 tbsp thick apple purée (page 158)
1 piece of raisin bread, toasted

Thick apple purée is great to spread on bread or toast instead of jam. Cut the toast into fingers to make it easy for little ones to eat.

rice cakes with fruit dip

5 cherries, stoned
1 tbsp thick apple purée (page 158)
2 plain unsalted rice cakes or corn cakes

Finely chop or mash the cherries and put into a bowl. Add the apple purée. Serve as a dip with the rice cakes. Babies also love eating cherries, but of course make sure you remove the stones and halve them first.

bacon and mushroom nibbles

1 rasher unsmoked streaky bacon or pancetta
4 button mushrooms
4 cocktail sticks

Remove the rind from the bacon – you don't need to with pancetta – and cut into four. Wrap each piece around a mushroom and push onto a cocktail stick. Bake in a medium oven, or grill, until the bacon is just crisp and cooked. Remove the cocktail sticks. Serve as is, or finely chop or lightly mash if necessary.

cucumber sticks with mint dip

¼ cucumber, peeled
2 tbsp natural full-fat yogurt
1 tbsp full-fat cream cheese
1–2 mint leaves, finely chopped.

Cut the cucumber into 1cm sticks. Mix the yogurt, cheese and mint together. Encourage your baby to dip the cucumber sticks into the minty yogurt to help her improve her coordination.

malt loaf with mashed bananas

¼ ripe large banana, peeled and mashed
1 slice of malt loaf

Spread the banana on the malt loaf and cut into bite-sized pieces. Malt loaf is quite high in sugar, so don't indulge them with this too often.

hot tuna toasts

**4 tbsp tinned tuna in oil,
drained and flaked
25g Cheddar cheese, grated
1 tsp natural full-fat yogurt
1 piece of wholemeal bread**

Mix the tuna, cheese and yogurt together. Spread onto the bread and cook under a medium grill until the top is golden and bubbling. Cut into finger-size pieces. Add a little finely chopped parsley or ripe avocado if you have any to hand.

fruit with prune purée

**6 ready-to-eat prunes
a little apple juice
½ ripe medium banana, peeled and
cut into chunks**

Heat the prunes in a small pan with the apple juice until they soften (approximately 5 minutes). Whiz them in a food processor or blender until smooth. Serve with chunks of banana, or any other soft fruit to dip into the purée.

soft flour tortillas with avocado

**2 tbsp full-fat cream cheese
1 soft flour tortilla
¼ ripe avocado, mashed**

Spread the cream cheese onto the tortilla, then top with the mashed avocado. Roll up the tortilla and cut into fine slices for your baby to nibble on. Add a little finely chopped fresh coriander to make it more zingy if you have some.

dried fruits with vanilla yogurt

**small handful of dried fruit, eg apple
or pear, finely chopped
50ml apple juice
2cm piece of vanilla pod
100ml natural full-fat yogurt**

Put the fruit to soak in the apple juice for at least half an hour. Slice the piece of vanilla pod in half, scrape the seeds into the yogurt and mix well. Mix the dried fruit into the yogurt and serve.

cottage cheese and pineapple

**3 tbsp full-fat cottage cheese
1-2 mint leaves, finely chopped
100g fresh pineapple, peeled and
cut into big chunks**

Mash the cottage cheese really well with the mint. Serve as a dip with the pineapple. You can leave the mint out and add a little crumbled cooked bacon or chicken instead if you prefer.

steamed vegetables with cottage cheese

**3 tbsp full-fat cottage cheese
1 tsp fresh parsley, finely chopped
handful of steamed vegetable sticks
eg carrots, courgettes, asparagus**

Mash the cottage cheese with the parsley and serve as a dip with the steamed vegetables. You could serve the vegetables with hummus instead of the cheese.

All quick bites make 1 portion
unless otherwise stated.

quick bites
snacks

 ½ ½ 9½

Vitamin B₁₂

pasta with pesto and tuna

75g cooked pasta
1 tsp pesto
30g tinned tuna in oil, drained and flaked

Mix everything together while the pasta is still hot. Serve as is or finely chop before serving. This works just as well with chopped cooked chicken instead of the tuna.

2½ C ½ 1 1 4½

cheesy peas

2 tbsp full-fat cream cheese
100g frozen peas, freshly cooked

Add the cream cheese to the peas while they are still hot, mash slightly, and stir well. Add some chopped fresh herbs, such as parsley, if you have any.

½ C ½ 1 1 3½

cream cheese and beetroot soldiers

1 tbsp full-fat cream cheese
1 piece of wholemeal bread
50g cooked beetroot, finely chopped

Spread the cream cheese on the bread and top with the beetroot. To serve, cut into little soldiers.

 1 2 ½ 16½

coronation chicken

75g cooked chicken, finely chopped
2 tbsp natural full-fat yogurt
1 tsp mango chutney, chopped

Mix all the ingredients together and serve with 50g cooked, cooled rice or pasta. Serve as is or cut up before serving if necessary.

 3 2 1½ 10

Vitamin B₁₂

sardines on toast

1 piece of brown toast
knob of unsalted butter
2 tinned boned sardines, mashed
freshly ground black pepper

Spread the toast with the butter and top with the mashed sardines. Grill until hot through and slice before serving with a pinch of ground black pepper.

1½ C ½ 1

apricots with cream cheese

4 dried apricots
50ml apple juice
1 tbsp full-fat cream cheese

Leave the apricots to soak in the apple juice for at least half an hour. Finely chop the apricots and mix with the cream cheese. You can add a little ground cinnamon to the cream cheese to make it more interesting.

tarragon chicken with wholemeal bread

75g cooked chicken, finely chopped
2 tbsp natural full-fat yogurt
pinch of fresh tarragon, finely chopped
1 slice of wholemeal bread, chopped
1 ripe tomato, finely chopped

Mix the finely chopped chicken with the yogurt and fresh tarragon and stir well. Serve with the small pieces of fresh bread and finely chopped ripe tomato.

bagels with ham and mozzarella

½ bagel
50g cooked ham, chopped
50g full-fat mozzarella cheese, grated
ripe avocado, peeled and mashed

Toast the bagel, top with the ham and cheese, then grill until the mozzarella is bubbling and golden. Slice before serving with some mashed avocado.

pasta with creamy tomato sauce

50ml tomato passata
75g pasta, freshly cooked
1 tbsp full-fat cream cheese

Heat the tomato passata in a pan, add the pasta, and stir well until heated through. Add the cream cheese. If necessary, finely chop before serving.

courgette and cottage cheese

1 small courgette, grated
1 tbsp olive oil, for frying
50g full-fat cottage cheese
freshly ground black pepper
1 tsp parsley, finely chopped

Fry the courgette in the oil until just cooked. Stir in the cottage cheese. Add some freshly ground black pepper and the finely chopped parsley, and serve with pieces of brown bread.

Vitamin B₁

couscous with ham and tomato

50g couscous, cooked
30g cooked ham, chopped
1 tomato, finely chopped
freshly ground black pepper
1 tsp fresh herbs, eg parsley, finely chopped

Mix the couscous, ham and tomato together, then season with freshly ground black pepper and finely chopped herbs. Finely chop before serving.

Vitamin B₁

pasta with courgette and bacon

75g pasta, freshly cooked
50g courgette, cooked and grated
5 tbsp tomato passata
1 rasher unsmoked streaky bacon,
rind removed, cooked and finely chopped

Mix all the ingredients together in the pan that the pasta was cooked in and heat gently until the sauce is hot. Serve as is or finely chop before serving.

All quick bites make 1 portion
unless otherwise stated.

fresh puddings

cocoa rice pudding

makes: 5 baby portions or 1 baby portion and 2 adult portions

storage: rice should never be reheated, but can be served cold up to 24 hours after cooking

3½

½

½

½

Vitamin B₁₂

1+

250ml full-fat milk or soya drink

250ml coconut milk

100ml water

2 tsp good cocoa powder

2 tsp golden caster sugar (or preferably omit)

½ tsp vanilla extract

150g short-grain pudding rice

little knob of unsalted butter

There are many variations of this recipe – why not try making a plain vanilla rice pudding, by omitting the cocoa and adding a split vanilla pod with the milk and water, and then swirling in some apple or banana purée? Do not serve coconut to babies if there is a family history of allergies.

1 Put the milk, coconut milk and water into a saucepan and bring the mixture up to the boil.

2 Put the cocoa in a bowl with the sugar (if using) and vanilla extract. Pour the hot milk over the cocoa mixture, stirring constantly. Pour back into the saucepan.

3 Add the rice and bring back to the boil. Reduce the heat and simmer for 15 to 20 minutes, stirring often to prevent the mixture from sticking on the bottom of the pan.

4 If necessary, add a few tablespoons of water in order to loosen the mixture a little.

5 Add butter, mix well and cook for 1 more minute.

tropical fruits with raspberry sauce

makes: 2 baby portions

storage: up to 24 hours in the refrigerator

1

½ ripe medium papaya

¼ small ripe melon

4 tbsp fresh orange juice

100g raspberries

Note: babies develop at different rates; do not feed chopped food to your baby until she is confident with chewing.

This is a brilliant way to encourage babies to eat fruit – not that most need much encouragement. You can make this quick and simple sauce out of lots of soft fruits; try strawberries or blueberries instead of raspberries.

1 Scoop the seeds out of the papaya and peel and cut the flesh into very small pieces. Peel the melon, removing any pips, and cut into very small pieces.

2 Put the papaya and melon into a bowl with 2 tbsp orange juice and mix gently.

3 Push the raspberries through a nylon sieve, scraping the bottom well. Mix with the remaining orange juice.

4 Serve half the fruit in a small bowl with half the raspberry sauce drizzled over it. Mash the fruits a little if your baby will find it easier.

raspberry and mango soup

½
½
9½ **C**
☑
Vitamin A
1+

makes: 3 baby portions or 1 baby portion and 1 adult portion

storage: up to 24 hours in the refrigerator

200g raspberries
100ml fresh orange juice
1 ripe mango

My girls love eating smoothies with spoons, so this seemed a logical progression. Don't make this soup too thin, or else dinner time will turn out to be a pretty messy experience! As with many fruity desserts, the ingredients in this are pretty interchangeable – just use whatever is in season.

1 Whiz the raspberries and orange juice in a hand-held blender (or food processor or blender) until smooth.
2 Slice the mango down either side of the stone and peel the skin from the flesh. Cut the mango into small pieces, then mash with a fork until it is just lumpy. Mix in the raspberry purée.

fruit trifle

3½
½
½
1
5 **C**
1+

makes: 3 baby portions or 1 baby portion and 1 adult portion

storage: up to 24 hours in the refrigerator

200g mixed soft fruit,
  eg raspberries, strawberries,
  blueberries, fresh or frozen
2 tbsp fresh orange juice
4 sponge fingers
150ml natural full-fat yogurt

This is really quick and easy. If you have any leftover muffin or fruit loaf you can use that instead of sponge fingers. Equally, you can use banana custard (see page 193) instead of yogurt.

1 Put the fruit and orange juice in a pan and heat gently until the fruits begin to burst. Lightly mash.
2 Arrange the sponge fingers in a small dish and spoon over three-quarters of the warm fruit. Leave to soak for at least 30 minutes. Lightly mash if necessary.
3 Gently swirl the remaining fruit through the yogurt and pour over the fruits and sponge to serve.

vanilla pears

makes 3–4 baby portions or 1 baby portion and 1 adult portion

storage up to 24 hours in the refrigerator

2 ripe pears, eg Williams
1 tsp soft brown sugar
1 tbsp lemon juice
1 vanilla pod, sliced
   lengthways (optional)
small knob of unsalted
   butter
natural full-fat yogurt,
   to serve

This is a really delicious wintry pudding, especially if you add a little pinch of ground ginger. If you have any left over, it's also very good cold served with yogurt or muesli for breakfast.

1 Preheat the oven to 180°C/350°F/gas mark 4.
2 Peel the pears with a sharp knife or peeler and then core them before cutting them into thin slices.
3 Put the pears in an ovenproof dish and then toss them with the sugar, lemon juice, vanilla pod and butter.
4 Bake the pears for approximately 20 minutes, basting occasionally, until tender and golden.
5 Remove the vanilla pod and serve as is, or finely chop or mash the pears before serving, if necessary.

baked bananas with raspberries

makes: 1 baby portion
storage: best eaten fresh

1 medium ripe banana
handful of raspberries
   (optional)
pinch of ground cinnamon
   (optional)
3 tbsp fresh orange juice

Bananas are always popular with babies. Baking intensifies their flavour and makes them even more irresistible. Bananas can be baked whole, in their skins; just cook them on a baking tray and let them cool before opening. They are also great mashed with natural full-fat yogurt.

1 Preheat the oven to 180°C/350°F/gas mark 4.
2 Lightly butter an ovenproof dish.
3 Peel the banana and slice in half lengthways.
4 Put the banana into the dish and sprinkle with the raspberries and cinnamon, if using. Pour over the orange juice.
5 Bake in the oven for 20 minutes, until soft. Cool slightly and serve, or finely chop or mash before serving.

quick bites
puddings

fruit with cinnamon cream cheese

small selection of soft fruit, eg banana,
¼ mango, ¼ peach
20g full-fat cream cheese
pinch of ground cinnamon

Peel the banana and mango. Beat the cream cheese with the cinnamon until smooth. Cut the fruit into slices and serve with the cheese as a dip or, if your baby is less confident with chewing, finely chop the fruit and mix into the cheese.

banana baked with apricots

½ small ripe banana, peeled
2–3 tinned apricot halves
small knob of unsalted butter

Put the fruit into a small baking dish and dot with the butter. Cover with foil and bake in a preheated oven at 180°C/350°F/gas mark 4 until the fruit is soft. Leave to cool. Mash lightly before serving.

autumn rice pudding

½ small ripe pear, peeled, cored and chopped
pinch of ground cinnamon
100g rice pudding (page 182)

Simmer the pear in 2 tbsp water until soft. Stir the pear and cinnamon into the rice pudding just before serving.

rice pudding with dried fruit purée

30g dried fruits, eg raisins, dates and prunes, finely chopped
50ml apple juice
100g rice pudding (page 232)

Heat the dried fruit and apple juice together in a pan for 5–10 minutes, then leave to stand for at least 10 minutes. Beat into a purée. Stir into the rice pudding just before serving.

baked almond peach

1 ripe peach, halved and stoned
1 tbsp ground almonds
small knob of unsalted butter

Put the peach in a roasting dish, sprinkle with ground almonds and dot with butter. Bake in a medium oven until soft and golden (5 minutes). Serve as is or finely chop then serve. Do not feed nuts to babies if there is any family history of allergies.

Vitamin B$_{12}$

nutty fruit yogurt

1 tbsp dried fruits, eg dates, raisins and apricots, finely chopped
100g natural full-fat yogurt
1 tbsp ground nuts

Heat the dried fruit in a pan with 1–2 tbsp water for 5–10 minutes, then leave to stand for at least 10 minutes. Beat into a purée. Mix all the ingredients together and leave to sit for 5 minutes. Do not feed nuts to babies if there is any family history of allergies.

strawberries with passionfruit

12 C ½

75g strawberries, hulled
1 passionfruit

Roughly mash the strawberries. Cut the passionfruit in half and scrape the flesh out over the strawberries.

apple and cheddar crackers

½ C 2 1 ½ 6

4 tbsp apple purée (page 158)
30g Cheddar cheese, finely diced
1–2 oat crackers

Serve the apple purée and cheese dice with the crackers. Only serve this to babies who are very confident with chewing. Alternatively, serve large pieces of cheese and apple with crackers.

apple purée with raisin toast

1 C ½ ½ 2½

1 slice of raisin bread, lightly toasted
60g natural full-fat yogurt
4 tbsp apple purée (page 158)

Break up the toast into tiny pieces and stir into the yogurt. Leave to soak for a few minutes, then swirl through the apple purée.

raisin bread with stewed fruit

 1 C

Vitamin B₁, B₁₂, A

1 slice of raisin bread
50ml full-fat milk
50g stewed fruit, eg plums

Tear the bread into tiny pieces and leave to soak in the milk for a few minutes. Stir the stewed plums into the mixture just before serving. Mash if necessary.

melon with passionfruit yogurt

3 C 1 ½ 2½

1 passionfruit, halved
50g natural full-fat yogurt
75g fresh ripe melon, cut into large pieces

Mix the passionfruit flesh into the yogurt. Serve the mixture as a dip with the melon fingers.

baby muesli bar with yogurt

 1 1½ 1 6

Vitamin B₁

1 baby muesli bar
50g natural full-fat yogurt

Break tiny pieces of the muesli bar into the yogurt. Alternatively, serve the muesli bar whole with a small pot of yogurt. If you like, add a few drops of vanilla extract.

All quick bites make 1 portion
unless otherwise stated.

puddings to freeze

berry sponge

makes: 10 baby portions

storage: up to 3 months in the freezer

125g unsalted butter, softened
75g golden caster sugar
2 eggs, lightly beaten
2 drops of vanilla extract
125g self-raising flour
175g mixed berries, eg blueberries, raspberries, cherries (stoned), fresh or frozen

If you can't get hold of any fresh berries, use a bag of the frozen forest fruits or summer berries instead. You can add the berries to the sponge mixture while they are still frozen.

1 Preheat the oven to 180°C/350°F/gas mark 4. Grease a deep 20cm round or square cake tin.
2 Beat together the butter and sugar until soft and fluffy. Gradually add the eggs, beating well. You may need to add a little flour to stop the mixture from curdling.
3 Beat in the vanilla extract, then fold in the flour. Add the berries and gently stir to mix through.
4 Spoon the mixture into the prepared tin. Bake for 25–30 minutes, until golden on top and spongy to touch.
5 Leave to cool in the tin for a few minutes before transferring to a cooling rack.
6 When cool, wrap up in foil and freeze or cut into slices and freeze individually.
7 Defrost thoroughly and serve or, if necessary, finely chop and serve.

banana and apple crumble

makes: 6 baby portions

storage: up to 3 months in the freezer

Vitamin B₁

3 medium cooking apples
juice and zest of 1 orange
1 tsp soft brown sugar
100g plain flour
50g unsalted butter
50g porridge oats
2 tsp golden caster sugar
pinch of ground cinnamon
2 small ripe bananas, peeled and finely chopped

Note: do not feed chopped food to your baby until she is confident with chewing.

Any fruits can be used in crumbles. Using bananas means that you can keep the amount of added sugar to a minimum, which is definitely no bad thing.

1 Peel, core and thinly slice the apples. Put them into a pan with the orange juice, zest and brown sugar. Heat gently until the apples are slightly soft – approximately 10 minutes.
2 Sieve the flour into a bowl and rub in the butter until the mixture resembles breadcrumbs. Stir in the oats, caster sugar, and cinnamon.
3 Put the fruit into a dish or into small ramekins and sprinkle over the crumble mixture.
4 Leave to cool, wrap in clingfilm or foil and freeze.
5 Thaw thoroughly. Preheat the oven to 180°C/350°F/gas mark 4. Bake in the oven for 25 minutes, until the crumble is crisp and golden.
6 Serve as is or, if necessary, finely chop and serve.

apple flapjacks

makes: 15 baby portions

storage: up to 3 months in the freezer

125g unsalted butter
75g soft brown sugar
2 tbsp golden syrup
350g porridge oats
½ tsp baking powder
2 eating apples, peeled, cored and grated
50g hazelnuts, toasted and ground

These are great flapjacks because they are soft, moist and slightly crumbly, rather than hard and chewy, which can be too much for many babies. The apple gives a natural sweetness so these flapjacks are not as sugar-laden as many shop-bought ones. Do not feed nuts to babies if there is any family history of allergies.

1 Preheat the oven to 180°C/350°F/gas mark 4. Grease a 23cm x 33cm Swiss roll tin.
2 Melt the butter, sugar and golden syrup together in a large saucepan over a low heat.
3 In a bowl, mix together the oats, baking powder, apples and ground hazelnuts, stirring well. Then add to the butter mixture and mix together.
4 Tip into the tin and flatten the surface. Bake for 20 minutes, until the edges are just beginning to turn golden. Cut into squares while still warm and leave to cool in the tin.
5 Layer with greaseproof paper and store in freezer bags. Freeze.
6 To serve, thaw thoroughly.

scones

makes: 8 baby portions

storage: up to 3 months in the freezer

225g self-raising flour
1 tbsp sugar
1 level tsp baking powder
50g butter
100ml milk, plus a little extra for brushing

This recipe makes eight standard-sized scones, but if you think your baby will only manage half a scone, just make them smaller!

1 Preheat the oven to 230°C/450°F/gas mark 8. Sieve the flour, sugar and baking powder into a bowl and then rub in the butter until the mixture resembles breadcrumbs.
2 Make a well in the centre, stir in the milk and bring together to form a soft dough.
3 Turn the mixture out onto a floured surface and knead very lightly. Roll out until about 2cm thick. Cut out eight rounds with a cutter.
4 Put the scones onto a baking sheet and brush with milk. Bake for 8–10 minutes, until golden brown and well-risen.
5 Leave to cool, freeze in an airtight container.
6 To serve, thaw thoroughly.

banana custard

Bananas are a perennially popular food for babies, although you can try this recipe with mango instead of banana if you prefer.

½

Vitamin B₁₂

1+

makes: 10 baby portions

storage: up to 3 months in the freezer

200ml full-fat milk or
  calcium-enriched soya drink
1 vanilla pod, split
  lengthways
3 large free-range egg yolks
1 tsp golden caster sugar
1 tbsp cornflour
2 medium ripe bananas
100g natural Greek yogurt

1 To make the custard, heat the milk with the vanilla pod in a saucepan until just below boiling point. Remove from heat and take out the vanilla pod.

2 In a bowl, mix the egg yolks, sugar and cornflour together. Pour the hot milk over the egg mixture, stirring constantly until smooth.

3 Return to the saucepan and heat, stirring constantly, until the mixture thickens. Do not allow it to boil or it will curdle.

4 Once the custard has thickened, leave it to cool.

5 Meanwhile, purée the bananas and yogurt together in a bowl with a hand-held blender (or in a food processor or blender). Gently fold together the cooled custard and banana mixture. Remove the vanilla pod.

6 Spoon the purée into ice-cube trays. Cover with foil or put into a freezer bag and seal. Freeze for at least four hours, until frozen. Transfer to freezer bags and return to the freezer.

7 To serve, thaw thoroughly. Heat gently until warm.

stewed plums

The plums must be ripe for this to be tasty without you having to add too much sugar. These stewed plums are great added to yogurt for a quick pudding, used as the base for a crumble, or even added to cereals for either pudding or breakfast.

½

3 C

makes: 4 baby portions or 2 baby portions and 1 adult portion

storage: up to 3 months in the freezer

12 ripe plums
juice of 2 oranges
pinch of ground cinnamon
1–2 tsp soft brown sugar
  (optional – add to taste)

1 Cut the plums in half, remove the stones and slice. Put the fruit into a saucepan, then add the orange juice and cinnamon.

2 Bring up to the boil, reduce the heat and simmer gently for 5–8 minutes, depending on the plums' ripeness, until they are lovely and soft in a sweet syrup. Add a little sugar if they are too tart.

3 Spoon the plums into ice-cube trays. Cover with foil or put into a freezer bag and seal. Freeze. When frozen, transfer to freezer bags and return to the freezer.

4 Thaw thoroughly. Heat the plums gently until warm then serve as is, or lightly mash if necessary.

During his second year, you will really begin to
notice how fast your toddler is developing. One of
the best things about his new-found self-awareness
is that he will share experiences with you as he
learns to gesture, talk and walk. This is often most
obvious at mealtimes where, as he becomes more
confident about feeding himself, he will begin to
express his likes and dislikes. Although this can be
challenging at times, you can help him to become
more sociable and to have an appreciation of good
food by feeding him at the same time as the rest of
the family eats. Most of the recipes in this book are
both family- and toddler-friendly, making it easy to
prepare the same meal for everyone.

1-2
years

what's happening to
your toddler

At this stage your toddler will be developing at an amazing rate. He will learn new things, however small, every day. For example, he will be constantly learning new words and by 18 months he will be able to say around 20 words, but will understand many more. It can be a challenging time for you as he becomes able to do more and more things for himself.

Your child will have been growing astonishingly fast, but at one to two years growth will level off to about 5–15cm per year, and he will gain approximately 25–50g in weight a week. (Your health professional will keep a check on this.) He will look more in proportion and 'adult'. As his first-year growth spurt diminishes, you may also notice a natural waning of his appetite at around 18 months. This is often combined with a new level of self-awareness – he will begin to express preferences and willful behaviour. However, he will find saying 'no', especially when he is able to feed himself, an important way to assert his independence.

This behaviour is most common at mealtimes and it can sometimes seem like he is barely eating enough to keep a sparrow alive! However, your toddler will also be becoming more and more active, particularly as he learns to walk, scramble up and down stairs and kick a ball. So energy-rich foods should be given at mealtimes and as little snacks. Because his appetite may be small, it is also vital to ensure that in the average week you have offered a wide range of foods, containing all the essential nutrients (*see* pages 12–27).

One of the delights of toddlerhood is being able to share experiences, as he learns to gesture and talk. This applies particularly to food because he can express likes or dislikes. Similarly, you can help to instil in him an interest in good food – this is especially important as eating requires him to sit still for more than two minutes! Make meals more relaxing by letting him learn to feed himself with his fingers or a spoon. At first, this may be a bit hit and miss, so it is a good idea to continue feeding him too until his co-ordination improves. Give him small portions in a shallow bowl; this is easier and more satisfying because he can finish them and ask for more.

A balanced diet will ensure that your toddler is getting all the nutrients he needs for healthy growth and development. This simply means a diet in which different amounts of a wide variety of foods from the five main food groups are eaten at different meals. The five main food groups are: bread, cereals and potatoes; fruit and vegetables; meat, fish and alternatives, such as tofu; foods containing fats and foods containing sugar; milk and dairy produce. A varied diet is essential because no single food provides all the nutrients your toddler needs, and it will also make mealtimes more interesting.

Just as adults have different nutritional needs at different stages of their lives, certain nutrients play a more central role in the diet as your toddler grows older. In particular, he will need plenty of energy. Energy-rich food should be given at breakfast time – slow-releasing carbohydrates, such as porridge with fresh fruit, are ideal because they will give your toddler a steady flow of energy until his next snack or meal. Healthy snacks make great energy boosters, but many processed, convenience foods, such as biscuits and crisps, only give short bursts of energy, often followed by a low in the form of a mood swing. The best way to ensure that your toddler is getting enough energy is to give him a good mix of protein, fat and carbohydrates throughout the day.

Protein is vital in toddlers' diets, as their bodies use it as building bricks for growth. Poultry, meat, fish, small amounts of dairy products and eggs are good sources of protein, but remember – whether your toddler is vegetarian or not – a mixture of beans, pulses, tofu, chopped nuts and grains will also provide a good source of protein. (Do not give nuts to toddlers under the age of three if there is any family history of food allergies.)

Your toddler may be vulnerable to iron deficiency during this year, which may cause anaemia. A toddler weaned on a broad range of foods is unlikely to be iron deficient (*see* pages 18–19).

which nutrients
are key

your toddler's
routine

your toddler's feeds

During your baby's first year, it is likely that you will have established a good feeding routine. This needs to be continued during toddlerhood. Your toddler will be far more secure and confident about food if he knows he will be given meals regularly. Most toddlers are very active and need energy to avoid becoming over-tired and over-hungry, which, as every parent knows, can lead to fussy eating. Remember that a drink or snack given just before a meal is likely to spoil your toddler's appetite. However, it is important for him to have a drink with his food; try to encourage him to drink water.

I follow the routine below my three children, making allowances for illnesses or holidays and I find that it works for all of us.

breakfast – around 7.30–8am
mid-morning snack – around 10am
lunch – around 12.30–1pm
mid-afternoon snack – around 3pm
supper – 5–5.30pm
bed – 7–7.30pm

your toddler's sleeps

At the age of 1, most toddlers are still having two sleeps during the day. During their second year this becomes less necessary, usually at around 15 months. Look out for signs that he does not want to sleep for as long as usual: it may take you longer to settle him for a day-time sleep, or he may wake up after only a short nap instead of the usual hour or so. With both of my girls it gradually became harder to settle them at night and they were waking up noticeably earlier in the morning. It is best to cut out one sleep at this stage because a sleep of up to an hour and a half, preferably after lunch, will be enough to recharge his batteries without affecting his night-time sleeps. Just make sure that he is awake before the middle of the afternoon so that he is still tired at bedtime.

refusing to eat

The best thing you can do if your child refuses to eat his meal is not to get uptight about it. Whatever happens, try not to put any pressure on him to eat; just remove the plate and do not offer anything else until the next meal. The worst thing that you can do is to force the issue, become over-anxious or offer an alternative. Toddlers pick up on this and can become uptight about eating. If he is hungry by the next meal, he should eat the food.

how long a toddler can go without food

At one to two years it is quite normal for your toddler's appetite to decrease as growth slows down. Often a baby between 6 months and 1 year will eat as much, and sometimes more, than a 2 year old. A toddler may go for a couple of days eating very little, but then make up for it by eating more later that week. A healthy child will not starve himself. However, it is important to make sure your child is eating a sensible amount to ensure he gets the nutrients he needs. If your toddler's appetite seems to have decreased dramatically and does not pick up over the week, contact your family doctor or state-registered dietician.

is good nutrition really important?

If a toddler does not eat a balanced diet, providing all the nutrients that he needs, he is less likely to achieve his potential in terms of growth, brain development, energy levels and moods. A poor diet may also have implications for his longer-term health. If your toddler will only eat a small range of foods and you suspect that he might not be getting a nutritionally balanced diet, try keeping a diary of what he eats and drinks for about two weeks. This may be a particularly useful exercise if your toddler eats away from home, for example, at a nursery or a relative's house. You may be pleasantly surprised by the true variety of his diet. If you are concerned about how to keep and make use of such a diary, talk to a state-registered dietician.

trouble shooting

sample meal planners

Toddlers in this age group are increasingly active, and need plenty of energy-rich foods, particularly at breakfast. Toddlers over one year old need a minimum of 350ml full-fat milk per day, inclusive of milk used in food; most toddlers need up to 565ml, with about 350ml of that being given as a drink. Snacks are important to this age group, but try to give your toddler fresh food rather than shop-bought convenience products – a little fruit is fine.

	breakfast	mid-am	lunch	mid-pm	supper	bed
menu 1	150ml milk, bacon and parsley bread, drink	grapes filled with cream cheese, drink	minty chicken with vegetables, filo parcels, drink	pieces of fresh fruit, drink	baked rice with squash, baked custard, drink	200ml milk
menu 2	150ml milk, apple, pear and banana smoothie, drink	pieces of fresh fruit, drink	herb scones, drink	warm pitta bread with peanut dip, drink	cheesy pasta bake, drink	200ml milk
menu 3	150ml milk, grated apple honey and bread, drink	drink	buttered peas with spaghetti, drink	pieces of fresh fruit, drink	pineapple and ham pizza, drink	200ml milk
menu 4	150ml milk, bacon and egg scramble, drink	grapes, drink	couscous with salad and tuna, drink	bread sticks with dips, drink	jacket potato with coleslaw, almond rice, drink	200ml milk
menu 5	150ml milk, eggy raisin bread, drink	pieces of fresh fruit, drink	avocado and cream cheese dip, drink	pieces of banana, drink	minty mash with grilled lamb, rice pudding with pears, drink	200ml milk
menu 6	Ready Brek with prunes, drink	pieces of peeled pear, drink	creamy tomato soup, drink	yogurt with dried fruit compote, drink	baked chicken with rice, drink	200ml milk

	breakfast	mid-am	lunch	mid-pm	supper	bed
menu 7	150ml milk, ham omelette, drink	raisin toast with apple purée, drink	carrot and cheese sandwich, drink	pieces of peeled pear, drink	new potatoes wrapped in bacon, apple pie, drink	200ml milk
menu 8	150ml milk, raspberry muffins, drink	rice cakes with nut butter, drink	rice with chicken and bacon, drink	pieces of peeled pear, drink	tuna, butter beans, tomato and lettuce, rhubarb crisp with custard, drink	200ml milk
menu 9	150ml milk, mango and banana smoothie, drink	pieces of fresh fruit, drink	lamb kebabs with mango, drink	corn thins with avocado, drink	moussaka stuffed aubergine, fruit jelly with fresh fruits, drink	200ml milk
menu 10	150ml milk, porridge, drink	pieces of fresh fruit, drink	tuna and pesto baked potatoes, strawberries and mango toasted oats, drink	pieces of fresh fruit, drink	sausage and apple pastry, drink	200ml milk
menu 11	150ml milk, bagel with cream cheese and apricot, drink	segments of satsuma, drink	pesto chicken, drink	pieces of banana, drink	lasagne, drink	200ml milk
menu 12	150ml milk, scrambled eggs with Cheddar cheese, drink	pieces of fresh fruit, drink	bubble and squeak, drink	pinwheel sandwiches, drink	pumpkin stew, pear and sesame yogurt, drink	200ml milk
menu 13	150ml milk, bacon and cheese on toast, drink	pieces of peeled pear, drink	lamb with a minty sauce, drink	drink	quick sausage and beans, drink	200ml milk
menu 14	150ml milk, yogurt with dried fruit compote, drink	drink	rich mushroom stew, drink	drink	plaice with a tomato sauce, berry compote with yogurt, drink	200ml milk

fresh breakfasts

bacon and parsley bread

makes: 10 toddler portions (approx 1kg loaf)

storage: best eaten fresh or keep in an airtight container for up to 3 days

400g plain white flour
400g wholemeal flour
100g Cheddar cheese, grated
6 rashers unsmoked back bacon (rind removed), grilled and finely chopped
25g sesame seeds (do not give seeds to toddlers under the age of three if there is a family history of food allergies)
handful of fresh parsley, chopped
approx 360ml warm water
1 tsp golden caster sugar
6g (1½ level tsp) dried yeast

vitamins B₁, B₆ – phosphorous

This is brilliant for breakfast with scrambled eggs, but is also lovely to use for eggy bread or sandwiches.

1 Grease a 1kg loaf tin with butter. Sift the white and wholemeal flour into a large bowl and mix in the cheese, bacon, sesame seeds and parsley.
2 Put 100ml of the warm water into a measuring jug, stir in the sugar and yeast and leave for 10–15 minutes, until a froth has formed.
3 Make a well in the flour mixture and pour in the yeast mixture. Mix with a wooden spoon, gradually adding the rest of the warm water. Use your hands to mix it, adding a little more warm water if necessary, until you have a smooth dough that comes away from the edges of the bowl.
4 On a floured surface, knead the dough briefly for 3–4 minutes until it is smooth and soft. Shape into an oblong and drop into the prepared tin. Sprinkle the surface with flour, cover with a warm damp cloth and leave to rise in a warm place for 30–40 minutes. Preheat the oven to 200°C/400°F/gas mark 6.
5 Bake the bread for 40 minutes, then remove from the tin and bake upside down on the shelf for 10–15 minutes to crisp up. When it is cooked, it will sound hollow when the bottom is tapped. Leave to cool on a wire rack.
6 Cut into thin slices, chop up each slice and serve.

mango and banana smoothie

makes: 6 toddler portions

storage: best eaten fresh or keep in the refrigerator for up to 24 hours

vitamin B₆

1 ripe medium mango
2 passionfruit
250ml orange juice
1 ripe small banana, roughly chopped

If you like, try adding a little full-fat natural yogurt for a creamier taste. Serve with toast or cereal.

1 Peel the mango and cut the flesh away from the stone. Put into a food processor or blender.
2 Cut the passionfruit in half and scoop the seeds straight into the blender. Add the orange juice and banana and whiz until smooth.

raspberry muffins

Make these with any soft fruits that you have to hand. Muffins are really easy to make so, if you have an older toddler, get him to help with the preparation of these.

2½

½

1 C

vitamin B₁₂

makes: 9 toddler portions (9 mini muffins)

storage: best eaten fresh or keep in an airtight container for up to 2 days or in the freezer for up to 3 months

185g plain flour
1½ tsp baking powder
80g golden caster sugar
1 medium egg
125ml full-fat milk
½ tsp vanilla extract
45g unsalted butter, melted
150g raspberries, fresh or frozen

1 Preheat the oven 200°C/400°F/gas mark 6. Butter a mini-muffin tray or line with paper cases.
2 Sift the flour into a bowl with the baking powder. Stir in the sugar.
3 In a separate bowl, whisk the egg, milk, vanilla and melted butter together.
4 Make a well in the centre of the dry ingredients. Pour in the milk mixture and mix gently until you have a wet, lumpy batter. Stir in the raspberries.
5 Spoon the batter into the muffin cases and bake in the hot oven for 10–12 minutes, until risen and golden. Cool on a wire rack.
6 If necessary, cut into smaller pieces before serving.

porridge

There are so many ways to jazz up plain porridge, you may like to try adding something to the mix before cooking, such as half a vanilla pod, split lengthways, for a creamy vanilla porridge (remove pod before serving). Alternatively, add one of the following to a bowl of porridge before serving: 1 tbsp puréed dried fruit such as prunes or apricots; half a ripe small banana, mashed; 1 tsp soft brown sugar or runny honey.

7½

1½

2

2

½ C

vitamins B₁, B₂, B₁₂, B₆
– phosphorous

makes: 2 toddler portions

storage: best eaten fresh or keep in the refrigerator for up to 24 hours

350ml full-fat milk or calcium-enriched soya drink
100g porridge oats

1 Put all the ingredients into a heavy-based saucepan and gently simmer for 5–10 minutes, stirring often, until the mixture has thickened.
2 Add a little more milk, soya drink or cooled, boiled water to thin if necessary.

bacon and egg scramble

makes: 2 toddler portions

storage: best eaten fresh

small knob of unsalted
  butter
4 rashers unsmoked streaky
  bacon (rind removed), very
  finely chopped
3 medium eggs
4 tbsp full-fat milk
1 tbsp fresh parsley, finely
  chopped (optional)
freshly ground black pepper

vitamins B₁, B₆
– phosphorous

12

1

2

½

This is a quick and easy way to make scrambled eggs a bit more interesting –
especially if you add a little parsley, which toddlers seem to love. You could
use back bacon for this, but it's best to avoid smoked bacon, which can be
too salty for toddlers.

1　Melt the butter in a heavy-based frying pan and fry the bacon until crisp and
   golden, approximately 5–10 minutes.
2　Meanwhile, whisk together in a bowl the eggs, milk, parsley and a little
   freshly ground black pepper.
3　Pour off the fat from the bacon pan.
4　Place the pan with the bacon bits over a gentle heat. Add the egg mixture
   and cook, stirring, until the eggs are scrambled and cooked through.
   Serve immediately.

eggy raisin bread

makes: 2 toddler portions

storage: best eaten fresh

1 tsp soft brown sugar
1 medium egg, slightly
  beaten
1 tbsp full-fat milk
few drops of vanilla extract
2 slices of fruit bread
small knob of unsalted
  butter, plus a little extra
  for greasing

vitamin B₁₂

4

½

½

½

This is an easy way to add a little extra protein to your toddler's diet. You
could just as easily make this without the sugar and use a savoury bread
instead of fruit bread.

1　Put the sugar, egg, milk and vanilla in a bowl and whisk together. Cut each
   slice of fruit bread into 4 triangles.
2　Heat a frying pan over a medium heat and grease with a little butter. Dip
   2 triangles of bread into the egg mixture and put into the hot frying pan.
3　Cook for 2 minutes on each side until golden and the egg is cooked through.
   Repeat with the remaining bread. Serve immediately. If necessary, cut into
   smaller pieces before serving.

quick bites breakfasts

Often it is a challenge to get everyone ready in the mornings, so quick breakfast ideas are essential.

All of the recipes make one toddler portion unless stated otherwise.

vitamins A, B₂, B₁₂, B₆ –
phosphorus

ham omelette

1 medium egg
small knob of unsalted butter
1 tsp olive oil
1 slice of cooked ham, finely chopped

Break the egg into a bowl and lightly whisk. Melt the butter and oil in a frying pan over a medium heat. Swirl the fat around the pan, then pour in the egg to cover the base of the pan. Using a wooden spoon, draw the edges of the omelette into the centre. When the omelette is cooked and there is no runny egg left in the pan, sprinkle over the ham and fold the omelette in half, then slide onto a plate. Chop into small pieces and serve. Try adding grated cheese, finely chopped cooked bacon, finely chopped herbs or finely chopped tomato.

Ready Brek with prunes

3 ready-to-eat prunes
75ml apple juice
30g Ready Brek
125ml full-fat milk

Prunes are high in fibre and minerals, particularly potassium and iron. Put the prunes into a bowl, add the apple juice and leave to soak for 10 minutes, then purée. Prepare the Ready Brek following the packet's instructions, using the full-fat milk. Swirl the puréed prunes through the Ready Brek.

vitamins B₁, B₆ –
phosphorous

bacon and cheese on toast

2 rashers unsmoked streaky bacon, rind removed
1 slice of white bread
15g Cheddar cheese, grated

Preheat the grill. Grill the bacon until cooked and slightly crisp. Cut into very small pieces. Grill the bread on one side, then scatter the bacon over the uncooked side. Top with the grated cheese and grill until slightly golden and bubbling. Cut into small pieces and serve.

vitamin B₆

apple, pear and banana smoothie

makes: 2 portions
1 eating apple, eg Cox's, peeled, cored and chopped
1 ripe pear, peeled, cored and chopped
1 ripe medium banana, chopped, or 2 ripe stoned plums, chopped
200ml apple juice

Put all of the ingredients into a jug and purée with a hand-held blender (or in a food processor or blender) until smooth.

stewed apple and blackberries

vitamins B₁, B₆ – phosphorous ✓ 1½ C ½ 1½

1 eating apple, eg Cox's
2 handfuls of ripe blackberries (75–100g)
1 tsp golden caster sugar, to taste
2 tbsp natural full-fat yogurt
½ plain bagel, chopped into bite-size pieces

Peel, core and slice the apple and put into a small saucepan with 2 tbsp water, the blackberries and sugar. Cook over a gentle heat until the apples are soft, then cool slightly. Purée with a hand-held blender (or in a food processor or blender) and return to the pan. Put into a bowl with the yogurt and serve with chunks of bagel.

bagel with cream cheese and apricot

½ C 1 ½ ½ 4

1 plain bagel
2 tbsp full-fat cream cheese
2 tinned breakfast apricots, drained

Breakfast apricots are different from ordinary tinned apricots as they have been dried and then soaked in juice, rather than syrup. When mashed, they make a less sugary alternative to marmalade or jam. Cut the bagel in half and spread each half with cream cheese. Mash the apricots well and spread them over the cream cheese. Cut into small pieces and serve.

fried bread with mushrooms

vitamin B₆ ✓ ½ ½ 2

1 tbsp olive oil
1 slice of white bread
15g unsalted butter
3 chestnut mushrooms (approx 75g), finely chopped

Heat the oil in a frying pan. Fry the bread on each side until golden – about 1–2 minutes each side. Cut into pieces and put onto a plate. Melt the butter in the frying pan, add the mushrooms and fry until soft and lightly golden – approximately 3–4 minutes. Spoon the mushrooms onto the fried bread. A little fat, especially olive oil, is good for toddlers as they need it for energy. Cut into small pieces and serve. Only serve to toddlers who are confident with chewing.

strawberries and mango with toasted oats

✓ 8 C 1 ½ 2½ vitamins A, B₁, B₆ – phosphorous

2 tbsp porridge oats
1 handful of fresh strawberries (approx 50g), hulled and finely chopped
¼ ripe small mango, peeled, stoned and finely chopped
1 tbsp full-fat natural yogurt

Dry-frying oats in a pan is a quick and easy way to make a crunchy topping for yogurt or fresh fruits. You can also toast chopped nuts and seeds in this way (do not give nuts to toddlers under the age of three if there is a family history of allergies). Heat a frying pan, add the oats and cook until lightly golden, stirring often. Cool. Put the chopped fruits into a bowl, top with the yogurt and sprinkle over the toasted oats.

scrambled egg with Cheddar cheese

✓ 1 ½ ½ 3 vitamins B₁, B₂, B₁₂, B₆, D – phosphorous

makes: 2 toddler portions
2 medium eggs
75ml full-fat milk
freshly ground black pepper
small knob of unsalted butter
50g Cheddar cheese, grated
1 tbsp fresh parsley, finely chopped (optional)
1 white or brown soft bun

Whisk the eggs and milk together with a little freshly ground black pepper. Melt the butter in a pan and add the egg mixture. Cook over a gentle heat, stirring with a wooden spoon, until the eggs begin to scramble. Sprinkle over the grated Cheddar and chopped parsley and continue to cook until the eggs are thoroughly cooked but not rubbery – approximately 3–4 minutes. Slice the bun in half and spoon the cheesy scrambled egg over the top. If necessary, cut into smaller pieces before serving.

fresh lunches

gnocchi, leeks and cheese sauce

makes: 4 toddler portions

storage: best eaten fresh

3

1

½

½

1½ **C**

vitamins A, B₁, B₆
– folic acid –
phosphorus

400g packet potato gnocchi
50g unsalted butter
2 small leeks, washed
  thoroughly, trimmed and
  very finely chopped
100ml no- or low-salt
  vegetable stock
  (page 332)
100g peas, fresh or frozen
80g Boursin with herbs
2 tbsp fresh parsley, chopped
freshly ground black pepper
2 tbsp Cheddar cheese, grated

Lunches that are as easy to make as this one are great. Add other soft vegetables too if you like; just chop them finely – courgettes or frozen sweetcorn would taste good.

1 Put a large pan of water on to boil, add the gnocchi and cook following the packet's instructions.
2 Meanwhile, melt the butter in a heavy-based pan and gently fry the leeks until soft and pale gold.
3 Add the stock, bring to the boil, then add the peas. Cook until the peas are done – approximately 2 minutes. Stir in the Boursin cheese and parsley and season with freshly ground black pepper.
4 Add the gnocchi and simmer for a few minutes. If necessary, cut into smaller pieces before serving and sprinkle with the grated Cheddar.

pesto chicken

14

½

1

1 **C**

vitamins B₂, B₆
– phosphorus

makes: 6 toddler portions

storage: best eaten fresh or keep in the refrigerator for up to 24 hours

4 chicken breasts
4 tbsp pesto
50g unsalted butter,
  softened
juice of ½ lemon
freshly ground black pepper

This is an easy way of adding a little extra flavour to chicken breasts, and the pesto mixture helps to keep the breasts juicy and succulent during cooking. Serve with the vegetables of your choice and a little pasta or potato.

1 Cut a slit into the side of each chicken breast, open the breast out and lay flat on a board.
2 Cover with clingfilm or greaseproof paper and bash with a rolling pin to flatten slightly.
3 In a bowl, mix together the pesto, butter, lemon juice and freshly ground black pepper.
4 Preheat the grill to high. Grill the flattened chicken pieces on one side for 4–5 minutes. Turn the chicken over and spread each breast with the pesto mixture. Grill for another 4–5 minutes, until cooked through. Cut into small pieces before serving.

couscous salad with tuna

7½
1½
½
1
½ C

makes: 4 toddler portions

storage: best eaten fresh or keep in the refrigerator for up to 3 days

200g couscous

400ml boiling no- or low-salt vegetable stock (page 332)

150g feta cheese

8 ripe baby tomatoes

½ cucumber, peeled

198g tin tuna in oil or water, drained and flaked

1-2 tbsp fresh basil, torn

vitamins B₁₂, B₆, D

Couscous is so quick to cook. By the time you have chopped up all the vegetables it will be ready. You can add pretty much any cooked vegetables that you have to hand to this dish; just be sure to chop them into small pieces for your toddler.

1 Put the couscous into a bowl, pour over the boiling stock, cover and leave for at least 10 minutes, or until the couscous has absorbed all of the liquid. Fluff up with a fork.

2 Meanwhile, cut the feta cheese, baby tomatoes and peeled cucumber into small pieces.

3 Add to the couscous with the drained tinned tuna and torn basil and mix together. If necessary, mash slightly before serving.

bubble and squeak

3
½
½
½
4 C

makes: 4 toddler portions

storage: best eaten fresh

550g white potatoes, peeled and halved

50g unsalted butter

50ml full-fat milk

450g cooked vegetables, eg cabbage, onions, leeks, carrots or sprouts, well drained and finely chopped

1 tbsp fresh parsley, finely chopped

freshly ground black pepper

vitamins B₁, B₆

You can add pretty much any cooked vegetables to this although leeks, cabbage or carrots seem to work best – nothing too watery is the rule. This would be delicious served with chopped cooked ham. Don't be too worried about flipping the bubble and squeak over; if it breaks, just turn over as many of the crispy bits as possible and cook the soft bits.

1 Bring a large pan of water to the boil and cook the potatoes until tender. Drain well and return to the pan.

2 Add half the butter and the milk and mash well.

3 Mix the cooked vegetables and parsley into the mash and season with freshly ground black pepper.

4 Melt the remaining butter in a heavy-based frying pan, then add the potato mixture, pressing it down well into the pan. Cook slowly over a low heat so a golden crust is formed on the bottom of the pan – approximately 5–10 minutes. Scrape up the bottom of the bubble and squeak and flip over to cook the other side for 5–10 minutes. Cut into small pieces before serving.

tuna and pesto baked potatoes

22

makes: 4 toddler portions

storage: best eaten fresh

1

1½

4 medium baking potatoes,
scrubbed

knob of unsalted butter

3 tbsp pesto

2

400g tinned tuna in water,
drained and flaked

2

100g Cheddar cheese, grated

handful of steamed sticks
of carrot and courgette,
to serve

nins B₁, B₁₂, B₆,
– phosphorous,

This makes a great weekend lunch for all the family. Once the potatoes are cooked, they take only minutes to prepare. Only serve raw vegetables to toddlers who are confident with chewing.

1 Preheat the oven to 180°C/350°F/gas mark 4. Bake the potatoes for 50 minutes, until crisp on the outside and soft and fluffy in the middle.

2 Cut the potatoes in half and scoop out the flesh. Mix the flesh thoroughly with the butter, pesto and tuna. Preheat the grill to high. Spoon the potato mixture back into the potato skins and sprinkle over the cheese. Grill for a few minutes, until the cheese is golden and bubbling.

3 Cut into smaller pieces before serving with steamed vegetable sticks. Only serve the skin to toddlers who are confident with chewing.

lamb with a minty sauce

5½

makes: 1 toddler portion

storage: best eaten fresh

½

1½

½

1 lamb chump chop,
trimmed

2 tbsp natural Greek yogurt

2 mint leaves, chopped

¼ cucumber, peeled
and grated

1 slice of white bread,
toasted and cut into fingers

vitamins B₁, B₂,
B₁₂, B₆ –
phosphorous

It does not take long to grill a lamb chop, making this a speedy way to feed your toddler some protein at lunchtime.

1 Preheat the grill to high and cook the lamb chop for 3–4 minutes on each side, until cooked through.

2 Mix together the yogurt, mint and cucumber.

3 Cut the lamb chop into very small pieces and serve with the bread soldiers and minty yogurt.

quick bites lunches

All of the recipes make one toddler portion unless stated otherwise.

avocado and cream cheese dip

½ ripe avocado, peeled, stoned and chopped
2 tbsp full-fat cream cheese
squeeze of lemon juice
1 soft flour tortilla or 1 slice white toast, cut into strips
5cm piece of cucumber, peeled and cut into sticks

It's best not to make this too far in advance, or it will go brown. Put the avocado in a bowl and mash with a fork until smooth. Add the cream cheese and lemon juice and mix until smooth. Serve with the tortilla or toast strips and cucumber sticks. Alternatively, spread on warm white toast. If necessary, cut into smaller pieces before serving. Only give this to toddlers who are confident with chewing.

vitamins B₁, B₆, B₁₂

guacamole with ham

2 tbsp guacamole
½ ripe avocado, peeled, stoned and chopped
1 slice of cooked ham, finely chopped
1 small plain bagel, halved and toasted

If you're buying the guacamole, check the label and avoid buying any with excessive added salt or sugar. It's best not to prepare this too far in advance, or it will go brown. Put the guacamole into a bowl with the avocado and mash together with a fork to form a rough purée. Stir in the finely chopped cooked ham. Spread onto the two halves of toasted bagel. If necessary, cut into smaller pieces before serving.

vitamins A B₂, B₆, B₁₂ – phosphorous

pasta with cheese and sweetcorn

50g pasta
75g sweetcorn, fresh or frozen
50g full-fat Cheddar cheese, grated
15g unsalted butter
small pinch of fresh parsley, finely chopped (optional)

Bring a medium pan of water to the boil. Add the pasta and cook following the packet's instructions. Stir in the sweetcorn a few minutes before the end of the cooking time, bring back to the boil and cook until both are cooked. Drain and return to the pan. Add the Cheddar and butter, then stir everything together. You could also add some chopped fresh herbs. If necessary, cut into smaller pieces before serving.

vitamins B₁, B₆, B₁₂ – phosphorous

pasta, avocado and tuna

50g pasta
70g tinned tuna in oil or water
½ ripe avocado, peeled, stoned and chopped
1 tbsp mayonnaise (optional)

Bring a medium pan of water to the boil and cook the pasta following the packet's instructions. Drain. Drain and flake the tuna and then add it to the pasta with the avocado. Mix together. You could add a little mayonnaise to help bind everything together if you wish. If necessary, cut into smaller pieces before serving immediately.

pineapple and ham pizza

1 C 1½ □ 1 ▣ ½ ⊠ 6½ ♀

1 slice of white bread
1 slice of cooked ham
1 slice of ripe fresh pineapple, peeled
and chopped
25g Cheddar cheese, grated

Ham and pineapple is one of the most popular pizza toppings among children. Preheat the grill. Toast the bread on one side. Turn over, top with the ham, then the pineapple and finally the grated cheese. Grill until the cheese is bubbling and hot. Leave to cool slightly, cut into small pieces and serve.

rice with chicken and bacon

vitamins B₁, B₆ – phosphorous ✓ 1 ▣ ½ ⊠ 8½ ♀

50g white Basmati rice
1 tbsp olive oil
2 rashers unsmoked streaky bacon,
rind removed, chopped
½ chicken breast, chopped
1 tbsp raisins

Put the rice into a saucepan and add 100ml cold water. Cover and bring to the boil, reduce to a simmer and cook for 11 minutes, still covered – or until the rice is cooked through. Remove from the heat and leave, still covered, for another 10 minutes. Meanwhile, heat the oil in a frying pan, add the bacon and cook for a few minutes. Then add the chicken breast and continue to cook, stirring occasionally, until it is just starting to turn golden and both the bacon and chicken are cooked through – approximately 10 minutes more. Add the raisins to the chicken with the cooked rice and mix everything together. If necessary, cut into smaller pieces before serving.

minty chicken with bite-size vegetables

vitamins A, B₁, B₆ ✓ 2 C 3½ ♀

1 tsp mint sauce
1 tbsp full-fat yogurt
2 tsp mayonnaise
½ cooked chicken breast, chopped
5cm piece of cucumber, peeled and
chopped into chunks
2 ripe tomatoes, chopped into
bite-size pieces

Put the mint sauce, yogurt and mayonnaise into a bowl and mix together. Add the chicken and stir thoroughly. Tip into a bowl and serve with the cucumber and tomato chunks. If your toddler is used to more pungent flavours, try adding a teaspoon of mango chutney instead of the mint sauce, and serving the chicken with some chunks of fruit, such as mango, as well as the vegetables. If necessary, cut into smaller pieces before serving. Only serve chunks of raw vegetables to toddlers who are confident with chewing.

buttered peas with spaghetti

vitamins B₁, B₆ – phosphorous ✓ 2 C 1 ▣ 1½ ⊠ 6 ♀

75g spaghetti
75g frozen peas or petits pois
15g unsalted butter
3 leaves of fresh mint or parsley, finely
chopped (optional)
1 tbsp grated Parmesan or Cheddar
cheese, (optional)

Bring a medium pan of water to the boil and cook the pasta following the packet's instructions. Stir in the peas a few minutes before the end of the cooking time, bring back to the boil and cook for the remaining time. Drain and return to the pan. Add the butter and a little finely chopped mint or parsley. You could add some grated Parmesan or Cheddar cheese as well. Cut into smaller pieces before serving.

lunches to freeze

squash, carrot and orange soup

1½

½

½

3C

vitamins A, B₆

makes: 8 toddler portions

storage: up to 3 months in the freezer

25g unsalted butter
2 tbsp olive oil
2 medium onions, chopped
2 medium carrots, peeled and cut into small chunks
2 sticks celery, finely chopped
1kg butternut squash, peeled, seeded and finely chopped
1 litre no- or low-salt veg stock (page 332), boiling
juice of 1 orange
freshly ground black pepper

A true winter-warming soup with a slightly sweet flavour that is always popular with toddlers.

1 In a heavy-based pan, melt the butter with the oil. Add the onions and cook gently for about 10 minutes, until soft but not coloured.

2 Add the carrots, celery and squash and cook for another 10 minutes, stirring occasionally. Add the stock, bring to the boil and cook for 20 minutes, until the vegetables are soft.

3 Purée in a food processor or blender, return to the pan to heat through, add the orange juice and season to taste with freshly ground black pepper. Leave to cool, pour into freezerproof containers or freezer bags and freeze.

4 Thaw thoroughly. Pour into a saucepan and reheat the soup gently until it is just boiling. Cool a little to serve.

creamy tomato soup

1½

½

½

2C

vitamins A, B₆

makes: 10 toddler portions

storage: up to 3 months in the freezer

10g unsalted butter
1 small red onion, chopped
1 garlic clove, crushed
1 small carrot, peeled and finely chopped
1 potato, peeled and chopped
1kg ripe tomatoes, chopped
2 tbsp tomato purée
600ml no- or low-salt vegetable stock (page 332)
freshly ground black pepper
fresh basil leaves, torn
300ml full-fat milk

If your toddler likes the taste or texture of shop-bought soups, such as the classic Heinz tomato soup, this may be a big hit.

1 Melt the butter in a large saucepan. Add the onion, garlic and carrot and cook until soft and golden – approximately 5 minutes. Add the potato and cook for another 5 minutes, stirring occasionally.

2 Add the tomatoes, tomato purée, stock, a little freshly ground black pepper and basil. Stir and bring to the boil, then simmer for 8–10 minutes, until the potatoes are soft.

3 Whiz with a hand-held blender (or in a food processor or blender) until smooth, then pass through a nylon sieve. Leave to cool, pour into freezerproof containers or freezer bags and freeze.

4 Thaw thoroughly. Pour into a saucepan, stir in the milk and reheat gently until just boiling. Cool a little and serve.

rich mushroom stew

makes: 5 toddler portions

storage: up to 4 months in the freezer

2 | 1/2 | 1/2

vitamins B₂, B₆

25g dried porcini

2 tbsp olive oil

4 shallots, peeled and finely
chopped

2 garlic cloves, crushed

600g fresh mushrooms, eg
field, oyster, brown caps etc

600ml no- or low-salt
vegetable stock (page 332)

2 tbsp fresh parsley,
chopped

freshly ground black pepper

boiled rice or mashed
potatoes, to serve

You could add more flavour by cooking the rice in diluted no- or low-salt vegetable stock.

1 Cover the dried mushrooms with 150ml boiling water. Soak for 30 minutes. Drain, reserving the soaking liquid, and finely chop. Heat 1 tbsp oil in a frying pan and cook the shallots and garlic until soft and pale gold. Tip onto a plate.

2 Finely chop the mushrooms. Heat the remaining oil in the frying pan and fry the fresh and dried mushrooms over a high heat, stirring often. When they begin to release their juices, add a little of the stock and bring to the boil. Add the remaining stock, shallots, garlic and porcini soaking liquid and simmer until the liquid has reduced and is syrupy – approximately 30 minutes.

3 Add the parsley and season well with freshly ground black pepper. Leave to cool completely, transfer to a freezerproof container, cover and freeze.

4 Thaw thoroughly. Transfer to a saucepan, heat through gently until just boiling. Serve with rice or mash.

lamb kebabs with mango

7½ | 1 | 2 | 2

vitamins B₆, B₁₂

makes 8 toddler portions

storage up to 6 months in the freezer

4 tbsp olive oil

1 tsp sesame oil

juice of ½ lemon

2 garlic cloves, finely chopped

2 shallots, peeled and
finely chopped

2 large handfuls of fresh
coriander, finely chopped

550g lamb neck fillet, cut
into small cubes

wooden skewers

1 ripe large mango, peeled,
stoned and cut into
small pieces

cooked Basmati rice, to serve

Freezing kebabs is an excellent way to have small portions ready to hand. Do not give nuts to toddlers under the age of 3 if there is any family history of food allergies. Remember – never refreeze raw meat that has already been frozen. Any pre-packaged meat will be labelled if it has already been frozen. Otherwise ask your butcher.

1 Mix the first 6 ingredients in a large freezerproof container.

2 Add the lamb, stir to coat thoroughly, then marinate for 15 minutes.

3 Thread the lamb onto skewers. Put back into the marinade, cover and freeze.

4 Thaw thoroughly. Preheat oven to 180°C/350°F/gas mark 4. Heat a griddle pan until hot, add a drop of olive oil and cook the kebabs for approximately 10 minutes, or until the lamb is cooked through, turning occasionally.

5 Remove the skewers, finely chop the lamb and serve with small pieces of mango and the rice.

herb scones

makes: 8 toddler portions
(8 scones)

storage: up to 3 months in
the freezer

4

½

1

225g self-raising flour
1 level tsp baking powder
pinch of mustard
50g unsalted butter, plus
    extra for greasing
75g Cheddar cheese, grated
1 tbsp fresh parsley,
    finely chopped
150ml full-fat milk

vitamin B₁₂
phosphorus

You can try many variations of these scones using different herbs, chopped
sundried tomatoes, cooked ham or cooked bacon.

1   Preheat the oven to 180°C/350°F/gas mark 4. Sift the flour into a bowl with
    the baking powder and mustard.
2   Rub in the butter with your fingertips, then stir in the parsley and all but
    1 tbsp of the cheese. Make a well and pour in the milk. Mix together to make
    a soft dough.
3   On a lightly floured surface, roll out to about 2.5cm thick and cut out
    6cm rounds. Put the scones onto a greased baking sheet, sprinkle with the
    reserved cheese and bake in the moderate oven for 12–14 minutes until risen
    and golden. Serve warm or leave to cool and place in a freezerproof
    container or freezer bag and freeze.
4   Thaw completely and reheat in the oven at 180°C/350°F/gas mark 4 for
    5 minutes or until warmed through.

lasagne

makes: 6 toddler portions

storage: up to 4 months in
the freezer

19½

1½

4½

3

1½

2 tbsp olive oil
500g lean beef, minced
2 carrots, peeled
2 medium red onions
2 garlic cloves, crushed
100g button or chestnut
    mushrooms, sliced
200ml low-salt veg stock
2 tbsp tomato purée
400g tin chopped tomatoes
1 tbsp fresh parsley, chopped
40g unsalted butter
40g plain flour
600ml full-fat milk
100g Cheddar cheese, grated
200g ready-to-cook lasagne
50g Parmesan, grated
cooked peas or green salad,
    to serve

vitamins A, B₁,B₂,
B₁₂, B₆ –
phosphorous

This is a fantastic all-in-one meal, high in protein and carbohydrate – just
serve it with some salad or peas.

1   Heat 1 tbsp olive oil in a heavy-based pan and brown the mince, stirring to
    break it up. Remove from the pan and reserve.
2   Finely chop the carrots and onions. Heat the remaining olive oil and fry
    the onions, garlic, carrots and mushrooms until soft and pale golden –
    approximately 10 minutes.
3   Add the stock and bring to the boil. Stir in the tomato purée, tomatoes,
    parsley and mince and simmer for 30 minutes until the sauce is thick.
4   Meanwhile, melt the butter in another pan. Stir in the flour and cook for
    1 minute. Remove from the heat and gradually whisk in the milk. Bring back
    to the boil, stirring constantly until the sauce is thick and smooth. Remove
    from the heat and stir in the Cheddar.
5   In an ovenproof and freezerproof dish, layer the meat sauce, lasagne sheets,
    then cheese sauce in turn until everything is used. End with a layer of cheese
    sauce sprinkled with Parmesan. Cool completely. Wrap in clingfilm and freeze.
6   Thaw thoroughly. Preheat the oven to 190°C/375°F/gas mark 5.
7   Cook in the oven for 30–35 minutes, until hot and golden. Cut into smaller
    pieces before serving.

quick bites
snacks

Snacks play an important part in toddlers' diets, contributing to their nutritional requirements and helping them to keep going between meals. But, of course, this is only if the snacks that you give them are healthy! Generally, I give my girls fresh fruit and vegetables as snacks. However, there are times when their moods change as a result of a drop in their blood sugar levels, and they need to eat something more substantial to give them enough energy to keep them going until the next meal. It is best not to give snacks too close to their next meal though.

All of the recipes make one toddler portion unless stated otherwise.

vitamins B_1, B_6 1 1 1 6½

warm pitta bread with peanut butter

1 small pitta bread
1 tbsp full-fat cream cheese
1 tsp smooth peanut butter (do not give nuts to toddlers under the age of 3 if there is a family history of allergies)

Warm pitta is lovely and soft and a very comforting snack for toddlers to chew, especially if they are teething. Peanut butter can be quite salty, so look for brands with no added salt (or sugar). Warm the pitta in a moderate oven (180°C/350°F/gas 4) for 5 minutes. Meanwhile, mix the cream cheese and peanut butter together. Spread on the warm pitta before cutting into fingers.

vitamin B_6 ½ 2½

corn thins with mashed avocado

½ ripe small avocado, peeled and stoned
2 low-salt corn thins

Corn thins are available in most supermarkets, alongside the cheese biscuits. They are a little more chewy than rice cakes and a bit tastier. It's best not to prepare the mashed avocado too far in advance, or it will go brown. Mash the avocado flesh with a fork in a bowl. Spread the mashed avocado onto the corn thins or, if you prefer, break them into pieces and serve with the mashed avocado as a dip.

½ 1 1 5½

breadsticks and dips

2 breadsticks
3 level tbsp hummus or guacamole

Breadsticks are a great 'occasional' snack either on their own or with dips. If you buy your dips, make sure you choose varieties with no (or very little) added salt or sugar, such as guacamole, salsa or hummus. You may find this snack a little messy to serve to one year olds. They are best off eating a little dip with a spoon, but as they get slightly older they tend to find dunking the breadsticks into the dips quite a novelty.

raisin toast with apple purée

1 slice of raisin bread
3 level tbsp apple purée (page 158)

Sweet, thick purées of mashed fruits or vegetables, such as banana or avocado, make a great alternative to sugar-laden jams. Simply toast the raisin bread and spread with the purée. Cut into fingers.

pineapple with ham

vitamins B₆, B₁₂

2 slices of fresh ripe
pineapple
1 slice of cooked ham

If your toddler is not fantastic at eating fresh fruit and needs a little encouragement, you may find teaming fruit with meat helps. Peel the pineapple and cut 2 slices of the flesh into small chunks. Cut the ham into small pieces and thread a piece of ham and pineapple onto a blunt stick. Repeat with the rest of the fruits and ham. Help your toddler remove the sticks before he eats the ham and pineapple.

vitamin B₆

rice cakes with nut butter

1 tbsp smooth nut butter, eg cashew nut butter (do not give nuts to toddlers under the age of 3 if there is a family history of allergies)
2 unsalted rice cakes

Look for nut butters from health food shops – they tend to have no added sugar or salt. There are so many other toppings that you could put onto rice cakes too, including low-salt yeast extract and honey. Spread the nut butter onto the rice cakes. If necessary, break into smaller pieces before serving.

yogurt with dried fruit compote

3 tbsp natural full-fat yogurt
2 tbsp dried fruit compote

Rather than rely on expensive little pots of fruit yogurts, that so often have a large amount of sugar added, make your own by adding fruit compotes or low-sugar jams to natural yogurt. Put the yogurt and dried fruit compote into a bowl and mix together.

vitamin B₆

grapes filled with cream cheese

5 big black or green
seedless grapes
1 tbsp full-fat cream cheese

Most children love to eat grapes – which is a good thing as they are absolutely packed with energy as well as vitamins and minerals. Rather than just giving your toddler a bowlful of grapes, combine them with some cream cheese to make a more substantial snack. Simply cut the grapes in half and then spread each half with a little of the cream cheese before serving them to your toddler. Only serve to toddlers who are confident with chewing.

vitamin B₆

grated apple, honey and bread

1 small apple, eg Cox's
1 tsp runny honey
1 slice of wholemeal bread

Peel, core and grate the apple into a small bowl. Add the honey and mix together well. Spread onto the slice of bread and cut into fingers.

fresh suppers

sausage and apple pastry

4½

makes: 8 toddler portions

storage: best eaten fresh or keep in the refrigerator for up to 2 days and serve cold

1

½

1

vitamin B$_6$

1 tbsp olive oil
450g sausage meat
1 large onion, chopped
1 garlic clove, crushed
2 eating apples, grated
2 sprigs fresh thyme or pinch dried thyme
100ml apple juice
100ml no- or low-salt vegetable stock (page 332)
freshly ground black pepper
450g ready-made puff pastry
full-fat milk, to glaze

Good-quality sausage meat with a high percentage of pork will taste better than the cheap stuff, and is also likely to have fewer chemical additives.

1 Preheat the oven to 220°C/425°F/gas mark 7. Heat the oil in a heavy-based pan and brown the sausage meat, stirring to break it up. Remove to a plate.

2 Add the onion and garlic to the pan and gently fry until the onion is soft, then add the apples and fry for a few minutes.

3 Return the meat to the pan with the thyme, apple juice, stock and some freshly ground black pepper, then simmer until all the liquid has gone. Cool.

4 On a floured surface, roll out the puff pastry into a rectangle about 2.5mm thick. Brush round the outside edge with milk, then lay on a baking sheet.

5 Spread the sausage mixture in the centre of the pastry, leaving a 2.5cm border all the way round. Fold the two short ends into the middle, overlapping slightly and pressing them together. Pinch the long sides together.

6 Brush the top with milk and bake for 15–20 minutes, then lower the heat to 180°C/350°F/gas mark 4 and cook for another 20 minutes, until golden and risen. Slice and serve warm. If necessary, cut into smaller pieces to serve.

corn pancakes

½

makes: 6 toddler portions (18 pancakes)

storage: best eaten fresh or keep uncooked batter in the refrigerator for up to 24 hours

200g tinned cooked sweetcorn
1 large egg
25g plain flour
5 tbsp full-fat milk
unsalted butter, for frying
4 slices cooked ham, chopped
green salad, to serve

If you are using fresh sweetcorn for this recipe you will need to blanch it first. And remember to leave a couple of hours aside for chilling the batter.

1 Drain the sweetcorn, then put half of it, the egg, flour and milk into a bowl and purée with a hand-held blender (or in a food processor or blender) to make a batter. Stir in the remaining sweetcorn. Cover and chill in the fridge for 2 hours.

2 Grease a heavy-based frying pan with a little butter and cook 2 tbsp of the mixture at a time for about 2 minutes on each side. Both sides should be golden and the pancakes cooked through.

3 Add a little more butter to the pan as you cook the pancakes. Serve, chopped up if necessary, with a little chopped cooked ham and salad.

chicken with herbs and cheese

10½

½

1

½

1½ C

☑

vitamin B₁,
B₆ – phosphorous

makes: 6 toddler portions

storage: keep in the refrigerator for up to 2 days

225g full-fat cream cheese
2 tbsp rosemary or mixture
   of fresh herbs, chopped
2 garlic cloves, crushed
zest of 1 unwaxed lemon
4 chicken breasts, skinless
cocktail sticks
750g new potatoes,
   scrubbed and halved
2 tbsp olive oil
freshly ground black pepper
steamed spring vegetables,
   to serve

A simple stuffing of cream cheese, herbs and garlic helps keep the chicken breasts succulent during cooking. Mascarpone, a rich Italian cream cheese also works well.

1   Preheat the oven to 200°C/400°F/gas mark 6. In a small bowl, mix together the cream cheese, herbs, garlic and lemon zest.

2   Cut a lengthways slit into the side of each chicken breast, to make a pocket. Stuff with the cheese mixture and seal with a cocktail stick. Cover and chill for 30 minutes.

3   Put the potatoes into a large roasting dish, drizzle with olive oil and season with freshly ground black pepper. Cook for 15 minutes in the hot oven, then push the potatoes to one side and rest the chicken alongside, with the top of the breast faced downwards. Cook in the top of the oven for 20–25 minutes, or until cooked through. Remove the cocktail sticks.

4   Cut into small pieces before serving with steamed vegetables.

anything goes rice

16½

2

2

2 C

☑

vitamins B₁, B₆ –
phosphorous

makes: 2 toddler portions

storage: best eaten fresh or keep in the refrigerator for up to 24 hours and serve at room temperature (do not reheat rice)

100g Basmati rice
200ml water
2 handfuls frozen peas
   (approx 90g)
1 cooked chicken breast,
   shredded
handful of cashew nuts,
   finely chopped (do not give
   nuts to toddlers under the
   age of 3 if there is a
   family history of allergies)
handful of raisins

I often give the girls rice with different things mixed in, such as cooked chopped lamb and little pieces of roasted butternut squash – both left over from a Sunday roast. This recipe, a combination of chicken, chopped nuts and raisins, is always popular.

1   Put the rice and water into a medium pan, cover with a tightly fitting lid and bring to the boil. Reduce the heat and simmer for 11 minutes, still covered. Remove from the heat and leave to stand for another 14 minutes without taking off the lid.

2   Boil the peas for a few minutes until just cooked.

3   Add the chicken to the rice with the peas, chopped nuts and raisins. Stir everything together and serve.

plaice with a tomato sauce

14½

makes: 4 toddler portions

storage: best eaten fresh

½

½

½

1½ **C**

min B₁, B₁₂, B₆ –
phosphorous

1 tbsp olive oil

1 onion, finely chopped

5 ripe tomatoes, chopped

freshly ground black pepper

handful of fresh parsley,
   finely chopped

4 small plaice fillets, skinned

2–3 tbsp crème fraîche

450g new potatoes,
   scrubbed, to serve

200g sugar snap peas,
   topped and tailed, to serve

This gorgeous fish dish is very easy to make and, thanks to the addition of crème fraîche, the sauce has a creamy texture that toddlers seem to absolutely love.

1 Heat the oil in a heavy-based saucepan. Add the onion and gently cook until soft – approximately 5–10 minutes.

2 Add the tomatoes, freshly ground black pepper, finely chopped parsley and fish. Cover the pan and then simmer for 10 minutes, or until the fish is cooked through.

3 Meanwhile, bring a pan of water to the boil, add the potatoes and cook until tender – approximately 12–15 minutes. A few minutes before they are cooked, add the sugar snap peas. Drain.

4 When the fish is cooked, stir in the crème fraîche and cook for a further 2 minutes.

5 Cut everything into small pieces before serving.

baked rice with squash

3½

1

½

3 **C**

vitamins A, B₆

makes: 8 toddler portions

storage: best eaten fresh or keep in the refrigerator for up to 2 days (do not reheat rice)

2 tbsp olive oil

1 large red onion, finely
   chopped

2 large leeks, washed
   thoroughly and finely sliced

2 garlic cloves, crushed

750g butternut squash,
   peeled and chopped

400g white Basmati rice

800ml no- or low-salt
   vegetable stock
   (page 332), boiling

freshly ground black pepper

If you need to satisfy ardent carnivores, just add some cooked shredded chicken to this dish.

1 Preheat the oven to 200°C/400°F/gas mark 6. Heat the olive oil in a large heavy-based casserole. Add the onion, leeks and garlic, then sauté until really soft – approximately 10 minutes.

2 Stir in the squash and rice and cook for 1 minute.

3 Pour over the boiling stock, cover with a tightly fitting lid or foil and bake in the oven for 30–35 minutes, until the rice is tender and the stock absorbed. Season to taste with freshly ground black pepper.

quick bites **suppers**

All of the recipes make one toddler portion unless stated otherwise.

 vitamin B₁₂

grilled white fish with pesto

1 small white fish fillet, eg sole
or plaice
1 tsp fresh pesto
freshly ground black pepper
1 lemon wedge (optional)
mash or new potatoes, to serve

Preheat the oven to 200°C/400°F/gas mark 6. Spread a little pesto onto each fish fillet. Season with a little freshly ground black pepper. Bake in the oven until the fish is cooked through – approximately 7 minutes. Squeeze a little lemon juice over (if that is your toddler's taste) and serve with mash or new potatoes. If necessary, cut the fish into smaller pieces before serving.

 vitamins A, B₁, B₂, B₆, B₁₂ –
phosphorous

chicken breast stuffed with mushrooms

makes: 2 toddler portions
2 tbsp olive oil
½ small onion, finely chopped
3 chestnut mushrooms (approx 75g),
finely chopped
2 tbsp full-fat cream cheese,
eg Boursin
freshly ground black pepper
1 chicken breast

Heat the oil in a heavy-based pan and fry the onion until soft and pale gold. Add the mushrooms and cook gently until they release their juices and are soft. Remove from the heat and allow to cool, then stir in the cream cheese and season with freshly ground black pepper. Leave to cool completely. Preheat oven to 180°C/350°F/gas mark 4. Carefully cut a pocket lengthways down the side of the chicken breast and fill with the mushroom mixture. Bake in the oven for approximately 25 minutes, or until cooked through. Cut into smaller pieces before serving.

 Vit B1

pitta bread with cottage cheese

½ pitta bread
1 tbsp full-fat cottage cheese
1 chive stalk, finely chopped
(optional)

Keep a packet of pittas in the freezer – you can slice and grill them almost as soon as you take them out. They are really handy for a quick snack or supper. Grill the pitta bread half with the cut side facing uppermost. When it is ready, mix the cottage cheese with the chopped chives and spread onto the pitta. Cut into small strips.

 vitamins A, B₁, B₆ – folic acid

jacket potato with coleslaw

1 small baking potato, scrubbed
1 medium carrot, peeled and grated
¼ small red cabbage, finely chopped
1 tbsp fresh parsley, finely chopped
1 tbsp raisins
1tbsp each of olive oil and lemon juice
knob of unsalted butter

Preheat the oven to 180°C/350°F/gas mark 4. Bake the potato for 1 hour until cooked. Meanwhile, mix the carrot, cabbage, parsley, raisins, olive oil and lemon juice together in a small bowl. Cut open the potato, top with the knob of butter and the coleslaw. Cut into smaller pieces before serving. Only serve the potato skins to toddlers who are confident with chewing.

new potatoes wrapped in bacon

✓ 1½ C ½ 🐟 ½ ⊗ 4 🍽️

vitamins B₁, B₆ – phosphorus

6 small new potatoes
3 rashers unsmoked streaky bacon (rind removed), cut in half lengthways
50g cooked peas, to serve

Preheat the oven to 180°C/350°F/gas mark 4. Bring a medium pan of water to the boil and cook the potatoes for 20 minutes. Drain and cool slightly. Wrap each potato in a strip of bacon – secure with a cocktail stick, if needed – then roast for 30 minutes, until the bacon is crisp and golden. Remove the cocktail stick. If necessary, cut into smaller pieces before serving with the peas.

tuna, butter beans, tomato and lettuce

✓ 1½ C 1 🐟 2 ⊗ 15½ 🍽️

vitamins B₆, B₁₂ – folic acid – phosphorus

70g tinned tuna in oil or water, drained and flaked
100g tinned cooked butter beans, washed, drained and finely chopped
1 ripe tomato, halved and finely chopped
2–3 iceberg lettuce leaves, shredded into tiny pieces
1 tbsp fresh parsley, finely chopped

Mix all the ingredients together in a bowl. Cover and leave to stand at room temperature for 10 minutes before serving.

aubergine and chicken in tomato sauce

 1½ C ½ 🥛 1½ 🐟 1½ ⊗ 10 🍽️

½ aubergine, cut into small cubes
½ chicken breast, cut into bite-size pieces
1 tbsp olive oil
freshly ground black pepper
½ quantity (250ml) storecupboard tomato sauce (page 332) or 250ml tomato passata
50g cooked pasta or cooked white Basmati rice, to serve

Preheat the oven to 190°C/375°F/gas mark 5. Put the aubergine and chicken into a small roasting tin and pour over the oil. Season with freshly ground black pepper and mix everything together. Roast in the oven for 20 minutes, or until the chicken is cooked through. Pour over the tomato sauce, mix well and roast for another 10 minutes. Serve with cooked pasta or rice.

minty mash with grilled lamb

✓ 3 C 4 🐟 1½ ⊗ 14½ 🍽️

vitamins B₁, B₂, B₆, B₁₂ – phosphorus

1 medium floury potato, peeled and cut into chunks
small knob of unsalted butter
1 tbsp full-fat milk
1 tsp mint sauce
1 small lamb chop (75g), trimmed

Bring a medium pan of water to the boil and cook the potato until soft, drain. Preheat the grill. Add the butter, milk and mint sauce to the cooked potatoes and mash until fluffy. Keep warm. Grill the lamb chop for approximately 3–4 minutes on each side, until cooked through, and cut into small pieces. Serve the lamb chop chunks with the minty mash.

mushroom and ham sauce with pasta

 ½ C 3 🥛 2½ 🐟 1 ⊗ 13½ 🍽️

50g macaroni
small knob of unsalted butter
75g chestnut mushrooms, washed, sliced
½ slice of cooked ham, finely chopped
¼ quantity (150ml) storecupboard white sauce (page 333)

Bring a medium pan of water to the boil and cook the macaroni following the packet's instructions. Drain and keep warm. Heat the butter in a frying pan and gently fry the mushrooms until soft and golden. Add the chopped ham and the white sauce and bring up to boiling point. Add the cooked macaroni and stir well. If necessary, chop into small pieces to serve.

suppers to freeze

moussaka stuffed aubergines

makes: 8 toddler portions

storage: up to 4 months in the freezer

6½

½

1½   4 small aubergines
       3 tbsp olive oil

½   freshly ground black pepper
       250g lean lamb, minced

½   2 medium red onions, chopped
       4 garlic cloves, crushed
       grating of fresh nutmeg
       250ml low-salt lamb stock or
vitamins B₁₂, B₆ –   no- or low-salt vegetable
phosphorus   stock (page 332)
       200ml tomato passata
       2 tbsp fresh parsley, chopped
       125ml natural Greek yogurt
       75g buffalo mozzarella

Never refreeze raw meat that has already been frozen.

1   Preheat the oven to 200°C/400°F/gas mark 6. Halve the aubergines, score the flesh with criss-cross lines, then drizzle over half the olive oil and season with pepper. Roast in the oven for about 20 minutes, until the flesh is cooked. Cool a little, then scoop out most of the flesh, leaving a 0.5cm layer.

2   Meanwhile, heat the remaining oil in a frying pan, then brown the mince. Transfer to a plate. In the same pan, sauté the onions and garlic until soft. Add the nutmeg, stock, passata, parsley and mince. Simmer for 20 minutes.

3   Mix the aubergine flesh into the mince and season with pepper. Cool.

4   Spoon the meat filling into the aubergine skins. Grate the mozzarella and mix with the yogurt, then spoon over the top. Wrap in foil and freeze.

5   Thaw thoroughly. Preheat the oven to 180°C/350°F/gas mark 4. Place the stuffed aubergines on a baking tray and cook in the oven for 20–25 minutes, until hot and slightly golden. Cut into smaller pieces before serving.

fish cakes

makes: 6 toddler portions (approx 18 fish cakes)

18½

½   **storage:** up to 4 months in the freezer

½   900g fish, eg salmon, cod,
          tuna, all bones removed

½   approx 300ml full-fat milk
       1kg potatoes, cooked, mashed

1   2 tbsp fresh parsley, chopped
       freshly ground black pepper
       4 tbsp plain flour, for dusting
vitamins B₁₂, B₆   2 medium eggs, beaten
– phosphorus   150g fine breadcrumbs
       olive oil, for frying

Fish cakes' crisp outsides and soft centres seem to be perennially popular with children. Serve with a lightly steamed green vegetable or a salad.

1   Cut the fish into pieces and put in a pan with just enough milk to cover. Bring to a gentle simmer, remove from the heat, cover and leave the fish to cool in the milk. Flake the fish into the potato with just a little of the poaching milk. Mix in the parsley and some freshly ground black pepper.

2   Shape a large tbsp of the mixture into a cake. Dip into the flour, then the egg, then the breadcrumbs and rest on a plate. Repeat with remaining mixture.

3   Put into a freezerproof container, with greaseproof paper between the layers, cover and freeze. Thaw thoroughly. Heat a little oil in a frying pan and fry the cakes until golden – 3–4 minutes each side – then cook them on their edges for a minute, until they're cooked and golden. Rest on kitchen paper for a minute. If necessary, cut into small pieces before serving.

quick sausage and beans

11½
2½

2
½
2

vitamins B₂, B₆, B₁₂ –
phosphorus

makes: 6 toddler portions

storage: up to 4 months in the freezer

2 tbsp olive oil
6 good-quality pork sausages
4 spring onions, sliced, or
1 medium onion, chopped
5 fresh tomatoes, chopped
3 x 400g tinned cooked
  beans eg 1 x haricot, 1 x
  cannellini 1 x chopped butter,
  drained and rinsed
freshly ground black pepper
500ml tomato passata
1 tbsp tomato purée
1 tsp English mustard
pinch of soft brown sugar
  (optional)

Generally, children love eating beans, and this is a great way to get them to eat varieties other than baked beans.

1 Preheat the oven to 180°C/350°F/gas mark 4. Heat 1 tbsp olive oil in a heavy-based frying pan and fry the sausages until golden – approximately 5 minutes. Transfer to a heavy-based casserole.

2 Add the remaining olive oil to the frying pan and sauté the spring onions and onion until soft. Add the fresh tomatoes and beans and season with freshly ground black pepper.

3 Cook for a couple of minutes, then stir in the passata, tomato purée, mustard and sugar, if using. Pour onto the sausages, stir, then cover and cook for 20–25 minutes in the oven, until the sausages are cooked and the sauce has thickened slightly.

4 Cool completely. Transfer to freezerproof containers and freeze.

5 Thaw thoroughly. Heat through in a pan until boiling. Cut into small pieces before serving.

pumpkin stew

2½
1½

½
1½

10

vitamins A, B₁, B₆
– phosphorus

makes: 8 toddler portions

storage: up to 4 months in the freezer

25g unsalted butter
1 tbsp olive oil
2 red onions, finely chopped
1 sprig rosemary
3 garlic cloves, thinly sliced
3 red peppers, deseeded and
  cut into large dice
1.4kg pumpkin or butternut
  squash, peeled and cubed
1 litre no- or low-salt veg
  stock (page 332)
1 tbsp tomato purée
2–3 sage leaves (optional)
freshly ground black pepper

Serve this mellow autumnal stew on its own for lunch or with mash and peas for a more substantial supper.

1 Heat the butter and olive oil in a heavy-based casserole, then fry the onions and rosemary for 5 minutes.

2 Add the garlic and peppers and cook over a low heat until the peppers are just soft – approximately 10 minutes.

3 Add the squash or pumpkin and cook for 5 minutes before adding the stock, tomato purée and sage, if using. Simmer for 35–45 minutes.

4 Remove the herbs and pour half of the stew into a bowl. Roughly purée with a hand-held blender (or in a food processor or blender). Return it to the casserole and season with black pepper to taste.

5 Cool completely. Transfer to freezerproof containers and freeze.

6 Thaw thoroughly. Heat gently in a saucepan until just boiling. Cool slightly before serving.

lamb with spices and apricots

makes: approx 8 toddler portions

storage: up to 4 months in the freezer

12

1

3½

1

vitamins B₆, B₁₂ – phosphorus

50g dried unsulphured apricots, finely chopped

juice of 1 large orange

4 tbsp olive oil

675g shoulder of lamb, in small cubes

1 Spanish onion, finely chopped

3 garlic cloves, crushed

5cm root ginger, peeled, grated

2 tbsp coriander seeds, toasted and ground

1 tsp cumin seeds, toasted and ground

400g tin chopped tomatoes

900ml low-salt chicken stock

freshly ground black pepper

This lamb and apricot dish is delicious served with couscous – a real toddler favourite – which you can steam over the stew to give it more flavour.

1 Soak the apricots in the orange juice for approximately 15 minutes. Drain and purée in a food processor or blender.

2 Heat 3 tbsp olive oil in a large heavy-based casserole and quickly brown the lamb. Transfer to a plate.

3 In the remaining oil, gently fry the onion, garlic and ginger for about 5 minutes until soft.

4 Add the coriander, cumin, tomatoes, stock, lamb and apricot purée, then season well with freshly ground black pepper. Bring to the boil, cover and simmer, stirring occasionally, for 1½ hours, or until the meat is tender. Cool completely.

5 Put into freezer bags or a freezerproof container and freeze.

6 Thaw thoroughly.

7 Reheat gently in a heavy-based casserole until just boiling. If necessary, cut into small pieces before serving.

cheesy pasta bake

makes: 4 toddler portions

storage: up to 4 months in the freezer

11½

1

2

3

½

vitamins B₆, B₁₂ – phosphorus

few sprigs of fresh thyme

1tbsp olive oil

2 red onions, finely chopped

freshly ground black pepper

25g unsalted butter

25g plain flour

300ml full-fat milk

300ml no- or low-salt veg stock (page 332)

100g Cheddar cheese, grated

50g Parmesan cheese, grated

300g penne, cooked

2 thick slices of white bread

handful of fresh parsley, finely chopped (optional)

The perfect dish when the only shop open is the local corner shop.

1 Remove the leaves from the thyme. Heat the oil in a frying pan. Add the onions and thyme, then cover and sweat until soft. Season with freshly ground black pepper.

2 To make the cheese sauce, put the butter, flour, milk and stock into a saucepan and whisk over a gentle heat until the sauce is thick and smooth. Season with freshly ground black pepper. Stir in half the cheeses.

3 Stir the onion and cooked pasta together and spoon into an ovenproof and freezerproof dish. Pour over the cheese sauce.

4 Crumb the bread using a food processor or blender. Mix together the remaining cheese, breadcrumbs and parsley and scatter over the pasta. Cool completely. Wrap in clingfilm or foil and freeze.

5 Thaw thoroughly. Bake in a preheated oven at 190°C/375°F/gas mark 5 for 25 minutes, until bubbling and golden. If necessary, cut into small pieces before serving.

fresh & frozen puddings

baked custard

6½

½

1

1½

vitamins B₂, B₆, B₁₂
– phosphorus

makes: 4 toddler portions

storage: best eaten fresh or keep in the refrigerator for up to 24 hours

3 medium eggs
1 medium egg yolk
50g golden caster sugar
½ tsp vanilla extract
450ml full-fat milk
pinch of grated nutmeg
berry compote, to serve
(optional)

This is a really quick and nutritious pudding, high in protein and calcium. Try serving it with some stewed fruit (*see* page 333) or a little jam.

1 Preheat the oven to 170°C/325°F/gas mark 3. Whisk the eggs, egg yolk, sugar and vanilla together briefly in a bowl, then add the milk and whisk again lightly.
2 Pour the mixture through a sieve into 4 ramekins.
3 Sprinkle the tops with a little grated nutmeg. Put the dishes into a roasting pan half-filled with boiling water.
4 Bake in the moderately slow oven for approximately 30 minutes, until a skin has formed on the top and the custard is set in the middle. If desired, serve with some berry compote.

fresh fruit salad

2½

vitamin B₆

makes: 2 toddler portions

storage: best eaten fresh or keep in the refrigerator for up to 24 hours

¼ ripe small melon
(approx 150g), eg Galia
or Canteloupe
2 handfuls of green or
black seedless grapes
(approx 100g)
2 handfuls of blueberries
(approx 100g)
50ml apple juice

Most toddlers of this age love fruit salad provided there aren't too many hard fruits. This is a lovely mixture of soft fruits with different textures.

1 Peel and chop the melon into bite-size pieces and put into a bowl.
2 Cut the grapes into quarters and add to the bowl along with the blueberries.
3 Pour over the apple juice. If necessary, mash before serving.

rice pudding with pears

2½

makes: 6 toddler portions

storage: best eaten fresh or cold within 24 hours (do not reheat rice)

½

1

½ C

vitamin B₁₂

2 large knobs of unsalted butter (approx 30g), plus extra for greasing

75g pudding rice

1–2 tbsp golden caster sugar

600ml full-fat milk

2 drops of vanilla extract

pinch of grated nutmeg

4 really ripe pears, peeled, cored and quartered

Make the most of the oven and cook some fruit alongside the pudding.

1   Preheat the oven to 110°C/225°F/gas mark ¼.
2   Butter an ovenproof dish.
3   Put the rice, sugar, milk and vanilla extract into the dish. Stir, then dot with a large knob of butter and sprinkle over grated nutmeg.
4   Bake in the very cool oven for 30 minutes, stir, and then continue to bake in the oven for another 1½ hours, until a brown skin forms and the rice is well cooked.
5   Meanwhile, put the pears in another buttered ovenproof dish. Dot with the remaining butter. Cook in the oven for 1½ hours. Cut into smaller pieces and serve with the rice pudding.

rhubarb crisp

2½

makes: 6 toddler portions

storage: best eaten fresh or keep in the refrigerator for up to 3 days or in the freezer for up to 3 months

½

½

1½

1 C

vitamin A

100g unsalted butter, diced and chilled, plus extra for greasing

165g plain flour plus 1 tbsp

large pinch of ground cinnamon

small pinch of grated nutmeg

pinch of salt

235g light soft brown sugar

750g rhubarb

juice and zest of 1 unwaxed orange

This is quite a sweet topping. You could always reduce the amount of sugar if you prefer, but as we hardly ever eat puddings I do not mind the sweetness, especially if it is on top of quite tart fruit such as rhubarb. As its name implies, the topping is a thin crisp layer rather than a thick layer of crumble.

1   Preheat oven to 180°C/350°F/gas mark 4. Butter a 1-litre ovenproof dish.
2   Sift 165g flour into a bowl with the cinnamon, nutmeg and salt.
3   Rub in the butter with your fingertips until the mixture resembles fine breadcrumbs. Stir in 175g light soft brown sugar.
4   Trim the rhubarb and cut into 2.5cm pieces. Put into the ovenproof dish with the remaining 1 tbsp flour, 4 tbsp sugar and the orange juice and zest. Mix everything together.
5   Sprinkle the crumble mixture over the fruit, making sure everything is covered. Bake in the oven for 25–30 minutes, until the top is crisp and golden and the fruit is tender.

apple pie

You may like to make a couple of these and pop one in the freezer. Serve with natural Greek yogurt or custard.

makes: 1 pie or 6 toddler portions

storage: best fresh or keep in the refrigerator for up to 3 days or freeze for up to 3 months

for the pastry:
175g plain flour
40g golden icing sugar
pinch of salt
75g unsalted butter, diced and chilled
2–4 tbsp water

vitamin B₆

for the filling:
675g cooking apples
225g eating apples, eg Cox's
juice and zest of 1 unwaxed lemon
40g golden caster sugar
½ tsp ground cinnamon
good pinch of grated nutmeg
full-fat milk, to glaze (optional)

1 Put the flour, icing sugar and salt into a food processor or blender, quickly turn on and off to aerate the flour. Add the butter and process until the mixture resembles fine breadcrumbs. Gradually add the water, with the processor on, until the pastry just draws together.
2 Alternatively, sift the dry ingredients together in a large bowl. Rub in the butter with your fingertips until the mixture resembles fine breadcrumbs. Gradually stir in the water, until the pastry just draws together.
3 Wrap in clingfilm and chill for 30 minutes.
4 Preheat the oven to 180°C/350°F/gas mark 4. Peel the apples, core and cut into thick slices and mix together in a bowl with the lemon juice and zest, sugar and spices. Spoon into the pie dish.
5 On a lightly floured surface, roll out the pastry to 2.5mm thick and 1cm bigger than the pie dish. Cut a 1cm-wide strip of pastry and place on the dampened dish lip. Cover the pie with the pastry lid, and cut a small slit in the middle.
6 Trim the pie and crimp the edges together. Glaze with a little milk, if using.
7 Bake in the oven for 35–40 minutes, until the pastry is light brown. Leave to cool slightly. If necessary, cut the pastry into small pieces before serving.

banana scones

Scones are very popular with toddlers, and particularly these banana ones, as they are very moist and easy to eat. They are lovely served with fresh fruit or just topped with some mashed banana or cream cheese.

makes: 12 toddler portions (12 scones)

storage: best eaten fresh or keep in an airtight container for up to 3 days or in the freezer for up to 3 months

225g self-raising flour
1 tsp baking powder
pinch ground cinnamon
50g unsalted butter, roughly chopped
2 tbsp light soft brown sugar
150ml full-fat milk
1 ripe large banana, roughly mashed

1 Preheat the oven to 180°C/350°F/gas mark 4. Sift the flour, baking powder and cinnamon into a bowl.
2 Rub in the butter with your fingertips, then stir in the sugar and make a well in the middle. Pour in the milk, stirring with a knife, then add the banana and mix well.
3 Drop dessertspoonfuls onto a greased baking sheet and bake in the moderate oven for 12–14 minutes, until golden brown and cooked through. Serve straight away. If necessary, cut into smaller pieces.

quick bites **puddings**

Pieces of fresh fruit and yogurt make the best and easiest every day puddings for toddlers in this age group. But at the same time, all toddlers like to be treated to an extra special pudding occasionally, as do the rest of the family. So here are some simple ideas.

All of the recipes make one toddler portion unless stated otherwise.

berry compote with yogurt

vitamin B₆ 10 **C** ½ 1½

125g berries, frozen
2 tbsp full-fat natural yogurt

For vegans, just serve the berry compote on its own. Put the berries into a small saucepan and heat gently until soft. Take off the heat. Carefully transfer half the berries to a jug and purée with a hand-held blender (or in a food processor or blender). Return the puréed berries to the pan and mix everything together. Leave to cool, spoon into a bowl and stir in the yogurt.

frozen yogurt with fresh fruit

vitamin B₆ 4 **C** 1 ½ 2

handful of fresh berries, eg raspberries, strawberries, blueberries
1 scoop of frozen natural yogurt

On a hot day, a scoop of frozen yogurt with fresh berries scattered over the top can be just what is needed. Chop the berries and hull if necessary, then put into a bowl. Mash with a fork, then spoon a scoop of frozen yogurt on top to serve.

pear and sesame yogurt

1 **C** 1 1 1 2½

1 ripe pear
1 sesame snap (do not give nuts or seeds to toddlers under the age of 3 if there is a family history of allergies)
2 tbsp full-fat natural yogurt

Core the pear, peel and grate the flesh. Put the sesame snap into a plastic bag and bash into small pieces with a rolling pin. Mix the pear, sesame snap and yogurt together in a bowl, then leave for 5 minutes before serving.

fruit jelly with fresh fruits

3 **C** ½ 2

makes: 5 toddler portions
135g packet of fruit jelly
approx 200ml fruit juice
100g fruit (except kiwi or papaya), fresh or frozen

When I tested this, I used raspberry jelly and frozen berries as the fruits – it went down a real treat! Make up the jelly following the packet's instructions, using fruit juice as well as water. Cut the fruit into small pieces and divide between 5 small jelly moulds or plastic cups. Pour the liquid jelly over the top and leave to set for at least 2 hours in a cool place.

3 **C** 1 🥚

2 sheets filo pastry
15g unsalted butter, melted
2 handfuls of berries (approx 100g),
eg blueberries, hulled and chopped
strawberries, fresh or frozen
raspberries

filo parcels

Preheat the oven to 180°C/350°F/gas mark 4. Take 1 filo sheet and brush all over with some of the melted butter. Place the second filo sheet on top and brush with a little more butter. Cut the sheets in half to make approximately 17.5cm squares. Arrange the berries in the middle of the filo squares and then bring the sides of filo up and around the berries, scrunching the pastry together in the middle to make a 'parcel'. Brush with the remaining melted butter, put on a greased baking tray and bake in the medium oven until golden – 5–10 minutes. Cut into smaller pieces before serving and remove any hard bits of pastry. Only serve filo pastry to toddlers who are confident with chewing.

2 **C** ½ 🥚

1 ripe small banana, peeled and halved
4 fresh raspberries (optional)

banana ice

Put the banana into a freezerproof bag and freeze for at least 4 hours. Put the frozen banana into a blender and then whiz for a few seconds, until roughly puréed. Serve immediately, with or without fresh raspberries scattered over the top.

vitamin B$_6$ ✓ 2 **C** 1 🥚

small knob of unsalted butter
1 level tsp soft brown sugar
1 ripe small banana, peeled and sliced
1 tbsp full-fat natural yogurt

warm banana with yogurt

This is a great pudding for a cold day or when your toddler is a little under the weather. There is something very comforting about warm bananas. Melt the butter and sugar in a small pan. Add the banana slices and cook gently until just soft around the edges. Serve with the yogurt. If necessary, lightly mash the banana slices before serving.

6½ **C** ½ 🗙 1 🥚

75g mixed berries, fresh or frozen
pinch of light soft brown sugar, or dash of
honey (optional)

warm fruit compote

Put the mixed berries in a pan with 1 tbsp cold water and the sugar or honey, if needed. Heat the compote gently until the berries are soft and just begin to give up their juices.

½ **C** 2 🥛 1 🐟 1 🗙 4½ 🥚

makes: 2 toddler portions
300ml full-fat milk
25g flaked rice
1 tbsp ground almonds (do not give nuts
to toddlers under the age of 3 if there is
a family history of allergies)
1 tsp golden caster sugar

almond rice

Put all of the ingredients into a heavy-based pan and bring to the boil. Reduce the heat and simmer gently for 10–12 minutes, until the rice is tender.

celebration **food**

Marmite and cheese straws

1

makes: 30 toddler portions
(30 straws)

storage: best eaten fresh or
keep in an airtight container
for up to 3 days or in the
freezer for up to 3 months

375g ready-rolled puff
pastry
75g Cheddar cheese, grated
1 tbsp Marmite
unsalted butter, for greasing

These are quick to make and very popular at children's parties – adults also
seem to find them rather moreish! For younger ones, cut them into slightly
shorter lengths.

1 Preheat the oven to 200°C/400°F/gas mark 6. Unroll the pastry and sprinkle
   over the grated cheese, then fold in half.
2 On a floured surface, roll the pastry out to its original size. Spread the surface
   evenly with the Marmite and fold in half again, with the long sides together.
   Press down firmly and then, using a sharp knife, cut into long, thin straws.
3 Twist each straw a few times and then put onto a greased baking tray.
4 Bake in the oven for 8–10 minutes, until risen and golden. Cool on a wire rack.

banana and date cake

3½

½

½

1

vitamins B₆, B₁₂

makes: 8 toddler portions

storage: best eaten fresh or
keep in an airtight container for
up to 3 days

3 medium eggs
175g soft brown sugar
200ml sunflower oil
175ml full-fat milk
125g plain flour
125g wholemeal flour
½ tsp bicarbonate of soda
1 tsp ground cinnamon
large pinch of grated nutmeg
1 tsp mixed spice
2 ripe bananas, mashed
250g dried dates, stoned,
   soaked and puréed
2 tbsp runny honey
   (optional)

Both my daughters had this cake at their first birthday parties. They
thoroughly enjoyed it and so did the adults. While toddlers are still pretty
unaware of chocolate and sweet-covered cakes make the most of it – it's
far less messy too!

1 Preheat the oven to 190°C/375°F/gas mark 5. Grease and lightly flour a
   20cm round loose-bottomed cake tin.
2 Put all the ingredients into a bowl, except the bananas, dates and honey, and
   mix together.
3 Stir in the mashed bananas and dates and then spoon into the prepared tin.
4 Bake for 45–60 minutes, until a skewer inserted in the centre of the cake
   comes out clean. Turn out and cool on a wire rack.
5 Make holes in the cake with a fork and then drizzle over the honey, if using.
   If necessary, cut into small pieces before serving.

white chocolate krispie cakes

½

makes: 20 toddler portions
(20 krispie cakes)

storage: best eaten fresh or
keep in an airtight container
for up to 3 days

150g white chocolate,
  roughly chopped
50g unsalted butter, roughly
  chopped
2 tbsp golden syrup
120g Rice Krispies

I made these for my daughter Jasmin's second birthday tea and every mum (OK, there were only four) asked for the recipe. They are rather sweet, it has to be said, but hey, we are celebrating.

1   Bring half a saucepan of water to simmering point, put the chocolate pieces, butter and syrup into a bowl and rest over (but not touching) the simmering water. Stir frequently, until the chocolate has melted. Remove from the heat.

2   Add the Rice Krispies and mix together well. Spoon into 20 paper cases. Leave to go completely cold.

3   Your toddler may be able to chew on one of these cakes quite happily, but if you are at all worried, break into small pieces before serving.

jam tarts

1

½ **C**

makes: 12 toddler portions
(12 jam tarts)

storage: best eaten fresh or
keep in an airtight container
for up to 3 days or in the
freezer for up to 3 months

180g plain flour
pinch salt
50g golden icing sugar
90g unsalted cold butter,
  cubed
1 medium egg yolk mixed
  with 2 tbsp cold water
few drops of vanilla extract
12–16 fresh berries, eg
  raspberries, blackcurrants,
  redcurrants
12–16 tsp fruit compote
  (page 333)

If you are pressed for time, you could always use ready-made, sweet shortcrust pastry.

1   Chill a jam tart tin. Sift the flour, salt and golden icing sugar into a food processor and whiz for a few seconds.

2   Add the butter and process until the mixture resembles breadcrumbs. Add the yolk (mixed with the water) and vanilla extract and mix until a ball forms.

3   On a floured surface, roll out to 2.5mm thick, and cut out 12–16 circles with a fluted 6cm cutter, using them to line your tart tin. Chill for 15 minutes.

4   Preheat the oven to 180°C/350°F/gas mark 4. Bake the tarts for 10 minutes.

5   Spoon a berry into each pastry case and top with fruit compote. Bake for another 5–8 minutes, until the pastry is golden.

6   Cool on a wire rack. If necessary, cut into small pieces before serving.

pinwheel sandwiches

3

½

½

½

makes: 2 toddler portions

storage: best eaten fresh

60g full-fat cream cheese

1 tsp fresh parsley, chopped

1 slice of cooked ham, very finely chopped

4 thin or medium slices of white bread, crusts removed

These are great sandwiches for children's parties. The pinwheel shape appeals to toddlers, and hopefully they will eat some savoury food rather than just overdosing on sweet things, which often seems to happen at parties!

1 In a bowl, beat the cream cheese until the mixture is soft, then stir in the parsley and ham.

2 Spread the cream cheese mixture evenly onto the four slices of bread.

3 Starting with a short end, tightly roll up one of the slices of bread. Chill for 15 minutes. Then, with a sharp knife, cut the 'log' into 6 pinwheel sandwiches. Repeat with the remaining slices of bread.

cheese and sesame biscuits

1½

½

makes: 35 toddler portions (35 biscuits)

storage: best eaten fresh or keep for up to 3 days in an airtight container or freeze for up to 3 months

150g unsalted butter, softened

175g Parmesan cheese, finely grated

175g plain flour, sifted

pinch of salt

1 tbsp olive oil

30–40g poppy seeds or sesame seeds, optional (do not give seeds or nuts to toddlers under the age of 3 if there is a family history of allergies)

The mixture for these biscuits can be made in advance and kept in the refrigerator or freezer until needed. The biscuits could also be frozen and just left to thaw before eating.

1 Put the butter in a large bowl and beat with a wooden spoon until it is soft and fluffy.

2 Add the cheese, flour, salt and olive oil and start to mix with a spoon. Use your hands to bring the dough into a ball and turn out onto a floured surface. Divide in half and roll each piece into a 25cm-long sausage shape.

3 Spread the seeds on a tray and roll the 'sausages' in them. Wrap loosely in cling film and chill in the refrigerator for 40 minutes. When firm, cut into 5mm-thin rounds.

4 Preheat the oven to 180°C/350°F/gas mark 4. Put the rounds onto a lightly greased baking tray and bake for about 12 minutes, until pale golden. Cool on a wire rack.

You will be much more aware of your toddler's emerging personality during this year. She will be determined to let you know how she feels, particularly about food. This is just her way of testing you: stick to your guns about acceptable behaviour; she will feel more secure if she knows the limits. Often, toddlers' appetites slacken off as growth slows, so she may seem fussier about food. However, she needs lots of energy for development and exploration. Healthy snacks in-between meals will help give her energy. Toddlers learn by example, so eating together, even if you just eat a small portion at her suppertime, will help.

2–3 years

what's happening to
your toddler

Many parents think that this is going to be the worst year – the 'terrible twos'. This negative anticipation can exacerbate the problem, which is rarely as bad as we expect. You will become more aware of your toddler's personality and individuality at this stage and, in trying to express this, her behaviour can often seem unreasonable. But it is a learning process: she is finding out about herself and testing you to establish boundaries and where she fits in. Rules are an important part of this – knowing your limits will make her feel more secure.

At this stage her physical agility will increase and she may be able to walk up and down stairs, jump, hop and walk backwards. She is expending more energy and will need foods that are high in slow-release energy, such as bananas, dried fruits and chopped nuts (do not give nuts to toddlers under the age of 3 if there is a family history of food allergies). During this year your toddler's hand–eye co-ordination should improve greatly, so self-feeding with a spoon will be much more successful. You can now introduce a fork, and chop food accordingly. She is likely to be able to eat most of her meal without any assistance.

By the age of 2, she will probably put at least two words together and have a larger vocabulary. Pointing will also enable her to communicate more. Teach your toddler by talking to her and showing her things. One of the best ways for her to learn is by example, particularly about food. A difficulty she may have at mealtimes is sitting still, but it will encourage her if you eat together.

Talking about the food you are eating and how it was made or grown will make meals more interesting and help to keep her focused. Try to get your toddler involved in the kitchen, too, even if it is just carrying things or watching you cook. Many toddlers love playing 'cooking' with kitchen utensils and having pretend meals with their toys.

This kind of involvement will help to avoid frustration when she doesn't have her own way or is unable to carry out certain tasks. Let her try things, even if you think the results may be unsuccessful, as this is how she will learn and in turn feel more confident and independent. By the end of this year you will find the frustrated outbursts few and far between.

Eating similar food to the rest of the family at shared mealtimes will not only make your life easier, it will also help to make her feel part of the family. But remember that while as a family you may be trying to reduce your fat intake, this kind of diet is not suitable for your toddler. She needs fat for energy and for the fat-soluble vitamins it contains. Good fat sources include full-fat dairy products, such as milk, cheese and yogurt, meat, chopped nuts and oils. If you are confident that your toddler is getting enough good fat in her diet, you can introduce semi-skimmed milk as a drink when your toddler is two.

Similarly, it is a mistake to give your toddler a high-fibre diet, particularly one containing large quantities of wholegrains or bran. These are very bulky foods that can hinder the absorption of important minerals, such as iron and calcium. However, high-fibre foods, such as brown rice or wholemeal bread, can be introduced gradually now, so that by the age of 5 your toddler will be used to a healthy adult diet. Just remember that high-fibre foods can be filling and toddlers have small tummies – give in moderation so that there is room for other foods.

A toddler's needs and abilities can be completely contradictory at this stage. While she needs lots of food for energy to fuel her increased physical activity and confidence, her attention span at meals and determination to test boundaries often means that very little gets eaten. The best way to keep her happy and energized throughout the day can be to take the view that a little food often is good: giving healthy, energy-boosting snacks when your toddler needs them. It is quite likely that your toddler will still need a nap during the day; giving a small snack or drink on waking can often increase her energy and improve her mood.

Your toddler needs a good calcium intake for the proper development of bones and teeth. The most obvious source of calcium is milk – she should be getting the recommended amount of 565ml per day, which includes milk used in cooking (see page 32). A toddler who is eating a broad and balanced diet should also be getting a plentiful supply of vitamins. If your toddler is having a fussy phase, or is a vegetarian or vegan, you may need to give her daily vitamin drops – but always consult your health care expert before doing so.

which nutrients
are key

your toddler's
routine

your toddler's feeds

There is no reason to deviate from the previous year's routine. However, at around this age your toddler may begin going to nursery or to a childminder and you may need to make some adjustments. A big part of my daughter Ella's routine at nursery is a mid-morning snack, which is a sociable and fun event. This tends to make her less interested in lunch, so I make up for it by giving her a more substantial mid-afternoon snack slightly earlier.

breakfast – around 7.30–8am
mid-morning snack – around 10am
lunch – around 12.30–1pm
mid-afternoon snack – around 3pm
supper – 5–5.30pm
bed – 7–7.30pm

your toddler's sleeps

During this year it becomes less necessary for your toddler to have a daytime sleep. You could start to reduce the amount of time that your toddler sleeps, for example, by cutting sleep time from 1½ hours to 45 minutes. However, with my second daughter Jasmin I cut out routine day-time sleeps altogether, but occasionally, if I feel she is particularly tired or has had a bad night's sleep – if she has been ill, for example – she has a short nap during the day. When you cut out sleeps it is important to allow for a 'quiet time' of at least 30 minutes during the day, where you may just sit quietly and read books or watch a short video. With my children I found this pause was normally enough to keep them going for the rest of the afternoon.

why do children become fussy eaters?

Toddlers who ate really well as babies may still become faddy eaters as they grow older. A toddler who has never vehemently expressed a preference or dislike for a particular food is rare, but one who frequently refuses food can be a real challenge. However, as long as your toddler does not show any signs of illness – such as weight loss, fatigue, weakness, fever, irritability (in which case you should seek advice from your family doctor) – try not to be too concerned. Around the time of the 'terrible twos', choosing what to eat and what not to eat, is just another way of asserting her budding independence and is normal. This problem can be exacerbated if toddlers are given too much choice or bribed or put under pressure to eat.

how to counteract fussy eating

There are a few ways to counteract fussy eating habits, but the most important is not to make too much of an issue of it. Just calmly remove the food without comment and don't offer an alternative. While it may be tempting to rely on favourite foods, try to offer a wide variety of foods, or even some new ones, as this will encourage your toddler out of the rut. If she won't eat green vegetables, such as peas, offer a spoonful with other acceptable foods for a few meals on the trot. If they are left, don't comment. A new food may have been rejected, but the more often you offer it, the more likely she will be to try it – some toddlers just take a while to get used to new tastes and textures. Try to offer her food when you know she is going to be hungry, and don't offer snacks if she has eaten little at the previous meal. Try to eat together and eat some of the same things – one of the most important ways she will learn is by watching you. Above all, remember you are in charge.

playing with food

Some toddlers need to play with food by touching and smelling it, especially when they are learning to feed themselves. They enjoy the experience of mashing it up or pulling it into pieces before eating it. Try to remain relaxed about this and don't rush your toddler; she may be a naturally slow eater. When the play no longer involves eating, end the meal. Just keep showing her how you eat with a knife and a fork, and be encouraging.

trouble shooting

portions: all servings are 1 portion.
drink: preferably water, tap or bottled.
Alternatively very diluted fruit juice.
breakfast: 7.30–8am; **mid-am:** 10am;
lunch: 12.30–1pm; **mid-pm:** 3pm;
supper: 5–5.30pm; **bed:** 7–7.30pm

sample meal planners

There is no reason to deviate from the eating routine given for the previous year. However, if your toddler begins going to nursery or a childminder's at this age, you may need to make some adjustments. For instance, a mid-morning snack at nursery can be a sociable event, but this can make her less interested in lunch, so give her a smaller lunch and then a larger mid-afternoon snack.

	breakfast	mid-am	lunch	mid-pm	supper	bed
menu 1	150ml milk, ham and cheese croissant, drink	pieces of peeled apple, drink	sticky chicken with mango, drink	drink	couscous with grated vegetables, drink	200ml milk
menu 2	150ml milk, muesli, drink	banana, drink	sweetcorn and coconut chowder, drink	drink	sausage stew, rhubarb and berries, drink	200ml milk
menu 3	150ml milk, porridge	piece of toast with a little unsalted butter, drink	herby potato cakes with bacon, drink	drink	mushroom and garlic stuffed bread, drink	200ml milk
menu 4	150ml milk, poached egg and English muffin, drink	pot of raw vegetables, drink	tomato sauce with gnocchi, drink	drink	fried parsley potatoes with poached egg, drink	200ml milk
menu 5	150ml milk, pineapple and passionfruit smoothie, porridge	muesli with blueberries, drink	chicken, apple and nut salad, drink	drink	Thai-spiced vegetables with rice, drink	200ml milk
menu 6	150ml milk, apricot scone, drink	peach and banana smoothie, drink	onion and potato tortilla, drink	pieces of peeled apple, drink	toad in the hole, drink	200ml milk

	breakfast	mid-am	lunch	mid-pm	supper	bed
menu 7	150ml milk, yogurt and cereal sundae, drink	grapes, drink	lamb stew with olives, drink	drink	penne with chicken and broccoli, drink	200ml milk
menu 8	150ml milk, grated apple with raisin toast, drink	drink	rice with tuna and sweetcorn, drink	pieces of peeled apple, drink	potato salad with olives, tomato and egg, orange and passionfruit sorbet, drink	200ml milk
menu 9	150ml milk, yogurt with banana, drink	drink	apple and hazelnut bread, drink	kiwi fruit in egg cup, drink	green vegetable crumble, drink	200ml milk
menu 10	150ml milk, toasted fruit bun, drink	grapes, drink	pea and bacon soup, drink	drink	chicken with parsley and garlic butter, drink	200ml milk
menu 11	150ml milk, doorstep with mushrooms, drink	drink	couscous with French beans and bacon, drink	grapes, drink	grilled salmon with steamed vegetables, drink	200ml milk
menu 12	150ml milk, warm fruit salad, drink	malt loaf with butter and pear, drink	grated carrot with pasta, drink	drink	hamburgers with cheese, apple bread and butter pudding, drink	200ml milk
menu 13	150ml milk, poached egg with toast soldiers, drink	scone with apple, drink	hummus and avocado dip, drink	drink	pork chop with parsnip and carrot mash, rice pudding with prunes, drink	200ml milk
menu 14	150ml milk, pear, kiwi fruit and melon salad, drink	piece of toast with a little unsalted butter, drink	egg mayonnaise fingers, drink	drink	crispy baked chicken, plums and custard, drink	200ml milk

fresh **breakfasts**

fruit salad with yogurt sauce

makes: 3 toddler portions

storage: best eaten fresh or keep in the refrigerator for up to 24 hours

200g fresh berries, eg blueberries, raspberries, hulled and sliced strawberries

200g ripe fresh watermelon

100ml orange juice

2 drops of vanilla extract

100ml full-fat natural yogurt

vitamin B₆

Any kind of fruit salad is popular with toddlers, as long as there is a good mix of crunchy and soft fruit. Watermelon seems to be universally loved for its colour and texture.

1 Place the berries in a bowl.

2 Peel the watermelon and cut into bite-size pieces, then add to the bowl with the orange juice. Using a large spoon, gently mix the fruit together and leave to marinate for at least 30 minutes.

3 Meanwhile, mix the vanilla extract and yogurt together, cover and leave in the refrigerator.

4 Serve the fruit at room temperature with the yogurt sauce over the top. If necessary, cut the fruit into smaller pieces or mash lightly before serving.

ham and cheese croissant

makes: 1 toddler portion

storage: best eaten fresh

1 croissant

1 slice of cooked ham, fat removed

25g Cheddar cheese, thinly sliced

mins B₁, B₂, B₆, B₁₂ – phosphorous

Filled croissants are great for weekend breakfasts, brunches or quick, lazy lunches. I keep a big pack of them in the freezer as they only take about half an hour to defrost.

1 Preheat the oven to 180°C/350°F/gas mark 4. Cut the croissant in half lengthways. Place the ham on top of one half and cover with the cheese.

2 Put the other half back on top and place on a baking sheet. Cook in the oven for 5–10 minutes, until the cheese is melted and the croissant is warm through. If necessary, cut into smaller pieces before serving.

apricot scones

makes: 9 toddler portions (approx 9 scones)

storage: best eaten fresh or keep in an airtight container for up to 3 days or freeze for up to 3 months

225g self-raising flour
pinch salt
1 level tsp baking powder
50g unsalted butter, plus
  extra for greasing
50g dried unsulphured
  apricots, finely chopped
150ml full-fat milk, plus
  extra for glazing

These are really quick and easy to make. You can use any kind of dried fruit as an alternative. They make great breakfast food, especially served with fruit or full-fat natural yogurt.

1 Preheat the oven to 180°C/350°F/gas mark 4.
2 Sift the flour into a bowl with the salt and baking powder. Rub in the butter with your fingertips until the mixture looks like breadcrumbs, and then stir in the apricots. Make a well in the centre and gradually add the milk, stirring with a knife until the mixture comes together.
3 Turn out onto a floured surface and knead lightly for a minute, then roll out to 2cm thick. Cut out approximately 9 x 5cm rounds and put them onto a lightly greased baking sheet. Brush the tops with milk and bake in the oven for 12–14 minutes, until risen and golden.
4 Cool on a wire rack. If necessary, cut into smaller pieces before serving.

muesli

makes: 10 toddler portions

storage: keep in an airtight container for up to 4 weeks

vitamins B_1, B_6 – phosphorous

40g sunflower seeds, finely chopped
50g unsweetened shredded coconut
50g almonds, finely chopped
75g cashew nuts, finely chopped
300g rolled oats
4 tbsp wheatgerm
125g dried unsulphured apricots, finely chopped
75g dried blueberries or raisins
pinch of ground cinnamon
full-fat milk, natural yogurt or apple juice, to serve

Making muesli is not an exact science, you can use pretty much any nuts, or dried fruits that you like (do not give nuts or seeds to toddlers under the age of three if there is a family history of food allergies). Most nuts and seeds have a nicer flavour if lightly toasted. Do this in the oven or, as I prefer, in a frying pan – just watch them carefully as they can over-brown very quickly.

1 Dry fry the sunflower seeds until pale golden and tip into a large bowl.
2 Dry fry the coconut. Add to the bowl with all the other ingredients and mix together well.
3 Serve with milk, apple juice or yogurt.

poached egg and English muffin

8

1½

1

1

makes: 1 toddler portion

storage: best eaten fresh

1 medium egg
1 English muffin
small knob of unsalted
butter

tamins A, B₂, B₁₂ –
phosphorous

Muffins have a lovely dense texture and make an interesting change from ordinary toast. You could make this for lunch and serve it with some baked beans for a really nutritious meal.

1 Fill a small frying pan with water and bring to the boil. Turn the heat down to barely simmering. Crack the egg into the pan. Cook for 5 minutes, until the white is set and the yolk is firm, basting the top with the water as it cooks.

2 Meanwhile, split the muffin, then toast it under the grill and spread with a little butter.

3 Gently remove the egg from the pan with a slotted spoon, then rest the spoon on some kitchen paper to absorb the water. Place the egg on one half of the toasted muffin and then season with freshly ground black pepper.

4 Serve with the other half of muffin. If necessary, cut into smaller pieces before serving.

yogurt and cereal sundae

5½

1½

1½

3½

makes: 2 toddler portions

storage: best eaten fresh

100g raspberries, fresh or
frozen (defrosted)
100ml full-fat natural yogurt
100g granola (page 297)
full-fat milk, to serve (optional)

vitamins B₁, B₂, B₆
– phosphorous

If you have them, use two clear plastic cups to serve these sundaes as they would look really pretty. This is just as good made with ripe banana, strawberries or fresh apricots. Try adding a pinch of ground cinnamon to spice it up a little.

1 Mash the raspberries in a small bowl with a fork and swirl them through the yogurt.

2 Place a couple of spoonfuls of the yogurt into a small bowl or cup. Spoon an equal amount of the granola on top, then continue in layers. Repeat with a second cup. If necessary, cut the granola into smaller pieces before serving.

3 You may need to add a little milk to make it less dry.

quick bites breakfasts

All of the recipes make one toddler portion unless stated otherwise.

vitamin B₆

pineapple and passionfruit smoothie

makes: 2 toddler portions
½ ripe large pineapple, peeled
2 passionfruit
200ml apple juice

Cut the pineapple flesh into small chunks (making sure you remove any 'eyes') and put the flesh into a bowl. Halve the passionfruit and scoop the pulp into the bowl. Add the apple juice and whiz with a hand-held blender (or in a food processor or blender) until smooth. Where smoothies are concerned, it is a good idea to make enough for you as well as your toddler, as both of you can then benefit from a drink packed with nutrients. This smoothie is particularly high in vitamin C.

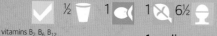

vitamins B₂, B₆, B₁₂

poached egg with toast soldiers

1 medium egg
1 slice of white toast

There are many ways to poach an egg, but this is one of my daughter Ella's favourites. Fill a shallow frying pan with water and bring up to simmering point. Crack the egg into the water and simmer for 5 minutes, or until the white is set and the yolk is firm, basting the top with the water as it cooks. Lift the egg out with a slotted spoon and rest on kitchen paper for a few seconds. Cut the toast into thin fingers and serve with the egg, chopped into small pieces, if necessary.

vitamins B₂, B₆, B₁₂ – phosphorous

yogurt with banana

½ ripe large banana
100ml full-fat natural yogurt
1 tsp runny honey

On the whole, breakfast recipes need to be quick to help busy mums and dads in the morning. This is really easy and universally popular. Mash the banana to a purée. Add the yogurt and honey and mix together.

phosphorous

grilled bacon with a wholemeal bun

2 rashers unsmoked back bacon, rind removed
1 wholemeal bun, halved
1 ripe small tomato, sliced
freshly ground black pepper

Grill the bacon until crisp, removing the rind if you prefer. Top one half of the wholemeal bun with the sliced tomato and season with a little freshly ground black pepper. Snip the bacon into pieces and put on top of the tomato. Cover with the other half of the bun. If necessary, cut into smaller pieces before serving. In season, try adding some sliced grilled mushrooms instead of, or as well as, the tomato.

vitamin B₆

2 tsp olive oil
2 large field mushrooms, thickly sliced
freshly ground black pepper
1 thick slice of white bread

doorstep with mushrooms

Make this when the lovely field mushrooms are in season. A thick slice of bread is a great energy booster. Heat the oil in a frying pan, add the sliced mushrooms and gently fry until they are soft and just beginning to give up their juices – approximately 5 minutes. Season lightly with freshly ground black pepper, then tip out over the slice of bread, so that it soaks up all the juices. If necessary, cut into smaller pieces before serving.

vitamin B₆

100ml tinned coconut milk
100g frozen exotic fruits
1 ripe large banana, chopped
juice of ½ lime

coconut milkshake

Check out the freezer section in your local supermarket for bags of exotic fruits. You will probably also find bags of frozen berries and summer fruits. (Do not serve nuts or nut products to toddlers under the age of 3 if there is a family history of allergies.) Put all the ingredients into a jug and purée with a hand-held blender (or in a food processor or blender) until smooth.

Vit B6 –

1 tbsp runny honey
2 tbsp apple juice
1 eating apple, peeled, cored, thinly sliced
1 slice pineapple, peeled, cored, cut in chunks
8 big seedless black grapes, halved

warm fruit salad

Toddlers enjoy the comfort of warm foods. Melt the honey with the apple juice in a small saucepan, add the sliced apples and cook them for 1–2 minutes. Stir in the pineapple chunks and grapes. Heat gently and stir until warmed through – approximately 2–3 minutes.

15g unsalted butter
½ eating apple, peeled, cored and grated
½ ripe pear, peeled, cored and grated
pinch of ground cinnamon (optional)
1 slice of raisin bread

grated apples with raisin toast

Heat the butter in a small saucepan, add the apple, pear and cinnamon and cook gently, stirring, for approximately 2–3 minutes. Toast the raisin bread and top with the warm fruit mixture. Cut into pieces and serve.

vitamins A, B₆

1 ripe pear, peeled and cored
1 small slice of ripe melon (approx 100g flesh), peeled
1 ripe kiwi fruit, peeled and chopped
50ml apple juice

pear, kiwi fruit and melon salad

These fruits have a cool texture, so are delicious for summer breakfasts. Chop the pear and melon into small pieces. Put into a bowl with the kiwi fruit. Pour over the apple juice. If necessary, lightly mash before serving.

1 fruit bun
small knob of unsalted butter
1 eating apple, eg Cox's, peeled and finely chopped

toasted fruit bun

Look in your supermarket for yeast buns that have lots of dried fruit and very little sugar. Cut the bun in half and put into your toaster to toast. Spread the toasted halves with a little butter. If necessary, cut into smaller pieces before serving with the peeled, chopped apple.

fresh lunches

sticky chicken with mango

10

½

1

3 C

vitamin B$_6$
– phosphorous

makes: 3 toddler portions

storage: best eaten fresh or keep in the refrigerator for up to 24 hours

2 chicken breasts
2 garlic cloves, crushed
2 tbsp runny honey
1 tbsp sweet soy sauce or light soy sauce
juice of 1 lime
1 ripe mango, peeled, stoned and finely sliced
3–4 fingers of white or brown bread, to serve

This dish is always a hit with my children and their friends. They love to hold the sticky chicken and alternately munch on chicken, mango and fingers of bread.

1　Slice the chicken into thin strips (approximately 8 slices per breast).
2　In a bowl, mix together the garlic, honey, sweet soy sauce and lime juice. Add the chicken and marinate for at least 30 minutes, or preferably 1–2 hours.
3　Heat a griddle pan until really hot and cook the chicken over a medium heat, turning the pieces after about 1–2 minutes, then cook for another 2–3 minutes until cooked through. The honey and sweet soy should caramelize, making the chicken nice and sticky.
4　Serve the sticky chicken with pieces of mango and fingers of bread. If necessary, cut into smaller pieces before serving.

onion and potato tortilla

9½

1½

1½

1½

1 C

vitamins A, B$_2$,
B$_6$, B$_{12}$
– phosphorous

makes: 6 toddler portions

storage: best eaten fresh or keep in the refrigerator for up to 2 days

8 medium eggs, beaten
75g full-fat Cheddar cheese, grated (or half of each Parmesan and Cheddar)
freshly ground black pepper
2 tbsp olive oil
1 large onion, sliced
150g potatoes, finely diced
50g baby spinach leaves

Once you have tried this recipe, have a go at experimenting with other vegetables. You may find that toddlers prefer this cut into small pieces and served with a dipping sauce.

1　In a bowl, mix the eggs with half the cheese and season with freshly ground black pepper.
2　Heat the oil in a heavy-based frying pan. Add the onion, cover and sauté until it is very soft and beginning to caramelize – approximately 10 minutes.
3　Add the potatoes and gently fry until soft – approximately 10 minutes.
4　Add the spinach, wilt and pour in the egg mixture, then sprinkle the remaining cheese over the top.
5　Cook over a low heat until the tortilla begins to set, then place under a medium grill and cook until pale golden. Wait a few minutes before turning out. If necessary, cut into smaller pieces before serving.

herby potato cakes with bacon

Typical Scottish fare, these potato cakes make a good breakfast served simply with a little butter. For lunch, try serving them with grilled bacon or sausages and grilled tomatoes.

10½

1½

2

½

6 C

vitamins A, B₁, B₆
– phosphorous

makes: 4 toddler portions

storage: keep in the refrigerator for up to 2 days

450g potatoes, peeled and chopped
50g unsalted butter, plus extra for greasing
75g plain flour
2 tbsp fresh parsley, chopped
½ tsp baking powder
freshly ground black pepper
8 rashers unsmoked back bacon, rind removed, grilled and chopped
8 tomatoes, grilled and chopped

1. Boil the potatoes until they are tender – this should take approximately 15 minutes. Drain, then return them to the heat for a minute in order to dry them.
2. Add the butter and mash well. Add the flour, parsley and baking powder. Season with freshly ground black pepper and mix thoroughly.
3. Flour the work surface. Pat the dough out to 1cm thick and cut out 8 x 6cm circles.
4. Lightly butter a heavy-based frying pan, heat and fry the potato cakes for 2–3 minutes on each side, until golden. If necessary, cut into smaller pieces before serving immediately with bacon and tomatoes.

quick muffin pizzas

These pizzas are perfect for those occasions when you do not have the time to make your own pizza base. You could also try using specialty breads such as olive bread or pitta.

18

1

1

2½

4½ C

vitamins A, B₁,
B₆, B₁₂
– phosphorous

makes: 1 toddler portion

storage: best eaten fresh

1 English muffin
1 tsp tomato purée
1 ripe tomato, thinly sliced
¼ courgette, thinly sliced
25g full-fat cheese, eg buffalo mozzarella or Cheddar, grated

1. Preheat the grill. Cut the muffin in half and spread with the tomato purée.
2. Top with the tomato and courgette slices, then sprinkle over the cheese.
3. Grill for 3–4 minutes, until the cheese is golden and bubbling and the pizza is hot through. If necessary, cut into smaller pieces before serving.

Jane's fish finger pie

makes: 4 toddler portions

storage: best eaten fresh

550g floury potatoes, peeled
  and chopped
knob of unsalted butter
50ml full-fat milk
8 x 100% cod fish fingers
415g tinned low-sugar baked
  beans or spaghetti hoops
75g Cheddar cheese, grated

14

1½

1½

2½

2

vitamins B₁,
B₆, B₁₂
– phosphorous

This fish finger pie is ridiculously easy to make and is always popular
with children of all ages. It is very nutritious, being packed with protein
and carbohydrate.

1 Preheat the oven to 180°C/350°F/gas mark 4.
2 Bring a pan of water to the boil and cook the potatoes until they are
  tender – approximately 15 minutes. Drain and mash with the butter
  and the milk.
3 Cook the fish fingers following the packet's instructions and put them into
  an ovenproof dish.
4 Pour over the baked beans or spaghetti and top with the mashed potato.
5 Sprinkle over the grated cheese and bake in the oven for 15 minutes, or until
  it is golden on top and hot through. If necessary, cut into smaller pieces
  before serving.

sausage and fennel pasta

makes: 6 toddler portions

storage: best eaten fresh or
keep in the refrigerator for up
to 2 days

2 tsp olive oil
3 shallots, finely chopped
2 garlic cloves, finely chopped
6 good-quality pork
  sausages (approx 400g),
  skinned
1 level tsp fennel seeds
150ml no- or low-salt
  vegetable stock
  (page 332)
400g tinned chopped
  tomatoes
freshly ground black pepper
400g pasta shells, cooked
fresh Parmesan cheese,
  grated, to serve

12½

1½

2

½

1½

vitamins B₆, B₁₂
– phosphorous

The fennel seeds add a subtle aromatic flavour to this dish. It is a good idea
to get your toddler used to different flavours from spices and herbs at an
early age, so that she accepts them more readily as she grows older.

1 Heat 1 tsp of the oil in a frying pan, and gently cook the shallots and garlic
  until soft, then reserve on a plate.
2 Heat the remaining oil and brown the sausage meat, breaking up any large
  pieces with a wooden spoon.
3 Add the fennel seeds and cook for 1 minute. Stir in the stock, then bring to
  the boil, stirring occasionally.
4 Add the tomatoes and cooked shallots and season with freshly ground black
  pepper. Simmer gently, uncovered, for 30 minutes.
5 Serve the sauce with the freshly cooked pasta and Parmesan. If necessary,
  cut into smaller pieces before serving.

quick bites lunches

All of the recipes make one toddler portion unless stated otherwise.

1 C   1 🥛   ½ 🐟   ½ 🧈   4 🥚

½ ripe small banana, peeled and mashed
1 tsp runny honey
25g full-fat cream cheese
2 slices of raisin or wholemeal bread

banana and honey sandwich

Mix the banana and honey together in a small bowl. Spread a slice of bread with cream cheese and top with the banana mix, then top with the other slice of bread. Cut into 4 triangles and serve.

2 C   1 🥛   1½ 🐟   1½ 🧈   6½ 🥚

½ ripe avocado, peeled and stoned
4 tbsp hummus
2 breadsticks
1 small carrot, peeled and cut into sticks

hummus and avocado dip

It's best not to make this dip too far in advance or it will go brown. Put the avocado and hummus into a bowl and mash with a fork until you have a rough purée. Serve as a dip with the breadsticks and carrot. To give the hummus a lovely sweet flavour, try adding a quarter of a roasted red pepper, skinned and finely chopped.

1 C   ½ 🥛   1 🐟   1½ 🧈   4½ 🥚

50g pasta
15g unsalted butter
2 tbsp raisins
1 small carrot, peeled and grated

grated carrot with pasta

Bring a medium pan of water to the boil. Add the pasta and cook following the packet's instructions. Drain. Heat the butter in a saucepan, add the raisins and grated carrot and cook gently for 4–5 minutes. Tip the cooked pasta into the pan, stir through and serve. By barely cooking the carrots you are keeping most of their nutrients, and the crunchy texture of grated carrot tends to be popular with children. If necessary, cut into smaller pieces before serving.

 1½   C   ½ 🧈   1½ 🥚
vitamin B$_6$

50g gnocchi
1 tbsp olive oil
1 spring onion, finely sliced
75ml passata (sieved tomato purée available from supermarkets)
1 tbsp full-fat cream cheese

tomato sauce with gnocchi

Bring a medium pan of water to the boil. Add the gnocchi and cook following the packet's instructions. Drain. Heat the olive oil in a saucepan, add the sliced spring onion and cook gently until soft – approximately 3–4 minutes. Add the passata and heat through for a few minutes, then stir in the cream cheese. Also, try adding one of the following variations, finely chopped: 1 slice cooked bacon or ham, half a cooked organic chicken breast, 2 fried mushrooms, 1 cooked broccoli floret or a small handful of green beans (trimmed) and heat through until the meat is hot. Serve with the gnocchi, all chopped into smaller pieces if necessary.

chicken, apple and nut salad

6½ C ½ 2 1 14½

½ cooked organic chicken breast
1 Granny Smith apple, peeled and cored
½ stick celery
3 leaves baby gem lettuce
2–3 walnuts, shelled
1 tbsp natural full-fat yogurt
1 tsp runny honey
slice of focaccia bread, to serve (optional)

Finely chop the cooked chicken, apple, celery, lettuce and walnuts. Put them in a bowl (do not give nuts to toddlers under the age of 3 if there is a family history of allergies). Mix together the yogurt and honey and drizzle over the salad. Toss everything together and serve with a slice of focaccia.

rice with tuna and sweetcorn

vitamins B$_1$, B$_6$, B$_{12}$, D, – phosphorous

½ C 1 1½ 14½

50g white Basmati rice
25g frozen sweetcorn
25g peas, fresh or frozen
70g tinned tuna in oil or water, drained and flaked

Put the rice into a saucepan, add 100ml cold water, cover and bring to the boil. Reduce to a simmer and cook for 11 minutes, still covered. Remove from the heat and leave, still covered, for another 10 minutes. Bring a small pan of water to the boil and cook the sweetcorn and peas, then drain. Next, drain the rice before stirring in the peas, sweetcorn and tuna.

Marmite toast with chunky salad

vitamins B$_1$, B$_2$, B$_6$ – phosphorous

1 C 1 1 4

1 slice of wholemeal bread
a little Marmite
5cm piece of cucumber, peeled and chopped into bite-size pieces
3 cherry tomatoes, halved
2 button mushrooms, quartered

Marmite is a good source of B vitamins, but it is quite salty so spread it thinly. Toast the bread on both sides and spread with the Marmite. Cut into fingers and serve with the vegetables.

egg mayonnaise fingers

vitamins B$_2$, B$_6$, B$_{12}$ – phosphorous

½ 1½ 1½ 7½

1 medium egg
1 tsp mayonnaise
1 slice wholemeal bread

Bring a small pan of water to the boil, add the egg and cook it for 8 minutes once it has returned to the boil. Remove the egg, cool, peel and place in a bowl – making sure the egg is totally cooked. Using a fork, mash the egg with the mayonnaise. Toast the bread and spread with the egg, then cut into fingers.

couscous with French beans and bacon

vitamins B$_1$, B$_6$ – phosphorous

1 C 1½ 5½ 9½

2 rashers streaky unsmoked bacon, rind removed
50g couscous
6 French beans, topped and tailed
3 ripe cherry tomatoes, quartered

Grill the bacon until cooked, then snip into bite-size pieces. Cook the couscous following the packet's instructions – try using no- or low-salt vegetable stock (*see* page 332), instead of water, to add more flavour. Bring a small pan of water to the boil and cook the beans until just done – approximately 2 minutes. Drain and cut into bite-size pieces. Tip the couscous into a bowl and mix through the tomatoes, bacon and beans.

lunches to freeze

lamb stew with olives

11

1

3

1½ **C**

vitamins B₁, B₂,
B₆, B₁₂
– phosphorous

makes: 9 toddler portions

storage: up to 4 months in
the freezer

4 tbsp olive oil
900g lean lamb shoulder, diced
2 medium onions, finely
    chopped
2 garlic cloves, chopped
100ml no- or low-salt
    vegetable stock (page 332)
400g tinned chopped
    tomatoes
400g tinned cherry tomatoes
large pinch of dark
    brown sugar
handful of fresh thyme sprigs
freshly ground black pepper
100g Kalamata olives,
    drained and stoned

Make sure you buy good quality olives, otherwise they can add a slightly sour taste to the stew. Serve with rice or mashed or new potatoes.

1 Preheat the oven to 150°C/300°F/gas mark 2. Heat a large heavy-based casserole until really hot. Add 2 tbsp oil and brown the lamb in batches. Transfer to a plate.
2 Heat the remaining oil and gently fry the onions and garlic until soft – approximately 5 minutes.
3 Add the stock and leave to bubble for a few minutes, stirring occasionally.
4 Add the lamb, chopped tomatoes, cherry tomatoes, sugar and three quarters of the thyme. Season with freshly ground black pepper.
5 Bring to the boil, cover and cook in the oven for 1½ hours. Stir in the olives and cook for another 20 minutes. Scatter over the remaining thyme leaves. Cool completely. Transfer to freezerproof containers or freezer bags. Freeze.
6 Thaw thoroughly. Gently heat until piping hot. If necessary, cut into smaller pieces before serving.

pea and bacon soup

6

3½

1

2 **C**

vitamin B₆

makes: 8 toddler portions

storage: up to 3 months in
the freezer

1 tbsp olive oil
6 rashers unsmoked streaky
    bacon, rind removed and
    finely chopped
1 onion, chopped
1 litre no- or low-salt
    vegetable stock (page 332)
800g peas, fresh or frozen
2 tbsp fresh mint, chopped
fresh Parmesan shavings

If you make this soup in the summer, be sure to use sweet fresh peas. I tend to sprinkle fresh Parmesan shavings on the top for extra flavour and a slight hint of saltiness.

1 Heat the oil in a heavy-based pan and fry the bacon over a gentle heat until cooked and just golden.
2 Add the onion and cook until soft – approximately 3–4 minutes.
3 Add the stock and peas and simmer gently for 25 minutes. Add 1 tbsp mint and cook for 2–3 minutes. Remove from the heat and cool slightly before whizzing in a food processor or blender.
4 Cool completely. Pour into freezerproof containers or freezer bags. Freeze.
5 Thaw thoroughly. Gently reheat until just boiling, add the remaining mint, scatter with the Parmesan shavings and serve.

baked fish in tomato sauce

22½

½

1

2½

vitamins B₆, B₁₂
– phosphorous

makes: 4 toddler portions

storage: up to 4 months in the freezer

2 tbsp olive oil
1 medium onion, finely
    chopped
2 garlic cloves, crushed
100g chestnut (or other)
    mushrooms, finely chopped
400g tinned chopped
    tomatoes
freshly ground black pepper
small handful of fresh basil
    leaves, torn
4 small pieces of white fish
    fillet eg cod, haddock
juice of ½ lemon

You could always make a larger quantity of the sauce and keep to use with chicken pieces or pork chops. Serve with mash or rice and green vegetables.

1   Preheat the oven to 180°C/350°F/gas mark 4. Heat the olive oil in a heavy-based pan and gently fry the onion until soft and golden. Add the garlic and mushrooms and cook for another 5 minutes, stirring occasionally.

2   Stir in the tomatoes, season with freshly ground black pepper and simmer gently for 20 minutes. Stir in the torn basil.

3   Check the fish for bones before placing it in a buttered ovenproof and freezerproof dish. Season with pepper, sprinkle with lemon juice and pour over the tomato sauce. Cook in the oven for 20–25 minutes. Cool completely. Wrap the dish in clingfilm or foil and freeze.

4   Thaw thoroughly. Cook at 180°C/350°F/gas mark 4 for 20 minutes, or until piping hot. If necessary, cut into smaller pieces, cool and check the fish again for bones before serving.

apple and hazelnut bread

6½

1½

1½

1

phosphorous

makes: approx 8 toddler
portions (900g loaf)

storage: up to 3 months in the freezer

approx 360ml warm water
1 tsp golden caster sugar
6g (2 level tsp) dried yeast
400g plain white flour
400g wholemeal flour
100g hazelnuts, toasted and
    finely chopped (do not give
    nuts to toddlers under the
    age of 3 if there is a
    family history of allergies)
50g dried apple, finely
    chopped

This easy-to-make loaf is deliciously nutty and moist.

1   Grease a 1kg loaf tin. Put 100ml warm water into a jug, stir in the sugar and yeast and leave for 10–15 minutes for a froth to form.

2   Sift the plain and wholemeal flour into a large bowl and mix in the nuts and apple. Make a well and pour in the yeast. Stir with a wooden spoon, gradually adding the rest of the warm water. Use your hands to mix it, adding a little more water if necessary, until you have a smooth dough.

3   Knead the dough briefly on a floured surface, shape it into an oblong and drop into the prepared tin. Sprinkle with flour, cover with a warm damp cloth and leave in a warm place for 30–40 minutes until doubled in size.

4   Preheat the oven to 200°C/400°F/gas mark 6.

5   Bake the bread for 40 minutes. Remove from the tin and bake upside down on the shelf for 10–15 minutes to crisp up. It is cooked if it sounds hollow when the bottom is tapped. Cool completely.

6   Slice, then wrap well in clingfilm or foil and freeze.

7   Thaw thoroughly. If necessary, cut into smaller pieces before serving.

macaroni bacon and cheese

19½

1½

1

4½

3 C

vitamins A, B₁, B₂,
B₆, B₁₂
– phosphorous

makes: 4 toddler portions

storage: up to 4 months in
the freezer

8 rashers unsmoked streaky
  bacon, rind removed
25g unsalted butter
1 medium onion, finely
  chopped
1 tbsp plain flour
600ml full-fat milk
150g Cheddar cheese, grated
freshly ground black pepper
200g macaroni, cooked
4 ripe tomatoes, halved
olive oil

This is a really satisfying variation on an old favourite, and is absolutely packed with protein.

1 Preheat the grill to hot. Grill the bacon until cooked and crisp.
2 Heat the butter in a pan and gently fry the onion until soft – approximately 5 minutes.
3 Stir in the flour and cook for a minute. Whisk in the milk and stir over a gentle heat until you have a smooth sauce.
4 Add the grated cheese, freshly ground black pepper and macaroni, then crumble in the bacon. Stir together and spoon into an ovenproof and freezerproof dish. Cool completely, wrap the dish in clingfilm or foil and freeze.
5 Thaw thoroughly. Preheat the oven to 180°C/350°F/gas mark 4.
6 Put the tomatoes on a baking sheet, drizzle with a little oil and roast alongside the macaroni cheese for 20 minutes, or until piping hot and golden. If necessary, cut into smaller pieces before serving.

sweetcorn and coconut chowder

4½

½

½

1 C

vitamin B₆

makes: 5 toddler portions

storage: up to 3 months in
the freezer

7 ears of fresh corn or 550g
  frozen sweetcorn, thawed
1 large onion, finely chopped
3 garlic cloves, finely chopped
2.5cm piece of root ginger,
  peeled and finely chopped
1 stick of lemon grass, outer
  leaves removed
1 large potato, peeled and
  cut into small chunks
1 knob of unsalted butter
400ml tinned full-fat
  coconut milk
300ml no- or low-salt
  vegetable stock (page 332)
2 tbsp fresh coriander, chopped
juice of ½ lime

This soup is thick and creamy and has a little texture from the corn and potatoes. For a vegan diet, just replace the butter with olive oil. Do not serve nut products to toddlers under the age of 3 if there is any family history of food allergies.

1 Preheat the oven to 200°C/400°F/gas mark 6. Peel the husks away from the fresh corn cobs and cut the kernels away.
2 Put the fresh or frozen corn into a heavy roasting dish with the onion, garlic, ginger, lemon grass and potato. Mix together, dot with butter and roast for 40 minutes, turning occasionally, until the vegetables are cooked and slightly soft. Remove the lemon grass.
3 Transfer half the vegetables to a bowl, add the coconut milk and stock, then purée with a hand-held blender (or in a food processor or blender). Transfer to a bowl with the remaining vegetables. Cool completely. Pour into freezerproof containers or freezer bags and freeze.
4 Thaw thoroughly. Gently reheat until boiling, add the coriander and lime juice. If necessary, lightly mash before serving.

quick bites snacks

Snacks play an important part in a toddler's diet. However, it is important not to rely on too many highly processed snacks, such as crisps and biscuits, that are often high in saturated fat, salt and sugar. Getting into this habit often results in a toddler becoming less interested in food at mealtimes, partly because she is not hungry and partly because the food is perceived to be less interesting than the attractively packaged snacks she has been munching during the day.

All of the recipes make one toddler portion unless stated otherwise.

vitamins B₆, B₁₂
– phosphorous

banana milk

1 ripe small banana, peeled and
roughly chopped
100ml full-fat milk
small pinch of ground cinnamon

Sometimes a thick milk drink is enough to keep your toddler satisfied until the next meal, particularly when made with bananas, which provide energy. You could also make this drink with other fruits, such as peaches or nectarines – just add a little natural yogurt to help thicken it slightly. Put the banana, milk and cinnamon into a food processor or blender and whiz until smooth.

muesli with blueberries

50g unsweetened muesli (do not
give nuts to toddlers under the
age of 3 if there is a family
history of allergies)
50g fresh blueberries
100ml full-fat milk

Unsweetened muesli is great for toddlers, especially if you add some fresh fruit. If the muesli you choose has large whole nuts, give it a quick whiz with a hand-held blender (or in a food processor or blender) before serving. Put the cereal into a bowl, add the blueberries and pour over the milk. Leave for a few minutes and then serve.

malt loaf with butter and pear

1 slice of malt loaf
small scraping of unsalted butter
1 ripe pear

Look for a good-quality malt loaf without too many additives. Spread a slice with butter and cut into strips. Core the pear, peel and cut into chunks. Serve with the malt loaf.

kiwi fruit in an egg cup

1 ripe kiwi fruit

Kiwi fruits are particularly rich in vitamins C and E. To help make them more fun to eat, cut the top off the fruit and stick the fruit into an egg cup. Serve with a spoon and let your toddler scoop out the flesh. The fruit must be ripe so that it is easy for the toddler to eat.

1 **C** ½ ½ ½ 2½

vitamins B₁, B₆

scone with apple

1 fruit scone, preferably home-made (page 156)
1 eating apple, eg Cox's

If you have the time, make a batch of home-made scones to keep in the freezer; they often taste better and will have far fewer additives than shop-bought ones. They make a great snack on a weekend afternoon, when your toddler may be eating supper slightly later in the day. Cut the fruit scone in half. Peel and core the apple and cut into chunks and serve with the scone.

2 1½ 1 6½

vitamin B₁₂ – phosphorous

oatcakes with cheese

30g Cheddar cheese
2 oatcakes

Suitable for vegetarians and vegans, oatcakes make a quick and easy snack for toddlers. Organic oatcakes are also now available. Cut the cheese into chunks and serve with the oatcakes. A couple of oatcakes and a few fresh grapes also make a great snack.

vitamins A, B₆ 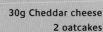 3 **C** ½ ½

pot of raw vegetables

1 small carrot
5cm piece of cucumber
4 ripe small cherry tomatoes

Snacks do not need to be complicated, they just need to be made using fresh ingredients, such as raw fresh vegetables or fruit. Peel the carrot, trim the ends and cut into small sticks. Cut the cucumber into similar sized sticks. Cut the tomatoes in half and mix with the other vegetables and serve in a small pot. It's especially important to stay with your toddler while she eats raw vegetables.

vitamins B₆, B₁₂ 1 ½ 4½

toast with paté

1 slice of wholemeal bread
2 tbsp meat or fish paté

Paté is the one food that I always spend a bit more on. Always read the label and look for one with a high meat percentage (around 70 per cent). Toast the slice of bread and spread with the paté. Cut into fingers and serve.

vitamin B₆ 11 **C** ½ 1½

peach and banana smoothie

1 ripe fresh peach
1 ripe small banana, peeled and roughly chopped
100ml apple juice

Cut the peach in half, remove the stone, roughly chop the flesh and put into a food processor or blender. Add the banana and apple juice and whiz until smooth. Pour into a plastic cup.

 1½ **C** ½ ½ 4

vitamins B₆, B₁₂ – phosphorous

cottage cheese dip

5cm piece of cucumber, peeled
2 tbsp natural full-fat cottage cheese
1 tbsp natural full-fat yogurt
1 tsp extra-virgin olive oil
few leaves of fresh coriander or parsley, or a chive leaf, chopped
3 baby corn, halved

Cut the cucumber in half and then into thin sticks. Mix the cottage cheese, yogurt, olive oil and herbs together and serve with the cucumber sticks and baby corn.

fresh **suppers**

Thai-spiced vegetables with rice

6

1

1½

½

3 **C**

vitamins A, B₁, B₆
– phosphorous

makes: 4 toddler portions

storage: best eaten fresh or keep Thai vegetables (not rice) in the refrigerator for up to 2 days

400ml tinned coconut milk

2–3 tsp Thai 7-spice powder

2 medium sweet potatoes, peeled and cut into chunks

2 carrots, peeled and sliced

½ aubergine, cut into chunks

125g fine green beans

zest of 1 unwaxed lime

200g white Basmati rice

This is real energy food for vegetarians. Add some fresh coriander if your toddler likes the flavour. Do not serve coconut milk to toddlers under the age of 3 if there is a family history of allergies.

1 Put the coconut milk and Thai 7-spice into a heavy-based saucepan and gently heat for a few minutes. Add the potatoes, carrots and aubergine and simmer for 15–20 minutes.

2 Add the green beans and cook for a few more minutes, until all the vegetables are cooked. Meanwhile, put the rice into a pan, add 400ml water and simmer for 14 minutes (covered). Remove from the heat and leave covered for 11 minutes.

3 Serve the rice in bowls with the coconut vegetables on top. If necessary, cut into smaller pieces before serving.

stir-fried marinated chicken

12½

½

1

4 **C**

vitamins A, B₆
– phosphorous

makes: 6 toddler portions

storage: best eaten fresh or keep in the refrigerator for up to 2 days (do not reheat rice)

4 chicken breasts (500g)

2 tsp dark soy sauce

2 tbsp hoi sin sauce

2 tsp sesame seeds

2.5cm root ginger, grated

1 tbsp runny honey

1 tbsp vegetable oil

2 spring onions, finely sliced

1 red pepper, seeded and cut into thin strips

2 medium carrots, peeled and cut into thin strips

50g mange-tout, thinly sliced

white Basmati rice, to serve

Don't be surprised if forks get abandoned, there seems to be something quite appealing about picking up crunchy pieces of vegetables and sticky chicken strips with little hands. Do not serve seeds to toddlers under the age of 3 if there is any family history of allergies.

1 Cut the chicken into thin 5mm wide strips. Mix together the soy sauce, hoi sin sauce, sesame seeds, ginger and honey. Pour over the chicken, cover and chill for 30 minutes.

2 Meanwhile, put the rice into a saucepan, add twice the volume of water and simmer for 14 minutes (covered). Remove from the heat and leave covered for 11 minutes.

3 Heat the oil in a wok. Add the chicken and stir-fry until golden and almost cooked. Pour over the remaining marinade and cook over a high heat for 2 minutes, until the chicken is cooked thoroughly.

4 Add the spring onions, pepper, carrots and mange-tout and stir-fry for a few more minutes. Serve with the cooked rice. If necessary, cut into smaller pieces before serving.

haddock with bacon and spinach

14½

1½

1½

1

1

makes: 6 toddler portions

storage: best eaten fresh

550g unsmoked haddock

1½ tbsp olive oil

6 rashers unsmoked back
    bacon, rind removed and
    chopped into small pieces

2 shallots, finely chopped

2 garlic cloves, finely chopped

knob of unsalted butter

225g baby spinach leaves

freshly ground black pepper

celeriac and potato mash,
    to serve

vitamins A, B$_1$,
B$_6$, B$_{12}$
– phosphorous

This requires nothing more complicated than shaking the frying pan for a few minutes. Make a mash of any vegetables that you fancy to go with the fish.

1   Check the haddock for bones. Heat most of the oil in a pan and fry the fish, skin side down, for 2 minutes. Turn over and fry for a few minutes more, until cooked.

2   Meanwhile, heat the remaining oil in another frying pan and fry the bacon until it starts to brown. Add the shallots and garlic and cook until golden and the bacon is cooked through.

3   Add the butter and spinach, then stir for a minute until the spinach has wilted. Season with freshly ground black pepper.

4   Serve the haddock on top of the bacon and spinach with some mash or rice. If necessary, cut into smaller pieces before serving.

chicken with herby mushrooms

19½

1½

2

½

½

makes: 4 toddler portions

storage: best eaten fresh or keep for up to 24 hours in the refrigerator

2 tbsp olive oil

4 small chicken pieces

2 medium red onions,
    finely sliced

2 garlic cloves, finely chopped

250g chestnut mushrooms,
    finely chopped

1 tbsp plain flour

600ml good low-salt chicken
    stock or no- or low-salt
    vegetable stock (page 332)

140ml double cream

2 tbsp fresh herbs, eg
    tarragon, parsley, chopped

freshly ground black pepper

mashed potato or rice,
    to serve

vitamins A, B$_1$,
B$_2$, B$_6$
– phosphorous

You can make this dish with any sort of chicken pieces and any type of mushrooms. However, I do prefer the wonderful nutty flavour of chestnut mushrooms, and my children seem to agree.

1   Preheat the oven to 180°C/350°F/gas mark 4. Heat 1 tbsp olive oil in a heavy-based casserole and brown the chicken pieces all over. Transfer to a plate.

2   Heat the remaining oil in a heavy-based frying pan and sauté the onions until soft – approximately 5 minutes. Add to the chicken.

3   Gently fry the garlic and mushrooms for 5 minutes in the casserole. Stir in the flour and cook for a minute.

4   Gradually add the stock, stirring constantly, and bring up to a gentle simmer. Return the chicken and onions to the pan, cover and transfer to the oven for 30–40 minutes, until the chicken is cooked through.

5   Remove from the oven and place on a low hob. Add the cream, herbs and freshly ground black pepper and heat through. Serve immediately if cool enough or keep warm for 10 minutes in a low oven. If necessary, cut into smaller pieces.

crispy baked chicken

18

1

1½

½ C

✓

vitamins B₆, B₁₂
– phosphorous

makes: 4 toddler portions

storage: best eaten fresh

1–2 tbsp olive oil,
   for greasing
4 chicken breasts
2 tbsp tomato ketchup
1 large egg, beaten
120g crisps (preferably with
   no added salt or low salt),
   crushed

If you feel tempted to give your toddler chicken nuggets, why not resist and make these instead?

1 Preheat the oven to 180°C/350°F/gas mark 4. Lightly oil a baking tray.

2 Lay the chicken breasts between 2 pieces of clingfilm and then bash them with a rolling pin in order to flatten them. Cut each breast into approximately 6 thin strips.

3 Brush the chicken strips with ketchup, then dip into beaten egg and finally roll in the crisps to coat thoroughly.

4 Put the chicken strips on the baking sheet and cook in the oven for 20 minutes, until crisp and golden. If necessary, cut into smaller pieces before serving.

toad in the hole

9½

1½

1½

1½

½ C

✓

vitamins B₆, B₁₂
– phosphorous

makes: 4 toddler portions

storage: best eaten fresh

170g plain flour, sifted
3 large eggs
285ml full-fat milk
2 tbsp cold water
2 tbsp sunflower oil
6 good-quality pork
   sausages
2 tbsp olive oil (optional)

for the gravy:
1 tbsp olive oil (optional)
2 medium onions,
   finely sliced
1–2 garlic cloves,
   finely chopped
1 tbsp plain flour
600ml low-salt chicken, beef,
   or no- or low-salt vegetable
   stock (page 332)
freshly ground black pepper

This recipe needs to be served with a good rich gravy. Cook a little broccoli or some stir-fried greens to make the meal complete.

1 Preheat the oven to 220°C/425°F/gas mark 7. Put the first 5 ingredients into a food processor or blender and whiz until smooth. Leave the batter for 30 minutes.

2 Preheat the grill to hot and cook the sausages until golden brown.

3 Transfer the sausages to a roasting tin with 2 tbsp sausage fat or olive oil. Heat the tin over a medium heat. When it is really hot, quickly pour in the batter and transfer to the highest shelf in the oven. Cook for 30–35 minutes, or until the batter is puffed up and golden brown.

4 To make the gravy, heat 1 tbsp sausage fat or olive oil in a heavy-based saucepan. Add the onions and garlic and sauté, stirring occasionally, until soft and light brown – approximately 5–10 minutes. Stir in the flour and cook for a couple of minutes before gradually adding the stock. Simmer for 5 minutes and then season with freshly ground black pepper.

5 If necessary, cut into smaller pieces before serving.

quick bites
suppers

All of the recipes make one toddler portion unless stated otherwise.

1 **C** ½ 2 ½ 11½

1 small carrot, peeled and chopped
1 small parsnip, peeled and chopped
15g knob of unsalted butter
1 medium pork chop (approx 100g)

pork chop with parsnip and carrot mash

Bring a small pan of water to the boil and cook the carrot and parsnip until soft – approximately 10 minutes. Drain, add the butter and roughly mash. Meanwhile, cook the pork chop under a preheated hot grill for approximately 4–5 minutes on each side, or until cooked through. If necessary, cut into smaller pieces before serving with the mash.

2 **C** 1½ ½ 12

vitamins B_1, B_6
– phosphorous

15g unsalted butter, softened
1 garlic clove, crushed
1 tbsp fresh parsley, chopped
1 chicken thigh, with skin
2–3 new potatoes, washed and quartered
1 tsp olive oil
freshly ground black pepper

chicken with parsley and garlic butter

Preheat the oven to 180°C/350°F/gas mark 4. Mix the butter, garlic and parsley together and push under the skin of the chicken thigh. Put into a small roasting tin with the potatoes and olive oil and season with freshly ground black pepper. Roast in the medium oven until the chicken and potatoes are cooked through – approximately 30–40 minutes. If necessary, cut into smaller pieces before serving.

1½ **C** 1½ ½ 10½

vitamin B_{12}
– phosphorous

1 medium potato, peeled
and halved
1 tbsp unsalted butter
1 tbsp fresh parsley, chopped
1 medium egg, poached (page 251)

fried parsley potatoes with poached egg

Bring a small pan of water to the boil and cook the potato for approximately 10 minutes, until still slightly firm in the centre. Drain, cool and cut into small cubes. Melt the butter in a heavy-based frying pan, add the potatoes and parsley and cook for 10–15 minutes, until the potato is cooked and golden. Serve with the poached egg, all chopped into small pieces if necessary.

3 **C** ½ 1 1½ 7½

3 medium new potatoes,
scrubbed
3 black Greek olives, stoned
and chopped
1 ripe small tomato,
finely chopped
1 medium egg, hardboiled
and quartered

potato salad with olives, tomato and egg

Bring a small pan of water to the boil and cook the potatoes until tender – approximately 10–12 minutes. Drain and cut into bite-size pieces. Put into a bowl with the chopped stoned olives and chopped tomato and top with the boiled egg quarters.

mushroom and garlic-stuffed bread

½ ▢ ½ ◖ ½ ⊠ 3½ ⊟

1 small, part-baked white or
wholemeal bread roll (available in
the freezer section of
most supermarkets)
15g unsalted butter
1 garlic clove, crushed
2 field mushrooms, halved

Preheat the oven to the temperature recommended for the bread. Make 4 slits into the top of the bread roll. Spread half of the butter in the slits. Melt the remaining butter in a small pan and gently fry the garlic and mushrooms briefly until the mushrooms are soft – approximately 5 minutes. Stuff the mushrooms into each slit, pouring over any pan juices. Bake in the preheated oven for the time recommended on the bread packet. Cut into small pieces, cool a little and serve.

sausage stew

½ C ½ ▢ 1 ◖ 1½ ⊠ 7½ ⊟

vitamins B₁, B₆

makes: 2 toddler portions
1 tsp olive oil
2 good pork sausages, skins removed
250ml storecupboard tomato sauce
(page 332) or 250ml passata
100g tinned cooked chickpeas, rinsed

Heat the oil in a heavy-based pan and fry the sausage meat, breaking it up with a wooden spoon as you go. When it is golden, add the tomato sauce. Bring to the boil, scraping the bottom to dislodge any bits that are sticking. Add the chickpeas and simmer for 10 minutes. Serve.

grilled salmon with steamed vegetables

vitamins B₁, B₆, B₁₂
– phosphorous

1 small piece of salmon fillet
(approx 75g), skinned
6 mange-tout
4 baby corn
1 tsp light soy sauce

Preheat the grill to high and cook the salmon for about 2–3 minutes on each side, until pale golden and cooked through. Meanwhile, cook the vegetables in a steamer over a pan of boiling water and cut into small pieces. Put the vegetables onto a small plate and flake over the salmon, checking carefully for bones. Sprinkle over the soy sauce and serve.

penne with chicken and broccoli

4 C 2½ ▢ 2½ ◖ 1 ⊠ 16½ ⊟

75g penne
100g mixed broccoli and
cauliflower florets
½ quantity (300ml) storecupboard white
sauce (page 333)
100g cooked chicken, shredded

Cook the penne following the packet's instructions. Steam the vegetables over a pan of boiling water until tender. Drain the pasta. Put the white sauce into a small, heavy-based pan and bring to simmering point. Stir in the pasta, vegetables and cooked chicken and bring back to simmering point, stirring often, until the chicken is heated through. If necessary, cut into small pieces before serving.

couscous with grated vegetables

3 C 1 ▢ ½ ◖ 2½ ⊠ 3½ ⊟

50g couscous
1 small carrot, peeled and grated
5cm piece of cucumber,
peeled and grated
50g baby spinach, finely shredded
1 tbsp extra-virgin olive oil
juice of ½ small lemon
1 tsp runny honey

Cook the couscous following the packet's instructions, then mix in the vegetables. In a small bowl, whisk together the olive oil, lemon and honey and pour over the couscous. Mix well and serve.

suppers to freeze

meatballs in tomato sauce

10½
1
3
2

makes: 10 toddler portions
(30 small meatballs)

storage: up to 4 months in
the freezer

4 tbsp olive oil
4 large onions, finely chopped
2 garlic cloves, chopped
1 tbsp balsamic vinegar
2 x 400g tin chopped tomatoes
300ml no- or low-salt
  vegetable stock (page 332)
freshly ground black pepper
large pinch of soft
  brown sugar
2 tbsp fresh parsley, chopped
2 tbsp basil leaves, torn
800g lean beef mince
2 tbsp fresh parsley, chopped
flour, for coating

vitamins B₆, B₁₂
– phosphorous

You can make meatballs in many ways, but I always come back to this recipe.

1 To make the tomato sauce, heat 2 tbsp oil in a heavy-based saucepan and sauté half the onions until soft. Add the garlic and sauté for a few minutes before adding the balsamic vinegar. Cook for a minute.

2 Stir in the tomatoes and stock. Season with a pinch of salt, black pepper and sugar, then simmer, uncovered, for 20 minutes. Add the parsley and basil.

3 For the meatballs, heat the remaining oil in a frying pan and sauté the remaining onions until soft. Transfer to a bowl and cool. Mix in the mince, parsley and seasoning. Lightly flour your hands and make small meatballs. Roll each in flour.

4 Heat 2 tbsp oil in a heavy-based frying pan and brown the meatballs in batches. Drain on kitchen paper. Add the meatballs to the sauce, cover and simmer for 15 minutes. Turn the meatballs, then cook, uncovered for 10–15 minutes. Cool completely. Spoon into freezerproof containers or freezer bags. Freeze.

5 Thaw thoroughly. Gently heat in a saucepan until boiling. If necessary, cut into smaller pieces before serving.

smoked haddock soup

12½
½
1
1
2

makes: 6 toddler portions

storage: up to 3 months in
the freezer

450g smoked haddock fillets
450ml full-fat milk
450ml water
2 small onions
40g unsalted butter
2 medium potatoes, peeled
  and cubed
2 ripe tomatoes, skinned,
  seeded and chopped
freshly ground black pepper
1 tbsp fresh parsley, chopped

vitamins B₁, B₆, B₁₂
– phosphorous

Many toddlers will love this soup and its smoky flavour.

1 Put the fish into a saucepan with the milk, water and 1 onion. Simmer very gently for 5 minutes, until the fish is cooked, then leave to stand for 10 minutes. Strain and reserve the liquid and fish separately.

2 Finely chop the remaining onion. Melt the butter in a large pan and cook the onion until soft, then add the potatoes and cook for a few minutes, stirring.

3 Pour over the poaching liquid and cook until the potato is soft. Purée with a hand-held blender (or in a food processor or blender). Return to the pan.

4 Flake the cooked fish, removing any bones. Stir into the soup with the tomatoes, freshly ground black pepper and parsley. Leave to cool completely, then pour into freezerproof containers and freeze.

5 Defrost thoroughly, then heat through until boiling. Cool a little to serve.

beef burgers with cheese

15½

makes: approx 6 toddler portions (12 small burgers)

1

storage: up to 4 months in the freezer

4

1 tbsp olive oil

1

1 medium red onion,
    finely chopped

500g good-quality lean
    beef mince

vitamins B₁, B₆, B₁₂
– phosphorous

1 medium egg, beaten

freshly ground black pepper

75g Cheddar cheese, finely
    chopped (optional)

bread rolls, shredded
    lettuce, cheese slices,
    tomato slices, to serve

It does not take long to mix together some minced beef with a few seasonings to make beef burgers – giving you peace of mind as you know exactly what went into them. Never refreeze raw meat that has already been frozen.

1 Heat the oil in a frying pan and sauté the onion until soft – approximately 5 minutes. Transfer to a large bowl and cool.

2 Add the mince and egg and season lightly with freshly ground black pepper. Mix well with the cheese, if using.

3 Wet your hands slightly and make small beef burgers. Layer in a freezerproof container between sheets of greaseproof paper and freeze.

4 Thaw thoroughly. Keep the burgers at room temperature for 30 minutes before cooking.

5 Grill the burgers for 3–4 minutes on each side, until cooked through.

6 Serve with bread rolls, lettuce and cheese and tomato slices. If necessary, cut into smaller pieces before serving.

lamb stew

16½

makes: 8 toddler portions

storage: up to 4 months in the freezer

1½

1

4 tbsp olive oil

2½

150g unsmoked back bacon,
    rind removed, chopped

900g lean lamb shoulder,
    diced

vitamins B₁, B₆, B₁₂
– phosphorous

2 medium onions,
    finely chopped

2 garlic cloves, finely chopped

100ml no- or low-salt
    vegetable stock (page 332)

400g tin chopped tomatoes

400g tin cherry tomatoes

large pinch of dark
    brown sugar

handful of fresh thyme sprigs

freshly ground black pepper

You may like to add some mushrooms or olives to this stew. I often serve it with a creamy plain or pesto mash, but it is also great with rice.

1 Preheat the oven to 150°C/300°F/gas mark 2. Heat a large heavy-based casserole until hot. Add 2 tbsp olive oil and brown the bacon and lamb. Transfer to a plate.

2 Heat the remaining oil and gently sweat the onions and garlic until soft – approximately 5 minutes.

3 Add the stock and leave to bubble for a few minutes, stirring occasionally.

4 Add the lamb, bacon, chopped tomatoes, cherry tomatoes, sugar and most of the thyme. Season with freshly ground black pepper.

5 Bring to the boil, cover and cook in the oven for 1 hour 50 minutes, stirring occasionally. Scatter over the remaining fresh thyme leaves and season. Cool completely. Transfer to freezerproof containers, cover and freeze.

6 Thaw thoroughly. Gently heat until boiling. If necessary, cut into smaller pieces before serving.

green vegetable crumble

makes: 5 toddler portions

storage: up to 4 months in the freezer

10

2

2

3

6 C

vitamins A, B₁, B₂, B₆, B₁₂ folic acid – phosphorous

2 heads broccoli, in florets
2 leeks, washed and sliced
200g green beans, topped and tailed
250g fresh spinach, washed
30g unsalted butter
30g plain flour
400ml full-fat milk
75g Cheddar cheese, grated
freshly ground black pepper
2 tbsp fresh herbs, chopped
50g fresh breadcrumbs
50g nuts, finely chopped
25g Parmesan cheese, grated

A variety of textures make this crumble popular with toddlers. Do not give nuts to children under the age of 3 if there is a family history of food allergies.

1 Steam or boil the broccoli, leeks and beans separately until just tender. Drain.
2 Wilt the spinach in a pan with a tiny amount of water. Drain thoroughly in a sieve, pressing with a wooden spoon. Roughly chop and mix with other vegetables in an ovenproof and freezerproof dish.
3 Melt the butter in a pan, stir in the flour and cook for 1 minute. Gradually add the milk, stirring constantly, and simmer until the sauce is smooth and thickened. Stir in the cheese and add pepper. Pour over the vegetables.
4 Mix together the herbs, breadcrumbs, nuts and Parmesan and scatter over the top. Cool completely. Wrap the dish in clingfilm or foil and freeze.
5 Thaw thoroughly. Cook in a preheated oven at 180°C/350°F/gas mark 4 for 20–25 minutes, until piping hot and the topping is golden. If necessary, cut into smaller pieces before serving.

creamy chicken and leek pie

makes: 8 toddler portions

storage: up to 4 months in the freezer

24

1½

2½

½

2 C

vitamins A, B₁, B₂, B₆ – phosphorous

1.25kg whole chicken
2 medium onions, quartered
1 large carrot, peeled and cut into chunks
bunch of fresh herbs, eg rosemary, thyme and parsley
salt and 4 peppercorns
3 tbsp olive oil
130g pancetta, cubed
250g chestnut mushrooms, chopped
25g unsalted butter
3 medium leeks, finely sliced
25g plain flour
4 tbsp double cream (optional)
1 x 375g pack puff pastry

This is a richly satisfying supper that is packed with protein.

1 Put the chicken in a casserole with the onions, carrot, half the herbs, a pinch of salt and the peppercorns. Cover with water and a lid. Bring to the boil. Simmer for 1 hour. Pierce a thigh with a knife to see if the juices run clear, then leave to cool. Remove the meat from the bones, cut into small chunks then put into a freezerproof pie dish. Skim any fat off stock, strain and reserve 565ml.
2 Heat the olive oil in heavy-based saucepan. Add the pancetta and mushrooms and cook until golden – about 5 minutes. Transfer to a bowl and cool.
3 Heat the butter in the pan and sauté the leeks until soft. Stir in the flour and cook for 2 minutes, then gradually add the stock and stir, until sauce thickens.
4 Chop the remaining herbs, and add with some seasoning. Cool completely. Add the cream (if using) and the mushroom and pancetta mixture. Mix well.
5 Pour the cool sauce over the cool chicken.
6 Cut thin strips of the pastry and place on the dampened pie dish lip. Rest the remaining pastry sheet over the pie. Crimp the edges together and trim. Make a small slit in the lid and wrap in clingfilm or foil and freeze.
7 Thaw thoroughly. Cook in a preheated oven at 190°C/375°F/gas mark 5 for about 30 minutes, until piping hot and the pastry is puffed and golden. If necessary, cut into smaller pieces before serving.

fresh & frozen puddings

banana and toffee ice-cream

makes: 8 toddler portions

storage: up to 3 months in the freezer

2½

½

½

1 **C**

vitamin B₆

150ml full-fat milk
juice of ½ lemon
125g golden caster sugar
300g full-fat cream cheese
3 very ripe bananas, peeled,
   and roughly chopped
2 x 45g Crunchie bars

Use the ripest bananas you can find to give the best flavour. This has to be one of the easiest ways to make ice-cream – and one of the tastiest.

1 Put all of the ingredients, except the Crunchie bars, into a food processor or blender and whiz until really smooth.
2 Roughly crush the Crunchie bars into very small pieces.
3 Tip into a freezerproof bowl, add the Crunchie pieces, stir once, cover and freeze for at least 6 hours.
4 Leave at room temperature for 5 minutes before serving.

apple and blackberry crumble

makes: 6 toddler portions

storage: best eaten fresh or freeze for up to 4 months

2½

½

½

½

1 **C**

100g plain flour, plus 1 tbsp
25g hazelnuts, toasted and
   finely chopped
50g unsalted butter, chilled
   and diced
1 medium egg yolk
3 apples, eg Bramley, peeled,
   cored and sliced
100g blackberries
3 tbsp light soft brown sugar

for the crumble topping:
50g unsalted butter, chilled
   and diced
75g white flour
50g soft brown sugar
25g hazelnuts, toasted and
   finely chopped

This makes a change from the traditional crumble. It is a tart with a crumble topping. You could use any fruit that is in season. Do not give nuts to toddlers under the age of 3 if there is any family history of food allergies.

1 Put the flour and nuts into a food processor or blender, add the butter and process until the mixture resembles fine breadcrumbs. (Alternatively, rub in the butter with your fingertips.)
2 Add the egg yolk and a little water, if necessary, and process until the pastry just draws together. Knead briefly on a lightly floured surface to form a flat 22cm round.
3 Line a chilled 20cm loose-bottomed tin with the pastry, trim the edges with a generous hand and chill for 30 minutes. Line with baking paper and baking beans and bake blind in a preheated oven at 180°C/350°F/gas mark 4 for 10 minutes, then remove the paper and beans and bake for a further 5 minutes.
4 In a bowl, mix together the apples, blackberries, soft brown sugar and 1 tbsp flour. Spoon into the pastry case.
5 For the topping, rub the butter into the flour (or in a food processor or blender) until the mixture resembles fine breadcrumbs. Stir in the remaining ingredients. Sprinkle over the fruit and bake at 180°C/350°F/gas mark 4 for 20–25 minutes.

quick bites puddings

Try not to make a habit of always offering something sweet after a savoury course, as most toddlers will very quickly learn that if they don't eat their main course they can still fill up on pudding.

All of the recipes make one toddler portion unless stated otherwise.

1½ **C** 2 1 ½ 5½

banana pasta

makes: 3 toddler portions
600ml full-fat milk
25g golden caster sugar
100g macaroni
2 ripe small bananas, peeled and sliced

Bring the milk and sugar to the boil in a heavy-based pan. Add the macaroni and bring back to the boil. Continue to simmer, stirring often, until the pasta is tender – approximately 10–15 minutes. Spoon into a bowl, add the sliced bananas and serve.

1 **C** ½ ½ ½ 3½

quick passionfruit trifle

1 ripe passionfruit
2 sponge fingers, broken
into pieces
2 tbsp natural full-fat yogurt

Passionfruit are a good source of both beta-carotene and vitamin C. Cut the passionfruit in half and scoop out the pulp. Put the sponge fingers into the bottom of a small plastic bowl. Top with the yogurt and then the passionfruit pulp. Cover and leave for at least 10–15 minutes for the sponge fingers to soak up all the juices.

 1 ½ ½ 2½

phosphorous

rice pudding with prunes

1 portion of home-made rice
pudding (page 232)
or 100g tinned rice pudding
3 ready-to-eat prunes

Chop the prunes into very small pieces and simply stir into the rice pudding before serving. Do not reheat home-made rice pudding.

1½ ½ ½ 4

vitamin B₆ –
phosphorous

yogurt with honey and raisins

1 tbsp nuts, eg cashews,
hazelnuts, almonds (do not give
nuts to toddlers under the age
of 3 if there is a family history
of allergies)
3 tbsp natural full-fat yogurt
1 tsp runny honey
1 tbsp raisins

Finely chop the nuts and put into a bowl. Add the yogurt, honey and raisins and mix together.

orange and passionfruit sorbet

5

makes: 10 toddler portions
juice of 1kg fresh oranges
125g golden caster sugar
5 passionfruit

This is how sorbets should taste – full of flavour. The reason for this is because it is made of pure, fresh fruit juice without any added water. It does contain sugar, as this is a vital ingredient for determining the soft and creamy texture. Put the juice in a pan, scoop out any pips, then add the sugar and heat gently until all the sugar is dissolved, stirring occasionally. Leave to cool. Put a sieve over the pan. Halve the passionfruit and scrape the flesh into the sieve. Press it through with a wooden spoon. Stir well, then freeze in an ice-cream machine or pour the mixture into a freezerproof container, cover and freeze for 2 hours. Remove the sorbet from the freezer and whiz in a food processor or blender, then return it to the freezer for another 2 hours. Repeat the process. Freeze for at least 6 hours. Leave at room temperature for 5 minutes before serving.

plums and custard

½ C 1½ ½ 3½

vitamins B₂, B₆,
2 – phosphorous

makes: 2 toddler portions
1 tbsp custard powder
2 tsp golden caster sugar
300ml full-fat milk
2 ripe plums, halved and stoned

Make the custard following the packet's instructions. Chop the plums into very small pieces and divide the fruit between 2 bowls. Cover each with custard. When it is in season, try using stewed rhubarb instead of the plums; it goes really well with custard.

peach with dried papaya

6 C 1 1

1 ripe peach
2 pieces of dried papaya, finely chopped
full-fat natural yogurt, to serve

Peel the peach if necessary. Cut in half and remove the stone. Cut the flesh into small pieces and put into a bowl. Scatter over the dried papaya. If you are serving this to a vegan toddler, keep as it is. Alternatively, you may like to add a dollop of natural yogurt.

rhubarb and berries

4 C 1 6½

makes: 2 toddler portions
200g fresh rhubarb
handful of blueberries (approx 50g)
4 ripe strawberries, hulled, chopped
75ml apple juice
1–2 tbsp golden caster sugar – enough to taste

Trim the rhubarb and chop into small pieces. Put it into a saucepan. Add the berries, 50ml water and the apple juice and simmer for 5 minutes, or until the rhubarb is just tender. Stir in the caster sugar to taste. Transfer the fruit into small bowls to serve.

nectarine crumble

vitamin B₆ –
phosphorous

1 ripe nectarine
2 tbsp home-made granola (page 297; do not give nuts to toddlers under the age of 3 if there is a family history of allergies)
small knob of unsalted butter

If you don't have home-made granola to hand, use a bought cereal. Preheat the oven to 180°C/350°F/ gas mark 4. Cut the nectarine in half and remove the stone. Put each half in a small ovenproof dish. Spoon the granola on top of the fruit. Dot with butter and bake for 15 minutes, until the nectarine is soft and the topping is crunchy. If necessary, cut into smaller pieces before serving.

celebration food

pink meringues

makes: 20 toddler portions (approx 40 meringues)

storage: keep in an airtight container for up to 2 weeks or freeze for up to 3 months

175g golden caster sugar

a couple of drops pink food colouring

3 medium egg whites

When I served these for Jasmin's birthday tea her eyes nearly popped out of her head. You do need to use a good quality food colouring otherwise the colour can vanish on cooking.

1 Preheat the oven to 110°C/225°F/gas mark ¼. Line 2 baking trays with non-stick baking parchment.
2 Put the sugar into a bowl, add the food colouring and mix together.
3 Put the egg whites into a clean, grease-free bowl and whisk until stiff peaks form. Add a little of the coloured sugar and whisk, then continue to add the sugar, whisking after each addition – whisk quickly to prevent the egg whites from collapsing.
4 Put little spoonfuls of the mixture onto the trays, leaving a small space between each. Put the trays into the oven and bake for 1 hour, then turn off the oven and leave to cool.
5 When cool, peel away the paper.

bicycle pump

2½

½

1

makes: 10 toddler portions

storage: keep in the refrigerator for up to 2 days

135g packet of flavoured jelly
410g tinned evaporated milk

vitamin B₆

This works best with a red- or black-coloured jelly, such as strawberry, raspberry or blackcurrant. If you don't have an electric whisk, you could try whisking it by hand, but it may take quite a while!

1 Put the jelly into a small saucepan with 2 tbsp water and melt over a very gentle heat. Do not allow it to boil or simmer. Keep warm.
2 Meanwhile, put the evaporated milk into a large bowl and whisk with an electric whisk for about 10 minutes, until thick and mousse-like and almost tripled in volume. Continue to whisk and slowly pour in the melted jelly so that the mousse is evenly coloured. Quickly pour into a clear bowl and leave in the refrigerator for at least 2 hours, until set.

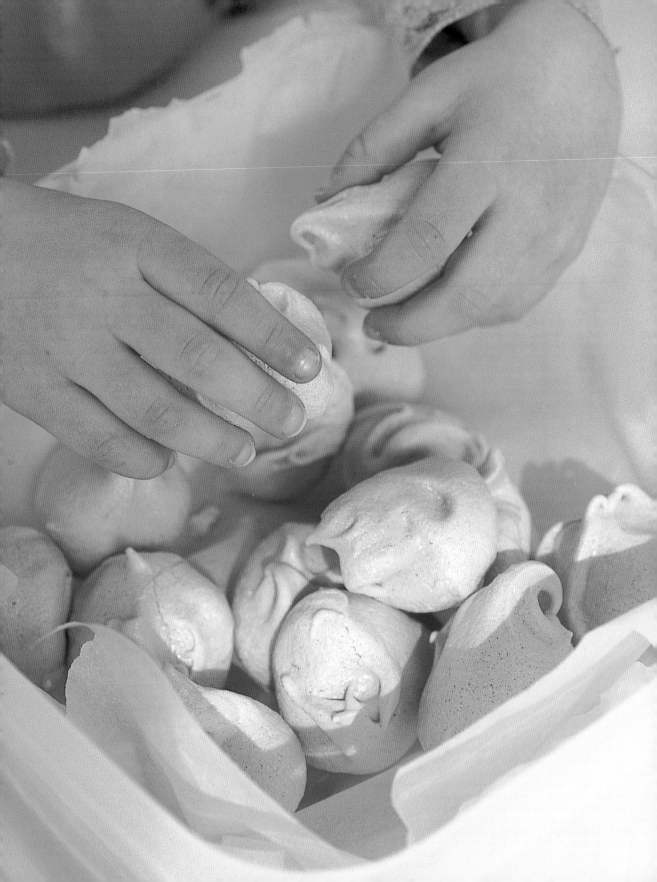

banana and apricot tea bread

2½

makes: approx 10 toddler
portions (approx 1kg loaf)

½

storage: best eaten fresh or
keep in airtight container for
up to 3 days or freeze for up
to 3 months

½

1

vitamins B₆, B₁₂

100g unsalted butter, melted,
  plus extra for greasing
3 large bananas
  (450g unpeeled weight)
juice of ½ lemon
2 large eggs
150g golden caster sugar
½ tsp salt
200g self-raising flour, sifted
50g dried unsulphured
  apricots, finely chopped
50g dried cranberries,
  finely chopped
75g sifted icing sugar, to glaze
juice of ½ lemon, to glaze

Really ripe bananas, even ones with blackened skin, give the best banana flavour. If you do not have any dried cranberries, just use 50g more dried unsulphured apricots.

1 Preheat the oven to 180°C/350°F/gas mark 4. Grease and line a 1kg loaf tin or butter 10 mini loaf tins.

2 Whiz the bananas in a food processor or blender with the lemon juice until really smooth.

3 Whisk the eggs until foamy, then add the sugar, a little at a time, and the melted butter and salt. Fold in the flour alternately with the banana mixture. Stir in the apricots and cranberries.

4 Spoon into the loaf tin and bake in the oven for 50–55 minutes (or 25 minutes for the mini loaf tins). Turn out and cool on a wire rack.

5 To make the glaze, mix together the icing sugar and lemon juice and drizzle over the top.

fruit cookies

1

makes: 20 toddler portions
(approx 20 cookies)

storage: keep in an airtight
container for up to 3 days or
freeze for up to 3 months

100g unsalted butter,
  softened, plus 2 tbsp for
  the topping and extra
  for greasing
100g golden caster sugar,
  plus 2 tbsp for the topping
1 large egg
175g plain flour, sifted
50g ground almonds
1 tsp ground mixed spice
75g currants

Ella calls these squashed-fly cookies. They are sweet but not too messy to eat – something I am sure many parents consider when planning a celebration that involves toddlers! Once cooked, these can be frozen and just thawed when needed.

1 In a bowl, beat the butter and sugar together until pale and fluffy. Add the egg and beat well.

2 Add the flour, ground almonds, mixed spice and currants and mix to a firm dough. Cover and chill for 15–20 minutes.

3 Preheat the oven to 180°C/350°F/gas mark 4. Grease a baking tray. On a lightly floured surface, roll out the dough to 3–4mm thick. Use a 5cm biscuit cutter to cut out rounds and place on the tray.

4 Brush the biscuits with a little melted butter and sprinkle with sugar. Bake in the oven for 8–10 minutes, until lightly golden. Cool on a wire rack.

lemon drizzle cake

2

½

vitamin B$_6$

makes: 10 toddler portions

storage: keep in an airtight container for up to 4 days or freeze for up to 3 months

175g unsalted butter, softened

175g golden caster sugar

grated zest and juice of 1 unwaxed lemon

2 medium eggs, beaten

3–4 tbsp full-fat milk

175g self-raising flour, sifted

2 tbsp golden icing sugar, sifted

You could make an orange drizzle cake instead of this lemon cake – just use the zest of 2 unwaxed oranges in the cake mix and the juice of 1 orange for the topping.

1 Preheat the oven to 180°C/350°F/gas mark 4. Grease and line the bottom of a 900g loaf tin.

2 Beat the butter, sugar and lemon zest together in a bowl until light and fluffy. Gradually beat in the eggs and milk.

3 Fold the flour into the mixture. Spoon into the prepared tin. Bake in the oven for 45–55 minutes, until the cake is golden and firm to touch.

4 Mix together the lemon juice and icing sugar.

5 Poke a cocktail stick all over the hot cake and then pour over the lemon icing immediately.

6 Cool in the tin for 5 minutes, then turn out onto a wire rack.

piggies in blankets

2

makes: 25 toddler portions

storage: keep in the refrigerator for up to 2 days or freeze for up to 3 months

40g unsalted butter, plus extra for greasing

225g self-raising flour

pinch of salt

½ tsp baking powder

50g sundried tomatoes, finely chopped

25g fresh parsley, chopped

75g Cheddar cheese, grated

150ml full-fat milk, plus extra for glazing

25 chipolata sausages, cooked and cooled

These little sausages wrapped in a herby scone mixture make a great alternative to sausage rolls.

1 Preheat the oven to 200°C/400°F/gas mark 6. Grease a baking sheet. Sift the flour, salt and baking powder into a bowl.

2 Rub in the butter with your fingertips or in a food processor or blender until the mixture resembles breadcrumbs. Stir in the tomatoes, parsley and cheese. Make a well in the centre, then mix in enough milk to form a soft dough.

3 On a lightly floured surface, roll into a square, 6mm thick. Cut into 25 smaller squares.

4 Wrap each chipolata in a square of dough, then use a little milk to stick down the edges. Put on the baking sheet and brush the tops with milk. Bake in the oven for 8–10 minutes, until risen and golden. Serve warm.

5 If necessary, cut into smaller pieces before serving.

Now is the time to get your toddler involved in all aspects of food, not just mealtimes. Encourage his interest by taking him to stimulating places, such as farmers' markets, where he will be able to taste seasonal produce. Or involve him in the preparation of meals. Toddlers at this stage get bored quickly, particularly at mealtimes, so don't insist he eats everything; just serve smaller portions so that he has the satisfaction of finishing a meal and asking for more. And he will really pick up on your attitude to food: try to be relaxed and encourage him to eat well by giving him the wide variety of foods that you eat yourself. What you do now will set him up for the rest of his life.

3–4 years

what's happening to
your toddler

During this year you will notice that your toddler is becoming more self aware. If he is anything like my 3-year-old he will be chatting for Britain, with a favourite word being 'why' – in Ella's case, partly because she is naturally inquisitive, but also because she likes to keep me talking!

Your toddler will be more independent and sure of himself. He will like to play with siblings and other children, but he will also be content to play by himself. He will love to do 'grown-up' things, such as choosing and paying for goods in a shop. Encourage this when you are out shopping for food and, if you get the chance, go to farmers' markets, where he may be able to taste as well as look at food.

Of course, his physical skills will have improved. He will enjoy hopping, skipping and running. He will also be more capable of carrying out everyday tasks – for example, he will probably be able to dress himself (albeit haphazardly), and feed himself quite easily, perhaps even using a big knife and fork. Mealtimes should become less challenging, especially as he becomes more reasonable and willing to accept substitutes – for example, if he asks for a banana but you only have an apple.

At this age, toddlers will have a fairly clear idea of what they do and don't enjoy and will be able to let you know this. They think more deeply than they have before but will get bored quickly, often at mealtimes: when they have lost interest, don't drag things out by insisting plates are cleared. If you offer varied and interesting meals, most inquisitive toddlers will take up the challenge. Try offering fun foods such as cherry tomatoes, little cheeses or small bread rolls rather than processed foods aimed at children.

Your toddler will also become far more aware of others, learning from them, but also acknowledging how they feel about things. At this stage, your attitude to food will really have an effect on him. Having a relaxed but healthy approach to eating is vital. You can also encourage him to eat well by simply giving him the same wide variety of foods that you eat yourself. What he eats in his formative years may have some impact on his health later in life.

By the age of three, you will notice your toddler becoming more interested in the food that he eats. The main concern at this stage can be what your toddler is eating while he is out of your care, for example at friends, grandparents or a nursery. You will also begin to notice some of the effects of peer pressure – my daughter Ella has become aware of the kinds of convenience foods available and looks for them when we go shopping, even though I don't keep them in the house.

If your toddler is eating less than usual, this may be because he has been eating foods such as crisps, that are too energy-dense, without enough other nutrients. You may also see other behavioural changes, particularly those induced by the over-consumption of sugar or additives. I am aware that Ella becomes 'hyper' after children's parties, where she has eaten lots of high-sugar foods such as cakes, sweets and biscuits.

Of course, regular sugar consumption can also cause tooth decay. It can be more problematic and unrealistic to completely ban all sugary foods. Giving a few sugary foods every now and then is fine. If, like Ella, your toddler has a sweet tooth, give other sweet foods, such as fruit-based smoothies or milkshakes, chunks of fresh fruit, handfuls of dried fruits or low-sugar muesli bars (do not give nuts to toddlers under the age of 3 if there is a family history of food allergies).

At this stage, your toddler is likely to be active and full of energy. Playing outside is something that should be encouraged, not only because it is good for your child's well-being but also because it has important nutritional benefits. The main source of vitamin D for most toddlers is from the action of sunlight on their skin. Vitamin D, along with calcium, is needed to help make bones stronger. However, if you live in a more northerly country, or your toddler is kept covered for religious or medical reasons, or if he is on a restricted diet, such as vegan, you should speak to your family doctor or registered dietician about vitamin D supplements.

which nutrients
are key

your toddler's
routine

your toddler's feeds

Snacks will be more of a contentious issue, as your toddler becomes aware of the types of foods available – and junk food in particular. It is really important to always try and offer healthy snacks. Make sure that they are given at least two hours before the next meal, so that they do not spoil your toddler's appetite.

Continue with the previous two years' routine:
breakfast – around 7.30–8am
mid-morning snack – around 10am
lunch – around 12.30–1pm
mid-afternoon snack – around 3pm
supper – 5–5.30pm
bed – 7–7.30 pm

your toddler's sleeps

It is unlikely, between three and four years old, that your toddler will need a sleep during the day. However, he will be a lot more active and inquisitive, and he can become overtired. Ella, my oldest, at 3½ years old, still had a quiet time during the day, usually after lunch, when she was happy to sit and look at books or watch a video by herself for at least half an hour. It is important for toddlers to feel relaxed about spending some quiet time on their own.

how important is variety?

From the age of 1, your goal should be to gradually increase the variety of foods included in your toddler's diet, so that by the age of 4 he is eating as wide a variety of foods as possible. Although variety is best, inevitably there will be times when it seems he has eaten the same thing for two or three days in a row. Some parents worry that it will affect their toddler's nutritional intake, but many studies have shown that even if a toddler eats the same healthy meals for a few consecutive days, they will usually manage to consume the right kind of food for normal growth and development.

constipation

Almost all toddlers will suffer from constipation at some point. It is likely that your toddler is suffering if he finds it difficult to go the toilet, passing only hard and dry faeces infrequently. Stools should always be quite soft and not cause pain or discomfort. However, constipation is normally a short-term problem. Try to give him more fresh fruit, vegetables, wholemeal bread and other fibre-rich foods that toddlers like, such as low-sugar baked beans and high-fibre white bread. It is also very important to get him to drink lots of water, as this will help with bowel movement: sometimes constipation is just the result of insufficient fluid. If the problem persists for more than a week, seek advice from your family doctor or registered dietician.

toddler diarrhoea

Toddler diarrhoea is also relatively common. There are several possible causes, but the most likely is a change in diet. If your toddler has eaten more fruit, fruit juice, sugary drinks or dried fruit than usual, he is likely to suffer from diarrhoea. The most important thing to do is to make sure he drinks enough fluids to compensate for those lost, or he may become dehydrated surprisingly quickly. Diarrhoea may sometimes be accompanied by a fever, lack of appetite, vomiting and abdominal pain. If your child shows any of these symptoms, consult your family doctor.

trouble shooting

sample meal planners

By the age of 4, your child should be eating more or less the same variety of foods as the rest of the family, so try to vary his diet as much as possible in this year. This will have the added bonus of encouraging his interest in mealtimes – by the time they are 3, toddlers can get bored easily, so meals with challenging textures and 'naturally' toddler-size foods, such as cherry tomatoes, individual home-made tarts or vegetable sticks, can appeal.

	breakfast	mid-am	lunch	mid-pm	supper	bed
menu 1	150ml milk, banana and chocolate pastry, drink	orange segments, drink	smoked mackerel paté, drink	drink	courgette cream cheese pasta, raspberry yogurt ice, drink	200ml milk
menu 2	150ml milk, dried fruit compote, drink	apple, drink	quick tomato chicken, drink	drink	home-made pizza, very quick apple crumble, drink	200ml milk
menu 3	150ml milk, fried bread and eggs, drink	drink	chickpea and bacon soup, drink	pear, drink	lamb burgers with lemony beans, grilled fruits, drink	200ml milk
menu 4	150ml milk, granola, drink	grapes, drink	warm bacon with beans, drink	drink	couscous with roasted ratatouille, drink	200ml milk
menu 5	150ml milk, boiled egg with soldiers, drink	banana, drink	tomato, mozzarella and basil on ciabatta, drink	drink	baked beans and cheese on toast, drink	200ml milk
menu 6	150ml milk, bacon eggy bread, drink	drink	roasted vegetables with pasta bake, drink	drink	lamb koftas, drink	200ml milk

	breakfast	mid-am	lunch	mid-pm	supper	bed
menu 7	150ml milk, blueberry buttermilk pancake, drink	banana, drink	noodles with peanuts, drink	drink	lamb chop with French beans, choc chip steamed pudding, drink	200ml milk
menu 8	150ml milk, kedgeree, drink	drink	cottage cheese and olive bagel, drink	grapes, drink	tortellini with cauliflower and cheese, fruit with raspberry dipping sauce, drink	200ml milk
menu 9	150ml milk, grilled kipper, drink	cereal bar with melon, drink	courgettes with rosemary and pasta, drink	satsuma, drink	roast chicken with tomatoes and beans, drink	200ml milk
menu 10	150ml milk, porridge, drink	pitta bread with cottage cheese, drink	vegetable korma, drink	satsuma, drink	broccoli, chickpeas, bacon and red pepper, drink	200ml milk
menu 11	150ml milk, mango smoothie, toast, drink	drink	sardine and tomato toast, drink	piece of fresh fruit, drink	beef stew with mushrooms, drink	200ml milk
menu 12	150ml milk, muesli with fresh raspberries, drink	drink	Mediterranean bean stew, drink	satsuma, drink	potato wedges with fish fingers, Malteser and caramel ice-cream, drink	200ml milk
menu 13	150ml milk, crunchy yogurt, drink	drink	noodles with peanut sauce, drink	piece of fresh fruit, drink	lentil and root vegetable stew, drink	200ml milk
menu 14	150ml milk, boiled egg with soldiers, mango smoothie, drink	drink	roasted vegetable and pasta bake, drink	piece of fresh fruit, drink	garlic prawns in white sauce with pasta, drink	200ml milk

fresh breakfasts

blueberry buttermilk pancakes

makes: 7 toddler portions (14 pancakes)

3½

storage: best eaten fresh or keep in the refrigerator for up to 2 days

½

½

1

1

vitamin B₁₂ – phosphorous

15g unsalted butter
1 medium egg
284ml buttermilk
2 drops vanilla extract
125g plain flour
1 tsp bicarbonate of soda
100g dried pears, finely chopped
150g fresh blueberries
2 tsp vegetable oil

These are really popular with toddlers. If you can't get hold of blueberries, just add a little more pear. To really gild the lily, try serving them with a little golden or maple syrup.

1 Melt the butter in a small pan over a gentle heat.
2 In a mixing bowl, whisk together the egg, buttermilk, vanilla extract and melted butter.
3 Sift the flour and bicarbonate of soda into a separate bowl, mix, then add the egg mixture and mix together. Don't worry if the batter is lumpy.
4 Stir in the dried pears and blueberries.
5 Heat 1 tsp oil in a heavy-based frying pan. Spoon 1–2 tbsp of batter for each pancake into the pan and cook for 2–3 minutes, then flip over and cook for a further 1–2 minutes until the pancakes are lightly browned. Keep warm in a low oven in-between sheets of greaseproof paper while you cook the rest, adding the second teaspoon of oil when you have cooked half the pancakes.

banana and chocolate pastries

makes: 6 toddler portions (6 pastries)

2½

storage: best eaten fresh or keep in an airtight container for up to 2 days

½

1

vitamin B₆ – folic acid

1 x 280g tube *pain au chocolat* dough (available from supermarkets)
2 ripe large bananas, sliced
handful of raspberries, fresh or frozen (defrosted)
apricot jam, to glaze

These are definitely designed to be a treat rather than the norm. Instead of bananas and raspberries, you could try finely chopped breakfast apricots – dried apricots soaked in juice, which have a wonderful texture and flavour.

1 Preheat the oven to 190°C/375°F/gas mark 5. Remove the dough and little bag of chocolate sticks from the tube, then cut along the dough's perforated lines.
2 Put 3 banana slices into the middle of each rectangle of pastry, top with 2–3 chocolate sticks and a few raspberries, and put onto a baking sheet.
3 Bake the pastries for 8–12 minutes, until risen and golden.
4 Warm some apricot jam in a small pan and brush it over the top of the cooked pastries. If necessary, cut into smaller pieces before serving.

kedgeree

makes: 4 toddler portions

storage: best eaten fresh

300ml full-fat milk
350g unsmoked haddock
3 medium eggs, soft to
  hardboiled (page 199),
  roughly chopped
50g unsalted butter
150g long grain white or
  brown rice, freshly cooked
2 tbsp fresh parsley, chopped
freshly ground black pepper

vitamins A, B₁, B₂,
B₆, B₁₂ – folic acid
– phosphorous

You could make this with salmon instead of haddock. Originally an Indian dish, it would have been served slightly spiced. Try adding a little mild curry powder to the butter and cooking for a minute before adding the rest of the ingredients. The rice should be freshly cooked – it is important not to reheat rice.

1 Put the milk and 300ml water into a wide pan with the haddock and bring up to the boil. When it boils, turn the heat off and leave to stand for 15 minutes.
2 Lift the fish from the pan and flake onto a plate, carefully removing any bones and skin.
3 Roughly chop up the boiled eggs.
4 Heat the butter in a pan and add the cooked rice, flaked haddock, chopped boiled eggs and parsley. Stir gently until hot through, then season with freshly ground black pepper.

fried bread and eggs

makes: 2 toddler portions

storage: best eaten fresh

2 slices of sliced bread
25g unsalted butter
1 tbsp olive oil
2 medium eggs

vitamins A, B₂, B₆,
B₁₂ – folic acid –
phosphorous

This is a neat way to serve fried eggs. You can experiment with different types of bread, but pre-sliced does seem to work best. This makes a great breakfast, with plenty of protein and carbohydrate.

1 Using a 7.5cm cutter, cut out a circle from the centre of each piece of bread. Reserve the circles.
2 Melt the butter and oil in a large frying pan. When it foams, add the bread and cut-out rounds and fry on one side until golden brown – approximately 2–3 minutes.
3 Turn the pieces over and carefully break an egg into the circular hole in each slice of bread. Spoon some of the hot fat over the yolk in order to help cook it. Cook over a gentle heat until the eggs are completely cooked through – approximately 4 minutes.
4 Transfer to plates and put the fried bread lids onto the eggs. If necessary, cut into smaller pieces before serving.

granola

5½

2

2½

½

vitamins B₁, B₆, B₁₂
– phosphorous

makes: 11 toddler portions

storage: keep in an airtight container for up to 4 weeks

unsalted butter, for greasing
350g porridge oats
50g wheatgerm
50g unsweetened shredded
  coconut
50g sesame seeds
75g sunflower seeds
75g hazelnuts, finely
  chopped
125ml sunflower oil
75ml runny honey
½ tsp vanilla extract
175g dried fruit, chopped
  into small pieces

This crunchier version of muesli is excellent served with fruit, full-fat natural yogurt or full-fat milk for breakfast. You can adapt the recipe according to the kind of nuts or dried fruits you have in the house. But remember, do not give nuts or seeds to toddlers under the age of 3 if there is any family history of allergies.

1 Preheat the oven to 150°C/300°F/gas mark 2. Grease a large baking tin.

2 In a large bowl, mix the oats, wheatgerm, coconut, sesame seeds, sunflower seeds and hazelnuts.

3 In a large saucepan, combine the oil, honey and vanilla. Heat gently until the honey has melted. Pour the honey mixture into the bowl containing the dry ingredients and mix thoroughly. Spread the mixture out in the tin. Bake in the oven for 35–45 minutes, stirring the mixture every 10 minutes.

4 Cool, then add the dried fruit.

dried fruit compote

1

1

1

copper

makes: 11 toddler portions

storage: keep in the refrigerator for up to 3 days

100g ready-to-eat prunes
100g dried apples
100g dried apricots
100g dried mango
50g dried pineapple
200ml apple juice
pinch of ground cinnamon
  (optional)
2 ripe pears, peeled, cored
  and chopped

You can use pretty much any kind of dried fruit. Serve this compote cold for breakfast with muesli (*see* page 152) or full-fat natural yogurt. Alternatively, serve it warm with custard on cold days.

1 Cut all the dried fruit into small pieces and put into a large saucepan.

2 Add the juice, 300ml water and cinnamon, if using, and bring to the boil. Simmer over a gentle heat for 15 minutes.

3 Add the fresh pear and simmer for another 5 minutes. Cool completely, then marinate for at least an hour before serving.

quick bites
breakfasts

All of the recipes make one toddler portion unless otherwise stated.

mango smoothie

vitamin B$_6$
– folic acid

makes: 2 toddler portions
½ ripe large mango, peeled
and stoned
1 ripe small banana, peeled and
cut into chunks
200ml orange juice
approx 50g berries, eg blueberries

Look for tree-ripened mangoes, as they should be ripe and ready to eat with the best flavour. Often Asian supermarkets have really good fruit to choose from, so it's worth looking around for your fruit if you have the time. Cut the mango into small pieces and put into a bowl. Add the banana chunks, orange juice and berries and whiz with a hand-held blender (or in a food processor or blender) until smooth.

hot chocolate

vitamins A, B$_2$, B$_6$,
B$_{12}$ – phosphorous

approx 200ml full-fat milk
2–3 tsp drinking chocolate powder

Use a good-quality hot chocolate powder that relies on chocolate for flavour rather than sugar. This is a great drink for cold wintry mornings. Make it following the packet's instructions.

muesli with fresh raspberries

makes: 2 toddler portions
100g muesli (do not give nuts to
toddlers under the age of 3 if there is a
family history of allergies)
approx 50g raspberries,
fresh or frozen (defrosted)
100ml full-fat milk

If necessary, whiz the muesli, then put it into a bowl. Lightly mash the raspberries and scatter over the muesli. Pour over the milk. The mashed raspberries will make the milk go a lovely pink colour.

crunchy yogurt

vitamins B$_2$, B$_6$, B$_{12}$
– phosphorous

1 children's muesli bar (do not
give nuts to toddlers under the
age of 3 if there is a family
history of allergies)
½ ripe small pear, cored, peeled
and chopped
100ml natural full-fat yogurt
approx 50ml full-fat milk

Lots of unsweetened or low-sugar muesli bars are available that make great breakfast stand-bys. This is an easy way of using them to make a more substantial breakfast. Crumble the muesli bar into a bowl. Add the chopped pear and yogurt and mix together. If it's a little too thick, thin with some milk.

boiled egg with soldiers

vitamins A, B₂, B₆, B₁₂ – folic acid – phosphorous

½ 1 1 6½

1 medium egg
small knob of unsalted butter
1 slice wholemeal bread, toasted

Children love boiled eggs, especially if you serve them in some fun egg cups. Bring a small pan of water to the boil. Add the egg and simmer for 6 minutes, or until completely cooked, then transfer to an egg cup. Immediately chop the top off. Butter the toast – you could also spread it with Marmite if you prefer – cut into fingers and serve with the egg.

berry milkshake

vitamins B₂, B₆, B₁₂ – phosphorous

10 C 1 ½ 2½

makes: 2 toddler portions
approx 125g berries, fresh or frozen (defrosted)
200ml full-fat milk
½ ripe medium banana (optional)

Any combination of soft fruits will work well for this milkshake. You can add a little banana or a few crushed ice cubes if you would like a drink that is a bit thicker. Simply put the fruits and milk together into a jug and purée them with a hand-held blender (or in a food processor or blender) until you have a smooth milkshake.

grilled kipper

vitamins B₆, B₁₂, D – folic acid – phosphorous

1 1 6½

1 kipper fillet
25g unsalted butter, melted
1 slice of granary toast

When choosing kippers, look for ones that are plump and oily and have a nice smoky smell. Covering the grill-pan with foil prevents the smell from recurring when you grill other foods. Preheat the grill. Line the pan with foil and brush it with half the melted butter. Put the kipper, skin side up, onto the foil and grill for 1 minute. Turn over the kipper, brush the flesh with the remaining melted butter and grill for a further 4–5 minutes, until cooked through. Double-check for bones, then serve with toast. If necessary, flake into small pieces to serve.

croissant with apple

vitamin B₆ – folic acid

1 C ½ ½ 2

1 croissant
1 eating apple, eg Cox's

Preheat the oven to 180°C/350°F/gas mark 4. Place the croissant on a baking tray and warm through for 4–5 minutes. Peel, core and chop the apple and serve with the croissant. Or you could do as they do in France and let your toddler dunk the croissant into some hot chocolate (*see* page 298).

bacon eggy bread

vitamins B₂, B₆, D – folic acid – phosphorous

1 1 1 6

1 medium egg, whisked
2 tbsp full-fat milk
freshly ground black pepper
1 slice of bacon and parsley bread (page 202) or other savoury bread of your choice
small knob of unsalted butter

In a shallow bowl, whisk together the egg and milk with a little freshly ground black pepper. Dip the bread into the egg mixture, making sure it is completely coated. Heat the butter in a frying pan, then cook the bread for 2–3 minutes on each side, until just starting to go golden. Cut into fingers to serve.

fresh lunches

noodles with peanut sauce

makes: 4 toddler portions

storage: best eaten fresh or keep in fridge for up to 2 days

2½

1½

1½

3 C

vitamins B₁, B₆ – folic acid – phosphorous

1 tbsp olive oil

1 garlic clove, peeled, crushed

4 spring onions, finely sliced

½ orange pepper, deseeded and thinly sliced

100g mange-tout, thinly sliced

100g creamed coconut

300ml no- or low-salt vegetable stock (page 332)

4 tbsp crunchy peanut butter

juice of ½ lime

freshly ground black pepper

250–300g medium egg thread noodles

1 tbsp sesame seeds, toasted

Nuts are a great source of protein, especially for vegetarians and vegans. Serve with some stir-fried green vegetables or steamed vegetables. You do not need to serve vegetables with this dish as it is already packed with them. Do not give nuts or seeds to toddlers under the age of 3 if there is any family history of allergies.

1 Heat the oil in a heavy-based saucepan and fry the garlic and spring onions for a minute. Add the orange pepper and mange-tout and fry for a minute.

2 Roughly chop the creamed coconut. Add the stock and coconut. Stir in the peanut butter, then simmer for 2–3 minutes, stirring often.

3 Stir in the lime juice and season with freshly ground black pepper.

4 Meanwhile, boil a large pan of water and cook the noodles following the packet's instructions.

5 Drain, and add the noodles to the pan with the peanut sauce, then stir well. Sprinkle over the toasted sesame seeds. If necessary, cut into smaller pieces before serving immediately.

smoked mackerel paté

makes: 6 toddler portions

storage: keep in the refrigerator for up to 2 days

6½

½

½

vitamins B₂, B₆, B₁₂, D – phosphorous

2 garlic cloves, peeled and crushed

400g smoked mackerel fillets (approx 3 fillets), flaked

4 tbsp full-fat natural yogurt

juice of ½ lemon

wholemeal toast, to serve

carrot, cucumber and celery sticks, to serve

tomato chunks, to serve

Oily fish, such as mackerel, is great brain food and it is fine to offer your toddler smoked fish occasionally, as long as it is not a regular occurrence.

1 Put the first four ingredients into a bowl and purée with a hand-held blender (or in a food processor or blender) until smooth.

2 Cover and chill for 10 minutes, or serve immediately with toast, carrot, cucumber and celery sticks, and tomato chunks.

baked eggs

9½

1

1½

2

1

makes: 2 toddler portions

storage: best eaten fresh

knob of unsalted butter

½ small leek, washed and
   finely sliced

2 medium eggs

freshly ground black pepper

50g Cheddar cheese, grated

vitamins A,, B$_2$, B$_6$,
B$_{12}$, D – folic acid
   – phosphorous

These are quick and easy and toddlers love the fact that they are served in individual dishes. You could try using some gently fried mushrooms, or cooked flaked haddock or smoked salmon trimmings, instead of the leeks.

1 Preheat the oven to 180°C/350°F/gas mark 4. Melt the butter in a small pan and fry the leek over a gentle heat until soft – approximately 4–5 minutes.

2 Butter 2 ramekins or small ovenproof dishes. Divide the leek mixture between the dishes, then crack an egg over each and season with freshly ground black pepper. Sprinkle over the grated cheese.

3 Put the ramekins into a roasting tin and pour boiling water into the tin to come about halfway up the sides of the dishes. Bake for 15–18 minutes, or until the egg is completely cooked through.

Mediterranean bean stew

6½

1½

1

1½

3

makes: 6 toddler portions

storage: keep in the
refrigerator for up to 3 days

50g unsalted butter

3 medium leeks, washed and
   finely sliced

1 medium red onion, sliced

2 tbsp olive oil

1 red pepper, chopped

2 garlic cloves, crushed

200g courgettes, cut in chunks

400g tinned tomatoes

1 tbsp tomato purée

400g tinned cooked butter
   beans, drained and rinsed

300g tinned cooked cannellini
   beans, drained and rinsed

200ml no- or low-salt
   vegetable stock (page 332)

handful of fresh basil leaves,
   torn, or parsley, chopped

3 tbsp Parmesan or Cheddar
   cheese, grated, to serve

brown or white bread

vitamins A, B$_1$, B$_6$ –
   folic acid –
   phosphorous

This is a hearty vegetarian dish that can be made in advance and kept in the refrigerator until needed. Serve with bread for a complete meal.

1 Heat the butter in a large casserole and fry the leeks and onion until soft and pale golden – approximately 5 minutes. Remove from the pan and reserve.

2 Heat the oil in the casserole and gently fry the red pepper for 4–5 minutes, until soft and golden. Add the garlic and fry for 1 more minute.

3 Add the courgettes, tomatoes and purée and cook for a few minutes. Add the beans and stock and return the leeks and onions to the pan. Stir well and bring to the boil. Simmer for 20 minutes.

4 Stir in the basil or parsley and cook for another 5 minutes. Season with freshly ground black pepper and serve in bowls with grated cheese over the top and bread to mop up the juices.

souffléd baked potatoes

8

makes: 8 toddler portions

storage: best eaten fresh

1

1½

1

1

vitamins B₂, B₆, B₁₂,
– folic acid –
phosphorous

4 baking potatoes, scrubbed
olive oil
4 tbsp full-fat milk
25g unsalted butter
30g Cheddar cheese, grated
2 medium eggs, separated
freshly ground black pepper
2 rashers unsmoked streaky
    bacon, rind removed,
    grilled and chopped
1 tbsp fresh parsley, chopped

These are a little more special than a plain jacket potato, and are a good way of encouraging your toddler to enjoy eggs.

1 Preheat the oven to 200°C/400°F/gas mark 6. Rub a little olive oil into the potatoes, then cook in the oven for 1 hour until the skins are crisp and the insides are soft.

2 Slice the potatoes in half and carefully scoop out the flesh into a bowl, reserving the skins.

3 Add the milk and butter to the flesh and mash the potatoes well. Add the cheese, egg yolks and some pepper, then mash again. Stir in the bacon and fresh parsley.

4 Whisk the egg whites in a grease-free bowl until stiff and then fold them into the potato mixture. Spoon this mixture back into the reserved potato skins and put onto a baking tray. Cook in the hot oven for a further 20 minutes, until risen and golden.

quick tomato chicken

18½

makes: 3 toddler portions

storage: best eaten fresh or keep in the refrigerator for up to 2 days

2

2½

2

vitamins B₁, B₆ –
folic acid –
phosphorous

2 tbsp olive oil
10g unsalted butter
2 chicken breasts, skinned
    and cut into bite-size pieces
300ml passata (sieved
    tomato purée available
    from supermarkets)
large handful of fresh basil
    leaves, torn
400g spaghetti or tagliatelle
4 tbsp full-fat crème fraîche,
    cream cheese or Greek
    yogurt
freshly ground black pepper

Billy, who has been assisting me on this book, was served something similar to this for supper at a friend's house. She was so enthusiastic about it that I had a go – it is delicious.

1 Heat the oil and butter together in a frying pan, then fry the chicken pieces until golden. Add the passata and basil and simmer for 5–8 minutes, until the chicken is cooked through.

2 Meanwhile, boil a large pan of water and cook the spaghetti or tagliatelle following the packet's instructions. Drain.

3 When the chicken is cooked, stir in the crème fraîche and season with pepper. Serve with the spaghetti or tagliatelle. If necessary, cut into smaller pieces before serving.

quick bites lunches

All of the recipes make one toddler portion unless stated otherwise.

sardine and tomato toast

1½ **C** 2 1½ 1 6½

1 slice of wholemeal bread
3 tinned sardines in oil, drained and
lightly mashed
1 juicy ripe tomato, finely chopped
lemon wedge (optional)

Tinned sardines are a great source of calcium and, like other oily fish, they are also high in essential fats and zinc. Preheat the grill, then grill the bread on one side. Turn over and top with the mashed sardines, then sprinkle over the tomato. Return to the grill and cook for 3–4 minutes until hot through. Your toddler may like to squeeze some lemon juice over the top. Cut into pieces.

creamy beetroot dip

½ **C** ½ ½ ½ 2½

2 small beetroots
(approx 75g), cooked
2 tbsp full-fat cream cheese
3 fresh chives, finely snipped
1 slice of granary toast

Chop the beetroots into tiny pieces and put into a bowl. Add the cream cheese and chives and mash really well with a fork. Serve the dip with toast fingers. If this goes down well with your toddler, try using it as a sauce for pasta – just add it when the pasta is still hot and stir thoroughly.

courgettes and rosemary with pasta

✓ 1½ **C** ½ ½ 3½

vitamins A, B₂ B₁₂ –
folic acid –
phosphorous

50g pasta
15g unsalted butter
1 sprig of rosemary
1 courgette, grated
50g buffalo mozzarella or full-fat
cream cheese (optional)

Bring a medium pan of water to the boil. Add the pasta and cook following the packet's instructions, then drain. Heat the butter in the pan, add the rosemary sprig and grated courgette and cook gently for 4–5 minutes, stirring occasionally. Return the pasta to the pan and heat through briefly. Remove the rosemary before serving. If you like, you could add the mozzarella or cream cheese to make the sauce creamier.

noodles with peanuts

✓ ½ **C** 2 1 10

vitamins B₁, B₆ –
folic acid –
phosphorous

50g medium egg noodles
1 tsp sesame oil
1 spring onion, finely chopped
1 tbsp smooth peanut butter
25g peanuts, finely chopped
1 tsp lime juice

Bring a medium pan of water to the boil and cook the noodles following the packet's instructions, then drain. Heat the oil in a pan and gently fry the spring onion until soft. Add the peanut butter, peanuts and lime juice. Add the noodles and toss everything together to mix thoroughly. If necessary, chop into small pieces before serving. Do not serve nuts, seeds or their products to toddlers under the age of 3 if there is any family history of allergies.

new potatoes with bacon and pesto

vitamins B₁, B₆ – folic acid

6 medium new potatoes
2 rashers unsmoked streaky bacon, rind removed
1 tbsp pesto (or less if this is too strong for your toddler)

Cut the potatoes into small pieces. Bring a small pan of water to the boil, add the potatoes and cook until just tender – approximately 10–12 minutes. Drain and return the potatoes to the pan. Preheat the grill. Grill the bacon until cooked and slightly golden around the edges. Chop the bacon into small pieces and add to the potatoes with the pesto, then mix everything together.

tomato, mozzarella and basil on ciabatta

vitamins A, B₁, B₆, B₁₂ – folic acid – phosphorous

1 soft ciabatta roll
1 tbsp olive oil
1 ripe tomato, thinly sliced
3 thin slices buffalo mozzarella (approx 50g)
2 fresh basil leaves

Cut the ciabatta roll in half, and drizzle each half with the olive oil. Place the tomato slices onto one half, with the mozzarella and basil on top. Place the other half on top, squidge down and cut into small pieces.

cottage cheese and olive bagel

50g full-fat cottage cheese
4 Kalamata olives, stoned and finely chopped
1 plain bagel, sliced in half
1 ripe small tomato, chopped into bite-size pieces

Bagels are soft but chewy enough to make them interesting. If you are feeling adventurous, look for flavoured varieties, such as onion bagels. Mix the cottage cheese and chopped olives together in a small bowl. Toast the bagel halves and top with the cheese mixture. Serve with the tomato pieces.

Camargue rice with apricots and feta

50g Camargue red rice
3 small broccoli florets
2 dried unsulphured apricots, finely chopped
30g feta cheese, crumbled

Cook the rice following the packet's instructions, then drain. Bring a pan of water to the boil and steam the broccoli for a few minutes until just tender, then cut into small pieces. While the rice is still warm, mix through the broccoli, apricots and feta. Serve immediately.

warm bacon with beans

2 broccoli florets
2 tsp olive oil
2 rashers unsmoked streaky bacon, rind removed and chopped
100g tinned cooked cannellini beans, drained and rinsed

Steam the broccoli for a few minutes over a pan of boiling water until just tender. Cut into small pieces. Heat the olive oil in a saucepan, add the bacon and fry until lightly golden and cooked. Add the cannellini beans and broccoli, then heat through briefly.

lunches to freeze

easy mini quiches

Toddlers love miniature foods, so these quiches are always popular.

makes: 12 toddler portions (12 mini quiches)

storage: up to 4 months in the freezer

175g plain flour, sifted
pinch of salt
90g unsalted butter, chilled
  and diced, plus 15g for
  the filling
1 medium egg yolk
  plus 1 tbsp cold water
1 medium leek, washed and
  finely chopped
1 large courgette, sliced
50g Gruyère cheese, grated
sprig of rosemary
2 large eggs, beaten
200ml full-fat milk

vitamins B₆, B₁₂

1 Chill a muffin tin. Put the flour and a pinch of salt into a food processor or blender and whiz to aerate. Add 90g butter and process until the mixture resembles fine breadcrumbs (or rub the butter in with your fingertips). Add the egg yolk and, if necessary, water, and process until the pastry just draws together.

2 Roll out the pastry to 2.5mm thick and cut out circles to line your muffin tin. Chill for 1 hour. Preheat the oven to 180°C/350°F/gas mark 4. Heat 15g butter in a frying pan and sweat the leek for 5 minutes. Add the courgette and brown a little, turning often. Spoon into the pastry cases and sprinkle with cheese.

3 Chop the rosemary leaves. Whisk the milk into the eggs with the herbs and season with black pepper. Pour over the filling. Cook for 18–20 minutes, or until the filling is golden and puffy. Cool, then freeze in a freezerproof container.

4 Thaw thoroughly. Warm through in the oven at 180°C/350°F/gas mark 4 for 10 minutes. If necessary, cut into smaller pieces before serving.

carrot and coriander soup

makes: 6 toddler portions

storage: up to 3 months in the freezer

800g large carrots, peeled
2 medium onions
25g unsalted butter
1 tbsp olive oil
2 sticks celery, chopped
2 garlic cloves, chopped
2cm piece of fresh root
  ginger, finely chopped
1 tbsp runny honey
2 tbsp fresh coriander
2–3 tbsp double cream

vitamins A, B₆

This is one of my girls' favourites, and I have not found a toddler yet who dislikes it. Making soups yourself has the advantage that you can leave the texture quite thick, making it easier for toddlers to spoon it up!

1 Thinly slice the carrots and finely chop the onions.

2 Melt the butter and oil together in a large heavy-based saucepan. Add the carrots, onions, celery, garlic and ginger. Cover and sweat over a gentle heat for 20 minutes. Add 750ml water, the honey and freshly ground black pepper, then simmer until the vegetables are soft – about 10 minutes.

3 Purée until smooth using a hand-held blender (or in a processor or blender).

4 Cool completely, then transfer to freezerproof containers or freezer bags and freeze.

5 Thaw thoroughly. Reheat gently until boiling, adding more water to make the desired consistency. Chop the coriander and add with the cream.

chickpea and bacon soup

You could always make a larger quantity of the soup (without the pasta) and keep to use with chicken pieces or pork chops. This is delicious served with mash, or rice and green vegetables.

makes: approx 10 toddler portions

storage: up to 3 months in the freezer

6

1

1

2

vitamins A, B₁, B₆

1 tbsp olive oil
1 large onion, finely chopped
2 garlic cloves, finely chopped
2 sticks celery, finely chopped
2 medium carrots, chopped
130g pancetta or unsmoked streaky bacon
400g tin chopped tomatoes
2 x 400g tin cooked chickpeas, drained and rinsed
1 litre no- or low-salt vegetable stock (page 332)
freshly ground black pepper
100g small pasta

1 Heat the oil in a heavy-based saucepan. Sauté the onion, garlic, celery and carrots until soft – approximately 5–10 minutes. Transfer to a plate.
2 Cut the pancetta or bacon into small cubes and add to the pan. Fry until golden and crisp – approximately 5 minutes.
3 Add the cooked vegetables, tomatoes, chickpeas and stock, season with freshly ground black pepper and simmer for 10 minutes.
4 Put a third of the soup into a bowl and purée with a hand-held blender (or in a food processor or blender). Pour in the remaining soup, stir and cool completely. Pour into freezerproof containers or freezer bags and freeze.
5 Thaw thoroughly. Add the pasta and gently reheat in a saucepan until boiling and the pasta is cooked.

roasted veg and pasta bake

This protein-packed lunch is a great way to serve vegetables to toddlers.

makes: 4 toddler portions

storage: up to 3 months in the freezer

10½

1½

2

2

6

vitamins A, B₆, B₁₂ – folic acid – phosphorous

1 large red onion
1 large aubergine
1 large courgette
1 red and 1 orange pepper, seeded and sliced
2 tbsp olive oil
2–3 tbsp pesto
125ml double cream
50ml full-fat milk
freshly ground black pepper
250g pasta, cooked
75g Cheddar cheese, grated
handful of parsley, chopped

1 Preheat the oven to 190°C /375°F/gas mark 5. Cut the onion into thin wedges and cut the aubergine and courgettes into 2cm chunks.
2 Put all the vegetables into a roasting dish, drizzle with olive oil and roast in the oven for 40 minutes, until cooked and golden-edged.
3 Put the pesto, cream and milk into a saucepan, season with freshly ground black pepper, then heat gently for 2 minutes, stirring.
4 Mix the pasta and vegetables into the sauce. Spoon the mixture into 4 ovenproof and freezerproof dishes, sprinkle with cheese and parsley. Cool completely. Wrap in clingfilm or foil and freeze.
5 Thaw thoroughly. Preheat the oven to 190°C/375°F/gas mark 5. Cook for 15–20 minutes, until piping hot and golden. If necessary, cut into smaller pieces before serving.

shepherd's pie

16

2

4

½

3 **C**

vitamins A, B₁, B₂, B₆, B₁₂ – folic acid – phosphorous

makes: 6 toddler portions

storage: up to 4 months in the freezer

2 tbsp olive oil
550g lean lamb mince
1 medium leek
2 medium carrots
100g mushrooms
1 garlic clove, crushed
200g tinned cooked kidney
  beans, drained and rinsed
400g tinned tomatoes
2 tbsp fresh herbs, chopped
freshly ground black pepper
300ml water
900g potatoes
3–4 tbsp full-fat milk
knob of unsalted butter

Toddlers love this nutritious British classic.

1 Preheat the oven to 180°C/350°F/gas mark 4. Heat 1 tbsp olive oil in a heavy-based casserole and brown the mince. Reserve on a plate.

2 Wash the leek and peel the carrots, then dice them. Wash and thinly slice the mushrooms. Heat the remaining oil and fry the leek and carrots until soft and pale golden. Add the mushrooms and garlic and fry for 5 minutes, stirring often.

3 Add the kidney beans, tomatoes and herbs, and stir well. Stir in the water and mince. Season with black pepper, then simmer gently for 35 minutes.

4 Meanwhile, peel and halve the potatoes and cook them in a pan of boiling water until tender. Drain and mash with the butter and most of the milk.

5 Put the mince into a freezerproof pie dish, then top with the potato. Brush with a little milk. Cool completely. Wrap in clingfilm or foil and freeze.

6 Thaw thoroughly. Cook in a preheated oven at 180°C/350°F/gas mark 4 for 30–35 minutes, until the top is golden and crunchy.

vegetable korma

4½

2

1½

1

3 **C**

vitamins B₁, B₆, – folic acid – phosphorous

makes: 6 toddler portions

storage: up to 4 months in the freezer

2 medium onions
5 garlic cloves
8cm piece of root ginger
2 medium parsnips
1 medium swede
2 small turnips
2 medium potatoes
50g unsalted butter
2 tbsp sunflower oil
3 tsp mild curry powder
200g creamed coconut
1.2 litres no- or low-salt veg
  stock (page 332), boiling
freshly ground black pepper
4 tbsp full-fat natural yogurt
fresh coriander leaves
50g roasted cashews
brown or white rice, to serve

Do not give nuts or their products to toddlers under the age of 3 if there is a family history of food allergies.

1 Peel and finely chop the onion, garlic and ginger. Peel and dice the remaining vegetables. Heat the butter and oil in a heavy-based saucepan and sauté the onions for 5 minutes.

2 Add the garlic and ginger and cook for a few minutes, then add the curry powder and cook for a minute. Add the peeled and diced vegetables and cook for 10 minutes, stirring often.

3 Chop the coconut, put it into a bowl and dissolve in the boiling stock. Add to the vegetables, season with freshly ground black pepper, then simmer for 1 hour, stirring occasionally. Leave to cool, transfer to a freezerproof container and freeze.

4 Thaw thoroughly, put into a saucepan and bring to the boil. Just before serving, stir in the yogurt and adjust the seasoning. Finely chop the coriander and cashew nuts, then sprinkle them over the korma. Serve with the cooked rice.

quick bites
snacks

Some of the problems associated with children's eating habits are linked to snacking. Often parents give children snacks without realizing how high in sugar and fat they are. Such snacks spoil the children's appetites and provide empty calories, which give a short-lived burst of energy but have little nutritional value. Bite-size pieces of fruits and vegetables make the best snacks, with more substantial snacks given when a toddler needs a quick energy fix.

All of the recipes make one toddler portion unless otherwise stated.

vitamins A, B$_1$, B$_6$, E folic acid – phosphorus

 1   2   2½   4½

40g Brazil nuts
50g dried mango with no added sugar

dried mango with Brazil nuts

Just one Brazil nut can provide your toddler with all the mineral selenium he needs (selenium helps boost the immune system). There are many dried fruits to choose from – offer a variety to your toddler so that he benefits from the nutrients each one gives. Dried mango is a great source of beta-carotene and vitamin C. Chop the nuts and mango into bite-size pieces and mix. Do not give nuts to toddlers under the age of 3 if there is any history of food allergies.

vitamins B$_2$, B$_6$, B$_{12}$, – folic acid – phosphorous

 2½ C ½ 1

1 scoop of home-made ice-cream (page 276)
handful of fresh ripe berries, eg raspberries, strawberries

home-made ice-cream with fresh fruits

Good-quality home-made ice-cream, made with cream, unrefined sugar and fresh fruit, is delicious. In small quantities it's fine for your toddler – much better than many of the cheap children's ready-made ice-creams, which often contain hydrated fats, chemical additives, lots of sugar and other baddies. Serve the ice-cream in a pretty plastic bowl or cup and scatter over the fruit. Often an attractive bowl and spoon are all that is needed to make this treat extra exciting and enticing.

vitamin B$_{12}$ – folic acid

 ½ 3

½ pitta bread
1 tbsp full-fat cottage cheese
1 chive stalk, finely chopped (optional)

pitta bread with cottage cheese

Keep a packet of pittas in the freezer – you can slice and grill them almost as soon as you take them out. They are really handy for a quick snack or lunch. Grill the pitta bread half, with the cut side facing uppermost. When it is ready, mix the cottage cheese with the chopped chives and spread onto the pitta. Cut into small strips.

½ C ½ 🍶

10g unsalted butter
½ fresh, or equivalent of frozen, corn on the cob

corn with butter

As much as possible, make your toddler's snacks fresh fruits or vegetables. To make this corn on the cob, melt the butter in a small saucepan. Bring a large pan of salted water to the boil and boil or steam the corn on the cob until it is just tender. Drain and serve with melted butter drizzled over the top.

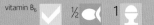

vitamin B₆ – phosphorus ✓ ½ 🥤 1 🐟 ½ 🚫 2½ 🍶

1 large slice of ripe Galia melon
1 cereal bar

cereal bar with melon

Cut the skin away from the melon, then cut the fruit flesh into chunks. Chop the cereal bar into small pieces and mix with the melon in a small pot. (There are many good cereal bars on the market – try to look for ones that don't have too much added sugar and be aware that sugar can come in many guises including syrup, honey and dextrose.)

vitamin B₆ ✓ ½ 🐟 1 🍶

1 tbsp vegetable oil
100g dried corn kernels

popcorn

Heat the oil in a saucepan until hot. Add the corn kernels in a single layer and put the lid on the pan. When the kernels begin to pop, reduce the heat and shake gently. When the popping stops, remove the pan from the heat. Allow to cool slightly. Serve 40g cooked popcorn per toddler and keep the rest in an airtight container. Always supervise your toddler when they are eating popcorn.

vitamin B₆ – folic acid ✓ 3 C ½ 🚫 ½ 🍶

1 seedless satsuma
2 tbsp raisins

frozen satsumas with raisins

We all know that oranges and satsumas are good sources of vitamin C, but many of us do not realize that they also provide a good supply of potassium and they even have a little folic acid. This may seem like an easy snack to suggest, but something as obvious as a handful of raisins and a satsuma can be forgotten. Peel the satsuma, scatter the segments in a freezerproof container, cover and freeze. Serve with a little pot of raisins. Frozen segments make a great thirst-quencher on a hot day.

2 C ½ 🥤 ½ 🐟 1 🍶

makes: 3 toddler portions
100ml natural full-fat yogurt
400ml fresh apple juice

ice lollies

During the summer, toddlers will inevitably ask for lollies. You can choose whether you keep these for a pudding or an occasional snack. They are a great way of cooling little ones down. Put the yogurt into a large jug and gradually whisk in the apple juice. Divide the mixture between ice cube trays, lolly pop containers or small paper cups. Insert a lolly pop stick into the middle of each and freeze for 3–4 hours, or until firm.

fresh suppers

sticky salmon

makes: 4 toddler portions

storage: best eaten fresh or keep in the refrigerator for up to 2 days

vitamins B₆, B₁₂ – phosphorous

4 salmon fillets (450g)
lemon or lime wedges

for the marinade:
5cm root ginger, peeled and grated
2 garlic cloves, crushed
1 tbsp light soy sauce
juice of ½ lemon
1 tsp sesame oil
a little olive oil

A tasty marinade can help to entice the slightly less willing to get stuck into eating fish. Some rice or a few noodles and a steamed green vegetable would make the meal complete. Do not serve seeds or their oils to toddlers under the age of 3 if there is any family history of allergies.

1 Preheat the oven to 220°C/425°F/gas mark 7. Mix together the marinade ingredients and pour over the salmon in a non-metallic bowl. Cover and chill for 30–60 minutes.

2 Take the salmon out of the marinade and place on a roasting tray. Pour over the marinade and roast in the oven for approximately 10–12 minutes, or until the fish is cooked through. If necessary, cut into smaller pieces before serving with the citrus wedges.

lamb koftas

makes: 6 toddler portions (12 small koftas)

storage: keep uncooked in the refrigerator for up to 2 days or keep cooked in the refrigerator for up to 3 days

vitamins B₆, B₁₂ – phosphorous

250g lean lamb mince
2 onions, finely chopped
2 garlic cloves, roughly chopped
2 tsp mixed spice
2 slices white bread, crumbed
2 tbsp fresh parsley, chopped
1 tbsp fresh mint, chopped
1 medium egg, beaten
2 tbsp pine nuts, chopped and toasted
seasoned flour

I tend to serve these little lamb koftas with cherry tomatoes, strips of pitta bread and a dip of full-fat natural yogurt mixed with chopped fresh mint. Remember to soak the sticks in water before cooking, to prevent them from catching fire under the grill. Do not serve nuts to toddlers under the age of 3 if there is any family history of allergies.

1 Put the first seven ingredients into a food processor or blender and whiz together for a couple of minutes.

2 Transfer to a bowl, add the egg and chopped pine nuts, mix well and mould into 12 sausage shapes. Cover and refrigerate for 30 minutes.

3 Roll in seasoned flour. Stick a skewer into each (which is traditional) or leave as they are, then grill or shallow fry for 3–4 minutes on each side, until cooked through (8–10 minutes in total).

4 If you wish, mix together some yogurt and mint and serve with the lamb koftas, cherry tomatoes and pitta bread. If necessary, cut into smaller pieces before serving.

lamb chops in herb crust

makes: 4 toddler portions

storage: best eaten fresh or keep in the refrigerator for up to 24 hours and serve at room temperature

4 lamb chops, approx
  1cm thick
50g white or brown fine
  breadcrumbs
small handful of fresh
  parsley, chopped
handful of cheese, eg fresh
  Parmesan, finely grated
2 medium eggs, beaten
olive oil, for frying

vitamins B₆, B₁₂ – phosphorous

Many toddlers love the texture of a crunchy coating. Serve these chops with some freshly cooked green vegetables and potatoes or a few fingers of bread to make the meal complete.

1 Put the chops in a plastic bag and flatten with a rolling pin. You may like to cut out the bone at this point (alternatively, cut the meat into small pieces once it is cooked).

2 Mix together the breadcrumbs and parsley in a bowl. Dip the chops into the grated cheese – pressing it into the meat, then into the beaten eggs and finally the breadcrumb mixture.

3 Heat the oil in a large heavy-based frying pan over a medium heat and brown the chops on one side – approximately 3–4 minutes. Do not move them earlier, as the coating will stick to the pan. Turn over and brown the other side for another 3–4 minutes, or until cooked through.

4 Rest on kitchen paper for 2 minutes. If necessary, cut into smaller pieces before serving.

courgette cream cheese pasta

makes: 4 toddler portions

storage: best eaten fresh

300g tagliatelle
2 tbsp olive oil
6 small courgettes, very
  thinly sliced lengthways
2 garlic cloves, finely chopped
2 sprigs of fresh rosemary,
  leaves only, chopped
200g full-fat cream cheese,
  roughly chopped
freshly ground black pepper
juice of ½ lemon

vitamins A, B₁, B₆ – folic acid – phosphorous

This also works really well with half cream cheese and half goat's cheese, which some toddlers will love and others will hate, it's just a case of experimenting to see what they like.

1 Bring a large pan of water to the boil, add the tagliatelle and cook following the packet's instructions.

2 Heat the oil in a large frying pan. Add the courgettes, garlic and rosemary and sauté until just soft, but not golden.

3 Add the cream cheese and cooked tagliatelle, and season well with freshly ground black pepper, then add lemon juice to taste. If necessary, cut into smaller pieces before serving.

Thai green chicken and peas

15½

½

1

vitamin B$_6$ –
phosphorous

makes: 5 toddler portions

storage: keep in the
refrigerator for up to 3 days

2 tbsp groundnut or
vegetable oil

500g chicken meat, cut into
small pieces

1–2 tbsp Thai green curry
paste

400ml tinned coconut milk

200ml no- or low-salt
vegetable stock (page 332)

2 fresh lime leaves or juice
of ½ lime

large handful of basil
leaves, torn

salt and freshly ground
black pepper

You may like to add just 1 tbsp of the Thai green curry paste the first time
you make this for your toddler – although, if he's anything like my daughter
Ella he will be quite happy with the heat from 2 tbsp paste. Alternatively, if
you want to make the curry quite hot for the rest of the family but not too
spicy for your toddler, take a little of the juices out of the pan and dilute
them with more coconut milk for him. You could bulk the dish out by adding
chopped vegetables about 5 minutes before the end of the cooking. Do
not serve nut products to toddlers under the age of 3 if there is a family
history of allergies.

1 Heat 1 tbsp oil in a heavy-based saucepan. Fry the chicken pieces until they
come away from the pan easily – approximately 2–3 minutes. Turn over and
cook until just golden – approximately 3–4 minutes more.

2 Stir in the Thai green curry paste and cook for a few more minutes. Add the
coconut milk, vegetable stock and lime leaves or lime juice. Gently simmer
for 10 minutes.

3 Add the basil and season. If necessary, cut into smaller pieces before serving.

herby roast chicken

10

½

1

3 C

vitamins B$_1$, B$_6$
– folic acid –
phosphorous

makes: 8 toddler portions

storage: keep in the
refrigerator for up to 2 days

2 seedless oranges,
cut into wedges

6 sprigs of fresh rosemary

handful of fresh thyme
sprigs

2 large knobs of unsalted
butter

1 chicken (approx 1.8kg)

salt and freshly ground
black pepper

olive oil

700g new potatoes,
scrubbed

peas or green beans,
to serve

A roast chicken normally provides you with a few extra meals when you can
use up any leftover meat.

1 Preheat the oven to 180°C/350°F/gas mark 4. Push the orange wedges, half
the herbs and a good knob of butter inside the chicken.

2 Stuff the remaining butter and herbs under the skin of the chicken breasts.
Season the bird.

3 Heat the oil in a large roasting tin and add the chicken. Roast for 15 minutes
per 450g plus an extra 15 minutes.

4 30 minutes before the end of cooking, add the potatoes to the roasting tin
and continue to cook.

5 Remove the chicken and potatoes from the oven when the chicken is
thoroughly cooked. Place the chicken on a plate to rest for 5 minutes before
carving, while keeping the potatoes warm. Serve slices of the chicken with
the potatoes and green vegetables. If necessary, cut into smaller pieces
before serving.

quick bites **suppers**

All of the recipes make one toddler portion unless stated otherwise.

1 C 1 ½ 4

vitamin A, B₁, B₆, B₁₂
– folic acid –
phosphorous

2 new potatoes, scrubbed
and quartered
8 thin French beans, topped
and tailed
1 small carrot, peeled and cut into chunks
1 medium lamb chop (approx 75g)
1 tsp mint sauce (optional)

lamb chop with beans, carrots and potatoes

Bring a pan of water to the boil, add the potatoes and simmer gently for 10 minutes or until tender, then drain. Steam the other vegetables over boiling water for 5 minutes, or until tender. Meanwhile, grill the lamb chop under a hot grill for 3–4 minutes each side, until cooked through. Serve the lamb with the vegetables and, if you like, the mint sauce. If necessary, cut into smaller pieces before serving.

1½ C 2 1 ½ 8½

75g tortellini
3 cauliflower florets, cut into
small pieces
50g Cheddar cheese, grated

tortellini with cauliflower and cheese

Bring a pan of water to the boil and cook the tortellini following the packet's instructions, then drain. Steam the cauliflower over the boiling water until tender. Chop the cauliflower into small pieces and add to the drained tortellini. Stir in the grated cheese. If necessary, cut into smaller pieces before serving.

 ½  ½ 6½

vitamin B₁, B₂, B₆ –
phosphorous

½ chicken breast, cut into
bite-size pieces
2 tsp olive oil
freshly ground black pepper
100ml passata (sieved tomato
purée available in supermarkets)
75g tinned cooked cannellini
beans, rinsed and drained
pinch soft brown sugar
a few fresh coriander leaves,
chopped (optional)

roasted chicken with beans and tomato

Preheat the oven to 190°C/375°F/gas mark 5. Put the chicken pieces into an ovenproof dish with the olive oil, season with freshly ground black pepper and mix well. Roast in the moderately hot oven for 15 minutes until the pieces are pale golden. Stir in the passata, beans, sugar and coriander and return the chicken to the oven for 15 minutes, or until it is cooked and the sauce hot through. If necessary, cut into smaller pieces before serving.

potato wedges with fish fingers

vitamins B₁, B₆, B₁₂ – folic acid – phosphorous

vitamins B₁, B₆, B₁₂ – folic acid – phosphorous ½ 4

small baking potato,
scrubbed and cut into wedges
2 tsp olive oil
freshly ground black pepper
2 x 100% cod fish fingers

Preheat the oven to 180°C/350°F/gas mark 4. Put the potato wedges into a small roasting tray, pour over the oil and season with freshly ground black pepper. Mix well and roast for 30 minutes. Add the fish fingers to the roasting tray alongside the wedges and cook following the packet's instructions. Serve the wedges with the fish fingers. If necessary, cut into smaller pieces before serving.

broccoli, chickpeas, bacon and red pepper

6 C 1 ½ 4½

vitamins A, B₁, B₆ – folic acid – phosphorous

2 rashers unsmoked
streaky bacon, rind removed
2 broccoli florets
80g tinned cooked chickpeas,
rinsed and drained
½ red pepper, seeded and finely chopped

Preheat the grill and cook the bacon until just golden and slightly crisp. Chop into small pieces and put into a bowl. Steam the broccoli over boiling water until just tender, then chop up and add to the bacon with the chickpeas and red pepper. Pour into a saucepan and heat through. If necessary, cut into smaller pieces before serving.

baked beans and cheese on toast

2 1 ½ 6½

vitamins A, B₁, B₆, B₁₂ – folic acid – phosphorous

1 slice of white or brown bread
small knob of unsalted butter
40g full-fat Cheddar cheese, grated
100g low-sugar baked beans

Preheat the grill and toast the bread on one side. Spread the untoasted side with butter and cover with the cheese. Grill until bubbling and melted. Meanwhile, warm though the baked beans and serve with the cheese on toast. If necessary, cut into smaller pieces before serving.

garlic prawns in white sauce with pasta

vitamins A, B₁, B₂, B₆, B₁₂ – folic acid – phosphorous

1 ½ 4

75g penne
15g unsalted butter
1 small garlic clove, crushed
6 raw medium prawns, shelled
½ quantity (300ml) storecupboard
white sauce (page 333)

Bring a large pan of water to the boil and cook the pasta following the packet's instructions, then drain. Melt the butter in a small saucepan, add the garlic and prawns and cook until the prawns are just pink – this will only take a few minutes. Add the white sauce and heat through. Stir in the pasta and heat through for another couple of minutes. If necessary, cut into smaller pieces before serving.

couscous with oven-roasted ratatouille

3 C ½ 1½ 2½

vitamins B₁, B₆ – folic acid

makes: 2 toddler portions
1 ripe small tomato,
chopped into small pieces
1 small courgette, thinly sliced
½ aubergine, chopped into small cubes
1 tbsp olive oil
freshly ground black pepper
50ml passata (sieved tomato purée
available at supermarkets)
50g couscous

Preheat the oven to 190°C/375°F/gas mark 5. Put all the vegetables into a small roasting tray, pour over the oil and season with freshly ground black pepper. Mix well and roast for 25 minutes. Add the passata, stir well and roast for a further 5 minutes. Meanwhile, make the couscous following the packet's instructions. Serve with the roasted ratatouille. If necessary, cut into smaller pieces before serving.

suppers to freeze

beef stew with mushrooms

Kids love the sweetness of the prunes in this otherwise richly savoury dish.

14

2

4

½ C

vitamins A, B₆,
B₁₂
– phosphorous

makes: 8 toddler portions

storage: up to 4 months in the freezer

4 tbsp olive oil
2 medium onions, sliced
2 carrots, finely chopped
sprig of thyme
25g unsalted butter
250g field mushrooms, sliced
2 tbsp fresh parsley, chopped
750g lean stewing steak
2 tbsp flour, seasoned
500ml no- or low-salt
   vegetable stock (page 332)
1 tbsp tomato purée
2 tsp English mustard
   (optional)
200g prunes, stoned

1 Preheat the oven to 150°C/300°F/gas mark 2. Heat 2 tbsp oil in a frying pan and fry the onions and carrots until soft and pale golden, then tip them into a casserole with the thyme. Add the butter to the frying pan and sauté the mushrooms until they begin to give up their juices, then stir in the parsley and tip into the casserole.

2 Cut the stewing steak into chunks. Turn the chunks in the flour. Heat the remaining oil in the pan until hot and brown the meat. Add to the casserole.

3 Stir any remaining flour into the frying pan with 150ml water and leave to bubble for a few minutes. Add the stock, tomato purée and mustard (if using), then pour into the casserole. Chop the prunes and add, stir well. Cover and cook in the oven for 1 hour 45 minutes – stir occasionally to prevent the meat overbrowning. You may also need to add more stock.

4 Cool completely, transfer to freezerproof containers and freeze. To serve, thaw thoroughly. Gently heat until boiling. If necessary, cut into smaller pieces.

home-made pizzas

These pizzas are so tasty that they might not make it to the freezer! Try adding herbs, cheese or tomato purée to the base.

6½

½

1

2

vitamin B₆
– phosphorous

makes: 4 toddler portions

storage: up to 3 months in the freezer

200g self-raising flour
100ml full-fat milk or
   soya drink
50ml olive oil, plus extra
4 tbsp tomato passata
2 chestnut mushrooms,
   finely sliced
1 slice of cooked ham,
   finely chopped
50g Cheddar cheese, grated

1 Preheat the oven to 180°C/350°F/gas mark 4. Sift the flour into a bowl and make a well in the centre. Pour in the milk and olive oil and, using a fork, draw the mixture together into a dough. Tip the dough out onto a floured surface and divide into four. Roll each chunk into a ball and roll out to a flat circle (10cm diameter), then press it flatter still on a lightly greased baking sheet.

2 Spread 1 tbsp tomato passata on each circle and top with the mushrooms and ham. Sprinkle over a little cheese and bake for 5–10 minutes. Cool completely. Wrap in clingfilm or foil and freeze.

3 Thaw thoroughly. Reheat in a preheated oven at 170°C/ 325°F/ gas mark 3 for 5 minutes or until hot through and bubbling on top.

chicken, olive and bean stew

18

1½

1½

½

1 C

vitamins B₁, B₆ –
phosphorous

makes: 8 toddler portions

storage: up to 4 months in
the freezer

850g chicken breast, skinned
large pinch of paprika
3 tsp ground coriander
freshly ground black pepper
3 tbsp olive oil
1 onion, finely chopped
300g tinned cooked black-
    eyed beans
400g tinned cooked
    cannellini beans
250ml low-salt veg stock
400g tinned cherry tomatoes
2 tbsp tomato purée
125g Kalamata olives
handful of fresh coriander
1 tbsp balsamic vinegar

This is a great way to get your toddler used to the more intense flavours of
ingredients such as olives.

1 Cut the chicken into small chunks and put them in a bowl with the paprika
and coriander. Season with freshly ground black pepper and mix well.

2 Heat 1½ tbsp oil in a heavy-based casserole. Brown the chicken and reserve.
Add the remaining oil to the pan and sweat the onion until soft.

3 Drain and rinse the beans. Add the chicken, beans, stock, tomatoes and
tomato purée to the onion, then simmer for 20 minutes. Stone and chop the
olives and chop the coriander.

4 Add the olives, vinegar and coriander and simmer for 5–10 minutes more,
until the chicken is cooked. Cool completely, transfer to freezerproof
containers and freeze.

5 Thaw thoroughly. Heat gently in a saucepan until boiling.

6 Serve with couscous, rice or mashed potato. If necessary, cut into smaller
pieces before serving.

lentil and root vegetable stew

5½

1½

1

½

3 C

vitamin A, B₁, B₆ –
folic acid –
phosphorous

makes: 8 toddler portions

storage: up to 4 months in
the freezer

2 tbsp olive oil
25g unsalted butter
1 red onion, finely chopped
2 medium leeks, finely sliced
2 garlic cloves, crushed
2 large parsnips, peeled
2 large carrots, peeled
2 sweet potatoes, peeled
100g split red lentils
1 bay leaf
1 sprig of rosemary
850ml no- or low-salt
    vegetable stock (page 332)
410g tinned cooked butter
    beans, drained and rinsed
2 courgettes, sliced
handful of fresh parsley

This is a great dish to serve to your toddler on a cold winter's night.

1 Heat the oil and butter together in a heavy-based saucepan. Gently fry
the onion, leeks and garlic until soft, but not browned – approximately
5 minutes.

2 Cut the parsnips, carrots and sweet potatoes into bite-size chunks, then add
to the pan to lightly brown.

3 Stir in the lentils, bay leaf, rosemary and stock. Cover and gently simmer for
45 minutes.

4 Add the butter beans and courgettes, then simmer for 15 minutes more,
until just tender.

5 Chop the parsley and add to the stew. Season with freshly ground black
pepper. Leave to cool completely. Transfer to a freezerproof container
and freeze.

6 Thaw completely. Heat through thoroughly until boiling. If necessary, chop
into smaller pieces before serving.

lamb burgers with lemony beans

9½

1½

2½

vitamins B₁, B₁₂
– folic acid –
phosphorous

makes: 7 toddler portions
(approx 14 burgers)

storage: up to 3 months in
the freezer

4 tbsp olive oil, plus 3 tbsp
  for the beans
3 garlic cloves, finely chopped
800g lean lamb mince
1 tbsp runny honey
1 tbsp lemon juice
2 tsp ground cumin
2 tsp ground coriander
4 tbsp fresh mint, chopped
4 tbsp pine nuts, toasted
600g tinned cooked
  cannellini beans, drained
juice of ½–1 lemon
2 tbsp fresh parsley, chopped
2 tbsp fresh mint, chopped

I sometimes toss chopped baby spinach leaves and watercress in with the beans. Do not give nuts to toddlers under the age of 3 if there is a family history of allergies. Never refreeze raw meat that has already been frozen.

1 To make the burgers, heat 2 tbsp olive oil in a frying pan and sauté the garlic for a few minutes until soft. Transfer to a large bowl.

2 Add the mince, honey, lemon juice, spices and mint and mix together. Flour your hands and shape the mixture into 14 balls. Cover and chill for 15 minutes.

3 Layer in a freezerproof container between greaseproof paper and freeze.

4 Thaw thoroughly. Heat a griddle or frying pan until really hot, add 2 tbsp olive oil and fry the burgers over a medium heat, until golden and cooked through – approximately 6–8 minutes on each side, turning occasionally. Alternatively, grill them. If necessary, cut into smaller pieces before serving.

5 Meanwhile, roughly chop the pine nuts. Blanch the cannellini beans in boiling water and drain. Mix with the olive oil, lemon juice, herbs and pine nuts.

6 Serve each toddler two burgers with a spoonful of the beans.

crispy vegetable bake

16½

2½

3

6

4

vitamins B₁, B₂,
B₆, B₁₂
– folic acid –
phosphorous

makes: 4 toddler portions

storage: up to four months in
the freezer

200g potatoes
200g parsnips
100g Gruyère cheese, grated
freshly ground black pepper
50g unsalted butter
2 leeks, washed and sliced
2 carrots, peeled and
  chopped
30g plain flour
565ml full-fat milk
100g Cheddar cheese, grated
2 tbsp parsley, chopped
200g green beans, cooked
  and chopped
200g frozen peas or
  sweetcorn, or a mixture

This highly nutritious dish is always popular with my daughter Ella.

1 Peel and parboil the potatoes and parsnips, then grate and mix together in a bowl with the Gruyère and some freshly ground black pepper.

2 Melt 25g butter in a pan and fry the leeks and carrots until soft and pale gold. Reserve.

3 Melt the remaining butter in the pan, stir in the flour and cook for 1 minute. Gradually add the milk, whisking constantly. Return to the heat and bring to the boil, stirring constantly until thick and smooth.

4 Stir in the Cheddar until melted. Add the parsley, leeks, carrots, beans and peas or sweetcorn. Tip into an ovenproof and freezerproof dish. Sprinkle the potato mixture on top. Cool completely. Wrap in foil or clingfilm and freeze.

5 Thaw thoroughly. Bake in a preheated oven at 180°C/350°F/gas mark 4 for 20–30 minutes, until golden.

fresh & frozen puddings

choc chip steamed pudding

3½ 👶
2 ❌
½ 🥛
½ 🥛

makes: 8 toddler portions

storage: best eaten fresh or keep in the refrigerator for up to 3 days

vitamins B₆, B₁₂

100g unsalted butter
100g light soft brown sugar
2 large eggs, beaten
1 tsp vanilla extract
170g plain flour
30g cocoa
2 heaped tsp baking powder
50g good-quality milk
  chocolate, finely chopped

for the sauce:
470g jar of Morello cherries
  in juice
2 tbsp soft brown sugar

If you do not fancy making the cherry sauce, serve with full-fat natural yogurt, vanilla ice-cream or custard instead. Do invest in a 900ml plastic pudding basin with lid: they are so easy to use. This pudding reheats well – just steam.

1 Butter a 900ml pudding basin. In a bowl, cream the butter and sugar together until pale and fluffy. Gradually beat in the eggs and vanilla extract until completely mixed in.

2 Sift the flour, cocoa and baking powder onto the egg mixture. Fold in. Stir in the chocolate and just enough cold water to make a loose dropping consistency.

3 Pour into the pudding basin. Cover with greaseproof paper or foil, with a fold in the centre to create space for the pudding to rise. Steam over boiling water for 1½ hours. Top up with boiling water as necessary. Turn out onto a warmed plate when cooked.

4 Meanwhile, to make the sauce, strain the cherry juice into a saucepan. Add the sugar and bring slowly to the boil. Simmer for 2 minutes.

5 Add three-quarters of the cherries and simmer for 2 minutes. Whiz with a hand-held blender or mash until smooth. Mix with the whole cherries and serve with the pudding. If necessary, cut into smaller pieces before serving.

raspberry smush

2½ 👶
½ ❌
½ 🥛
½ 🥛
4½ C

makes: 8 toddler portions

storage: freeze for up to 3 months

550g frozen raspberries
100g golden caster sugar
250g Greek yogurt

If it is the season for raspberries, have a go at 'pick-your-own' – they are much cheaper than their shop-bought counterparts and you could try to get your child to help. The first time my daughter Ella saw strawberries growing she thought someone had dropped them on the floor!

1 Put the frozen raspberries, sugar and yogurt together in a food processor or blender. Quickly whiz to make a quick and slightly chunky dessert.

2 Serve straight away – it will be semi-frozen.

banana and vanilla risotto

4½

½

½

1½

1

makes: 4 toddler portions

storage: best eaten fresh or keep in the refrigerator for up to 2 days (do not reheat rice)

750ml full-fat milk

25g light soft brown sugar

3–4 drops vanilla extract

50g unsalted butter

125g Arborio rice

2 ripe large bananas, chopped

freshly grated nutmeg

vitamins A, B₂, B₆, B₁₂ – phosphorous

This is a great source of carbohydrate, perfect for feeding the little ones before they go to bed, helping to ensure a good night's sleep – for you as well as them!

1 Put the milk, soft brown sugar and vanilla extract into a small saucepan and heat to simmering point.
2 Melt the butter in a heavy-based saucepan, add the Arborio rice and stir to coat the grains.
3 Add one of the chopped bananas and a ladleful of the hot milk and stir continuously, until all the milk is absorbed. Add another ladleful, and continue until the rice is *al dente*, with a creamy sauce.
4 Stir in the other chopped banana and sprinkle with nutmeg.

Eve's pudding

5½

1

½

1

1

makes: 6 toddler portions

storage: best eaten fresh or keep in the refrigerator for up to 24 hours

450g cooking apples

75g light soft brown sugar

zest of 1 unwaxed lemon

150g unsalted butter, plus extra for greasing

150g golden caster sugar

2 medium eggs, beaten

300g self-raising flour, sifted

4 tbsp full-fat milk

vitamins A, B₆, B₁₂

For a variation on this recipe, replace 25g of the flour with 25g ground almonds. Or add a pinch of ground cinnamon to the sponge mixture. You could also make this pudding with other soft fruits – fresh apricots or plums work particularly well – just make sure they are really ripe. Do not give nuts to toddlers under the age of 3 if there is any family history of allergies.

1 Preheat the oven to 180°C/350°F/gas mark 4, then butter a 900ml ovenproof dish.
2 Peel, core and finely slice the apples into the dish, sprinkle over the soft brown sugar and lemon zest. Mix well.
3 Cream the butter and caster sugar together in a bowl until pale and fluffy. Add the beaten eggs and beat well.
4 Fold in the flour and then stir in the milk.
5 Spoon this sponge mixture over the apples. Use a palette knife to smooth lightly over the top. Bake in the oven for 40–45 minutes, until the sponge is risen and golden.

pear and blueberry crisp

makes: 4 toddler portions

storage: best eaten fresh or store in fridge for 2–3 days

700g ripe pears
5 tbsp light soft brown sugar
100g blueberries
50g plain flour
pinch of ground cinnamon
pinch of freshly grated
  nutmeg
50g unsalted butter

vitamin B₆

I have also made this with blackberries and raspberries instead of the blueberries. This is delicious served warm with custard or cold with yogurt.

1 Preheat the oven to 200°C/400°F/gas mark 6. Peel the pears, core and cut them into chunks. Put into a saucepan with 1 tbsp sugar, a little water and the blueberries.

2 Cook over a low heat for 3–4 minutes, until the berry juice just begins to run. Tip into a small ovenproof dish or 2–3 ramekins.

3 Sift the remaining sugar, plus the flour, cinnamon and nutmeg into a bowl. Rub in the butter with your fingertips or in a food processor or blender until the mixture resembles fine breadcrumbs. Sprinkle over the fruit. Bake in the oven for 30 minutes, until golden.

grilled fruits

makes: 4 toddler portions

storage: best eaten fresh or keep for up to 2 days in the refrigerator

½ vanilla pod
4 tsp golden caster sugar
4 ripe peaches (or plums,
  nectarines, peeled pears,
  figs, etc), halved and stoned
4 tbsp Greek yogurt, to serve

A delicious pudding for summer months, when fruit is plentiful. Use anything you like really – it also works well with bananas. If you don't have a grill you can just as easily bake them in a hot oven.

1 Split the vanilla pod lengthways and scrape out the seeds into a small bowl. Add the sugar and mix well.

2 Put the fruit, cut side up, into an ovenproof dish and sprinkle over the sugar. Grill for 5–8 minutes, until softened and the tops are golden and bubbling.

3 Cool slightly before serving, ideally with a dollop of Greek yogurt. If necessary, cut into smaller pieces before serving.

quick bites puddings

I tend not to put a lot of emphasis on puddings, so the quicker they are to prepare and make the better.

All of the recipes make one toddler portion unless stated otherwise.

quick jam tarts with fruit

½ **C** 1½ ◖ 1 ⬮

makes: 12 toddler portions
375g ready-made sweet shortcrust pastry
12–16 raspberries, fresh or frozen
(defrosted)
12–16 tsp low-sugar good quality jam
(avoid those containing sorbitol)

Preheat the oven to 150°C/300°F/gas mark 2. Roll out the pastry to 2.5mm thick and cut out circles a little larger than the jam tart tins. Put in the tins, then place a raspberry in the middle of each pastry circle and top each with a teaspoon of jam. Cook for 18 minutes, until the pastry is golden. Leave to cool in the tins for a couple of minutes before lifting out. Cool on a wire rack.

fast strawberry ice-cream

4 **C** ½ ⬜ 1½ ⬮

makes: 3 toddler portions
200g frozen strawberries
60ml natural Greek yogurt
60ml crème fraîche
1–2 tbsp golden icing sugar

Take the berries out of the freezer 10 minutes before you want to eat the pudding. Put the berries into a food processor or blender, add the natural Greek yogurt, crème fraîche and icing sugar, and whiz until smooth. Serve the ice-cream immediately.

lemon yogurt

1½ ⬜ 1 ◖ 3½ ⬮

3–4 tbsp natural full-fat yogurt
1–2 tsp lemon curd

I rarely buy little pots of yogurt. I tend to add fruits and jams to natural yogurt to avoid giving the girls unnecessary flavourings, colours or too much sugar. Put the yogurt into a bowl, add the lemon curd and mix together.

fruit with a raspberry dipping sauce

vitamin B$_6$ – folic acid 4 **C** ½ ⬮

approx 100g raspberries, fresh or frozen
(defrosted)
1 small slice of ripe melon, eg
Canteloupe or Galia
3 ripe large strawberries, hulled
and halved

Put the raspberries into a bowl and mash with a fork until smooth. Spoon into a little serving dish. Peel the melon and cut the flesh into chunks. Put the melon and strawberries onto a little plate and serve with the crushed raspberries for dipping.

vitamins B₂, B₆ – phosphorous

½ C ½ ½ 1½

2 eating apples, eg Cox's
pinch of ground cinnamon
2 tbsp apple juice
3 tbsp crunchy granola (page 297;
do not give nuts to toddlers under
the age of 3 if there is any family
history of food allergies)

very quick apple crumble

If you don't have any home-made granola, buy a small bag of granola, preferably without too much added sugar. Preheat the oven to 180°C/350°F/gas mark 4. Peel, core and cut the apples into small pieces. Put the fruit into a saucepan with the cinnamon and apple juice and cook for 10 minutes, or until soft, then spoon into 2 ramekins. Top with the granola and bake for 10–15 minutes, until golden. Leave to cool slightly before serving.

folic acid – phosphorous

1½ C ½ 1½

50g good-quality plain or milk chocolate
1 thick slice of ripe pineapple
1 ripe small pear

pineapple and pear dipped in chocolate

This is a quick pudding, which I find especially handy when fussy toddlers come to tea – they tend to find room for a piece of fresh fruit dipped in chocolate. Break the chocolate into pieces and place in a bowl over a pan of gently simmering water until melted. Cut the slice of pineapple into small chunks. Core, peel and thickly slice the pear. Dip the fruit pieces into the melted chocolate and then rest on a cooling rack or piece of greaseproof paper, and leave in a cool place to dry for 20 minutes, or until the chocolate has set.

1 C 1 ½ 2½

vitamins B₂, B₆, ₂ – phosphorous

makes: 2 toddler portions
2 ripe pears
1 eating apple eg Cox's
50ml apple juice
1 tbsp custard powder
1 tbsp golden caster sugar
300ml full-fat milk

stewed fruits with custard

Peel the pears and apple, core and cut into chunks. Put the fruit into a saucepan with the apple juice. Simmer, covered, for 10–15 minutes, until the fruit is soft. Put the custard powder and sugar into a bowl and mix to a paste with 2 tbsp of the milk. Bring the remaining milk to the boil, gradually pour into the custard mix, whisking constantly, then return the custard to the pan and cook for a few minutes, until it is smooth and thick. Serve the stewed fruit with the custard.

Vit B6 –

4 C ½

makes: 3 toddler portions
1 ripe kiwi fruit
1 seedless orange
1 ripe small banana
2 tsp runny honey
6 wooden sticks, soaked in water

fruit kebabs

Line a grill-pan with foil. Preheat the grill to medium. Peel the kiwi fruit and cut the flesh into 1cm chunks. Peel and segment the orange. Cut the ripe banana into chunks. Skewer the fruit onto each wet, wooden stick, alternating the type of fruit as you go. Drizzle the honey onto the fruit and grill, turning occasionally, for 3–5 minutes, until the fruit is just starting to caramelize. Leave to cool slightly, then remove the fruit from the sticks and serve.

celebration food

vanilla strawberry cakes

makes: 10 toddler portions (10 cakes)

storage: keep for up to 3 days in an airtight container

6½

1

1

1½

2 C

vitamins A, B₁₂

125g unsalted butter, softened
125g golden caster sugar
2 drops of vanilla extract
2 large eggs
125g self-raising flour, sifted
1–2 tbsp full-fat milk
150g white chocolate, chopped
5 ripe strawberries, hulled and halved, or 10 whole raspberries

These fairy cakes are for the nostalgically–minded. You are doing better than me if you can wait until they have cooled down before you tuck in.

1   Preheat the oven to 180°C/350°F/gas mark 4. Line a muffin tin with some paper cases.
2   In a bowl, beat the butter, sugar and vanilla extract together until pale and fluffy. Beat in 1 egg and then 1 tbsp flour. Beat in the other egg, then gradually fold in the remaining flour.
3   Fill the paper cases with spoonfuls of the mixture and bake in the oven for 15 minutes. Cool on a wire rack.
4   Melt the chocolate in a bowl over a pan of gently simmering water and put a blob on top of each cake. Top each with half a strawberry and leave to set.

Malteser and caramel ice-cream

makes: 6 toddler portions

storage: up to 3 months in the freezer

4½

½

½

1

vitamins A, B₂, B₁₂

75g golden caster sugar
4 egg yolks, separated
600ml full-fat milk
2 drops of vanilla extract
450ml whipping cream
2 x 37g bags of Maltesers, crushed
2 x 50g caramel bars, roughly chopped

This special occasion ice-cream is quite soft and can be eaten 5 minutes after taking it out of the freezer.

1   Put the sugar and egg yolks in a bowl and beat until light and fluffy.
2   Put the milk and vanilla extract into a saucepan and bring to simmering point.
3   Pour the hot milk over the eggs and mix well. Pour back into the pan and gently heat, stirring constantly, until the custard is thick. Leave to cool.
4   Whisk the cream to soft peaks, then fold into the cooled custard. Pour into a freezerproof container and freeze for 1 hour, or until the ice-cream has just started to freeze and is slightly thick. Mix in the Maltesers and caramel bars and freeze for another 5 minutes.

lemon sandwich cookies

½

1 **C**

makes: 10 toddler portions

storage: keep in an airtight container for up to 1 week

125g self-raising flour
zest of 1 unwaxed lemon
60g golden caster sugar
75g unsalted butter, chilled
  and diced, plus extra
1 tbsp full-fat milk
golden icing sugar,
  for dusting

for the icing:
1 tbsp lemon juice
125g golden caster sugar
75g unsalted butter,
  softened

Sandwich the cookies together with the cream just before serving to prevent the crisp cookies from going soft.

1 Preheat the oven to 180°C/350°F/gas mark 4. Sift the flour into a bowl. Add the lemon zest and sugar.

2 Rub in the butter with your fingertips (or in a food processor or blender) until the mixture looks like breadcrumbs. Add the milk and mix until the dough comes together in a ball. Knead briefly on a floured surface until smooth, then refrigerate for 5 minutes.

3 Roll out on a floured surface to 3mm thick and cut into 5cm rounds and place on a greased baking sheet.

4 Bake for 6–8 minutes, until pale golden. Cool on the baking sheet, then lift gently onto a wire rack.

5 In a small bowl, mix the icing ingredients together well and chill for 5 minutes. Sandwich the biscuits together and dust with icing sugar. If necessary, cut into smaller pieces before serving.

triple chocolate cookies

1½

makes 15 toddler portions

storage keep in an airtight container for up to 4 days or freeze for 4 months

100g unsalted butter,
  softened
100g light muscovado sugar
few drops of vanilla extract
1 medium egg, beaten
2 tbsp golden syrup
150g self-raising flour
2 tbsp cocoa powder
100g mixture of milk, orange
  and white chocolate

You could use any chocolate chunks for these cookies, but the combination of white and orange chocolate is sublime.

1 Preheat the oven to 180°C/350°F/gas mark 4. In a bowl, cream the butter until very soft. Add the sugar and vanilla extract and beat well for a few minutes until pale and fluffy.

2 Gradually beat in the egg and stir in the golden syrup. Sift in the flour and cocoa and gently mix until incorporated.

3 Cut the chocolate into big chunks and gently but thoroughly stir it in.

4 Shape the mixture into 15 walnut-size balls, flatten the tops slightly, then place on a non-stick baking tray or tray lined with baking paper. Bake for 7 minutes – the mixture will continue to set as it cools.

5 Remove from the tray when the cookies are firm and cool on a wire rack.

chocolate-dipped flapjacks

makes: 16 toddler portions

storage: keep in an airtight container for up to 4 days or freeze for up to 4 months

75g unsalted butter, plus
   extra for greasing
75g golden caster sugar
2 tbsp golden syrup
175g rolled oats
75g good-quality milk
   chocolate

Dipped in a little chocolate, these flapjacks are extra special.

1 Preheat the oven to 180°C/350°F/gas mark 4. Butter a 20cm tin. Melt the butter, sugar and syrup in a large pan over a gentle heat. Stir well, then thoroughly mix in the oats.

2 Tip into the tin and level off. Bake for 15 minutes, until pale golden.

3 Cool slightly in the tin and mark into 8 fingers, then mark each finger diagonally so that you have 16 triangular flapjacks. Cool completely.

4 Melt the chocolate in a bowl over a pan of simmering water. Dip one end of each flapjack finger into the melted chocolate and leave to cool on a wire rack. If necessary, cut into smaller pieces before serving.

pancetta-wrapped fruit

makes: approx 10 toddler portions

storage: best eaten fresh or keep in the refrigerator for up to 2 days

vitamin B$_6$

½ fresh pineapple, peeled
1 ripe small mango, peeled
   and stoned
10–15 thin slices pancetta or
   unsmoked streaky bacon,
   rind removed
handful of ready-to-eat dried
   unsulphured apricots

for the sauce:
4 tbsp crunchy peanut butter
½ small onion, finely chopped
1 garlic clove, crushed
1 tsp fresh root ginger,
   peeled and finely chopped
2 tsp soft brown sugar
½ tsp mild chilli powder
40g creamed coconut,
   roughly chopped
150ml boiling water

These are a little different for a toddlers' party, but a good way of encouraging them to eat something savoury. Do not give nuts to toddlers under the age of 3 if there is any family history of allergies.

1 Preheat the oven to 190°C/375°F/gas mark 5. Cut the pineapple and mango into small chunks.

2 Cut the pancetta or bacon in half and wrap each piece around a chunk of fresh or dried fruit. Secure with a cocktail stick.

3 Put the pancetta-wrapped fruits on a baking tray and bake in the oven until the pancetta is just crisp and the fruit is starting to caramelize – approximately 15–20 minutes.

4 To make the peanut sauce, combine all the ingredients in a small pan and bring to the boil. It will spit violently but stir frequently for 10 minutes to prevent it from catching.

5 If necessary, remove the cocktail sticks and cut up the fruit before serving with the sauce as a dip.

toddler storecupboard
recipes

tomato sauce

makes: 500ml tomato sauce

storage: keep in the refrigerator for up to 3 days or freeze for up to 4 months

1 tbsp olive oil
1 large onion, finely chopped
1 garlic clove, crushed
500ml passata (sieved tomato
  purée available in supermarkets)
2 tbsp fresh herbs, eg thyme, basil,
  parsley, rosemary, chopped
freshly ground black pepper
milk, to glaze

This is a versatile sauce that can be served with pasta, noodles, rice or polenta or as a topping on pizzas. To make it a bit more substantial try adding a small tin of flaked cooked tuna, chopped cooked ham or shredded cooked chicken and heat through thoroughly.

1 Heat the oil in a heavy-based saucepan and fry the onion until soft and pale golden – approximately 5 minutes. Add the garlic, stir and cook for 1 more minute.
2 Stir in the passata, herbs and a little freshly ground black pepper and simmer for 10 minutes.
3 Whiz with a hand-held blender (or in a food processor or blender) until smooth. Alternatively, you can leave the sauce slightly chunky. If freezing, leave to cool completely, pour into a freezerproof container and freeze.
4 Thaw thoroughly. Gently heat through until boiling hot. Cool before serving.

no-salt vegetable stock

makes: 1 litre stock

storage: keep in the refrigerator for up to 2 days or freeze for up to 6 months

50g unsalted butter
1 large onion, finely chopped
1 large carrot, finely chopped
1 celery stick, finely chopped
1 large leek, washed thoroughly
  and finely chopped
few parsley stalks
leaves of a thyme sprig or torn
  basil (optional)
freshly ground black pepper

Make sure that you chop all of the vegetables quite finely, as the flavour of the finished stock will be much better if you do. You can chop them in a food processor or blender.

1 Melt the butter in large heavy-based saucepan. Add the chopped vegetables and cook over a low heat for 10–15 minutes, stirring occasionally.
2 Add the herbs and 1 litre cold water, bring to the boil and simmer for 15–20 minutes.
3 Strain and season to taste with freshly ground black pepper.
4 Leave to cool and then keep covered in the refrigerator or pour into freezer bags, label and freeze.
5 Thaw thoroughly before use.

white sauce

makes: approx 4–6 toddler portions
(approx 600ml white sauce)

storage: keep in the refrigerator
for up to 3 days or freeze for up to
3 months

40g unsalted butter
1 small onion, finely chopped
40g plain flour
600ml full-fat milk
freshly ground black pepper

for variations:
approx 50g Cheddar cheese, grated
handful of fresh herbs, chopped
approx 3 slices of freshly cooked
  ham or bacon, finely chopped
2 handfuls of sweetcorn
approx 100g tinned tuna in oil or
  water, drained and flaked
6 fried mushrooms, finely chopped
2 hard-boiled organic eggs and a
  handful of chives, finely chopped
1–2 tsp mild curry powder

Make a plain white sauce and then add ingredients from the variations list to jazz it up slightly for a complete meal.

1 Heat the butter in a heavy-based pan and fry the onion until soft.
2 Stir in the flour and cook for 1 minute, then gradually whisk in the milk, stirring constantly until you have a smooth sauce – approximately 5 minutes.
3 Add the other ingredients of your choice and heat through. Season to taste with freshly ground black pepper.
4 If freezing, leave to cool completely, pour into a freezerproof container and freeze.
5 Thaw thoroughly and gently heat through until boiling hot. Cool to serve.

stewed fruit compote

makes: approx 5 toddler portions

storage: keep in the refrigerator for up
to 3 days or freeze for up to 4 months

500g bag of frozen fruits, eg
summer berries, dark fruits
75ml water or orange juice
golden caster sugar, to taste

This can be added to yogurts, cereals and custards or used as a crumble base or under a sponge to make a pudding.

1 Put the frozen berries into a saucepan with the water or orange juice and sugar and bring up to a simmer. Cook for 5 minutes, until the fruits are just soft. Cool slightly.
2 Spoon half the berries into a jug and whiz to a purée with a hand-held blender (or in a food processor or blender).
3 Return to the pan and mix everything together.

index

acknowledgements

Thank you to the paediatric dieticians, health visitors, midwives and nutritionists for their invaluable contributions to this book, especially to Victoria Morris (paediatric dietician), Tanya Carr (registered dietician and consultant nutritionist), Fiona Hunter (nutritionist) and Wendy Robertson RGNRM.

Thank you to Billy, who helped me throughout with research, testing recipes and lots of support. Thanks to Kate Andrews for help with recipe testing and to Bill Reavell and Francesca Yorke – the photographs are wonderful.

Thanks to Juliet Harvey for beautiful props and to Becca, with whom I adore working.

Thanks also to all my friends, especially Annie. Thanks to my sister-in-law, Alison Mansell, for helpful research, and to all the beautiful children who modelled for the book.

Thank you all so much for all your efforts.

Amanda Grant